Hosay Trinidad

Hosay Trinidad

Muḥarram Performances in an Indo-Caribbean Diaspora

FRANK J. KOROM

PENN

University of Pennsylvania Press

Philadelphia

10 9 8 7 6 5 4 3 2 1

Published by
University of Pennsylvania Press
Philadelphia, Pennsylvania 19104–4011

Library of Congress Cataloging-in-Publication Data
Korom, Frank J.
  Hosay Trinidad : muḥarram performances in an Indo-Caribbean diaspora / Frank J.
Korom.
    p.   cm.
  Includes bibliographical references and index.
  ISBN 0-8122-3683-1 (alk. paper)—ISBN 0-8122-1825-6 (pbk. : alk. paper)
  1. Tenth of Muharram.   2. Shi'ah—Customs and practices.   3. Shi'ah—Trinidad and
Tobago.   4. Muslims—Trinidad and Tobago.   5. Trinidad and Tobago—Religious life and
customs.   I. Title.

BP194.5.T4 K67 2002
297.3'6—dc21   2002075894

Contents

Illustrations

A Note on Orthography

With a few minor modifications that should be obvious to the specialist, the transliteration of all terms in this work follows the guidelines set by the Library of Congress's series of *Cataloguing Service Bulletins*. For Arabic, see Bulletin 91; for Persian, see Bulletin 59; for Urdu, see Bulletin 120; and for Hindi, see Bulletin 64. Because many Perso-Arabic words are used in Hindi and Urdu, I do not necessarily use the etymological transliteration but opt for the form used in the sociolinguistic context under discussion when a term is used. For the reader's convenience, I have included a glossary of frequently cited terms. The Trinidadian spelling of words from Indian vernacular languages varies considerably because they are used primarily in an oral medium. I have attempted to render terms in a standardized way based on discussions with my consultants in the field, but when a word is quoted from a printed source, the spelling used by the author is cited.

Introduction

*On another occasion I invited one of my informants to witness the develop-
ment of photographic plates, . . . and he saw in the process . . . the actual embodiment of ripples into images, and regarded this as a demonstration of the
truth of his clan.*

—*Gregory Bateson,* Naven

*Diaspora consciousness is entirely a product of cultures and histories in colli-
sion and dialogue.*

—*James Clifford,* Diasporas

Taʿzīyeh/Muḥarram/Hosay

Each year during the first ten days of Muharram *(al-muḥarram)*, the first
month of the Islamic lunar calendar, Shiʻi Muslims throughout the world
join in a common observance to commemorate the martyrdom of the
Prophet Muhammad's grandson, the *imām* Husayn. Husayn died in
the seventh century on the plains of Karbala, in what is now contemporary Iraq. The dramatic commemoration, known variously as *taʿzīyeh*
in Iran, *muḥarram* in India, and *Hosay* in Trinidad, is the focal point in
the religious life of the Shiʻi mourning community. Because Imam
Husayn's suffering and death is seen as the most important tragedy in
history, the annual reactualization of the event is the central Shiʻi ritual
observance of the year. *Muḥarram* is a metahistorical phenomenon because the observance related to it makes possible individual identification with, and direct experience of, Imam Husayn's vicarious suffering.
During the observance, subjective apprehension is not spatially and
temporally bound, for the historical battle that occurred in 61 A.H./
680 C.E. is made present through the pious actions of Shiʻi Muslims the
world over.

The temporal and spatial transcendence of the tragedy fit in well with
the anthropological notions of liminality as developed by Arnold van
Gennep and elaborated by Victor Turner.[1] They place the passion of

Imam Husayn at Karbala in an atemporal and aspatial framework beyond all fixed points of classification. Turner sees liminality as a state of transition during which "liminal entities are neither here nor there; they are betwixt and between the positions assigned by law, custom, convention, and ceremonial." Moreover, the ambiguity of the liminal period "is frequently likened to death."[2] *Muḥarram*, being an annual rite of communal passage bridging each year to the next is thus a process of symbolic community death and rebirth, a ritual of renewal par excellence.[3] Although this is a universal overview applicable to the observances throughout the world, we find that the event is a complex, polysemic affair when viewed from an ethnographic perspective. In actuality, the ritual complex in context is comprised of a plethora of regional and local symbols; we find a variety of observances unique to given locales. In this book, I focus on local expressions of the Muharram rituals in Trinidad, but not without first situating them within the global development of Shiʻi popular piety in Iran and India, the geographic trajectory along which the rite passed during its lengthy odyssey that ended in the Caribbean.

As is the case with many Shiʻi observances, the various modes of ritual action expressed during the month of Muharram share the common aforementioned goal of identification with the martyr Imam Husayn. This identification pervades all domains of Shiʻi life. The pervasive notion of Husayn's drama providing an ideal model for human action in everyday affairs is what many scholars of Shiʻi Islam, following Michael Fischer, refer to as the "Karbala paradigm."[4] I situate my study within this model in Chapter 1 to show that Trinidadian Shiʻi Muslims act locally within a much broader transnational frame of reference, that is, from within a global ethos and worldview. Having stated this, however, I wish to note that the ways in which the goal of subjective apprehension is reached differ considerably in their performative aspects in Iran, India, and Trinidad, the three main sites of my study.

Participants share a common core of symbolic meaning but create separate emergent realities unique to their respective cultural, geographic, and linguistic environments. Common sense alone should tell us that the ritual performance of a shared core of faith and belief can take peculiar turns in specific geographic locations even when tied to a historical story or, to borrow Fredric Jameson's term, a "master narrative," with relatively stable motifs embedded in it.[5] But the ethnographic record also demonstrates that firm links with the original event are maintained in various religious contexts through processes of material and verbal enactment such as the building of cenotaphs and biers or the telling of the story of Imam Husayn's tragic death through numerous forms of narrative. These narrative events pertaining to Husayn's ordeal provide much of the collective global knowledge that serves as the basis for the construction and performance of lasting ritual reenactments on the local level.

Passages from dramatic *ta'zīyeh* scripts recited during staged "passion plays" in Iran suggest that salvation is guaranteed for all mourners because the *imām* is able to mediate between God and man on the Day of Judgment, the ultimate moment of reconciliation for one's deeds on earth. Interpreting the observance from this *emic*, or insider's, point of view concretizes the notion that participating in annual renewal on the human level is not only desirable but absolutely necessary in terms of the overall soteriological goal motivating the event. Participation in the annual *muharram* renewal is humankind's chief role and responsibility in this lifetime, according to the Shi'i perspective. Through participation in performances, systems of abstract theological meaning are shaped into emotional, experiential, and subjective local forms of knowledge comprehensible to the individual and his or her community. My study seeks to unravel the variety of local meanings attributed to *Hosay* in Trinidad. Thus the bulk of the study focuses on the Caribbean. To explicate fully the Trinidadian variant of *muharram*, however, I have provided the historical background of the rite's origins and observance in Iran and Iraq in Chapters 1 and 2 in order to inform my ethnographic observations included in the later chapters. Once having completed this task, I trace in Chapter 3 the rite's diffusion to South Asia, from where it was eventually transported to the Caribbean in the mid-nineteenth century via indentured laborers who were brought from India to work on colonial plantations under the British Raj.

Ta'zīyeh in Iran

In Iran, staged performance grew out of processional observances that were recorded by Muslim historiographers as early as the tenth century. The reactualizations first took place at locations where large numbers of people could gather, like crossroads or public squares. Ritual battles would take place in front of an audience while tableaux of bloodied martyrs moved past the stationary audience on wheeled platforms. In the sixteenth century, a private tradition of verbal martyr narration called *rauzeh khvānī* also began to flourish. These two traditions—public performance and private recitation—existed side by side but separately for nearly two hundred and fifty years. The two fused in the mid-eighteenth century to create what we know today as *ta'zīyeh*. *Ta'zīyeh*, like the *muharram* processions, developed historically as a communal event. The important element in the observance was participation. An audience member could not just observe passively. The viewer had to show emotion by weeping in order to experience the suffering of Husayn, and only in this way could he or she completely identify with the martyr.

In spite of the numerous historical changes that have contributed to the shaping of ta'zīyeh as we know it today, the soteriological purpose has remained constant: participation in the performance helps an individual to obtain salvation through the intercession of the martyr. The vicarious suffering and death of Husayn has been an instrument of redemption for all believers, and belief has been most readily manifested by performance participation. This underlying theological goal is central to the observance worldwide, and a host of scholars have identified it as the theological core complex of the Karbala paradigm adumbrated above. I intend to elucidate the paradigm as an overall frame for discussing the dialectics of the local and the global with regard to the rite's development in Trinidad.

Muḥarram in South Asia

Although many similarities exist between the Indic subcontinent and Iran in terms of performing muḥarram rituals, there are some great differences as well. A survey of Indian variations on the rite is the theme of Chapter 3, with special attention being paid to Banaras, where I first observed the event in the early 1980s.[6] Perhaps the greatest and most significant difference in muḥarram rituals as observed in Shi'i countries and in India lies in the use of the word ta'zīyeh (Ur. ta'zīyah). In Persian it is used to denote the ritual drama, or passion play, of Husayn's death. The term has a different meaning in South Asia, however. There it is the name given to the model tombs, the focal point of the public processions that take place during the event, and it is this aspect of the observance that becomes the dominating material feature of the rite in Trinidad. It is thus to India that we must look closely to identify the most salient aspects and morphological features of the observance in Trinidad.

As in Trinidad, there is not an emphasis on staged performance during the month of Muharram in India. Rather, the reenactment of Husayn's passion occurs as an unfolding social process within a larger symbolic space. The arena of performance, be it the house, the neighborhood, the village, or the city, becomes a microcosm of Karbala. Although Iran provides the underlying logic and symbolism for the event in the form of the Karbala paradigm, India provides the ritualistic precedent for the observance in Trinidad. Instead of staged drama, we find a greater emphasis on conveying the tragedy through the recitation of *marsīyahs* (martyr poems) and the singing of *nauhahs* (dirges) at *majālis* (sing. *majlis*), social gatherings for ritual mourning. The development of *marsīyah* composition and recitation in India is obviously an innovative continuation of the *rouzeh khvānī* tradition of Iran.[7] Although the private *majlis* is the central focus of the *muharram* observance in India, as it is elsewhere in South Asia, the public processional rituals that occur on the streets are also important on the level of popular piety. There is a distinct dialectic between these private and public spheres of action that is evident in Trinidad as well. But whereas India continues the verbal narrative tradition of Iran, Trinidad has transformed language to rhythm, replacing verbal performances with a series of drum "hands" to convey the tragic story in a nonverbal, musical fashion. I wish to suggest that these two spheres allow for the emergence of multilayered understandings of the event by different interpretive communities. To make this point, I introduce the notion of "esoteric" and "exoteric" interpretations of the rite depending largely on the interpreter's level of participatory intimacy with the rituals performed.

Again as in Trinidad, the ambulatory public observances and stationary private ones converge on the tenth of Muharram (*'āshūrā'*) in India, the culminating day when participants embark on a symbolic pilgrimage by carrying their *ta'zīyah*s in a huge procession to graveyards representing the plains of Karbala where Husayn was murdered. The *ta'zīyah*s are then buried ideally during the noonday hour, the legendary time of Husayn's last breath.[8] In some parts of India, the *ta'zīyah*s are immersed in rivers, oceans, or sacred tanks of water following the Hindu custom of deity immersion (*visarjan*) after a religious festival. The last point above indicates another important theme of my study: cultural accommodation. I wish to argue that the necessary process of a minority religious community adopting local customs has allowed the rituals to thrive creatively in each of the environments discussed. I refer to this process as "cultural creolization," an appropriate alternative to the outdated and problematic concept of syncretism.[9] Syncretism, according to the *Oxford English Dictionary*, suggests an "attempted union or reconciliation of diverse or opposite tenets or practices."[10] With its emphasis on an "attempted union," the dictionary definition suggests an inconsistency in doctrine and practice. More appropriately, exploring creolization and the concomitant concept of "decreolization" as an alternative to syncretism allows me to emphasize human agency, the conscious decisions made by human actors, in my analysis of a rite's historical transformation. Such work is sorely needed in ritual studies.

In their discussion of South Pacific spirit possession, Alan Howard and Jeannette Mageo follow Nicholas Thomas to argue that "parts of cultures often become metonyms for cultural continuity," which results in "specific segments of reconfigured historical experience" becoming tradition.[11] *Hosay* is one such metonym, an emblem of identity that is reworked constantly in different contexts. In stating this, however, I do not want to imply naive and syncretistic adaptations, for that would deny the essential role of human agency in the reinvention of tradition. For my purposes, the concept of creolization is more suitable to get at the "highly self-conscious and reflective" dimensions of cultural borrowing and subsequent reinvention to which Howard and Mageo refer.[12]

Hosay in Trinidad

The Trinidadian style of commemorating Husayn's martyrdom seems very different from the Iranian and Indian forms at first glance, and much of the scarce literature on the rite makes ample mention of its purported creole nature.[13] A closer look at the complex event reveals continuities with its older counterparts, constantly reminding us of its north Indian sources of origin. *Hosay,* as it is expressed today, is a direct by-product of earlier *muḥarram* observances that were brought to Trinidad by indentured East Indians who came to work on plantations as early as May 30, 1845. However, although the Indian origins of the rite can be observed clearly in Trinidad, there is no question that the ritual performance has gone through a fairly lengthy process of indigenization. The ethnographic portion of my text draws extensively on the words and opinions of the people involved in the rite.

While Trinidadian Shi'i Muslims ideally show emotion for Husayn through public displays of drumming to signify the incidents pertaining to Husayn's death and through the painstaking construction of the model tombs known as *tadjah*s, we also find that the observance becomes marked by gaiety and celebration for the revelers who participate in the public processions as audience members. The Trinidadian form of the rite becomes "carnivalized," to use Mikhail Bakhtin's term, so that it takes on aspects of observances occurring during periods of carnival in the Caribbean.[14] At least that is how it seems to the outside observer. I argue that while this might be true to a certain extent, these carnival aspects are not new elements in the Trinidadian variant of the rite because similar occasions for festive behavior were already noticeable in India and even in Iran. This is not to say, however, that the nature of the observance's outward appearance is uncontested in these countries. Indeed, the same sorts of ideological debate that emerge in

Trinidad each year as *Hosay* approaches find expression in India and Iran as well.

The craftsmen and others associated with the forty-day preparation of *Hosay* do not condone the merrymaking on the streets during the public processions. Nonetheless, the historical transformation of *muḥarram* from a predominantly solemn observance to a public celebration is a distinctive process on the island. It marks the event as a characteristic form of Trinidadian performance. Through it, East Indians participate in Creole culture, but they also reassert their own Indian ethnic identity by performing a tradition that is perceived to have come to Trinidad from India in an unaltered state. The various uses and understandings of tradition as something unchanging and frozen in time are a vehicle for the ongoing negotiation of ethnicity in a relatively new and multicultural nation-state.

The theme of identity politics is addressed most forcefully in Chapter 6, where I argue that the *Hosay* phenomenon manifests multiple discourses about national culture, race, and ethnic identity on the island. The domains of these discourses can best be visualized as a series of concentric circles starting from the center and radiating outward like the proverbial ripples on a pond. In his study of the *naven* ritual among the Iatmul of New Guinea, Gregory Bateson mentions that they also see the world and all its inhabitants as ripples and waves on the surface of water: "It is said secretly that men, pigs, trees, grass—all the objects in the world—are only patterns of waves. . . . On one occasion I took some Iatmul natives down to the coast and found one sitting by himself gazing with rapt attention at the sea. . . . He was gazing at the waves which were heaving and breaking when no wind was blowing, demonstrating the truth of his clan's myth."[15] Like Bateson's Iatmul friend, I too sat gazing pensively, but at a different ocean, with a friend in Trinidad as he wondered what India, the imaginary homeland of his ancestors, was like. I imagine ripples bursting out in concentric rings around my friends in Trinidad to connect them religiously and culturally with ever widening social circles. The image allows for the conceptualization of how the global becomes incorporated into the local. Roland Robertson cleverly refers to the process as one of "glocalization," which is a subtle blend of the local and the global.[16]

In Trinidad the rituals are at the center personal and subjective. From this subjective core, we move to the kinship unit or family circle within which ritualistic and customary activities occur in the esoteric, private realm of the "yard" compound. From here we move out to the tertiary ring of the small community of Shi'i worshippers on the island. In a largely Shi'i-populated country such as Iran, one would expect the circular ripples to end here, but Trinidad, being a polyethnic island, offers further ripples to consider. From the circle of the community of Shi'i worshippers, we move to the public or exoteric sphere of the fourth circle, which is the ethnic domain. It is on this level of discourse that non-Shi'i Indo-Trinidadians may claim the esoteric rite as a secular Indian pageant. Next comes the circle of the nation-state. As more and more Trinidadians of non-Indian descent become involved in the public display and performance of the *Hosay* rituals, the spectacle moves from the ethnic to the national realm. If we are to place *Hosay* in a transnational context, however, we need to engulf the inner circles with a globally constituted one that connects the innermost three spheres to the all-encompassing outer circle. Within this larger sphere of concentric circles, Caribbean Shi'i Muslims become part of a worldwide community of worshippers, for better or for worse. The fairly recent impact of orthodox Shi'i missionary activity on the island is the subject for my closing reflections in the epilogue on ideological challenges confronting *Hosay* participants after more than 150 years of residency.

In deploying the metaphor of ripples on a pond, I do not envision a seamless stream of harmonious continuity emanating from a quiet center. Rather, we may wish to imagine another pebble dropped at the periphery, which would lead to a collision between the rings bursting forth from the center and those moving inward from the periphery. This more complicated picture is more consonant with the quote from James Clifford that opened this Introduction. The image of colliding concentric rings offers an opportunity to look deeper at the contentions that have surrounded the event over time and across space.

The discourses revolving around issues of pious observance versus antinomian celebration and ethnic pageant versus national culture are serious points of contention in Trinidad, and it is through the discourses surrounding these debates that meanings and identities are negotiated on various levels. I argue that the levels of discourse described above can be identified very clearly. Essentially, the above circles can be reduced to three. On the most intimate level, the Shi'i families who lovingly nurture the *Hosay* observance collectively preserve the most esoteric (*bāṭin*) and symbolic level of the ritual complex's meaning. On the secondary level of Indo-Trinidadian ethnicity, Indians of other religious persuasions perpetuate the idea of *Hosay* as an Indian "cultural performance," in Milton Singer's term, divorced from its esoteric and sacred meanings.[17] Finally, on the tertiary level of the nation-state, non-Indian Trinidadians (most significantly those of African descent) see the performance as a purely secular and exoteric (*ẓāhir*) Trinidadian event with close parallels to the island's famous Carnival.[18] What I want to suggest is that the terminology used for the event, as well as the social organization of the yards within which the *tadjah*s are built, exemplifies the Caribbean nature of the performance quite well, providing ample evidence for cultural creolization. Having posited this, however, it is equally important to underscore the remarkable continuities that one finds as a result of the odyssey from Iran to India to Trinidad. These continuities suggest to me a cultural strategy of what the linguist Derek Bickerton calls decreolization along a pidgin/creole continuum.

Decreolization, as I use the term here, allows Indo-Trinidadians to resist the totalizing effects of creolization by consciously identifying concepts in Afro-Trinidadian culture to parallel their own Indic-inspired ones as a method of tolerance and accommodation. Bickerton, following Langacker, speaks of linguistic change in the process of decreolization proceeding through a phase of reanalysis during which "no overt change in surface structure occurs but the underlying structure is reinterpreted."[19] I do not assume, however, that changes in the expressive culture of Indo-Trinidadians are unidirectional in favor of the dominant social class. For as Christine Jourdan warns, "if decreolization means a move in the direction of a standard, it does not mean . . . a loss of other varieties" because "not all changes in creoles are in the direction of the acrolect."[20] Rather, actors in public ritual drama have a repertoire of options from which to choose, depending on the situational context of their performances, which allows for a relatively free flow of ideas in both directions. My findings argue against a movement toward standardization defined by the dominant class, and they are supported by Kean Gibson's recent study of Comfa religion and Creole language in Guyana.[21] Gibson draws upon the work of Robert LePage and Andrée Tabouret-Keller and shares my interest in developing a multidimensional approach that acknowledges the coexistence of more than one linguistic or religious system operating within any given polyethnic society.[22]

By applying the above linguistic model of culture viewed through a ritualistic lens, I aim to move beyond the binaries of extreme retentionism and extreme creolization, two positions that have plagued Caribbean anthropological debates.[23] In so doing, I am in agreement with Stuart Hall when he suggests that diasporic traditions retain strong links with their places of origin without harboring the illusion of any possibility of returning to the past. As he writes, "They are not and never will be unified in the old sense, because they are inevitably the products of several interlocking histories and cultures, belonging at the same time to several 'homes'—and thus to no particular home."[24] Hall's comment very clearly suggests that diasporic citizens are well aware that they may never go home to the motherland. It also suggests that they have the shifting option of expressing multiple allegiances in the negotiated form of various identities, be they religious, ethnic, national, or global. The imagined homeland abroad serves as a template for the bolstering of oscillating local identities, even while it remains largely unfathomable and incongruous to most.[25]

The Theoretical Scope of the Study and Its Relevance to the Field

As suggested in the above narrative, the observances have many levels of meaning that deserve close scholarly attention. Published works on the topic of *muḥarram* practices in Iran, India, and many other parts of the world are abundant, but no comprehensive monograph of the phenomenon in Trinidad currently exists. My aim is to fill this void with *Hosay Trinidad*. I trace the patterns of continuity and divergence mentioned above within the galaxy of *muḥarram* observances from their origins in the Middle East to the Caribbean via the Indian subcontinent as an example of transnational cultural production and flow. It was, after all, the military expeditions and expansions of Muslim conquerors from Central Asia that opened the door for the migration of the Shi‘ah from Persia to India in the fourteenth century. Moreover, it was the British colonial economy of indentured labor after the abolition of slavery in the nineteenth century that allowed for the rite's diffusion from the Indian subcontinent to Trinidad. These very facts force me to consider unequal power relationships as motive causes of ritual change in the social, political, and economic arenas within which rituals are publicly enacted. Although I need to situate my Trinidadian research in this broader historical and geographic context, the main thrust of my work focuses on Trinidad. Comparative materials prove useful for drawing structural and symbolic parallels between the three sites as well as for discussing the local/global dialectic. I am most interested, however, in focusing my discussion on the ritual complex as performed in Trinidad in order to present the first full explication of this understudied and neglected phenomenon.

I want to convey to the reader a sense of the creative processes, aesthetic evaluations, and community spirit that go into the making of the objects of veneration. At the same time, I want to address how these expressive practices are connected to contested social issues surrounding ethnic identity formation and the undying importance of racial relations in a nation-state still in the process of defining itself and its national culture. I hope that one of the major contributions of this study will be my interpretation of interethnic dialogue, cultural change, and religious persistence over centuries of historical interaction. On the theoretical level, I reflexively engage in an extended discussion of a diasporic culture in the making. Diaspora studies have grown immensely as an interdisciplinary field of inquiry over the past decade, and I situate my own position within that body of literature.[26] Diaspora scholars have been attracted by the notion of "hybridity" in recent years to talk about the ways that selves are situated on the margins of society in a transnational and deterritorialized world.[27] Although the idea of hybridity is an intriguing way to describe the "hyphenated" nature of diasporic identities and cultures, the term has some definitional problems because of its intentional ambiguity.[28] Moreover, Robert Young has shown that the term has a questionable colonial history not often acknowledged by contemporary theorists who use the concept.[29] Creolization also has a checkered colonial history, but it is a concept that has become well established in sociolinguistics, a field that provides one of the theoretical models that I employ in this book. My logic for using the creolization concept is that it is commonly used by creole makers themselves. People in Trinidad often evoke the word when talking about the dynamic processes involved in cultural mixing.

Essentially, the two terms have much in common, and I see hybridization as a postmodernist rendering of creolization. First, both terms emphasize a social process of mixture. Second, they both imply a strategy of empowerment used by "mixed" people to resist the hegemony of the dominant class. Homi Bhabha, for example, writes that hybridity is a "camouflage" that provides hybrid individuals with a "contesting antagonistic agency" to deal with the rules of social engagement.[30] Others also make much of the strength afforded by hybridity's "strategic biologism." Just as hybrid corn exhibits strength and resistance, the argument goes, the hybrid individual can persevere under a variety of conditions.[31] Camouflage and versatile strength are implied in the term *creolization* as well, because it provides creolized individuals a similar strategy for concealing certain things from the dominant class, thereby strengthening their own marginal positions in society.[32] My alternative is to opt for a more extended discussion of creolization, a well-established part of the Caribbeanist vocabulary, and a term that is still often used as a time-honored synonym for the more recent theoretical development of cultural hybridization.[33]

Caribbeanists earlier had opened up extensive discussions of the processes of cultural synthesis and multivalent identity formation through using the linguistic metaphor of creolization. Moreover, Ulf Hannerz states that "a concept of creole culture with its congeners may be our most promising root metaphor."[34] I build on this earlier corpus of work by employing linguistic and cultural models of creolization as a method to understand the complex phenomenon of Trinidadian racial and ethnic relations as exemplified through public displays of ritual behavior during *Hosay*. In my discussion, I employ, analyze, and interrogate the concept of creolization to understand the dynamics of indigenization on the local level. Simultaneously, I look at concepts of situated or emergent ethnicity as a viable strategy for allowing change to occur within a canonized form of global theology that remains open to innovative local interpretations. An *emic* model based on the Shi'i philosophical concept of *taqiyyah* (dissimulation), which allows believers to conceal their religious affiliation in particularly stressful contexts, combined with the *etic* s/x factor (esoteric/exoteric), provides a useful precedent for understanding indigenous modes of cultural and linguistic adaptation.[35] The concept of *taqiyyah* as a religiously based strategy for cultural adaptation in a multicultural environment fits well with current social scientific discourses concerning the fluid notion of ethnic identity. I believe it can provide a viable theoretical complement to linguistic models of creolization and Bhabha's concept of camouflage.

Sociolinguistic research over the past few decades has questioned the outdated and less useful devolutionary basis of language decay as the defining criterion of pidginization leading to creolization on a linear continuum.[36] The more recent movement to understand such mixed forms as dynamic and expansive systems has allowed researchers to look at grammar and syntax in the specific social contexts within which they formally develop. Looking at the development of cultural grammars both diachronically and syncronically in the context of convergence—not as devolving from complex to simpler forms but the reverse—signals, as Dell Hymes puts it, a shift to adaptive creativity.[37] It also provides richer possibilities for developing further the multidimensional approach advocated above. Such a strategic shift allows us better ways of explaining the negotiated and contested nature of cultural production. Similarly, a dynamic model of cultural grammars of maintenance, accommodation, and change allows me to look at the various modes of inflection that occur as religions and cultures increase their rate of encounter with other worldviews in the polyethnic environment of Trinidad. I therefore draw on this body of literature as well to counter certain misguided opinions about the decaying nature of Indian culture on the island.

The concept of creolization offers, in my opinion, the opportunity to account for the newly emergent and complex forms of culture that develop creatively through a synthetic process of convergence. In the context of *Hosay*, convergence can be understood either as the grafting of local elements and lexical labels borrowed from the socially dominant

group (the superstrate) onto a structural substrate derived from historical precedents originating in India and earlier in Iran or as a coming together of parallel traditions. I argue that in the former we notice aspects
of accommodation and acculturation as part of the creolization process,
while in the latter we see resistance to creolization by way of decreolization. I understand these concepts not as either/or propositions that are
mutually exclusive. Instead, one must see the processes as necessarily
complementary and working in tandem with one another. In other words,
creolization always implies decreolization; hence resistance can be accomplished through creative accommodation. What I mean by creative
accommodation is that what might seem like acculturation on the surface
may simultaneously be a valid form of resistance to total cultural absorption. Understanding the dialectics of creolization and decreolization
from this point of view allows us to think metaphorically of the theological, esoteric, or global level of *Hosay* as the grammar of the ritual, while
local innovations serve as the vocabulary of creative adaptation. I am
aware, however, that no such distinction can be absolute because influences flow in both directions. I therefore do not posit any clear-cut binary distinction. Instead, I use sociolinguistic ideas about creolization as
a heuristic for refining our understanding of cultural mixing in postcolonial contact zones, where diverse peoples come together to create local
culture anew out of historically descended practices. By using the linguistic analogy described above, I identify and analyze both latent continuities and manifest changes that have occurred within this performance
tradition over a fairly lengthy period of time and through space.

The idea of creolization, of course, raises important issues of authenticity, especially now that a virtually obscure and local rite has received
international attention through media exposure. Partially, I have been to
blame for this exposure due to the film on which I collaborated.[38] The
film and my previous publications on *Hosay* have, to a certain degree,
alerted not only Islamicists and anthropologists but also, and more significantly in terms of ideological impact, Shi'i missionaries to this relatively unknown Caribbean ritual phenomenon. Since 1994, for example,
orthodox Shi'i missionaries of East Indian descent from Canada have
started a campaign to reform *Hosay* so that it will more closely resemble
the rite as it is performed in Iran and other more conservative areas in
the Shi'i world. The missionaries aggressively argue that the Trinidadian
variant is not "correct," seeing it as an ill-informed deviation from the
Iranian model. In my epilogue, I analyze this most recent development
by situating the discourse of authenticity within the idea of emergent culture. By emergent culture, I mean "culture in the making," always in the
process of taking new forms to accommodate the needs of contemporary

sensibilities. Like identity and ethnicity, ritual is produced dialogically through ongoing negotiations between the various parties concerned, and it is precisely in these negotiations that we can observe how a ritual gradually changes and adapts to suit local needs through the conscious actions of individual social agents. The question then becomes the following: "How does the local respond to external forces of globalization?"

I address the dialectics of the local and the global by analyzing the subtle debates that take place annually between clerics and practitioners, as well as in the popular press, as the month of Muharram approaches. The transnational quality of the *muḥarram* phenomenon is most apparent in the debates and the rhetorical posturing resulting from them. My conclusion suggests that while recent global influences in the form of proselytizing activities place certain constraints on Trinidadian Shi'i practice, the local nonetheless is resilient enough to devise strategies of accommodation to external pressures and concerns. The ritual complex at the heart of this book is an important case study for describing how the local/global dialectic unfolds over time, but it also addresses some general issues of relevance to the study of festivity and public performance.

The *ta'ziyeh/muḥarram/Hosay* rite, however variegated in the three locations explored here, is an apt vehicle for expanding the discourse on festivity in general because it raises some broader issues concerning parades and power.[39] The rite also functions within an idiom of conspicuous display shared by many festive events. Language analogies are useful here as well, for all festivals share an expressive vocabulary. Writing about the "language of festivals," Roger Abrahams notes that they are "resounding times and elaborated places for excited exchange, for bringing out, passing around, for giving and receiving the most vital emblems of culture in an unashamed display of produce, of the plenitude the community may boast, precisely so that the community may boast. The emblems explode with meanings, for they are invested with the accumulated energies and experiences of past practice. They epitomize not only the seasonal passage but the history of the culture, a history spelled out in terms native to the group and appropriate to the place and the season."[40] He could easily have had the rituals discussed here in mind when he wrote the above passage. The Muharram rituals clearly manifest the transactional nature, emblematic multivalence, and collective history embodied in the festivals to which Abrahams alludes. Néstor García Canclini further adds that economies of consumption need to account for the reception of the products conspicuously displayed in the marketplace of culture.[41] I contribute to the concerns of Abrahams and Canclini by situating the Muharram ritual complex in the discourse of power relations that condition both the language of the event and how it is received, consumed, and interpreted by various agents present in the audience at the time of public display.

The fruits of my labor will be of interest to scholars in a number of disciplines within the humanities and social sciences, for I consider my study an interdisciplinary exercise. I blur genres to understand a very complicated and multivocalic performance event from both a textual and contextual point of view. To perform this feat successfully requires me to be somewhat of an academic *bricoleur*, but crossing disciplinary borders in the social and human sciences while using a variegated theoretical toolbox is absolutely necessary for the type of multisited study presented here.[42]

In short, my overall study demonstrates the remarkable resilience of the local vis-à-vis certain globalizing forces impinging upon it. Readers will find that my data fill a gap in studies on Indo-Muslim culture in Trinidad. Those especially interested in diasporic culture will benefit from the triangulation of my field sites, which has allowed me to tell a story that spans half the globe and more than 1300 years. I have intended, however, to keep the discussion in this work as free of jargon as possible to let the descriptive data speak on their own accord, for I believe, along with Paul Rabinow, that representational facts themselves are theoretically loaded.[43] Most importantly, it is my hope that because I have kept the text relatively accessible to a broader reading audience the people of St. James, Trinidad, who have befriended me over the past ten years will take the time to read this book. It is for them that I wrote it.

Chapter 1
Orientations and Overview

> **paradigm 1:** EXAMPLE, PATTERN; esp : *an outstandingly clear or typical example or archetype* **2** : *an example of a conjugation or declension showing a word in all its inflectional forms.*
>
> —*Webster's Ninth New Collegiate Dictionary (1986)*

The Karbala Paradigm

In June 1981 a bomb exploded in a Tehran meeting room during a high-level political meeting, killing over one hundred people. Among those who died in the explosion was Ayatollah Mohammed Beheshti, the leader of the Islamic Republican party. In 1986 this tragic event was commemorated with an Iranian postage stamp that identified a total of seventy-two killed in the explosion. The tally is equal to the number of people who traditionally are believed to have died with Imam Husayn ibn Ali, grandson of the Prophet Muhammad, "on the plain of sorrow and misfortune"[1] at Karbala in 61 A.H./680 C.E.[2] The stamp reads in both Persian and English: "Fifth Martyrdom Anniversary of 72 Companions of the Islamic Revolution." This powerful example demonstrates how the existential present can be explained and justified by reference to the historic past. Such popular symbolic techniques for the propagation of an officially sanctioned state ideology also instill a strong sense of religious ethos in those members of the global Shi'i community who pledge allegiance to Husayn. They remind believers that their supreme martyr's tragic demise is a recurrent phenomenon bridging past and present.[3]

The Karbala paradigm is a force as vital and potent today as it was during the first few centuries after the original event; it is one without parallel in human history.[4] The Karbala paradigm can be understood as, using Kenneth Burke's term, a "representative anecdote," or as Abrahams explains, "a proposition, not necessarily in narrative form, that is so conventionally recognized and understood that it can organize and analyze experience in common for those who draw on it together."[5] Indeed, every aspect of the pious Shi'i Muslim's life revolves around this anecdotal paradigm and is ordered by it. Moreover, it serves as a model for appropriate human behavior and as a rhetorical force to oppose tyrannical rulers.[6] But as we will see, the expression of the Karbala paradigm varies through time and space to make sense of contemporary sociopolitical realities. Variation in meaning and interpretation can best be gauged through a survey of the annual cultural performances that commemorate the martyrdom of Husayn.

During the first ten days of Muharram, Shi'i Muslims, regardless of where they reside, commonly observe Husayn's sacred commemoration. The tragic circumstances surrounding his redemptive suffering and vicarious death resonate throughout the Shi'i world, providing a central paradigm for a Shi'i theological emphasis on personal suffering as a method for the achievement of salvation. Indeed, there is great merit associated with weeping for Husayn, and even just remembering the event can absolve sin.[7] As Mahmoud Ayoub states in his richly detailed study of Shi'i redemptive suffering, "in the ritualistic moment, serial time becomes the bridge connecting primordial time and its special history with the timeless eternity of the future. This eternal fulfillment of time becomes the goal of human time and history."[8] Thus the Karbala event is enacted in numerous local ways wherever the Shi'ah reside in order to reap its soteriological benefits and often to bring about sociopolitical change. For this reason, the period of mourning during the month of Muharram is paramount, rewarding the pious participant with the benefits of Paradise. In the words of Elias Canetti, the suffering of Husayn and its commemoration become the essence of Shi'ism, which is "a religion of lament more concentrated and more extreme than any to be found elsewhere. . . . No faith has ever laid greater emphasis on lament. It is the highest religious duty, and many times more meritorious than any other good work."[9]

Muharram's metahistoricity provides an apt vehicle for what I wish to term "subjective apprehension."[10] Subjective apprehension is not an experience bound by time and space during the observance, for the implications of the seventh-century armed conflict between the *imām* and his foes are brought to bear on contemporary experience through ritual performance. As has been pointed out by one astute observer, "this places the passion of Imam Ḥusayn at Karbalā' at a time which is no time and in a space which is no space."[11] Again in the words of Ayoub, "all things are integrated into the drama of martyrdom and endowed with feelings and personality not very different from human feelings and emotions. Here we see myth attaining the highest expression, where men and inanimate things play an active role in a universal drama which transcends all limitations of time, space and human imagination."[12]

Because of the observance's timeless quality, the Shi'ah are able to measure continuously their own actions against the paradigmatic ones of Husayn. This is especially true whenever the community of believers regards itself as oppressed, a key theme we will find not only in Iran but in India and Trinidad as well. During the Iranian Islamic Revolution (1978–79), the slogans publicly chanted, painted on walls, or inscribed on headbands were in general variants of the following: "Every day is *'āshūrā*'; every place is Karbala; every month is Muharram."[13] Similar slogans were propagated in the media and displayed on posters during Iran's protracted war against Iraq (1980–88). Hans Kippenberg goes so far as to argue that "the traditional mourning rites and especially the Muharram-processions came to be powerful political manifestations against the Shah regime."[14] He further argues that people who died fighting against the Shah (and also later against Iraq) were considered martyrs similar to those in Husayn's camp who fell at Karbala in the seventh century. Everyday action thus takes on a ritual and performative dimension in the sense that participants in political street protests and processions conceive of their acts as part of a passion play *(ta'ziyeh)* linking them to the paradigmatic acts of the Karbala martyrs. The Iranian war maneuvers against Iraq in the Persian Gulf exemplify how the battle of Karbala still influences Iranians today. The military offensives were labeled Karbala-1, Karbala-2, and so forth, and the combined land and sea operations of August 1987 appropriately were termed "operation martyrdom."[15]

Such symbols, metaphors, and paradigms are transnational, ideologically connecting Shi'i adherents living in different parts of a loosely knit global community of worshippers stretching from Iran to Indonesia. Thus, much of what I have said so far is universally applicable to the observances throughout the world. But if we go beyond generalizations, we find that the event is a complicated and polysemic affair. In actuality, the student of the ritual complex in context is confronted with a plethora of regional and local symbols; hence we find a variety of observances unique to given locales.[16] We shall see that realizing subjective apprehension and identification with Husayn's passion is catalyzed through new and vital forms of practice in Iran, India, and Trinidad, even while remaining faithful to the Karbala paradigm.

Reenactments of Husayn's tragic death have been performed for centuries in what is today southern Iraq, the place of the martyr's violent death. They eventually extended far beyond their points of origin and moved via Iran, where they received official state sanction in the sixteenth century under the Safavids, to the Indian subcontinent and from there to the Caribbean basin. Even today, more than 1,300 years after Husayn's death, the rituals devoted to his sacrifice have not lost their potency. On the contrary, they seem to have become even more powerful. In some countries, the power of rituals performed during the month of Muharram has been channeled into the political arena and has been used as a psychological mechanism for mobilizing the masses against injustice and oppression. In other places, they provide more subtle "hidden transcripts," to invoke James Scott's term, that serve as methods of resistance to defy the hegemonic forces of the majority group.[17] Moreover, the rituals have often been used to subvert the authority of the ruling class, even if only symbolically at times.

As a general rule, the farther the rituals moved from their place of origin, the greater the influence of other cultures, religions, and customs on them became. Such changes may be regarded as the "declensions" of the paradigm. This notwithstanding, there are also remarkable continuities that we find in greatly separated areas of the world. Continuities as well as changes in ritual practice will be pointed out in due course as my study unfolds. For the moment, one example should suffice to make this point clear. Although the lament for the death of Husayn in the form of public self-mortification by ritual participants is prevalent in Iran, Iraq, and India, this aspect is not particularly visible at the two extreme ends of the ritual spectrum. In Trinidad and Indonesia, for instance, other forms of experiential remembering have replaced bodily punishment and pain. Nevertheless, the sacred period surrounding Husayn's annual death observance is still a ritual highly charged with unusual emotions in the Caribbean rim. Irrespective of the geopolitical arena in which the ritual complex takes shape, Husayn remains a spiritual and political redeemer, as well as a role model for participants.

Iran, more than any other country, has been influential in the expansion, diversification, and diffusion of Husayn's rituals into other geographical areas, especially in medieval times. Even earlier, when Persians began converting to Islam from the eighth century onward, strong pro-Shi'i sentiments were noticeable in the country. A sympathetic attitude toward the Shi'ah allowed the region to become a haven for many descendants of the Shi'i *imāms* who took refuge in the region to escape persecution by the Sunni majorities in other countries. It was not, however, until the sixteenth century—when they received royal patronage—that we observe the phenomenal growth of the rituals for Husayn. This aided, in turn, the spread of Shi'i doctrines across the Iranian plateau.

As noted above, the Muharram processions are especially powerful devices for conveying sociopolitical information and opinions, as they did during the massive demonstrations in Tehran and other Iranian cities during the 1978–79 revolutionary upheavals. The mixing of mourning slogans with political ones has been an old Muharram tradition, which allowed the designers of the revolution to draw upon the paradigm and present their claims in accordance with the Shi'i ritual calendar. Ayatollah Khomeini's revolution itself started on the day of *'āshūrā'* (June 3) in 1963 when he delivered a speech at the Fayziya Madrasa in the holy city of Qom. The speech, which followed an earlier one delivered on the occasion of the fortieth-day commemoration on April 3, 1963, of Iranian political martyrs who were killed by government troops for insurrection at the site, resulted in his exile. In his speech he boldly criticized the internal and external policies of the Shah and his government.[18] More than a decade later, on November 23, a week before the start of Muharram in 1978, Khomeini issued a declaration called "Muharram: The Triumph of Blood over the Sword" in order to bolster the claims of the revolution. The declaration was taped at his exile headquarters in Neauphle-le-Château, France, and distributed in Iran through an intricate network of mosques. The opening paragraph of the declaration is poignant and worth quoting at length:

With the approach of Muharram, we are about to begin the month of epic heroism and self sacrifice—the month in which blood triumphed over the sword, the month in which truth condemned falsehood for all eternity and branded the mark of disgrace upon the forehead of all oppressors and satanic governments; the month that has taught successive generations throughout history the path of victory over the bayonet; the month that proves the superpowers may be defeated by the word of truth; the month in which the leader of Muslims taught us how to struggle against all tyrants of history, showed us how the clenched fists of those who seek freedom, desire independence, and proclaim the truth may triumph over tanks, machine guns, and the armies of Satan, how the word of truth may obliterate falsehood.[19]

Less than two months after the Ayatollah's speech, the Shah left Iran with a box of Iranian soil in his hand on January 16, 1979, enabling Khomeini to return to his homeland after living in exile for fourteen years.

The Shah's abdication serves as a compelling example of the Karbala paradigm's power to organize collective social experiences. His departure from Iran also illustrates the persuasively effective use of the Karbala paradigm as an ideological tool for rallying the masses against tyranny and oppression. As Bruce Lincoln summarizes, "this myth was thus a useful instrument, one through which Iranian national identity could be continuously reconstructed along the same traditional pattern. Yet . . . the embattled Iranian 'ulama gave a radical new twist to the story as they identified the shah . . . with the quasi-demonic assassin and usurper Yazid."[20] Yazid becomes the arch-villain of the narrative, standing for any oppressive and unjust ruling force. By equating the Shah with the proto-typical villain, Iranian clerics were able to mobilize a successful popular movement to oppose what they understood to be an unjust rule. Lincoln goes on to point out a distinct shift in the use of the paradigm: "Thus interpreted, the Karbala myth no longer served primarily as the ancestral invocation through which Shi'i Iranians could define themselves in contradistinction to Sunni Arabs, but more important it became the revolutionary slogan through which the emerging movement of opposition to the shah was mobilized."[21] These two points—that is, ethnic and sectarian difference from Sunnis and oppositional ideology—are themes that reoccur historically both in South Asia and in the Caribbean, as the reader may note throughout this study.

While Muharram observances affect the entire Islamic community, albeit for different reasons, this widely publicized example amply demonstrates the powerful impact that the historical event has had on the collective psyche of Shi'i Muslims. Because Muharram rituals can be expressed both as religious mourning and as willful acts of public agitation, they have often been vehicles for political action and social mobilization. To return again to Khomeini's pronouncements, he urged his countrymen to make "Islam known to the people, then . . . create something akin to 'Ashura." He also said that protestors should still gather during Muharram to beat their breasts, but they should also "create out of it a wave of protest against the state of the government."[22] Moreover, after the Iraqi invasion of Iran in the fall of 1980, the theme of *'āshūrā'* was again invoked to mobilize people for the war efforts. Many of the Iranian combatants on the front lines in the war had the following inscriptions written on their helmets and headbands: "The epic-makers of *'āshūrā'* " or " *'āshūrā'* is the epic of faith, the epic of blood."[23] The historical epic of the rite's development and its emotive power to express sociopolitical discontent is a recurring theme in this book.[24]

The rituals of lamentation, so important to Shi'i Islam, are held mainly during the month of Muharram and the following month of Safar. They are observed especially on *'āshūrā'*, the day of Husayn's martyrdom, and on the twentieth of Safar, called *arba'īn*, the fortieth day after Husayn's death, when remembrances of a departed loved one are normatively held throughout the world by Muslims of all persuasions. These quintessential days, with their annual periodicity, punctuate the Karbala paradigm and serve constantly to remind the Shi'ah of their larger purpose in the cosmic picture. Before moving on to discuss the rituals at greater length in the next chapter, it is important to establish the logical and politicotheological significance of the Karbala paradigm through a brief recounting of the historical events leading up to Husayn's demise. I want to underscore the enduring narrative quality of the rite because Husayn's exemplary and paramount role in the Shi'i worldview serves as the master narrative that orders the lives of adherents and serves as a model for social and religious action. For this reason, I must delve into the events that are so vividly recalled each year during Muharram.

The Prehistory and History of Muharram

Although *'āshūrā'*, the tenth day of Muharram, was prior to the birth of Islam already a sacred day of fasting for Hebrews as Yom Kippur (Day of Atonement), the day takes on a new significance in the Islamic context.[25] Even before the tragedy at Karbala, Muslims observed *'āshūrā'* as a day of fasting during Muhammad's period in Medina.[26] But in terms of eschatology, the day takes on special cosmological and historical significance for the global Shi'i community, especially the Twelver branch of Shi'ism, because it was on this day that Husayn was killed for political reasons at Karbala.[27]

After Muhammad's death in midsummer of the year 11 A.H./632 C.E., a vacuum was created in the preexisting religiopolitical structure of the expanding body of believers in Medina because the Prophet never clearly specified who was to succeed him as caliph *(khalīfah)*, according to Sunni Muslims. The Shi'ah, however, claim that Muhammad ordered his son-in-law Ali to be his successor by appointment and testament. At any rate, an assembly of the most powerful men in Medina gathered together on the day that Muhammad died to decide who was to become the first *khalīfah* of Islam. Following a short deliberation, the council elected Abu Bakr, a close companion of the Prophet, to rule the Islamic world and guide the community of believers. Shi'i Muslims, of course, dispute this decision, arguing that the caliphate should be rooted within the House of the Prophet *(ahl al-bayt)*. They thus view Ali, husband of Muhammad's last surviving daughter Fatimah, to be the rightful heir to the Prophet's position as spiritual and political leader. The Shi'ah believe the Medina decision to elect Abu Bakr to be spurious because they argue that it was a divergence from a divinely mandated tradition dating from the beginning of time. It is said that Ali himself did not acknowledge Abu Bakr as *khalīfah* until after the death of Fatimah,[28] who only lived a short while after the death of her father—six months, seventy-five days, or forty days according to various traditions.[29] Even though Abu Bakr attempted to bring the Alids, those people who remained faithful to the House of the Prophet, into the fold, apostasy filled the empire. Popular opinion often claims that the faction that led to the birth of the Shi'i branch of Islam originated at this time.

Ali did, however, become caliph in 35 A.H./656 C.E., twenty-four years after Muhammad's death.[30] But there still remained factions in the growing Islamic Empire. Because the election of Ali took place in Medina, his support was strong there. Meccans, however, were not as sympathetic toward him. This relationship was further strained when Ali transferred his seat of power from Medina to Kufah in Iraq. Ali inadvertently isolated himself from the original home of Islam as a result of this move.

Syria also did not pledge allegiance *(bay'at)* to Ali; it refused to recognize him as caliph and remained loyal to the Umayyads. Ali's attempts to place his own governors in office in Syria during the year of his election backfired, for Syrians were staunch supporters of Muawiyah, who had ruled Syria before Ali was elected to the caliphate. This opposition caused severe problems for Ali's consolidation of power and threatened to undermine the unity of Islam. The conflict between the Umayyads under Muawiyah in Damascus and the House of the Prophet under Ali in Kufah ultimately led to a confrontation at Siffin in Iraq. The battle indecisively ended in a stalemate, and both parties returned to their respective seats with nothing more than uncertain compromises. The schism between Syria and Iraq intensified the following year when Egypt allied itself with Syria, leaving Ali's power considerably reduced, and his strength as a leader waned as a result. These reasons, along with many other sociopolitical factors and insurgence by the rebel Kharijites, a radical theocratic separatist group, led to a dual caliphate in 37 A.H./658 C.E. Muawiyah was recognized as caliph in Syria and Egypt, while Ali remained in charge at Kufah. Ali's remaining rule was fraught with difficulties. He was never able to regain the confidence of many who lost faith in him after Siffin, and the Kharijite insurgencies also added to the precariousness of his rule. Their rebellious attitude led to Ali's assassination at Kufah during Friday prayers by a Kharijite named Ibn Muljam in 40 A.H./661 C.E.[31] Theoretically, Muawiyah was left as the sole caliph. The fact that the historical record suggests that Ali was a weak ruler does not hinder Shi'i interpretation of his infallibility, a trait believed to be shared by all *imām*s

The question of a successor to Ali naturally became a major concern in Kufah, but the answer was ambiguous at best. It is claimed that when he was asked on his deathbed if his eldest son, Hasan, should become caliph by hereditary succession, Ali stated: "I do not command it, neither do I forbid. See ye to it."[32] Hasan thus succeeded his father in 40 A.H./661 C.E. Since Hasan was never officially elected at Medina, his web of influence did not extend far beyond Kufah. He was a weak ruler who kept a fairly low profile. Realizing Hasan's military passivity, Muawiyah prepared to attack Kufah, hoping to consolidate his power. His plan was an attempt to make the empire one political entity again. Rather than confront Muawiyah in battle, Hasan negotiated with the Umayyads and abdicated that same year. For a modest pension, Hasan agreed to move his retinue back to Medina, where he lived out the remaining years of his life comfortably.[33] At long last, Muawiyah was able to enter Kufah triumphantly. Having finally "tamed" the Eastern Provinces, he returned to the empire's sole capital, Damascus, to rule in the manner of an Arab *shaykh*—quiet but stern. Muawiyah reigned for the next twenty years as the undisputed caliph of Islam, even though conflicts with the Kharijites and Alids did arise from time to time.

So far, we have seen that the Shi'ah placed great emphasis on succession through an intrinsic form of transmission based on infallible guidance, whereas the Umayyads based it on election and consensus.[34] Muawiyah created a precedent for hereditary nomination, however, when he chose one of his sons, Yazid, to take the oath of fealty and become heir apparent. This shift from election to nomination changed the character of the caliphal office forever. It came to resemble a monarchy more than its original function as a seat of the "commander of the faithful."[35] Before Muawiyah died in 60 A.H./680 C.E., he warned Yazid that Husayn, the younger brother of Hasan, would be a problem for the empire. It is reported, however, that Muawiyah advised Yazid to deal gently with Husayn because the blood of the Prophet ran through his veins.[36] One Sunni source claims that Muawiyah conveyed a warning to Yazid, cautioning him to confront Husayn only in a good way, to let him move about freely, and to suffer him no harm. But Muawiyah also told Yazid that he should be respectfully stern with the grandson of the Prophet by means of diplomacy, not war. His final warning to Yazid was: "Be careful O my son, that you do not meet God with his blood, lest you be among those that will perish."[37] Both Sunni and Shi'i sources suggest that Muawiyah felt remorseful toward the end of his life that he had slighted the House of the Prophet. His newfound respect for Muhammad's family is most likely the reason why he advised Yazid to be lenient with Husayn. Unfortunately, Yazid did not heed his father's warning.

Husayn, living in Medina, had vowed to march back to Kufah in order to receive Iraqi support for his campaign after Muawiyah's death. Promises of support poured in from Kufah, and Husayn resolved to go there via Mecca to claim his regal rights. While in Mecca, Husayn sent an emissary named Muslim to Kufah to prepare for his coming. When Yazid learned of the plot, he sent Ubaydallah ibn Ziyad to Kufah to bring the situation under control.[38] Muslim was executed in Kufah along with later messengers sent by Husayn, who learned about these executions while on his way to Kufah but refused to turn back. Ibn Ziyad sent one thousand horsemen under the command of al-Hurr with the mission to check Husayn's movements and bring him back as a captive. They met near Karbala, at a place called Qadisiyyah, and al-Hurr informed Husayn of the impending doom awaiting him if he proceeded. Al-Hurr apparently meant Husayn no harm, for he attempted to convince him to take another road, one not leading to Kufah. At first, Husayn was inclined to accept his offer, but he refused on second thought because he had a pact with the Kufans.

Husayn reached Karbala on the second of Muharram in 61 A.H./680 C.E. He and his forces pitched camp there and made preparations for the rest of the journey. On the third, al-Hurr received word from ibn Ziyad by courier, that he should prevent Husayn's party from taking water from the Euphrates. Husayn was thus forced to pay homage to Yazid or die of thirst in the desert. Ibn Ziyad then sent Umar ibn Sad, the son of one of the Prophet's companions, to Karbala. Alhough ibn Sad attempted to turn down the task, ibn Ziyad forced him to go.[39] He thus proceeded to Karbala with four thousand men. Ibn Sad did not want to do battle with Husayn and hoped for peaceful reconciliation. But following the command of his superior officer, ibn Sad sent soldiers to guard the river against Husayn's access during the negotiations. Ibn Sad was, however, sympathetic to Husayn and therefore did not enforce this order strictly until the seventh, when he sent five hundred men to guard the banks of the Euphrates.[40] His congenial position and respectful attitude toward Husayn's party led to some partial agreements with the _imām_ concerning the future course of events. It is surmised that Husayn provided ibn Sad with three alternative courses of action: to allow Husayn to return, to confront Yazid, or to go freely to another land.[41] Ibn Sad then sent word to ibn Ziyad that reconciliation leading to peace would be for the best. It is purported that ibn Ziyad was at first inclined to accept Husayn's proposal but was eventually dissuaded by Shimr ibn Dhi-l Jawshan, who argued that accepting any of the options would be admitting to cowardice. Shimr was thus sent to Karbala with a letter demanding an unconditional surrender from Husayn and a strong suggestion for ibn Sad to comply with the order to destroy Husayn's party if he did not pledge allegiance to the caliph. If Husayn was not willing to accept this proposal, his punishment would be death.

Shimr passed on ibn Ziyad's message to ibn Sad on the ninth of Muharram. That day ibn Sad delivered the final ultimatum to Husayn, who asked that the battle be postponed until the next morning so that the small group could pray together one last time. Meanwhile, the order

to guard the river from Husayn's soldiers was stepped up again. It is reported, however, that Husayn's half brother and standard bearer, Abbas,
was able to fill twenty water skins with the help of fifty of Husayn's men
before the order was strictly enforced.[42] That evening Husayn gave a sermon and urged the others not to fight, for Yazid wanted only Husayn.
But out of piety and devotion to the *ahl al-bayt*, no one turned back. All
agreed to die as martyrs alongside Husayn. After prayers and the sermon, Husayn ordered a trench to be dug on one side of his encampment.
The trench was filled with reeds and kindling to create a protective bed
of flaming embers, allowing battle on only one side of the camp.[43]

The tragic battle began with a parley the next morning. Husayn's
party was hopelessly outnumbered and the result was a slaughter. Ibn
Sad, who wavered at first, is said to have shot the arrow that marked the
beginning of heavy fighting. Seeing the massacre that was being committed, al-Hurr defected to Husayn's side before midday, asking to be in the
front ranks of those to be killed. The fighting was fierce and bloody; even
small male children in Husayn's party were killed, according to sources
wishing to stress the extreme cruelty of the enemy.[44] Many of those mas-
sacred were still too young to handle weapons. Among these were
Hasan's sons Qasim[45] and Abdallah as well as other male members of the
House of the Prophet.[46] Husayn was the last to be killed, for no one was
willing to strike the death-dealing blow. He did, however, have multiple
wounds, because he was riddled with arrows "like a porcupine" and
pelted with stones during the fighting.[47] Finally, at the instigation of
Shimr, a swordsman approached the painfully swaying body of Husayn
and severed his left shoulder, while another stabbed him in the back with
a spear. It is reported that a soldier named Sinan ibn Anas al-Nakhi was
the one who severed Husayn's head in the end.[48]

The camp was pillaged, and Husayn's naked body ultimately was left
lying on the burning sand under the hot, noonday sun. Ayoub notes that
the survivors lamented loudly on the pillaged battlefield and that upon
seeing the dead bodies, Husayn's sister Zaynab hit her head on the tim-
ber of her carriage, "staining her face with the blood of sorrow."[49]
Husayn's head, along with his only surviving son and the female captives, was first transported to Kufah, then to Yazid's court in Damascus.[50]
Yazid had not expected such a gruesome outcome, nor did he wish to
take credit for this heinous victory. It is said that he was horrified by the
whole incident, and in compensation freed all of the captives, clothed
and fed them well, allowed them to lament for their dead, and arranged
for them all to be escorted back to Medina.

This brief historical overview should give the reader a sense of the
events that led to later hagiographic accounts of Husayn's tragedy,

which, from the Shi'i point of view, highlight the "destruction of family, community, government, and humanity."[51] Such inflated narratives emphasize the mournful, the oppressive, and the tragic. These tragic stories, and many others like them, provide a popular vehicle for the development of a powerful theological conception of Husayn as the paradigmatic martyr in Shi'i thought. Among the more heartrending stories that have been recounted by later hagiographers and are remembered annually today are the purported marriage of Qasim to Husayn's daughter Fatimah Kubra on the battlefield just prior to Qasim's death; the sacrificial death of Abbas, whose arms were severed as he was attempting to procure water for the parched women and children; and the death of Husayn's infant son Ali Asghar. I will have more to say about the importance of these scenes in the development of dramatic ritual reenactments, but first a few words on the importance of the figure of the *imām* are necessary in order to understand why Husayn became such a key symbol for the Shi'ah.

The Theological Significance of the *Imām*

The cultural construction of the *imām* figure in Shi'i Islam is a result of the interaction between historical, hagiographic, and theological forces. The impact of the *imām* on Shi'i thought and society has been so great that he is perceived to be an infallible center of sacredness or a "divine guide," as Ali Amir-Moezzi calls him.[52] Unlike the Sunni caliphate, the imamate is not seen primarily as a political office. Instead, the *imām* serves the Shi'i community in a spiritual capacity as the interpreter of religious teachings; he is the exegete par excellence. He is, for all practical purposes, a direct link in a chain of succession leading back to Creation itself. Therefore, his role as a conduit between the human realm and the sacred sphere throughout the ages is seen as a special, innate quality that only he possesses in any given lifetime. To understand why Husayn's martyrdom is so significant in the ritual year and in Shi'i eschatology, we must consider the concept of the *imām* in general.

Ayoub writes that "the *imām*s, for Shī'ī Muslims, may be thought of as a primordial idea in the mind of God which found temporal manifestation in persons occupying a position midway between human and divine beings."[53] This does not mean that these hereditary divine guides are something other than physically created sentient beings, for they are subject to death, just like any other human being. But their uniqueness rests in the critical place they occupy in maintaining the cosmic harmony of the universe. They are, first and foremost, products of divine thought, mirroring the Creator's mental blueprint of order for the world. Beginning, then, as pure thought in the worldly conception of the Divine, they became manifest as "luminous entities or conventicles of light in the loins of prophets and wombs of holy women until they reached actualization in the Prophet Muhammad."[54] The *imāms* are thus seen as "light upon light," an image used by the sixth *imām*, Jafar al-Sadiq, to describe the illuminated pattern of *imāmī* succession. The *imāms*, embodying pure light that has passed from the beginning of time through successive generations of prophets, are known as *al-nūr al-muhammadī*, the "light of Muhammad." The bearer of light, the interpreter of revelation, and the source of knowledge must be both physically and spiritually pure. He is further seen as the perfect man, the possessor of infallibility. This characteristic above all endows the *imām* with a special spiritual aura resulting from his gnosis, upon which he draws to fulfill his central religious duty.

Because the Twelver branch of the Shi'ah philosophically perceives religion to have mutually dependent external/exoteric *(ẓāhir)* and internal/esoteric *(bāṭin)* factors, there is a need for a spiritual leader who is entrusted with the divinely given metaphysical knowledge that allows him to act as an interpreter of God's revelations and the Prophet's teachings. The figure of the *imām* is the physical embodiment of God's primordial and divine trust *(amānah)*. He alone can communicate divine knowledge to humans, and therefore he must always be present in some form on earth. According to Seyyed Hossein Nasr, the basic task of each successive *imām*, above and beyond all other aspects of mundane life, is to guide the faithful from the external to the internal, toward the source of their existence.[55] The *imām* is, in this capacity, the entrusted being who guides the seeker of religious knowledge on an inner journey by performing the proper exegesis *(ta'vīl)* necessary to facilitate the adept's spiritual progress.[56]

Although the world can be without a prophet, it can never be without an *imām*, according to Shi'i theologians. The figure of the *imām* therefore must always be present on earth to serve as an interpreter of revelation. He is a vital link in a chain of authorities that must always be represented on earth, either physically or theoretically, in each successive generation. Only he has the capacity to understand and interpret that which no other earthly being can.[57] The role of the *imām*, then, is absolutely critical for the proper functioning of the world. Nasr suggests that the *imām*'s threefold functions and duties are "to rule over the community of Muslims as the representative of the Prophet, to interpret the religious sciences and the Law to men, especially their inner meaning, and to guide men in the spiritual life."[58] Ayoub adds that "if the concept or ideal of the *imām* embodies all spiritual and physical perfections for the Shi'is, then Imām Husayn can be regarded as the living perfection, or concretization of this ideal."[59] Husayn is, of course, an integral part of the chain of unbroken tradition, for he manifests the mystical light mentioned above and acts as the vicarious bearer of all the world's suffering. Indeed, the whole prophetic *silsilah* (chain) partakes in this suffering and pain, for hagiographic and legendary sources all point to the predetermination of Husayn's martyrdom. For example, when Husayn arrived at Karbala on the second of Muharram, it is reported that he prayed, knowing that he had arrived at the place of sorrow *(karb)* and calamity *(balā')* where his blood would be shed, according to his grandfather's prediction.[60]

Ayoub eloquently documents the eternal participation of all the prophets in Husayn's suffering.[61] Adam, Noah, Abraham, Jesus, and Muhammad each shared in the pain of the violent acts at Karbala. Their suffering, resulting from foreknowledge of the Karbala incident, has potent teleological significance, but it is merely a prelude to Husayn's own suffering and death. His self-sacrifice is the final act of the cosmic drama that encompasses all creatures—past, present, and future—in a recurrent test of faith and piety to guarantee the ultimate reward of vindication from all sinful acts performed on the face of the earth.[62] It is believed that even as a child Husayn had foreknowledge of his tragic end and knew of his unique, predetermined role in God's divine plan. It is written that when the Prophet was asked if he had explained Husayn's future fate to him, Muhammad replied: "No, his knowledge is my knowledge, and my knowledge is his, for we know of the recurrence of events before they occur."[63] It is important to my immediate concerns here that tradition states that Husayn learned after his death of his elevated yet humble status of being a mediator between man and God on *qiyāmat*, the Day of Judgment.

The social, theological, and psychological ramifications of Husayn's role as intercessor are far-reaching. The Mu'tāzilī scholar ibn Umar Zamakshari utilized the idea of *tashabbuh* (imitation)[64] to explain that "according to religious traditions anyone who weeps for Husayn is certainly destined to join him in eternity."[65] This idea is also expressed in certain key passages from *ta'ziyeh* scripts such as the following:

[The Prophet]: Sorrow not, dear grandchild; thou shalt be a mediator, too, in that day. At present thou art thirsty, but tomorrow thou shalt be the distributor of the water of Al Kauser [in Paradise].

[Gabriel, bringing the key of Paradise and delivering it to the Prophet]: He who has seen most trials, endured most afflictions, and been most patient in his sufferings, the same shall win the privilege of intercession. He shall raise the standard of intercession on the Day of Judgement who hath voluntarily put his head under the sword of trial, ready to have it cloven in two like the point of a pen.

Take thou this key of intercession from me, and give it to him who has under-gone the greatest trials.

[Gabriel, speaking for Allah]: The privilege of making intercession for sinners is exclusively his. Husain is, by My peculiar grace, the mediator for all.

[The Prophet, handing over the key]: Go thou and deliver from the flames every one who has in his life-time shed but a single tear for thee, every one who has in any way helped thee, every one who has performed a pilgrimage to thy shrine, or mourned for thee, and everyone who has written tragic verse for thee. Bear each and all with thee to Paradise.[66]

These illuminating passages, combined with Zamakshari's exegesis, clearly suggest that salvation is guaranteed for all mourners. They also reinforce the importance of making physical pilgrimages to Husayn's ac-tual tomb at Karbala.[67] Elizabeth Fernea, for example, writing about her observation of other participants on her pilgrimage to the sacred site, notes: "At first I wondered why on earth they had brought this sick child to Karbala in such heat, but the obvious answer came. Dying on pilgrim-age assures the soul immediate entrance into heaven."[68] Interpreting the observance from this indigenous point of view concretizes the notion that participating in annual renewal on the human level is not only desirable but also absolutely necessary.

Participation in the annual *muḥarram* renewal is humankind's chief role and responsibility in this lifetime. Through participation in the per-formance of passion, systems of abstract theological meaning are shaped into emotional, experiential, and subjective local forms of knowledge comprehensible to the individual and his community. Much of the sym-bolic and emotive potency that has motivated the continuation of this an-nual renewal is grounded in the narrativization of hagiographic history. To conclude this chapter, a few theoretical words on narrative and his-tory as a prolegomenon to my subsequent discussion are necessary.

The Narrativization of History

Hayden White has reminded us of a necessary theoretical and method-ological concern for the narrative quality of history.[69] History is, after all, a story that unfolds over time and is refashioned by scholars, raconteurs, and performers of ritual in the present. Insofar as history tells us a nar-rative about particular events believed to be empirically true, we must think of history as storytelling. History, from this point of view, is in-scribed in narrative, whether oral or written. Indeed, aspects of a com-munity's history are often conveyed and preserved through the telling of stories about important events that have transpired in the group's collective past: such storytelling provides a shared basis for remembering and understanding the significance of that past. It is also quite common for historic events to be communicated aurally through folkloric media such as songs or tales. This is the case with the events that transpired at Karbala, for conveying the historical tragedy in everyday discourse has proven insufficient in and of itself to induce the somber mood desired during the first ten days of Muharram each year. Other, more poetic, genres of conveying history, coupled with processional rituals and dramatic performances, have emerged in the Shi'i world to create an integrated semiotic system of oral/aural, visual, and visceral channels through which to preserve, remember, and experience the tragic story of Husayn.

While the inscription and embodiment of history in narrative form and visual representation offer keys to understanding mechanisms of transmission, it is also important to remember that narratives themselves have histories. These metahistories may provide interesting clues for understanding interrelationships between genres and motifs over time. My intention above has been to highlight chronologically the series of historical events that function as a master narrative for the global Shi'i community. In Iran, where *muharram* observances first developed into royally sanctioned ritual events during the sixteenth century, a unique Persian genre called *maqtal* developed as a literary medium for expressing emotionally the passion of Husayn and other Shi'i martyrs.[70] After recounting the early development of Iranian mourning traditions, I will return in the next chapter to the important role of vernacular narrative and drama in transmitting popular historical knowledge.

Chapter 2
Muharram Rituals in Iran
Past and Present

> *I shall exhaust my life weeping and sighing.*
> *In distress and grief I shall pass my lifetime.*
>
> —*Baḥrānī's* al-Fawādiḥ[1]

Performing Passion

Fernea provides a description of the events performed in honor of Husayn at his tomb in Karbala during the month of Muharram. After each "taaziya group" performed their preliminary rituals in "religious ecstasy," the processions began. She describes them as follows: "We could hear the chant of the group next in line, echoing and re-echoing within the great courtyard around the tomb. Then the new group emerged; a green banner and a black, lit by flickering torches held high, were borne forward by the hands of very old men and boys. . . . Then a score of young men, bare to the waist, wearing only black or white trousers and white head cloths, surged out, marching in strict rows of four. . . . Whatever I had expected, this was completely different, different in scope and quality from the taaziya I had seen in El Nahra."[2]

On one level, this quotation indicates the diversity found in the rite's performance in southern Iraq. On another, it hints at Fernea's sense of amazement and otherness as she witnesses an event that seems so foreign to her. Certainly the Muharram rituals do seem "different" to people of other faiths, but they are not so far removed from Western experience that they must be understood as wholly other. After all, the rituals bear strong resemblance to Christian penitents performing bodily mortification on Good Friday. Indeed, one scholar has recently posited that Christian influence from the Mediterranean region may have inspired the Shi'i tradition of flagellation.[3] Moreover, the passion plays to be discussed below would seem vaguely familiar to those who have witnessed the performance of dramas concerning Christ's passion at Oberamergau in Germany during the Christian Holy Week. But it would be a mistake to judge the forms discussed below from a solely Western perspective, for they have developed along a different set of performance principles that defy conventional Western categories of drama.

The study of the so-called "Persian passion play," the holy drama known as *ta'ziyeh* in Iran, is well developed. But even the word *drama* must be used cautiously here because the application of Aristotelian theatrical terminology is not entirely appropriate for the description of this phenomenon. *Ta'ziyeh* denotes an "expression of condolence" for Husayn, lamentation for all of the martyred *imām*s, the tragic event itself, and the Shi'i staged performance of the historical event.[4] Because it does not contain dialogue intended to convey plot in the Greek sense, the drama should be viewed as a distinct indigenous genre that is not equivalent to European theater. Rather, it has a metacommunicative quality resulting from the constant interaction between performers and audience. The *Sprechraum* of a *ta'ziyeh* performance is not limited to the stage, as it is in conventional Western theater, but is extended to include the entire space within which the audience is situated. Peter Chelkowski has suggested that the closest parallel in the West would be the unconscious avante-garde of Grotowski's "poor theatre," which also attempts to burst bound performance space open to allow for audience participation.[5] The viewer takes part in a discourse and thus becomes a conarrator. There is no concrete experience of dramatic time during the event, as there is in theatrical dialogue. There is, rather, a suspension of time in *ta'ziyeh* discourse, for past, present, and future coexist simultaneously in its performance, thereby allowing the original event, the existential reactualization, and the future goal of salvation to merge into one experiential event.

Let us be content in saying that *ta'ziyeh* is a distinct Iranian performance genre not easily explained in European dramatic terms.[6] It is wiser to attempt to understand the genre in indigenous terms. To do so, we must go back to pre-Islamic times to glean glimpses of a Persian tragic ethos that was incorporated into Shi'i Islam after the nation officially adopted the religion in Safavid Persia (1501–1722 C.E.).

The Emergence and Early Development of Mourning Rites in Iran

Ta'ziyeh has a long history of development in Iran. The rite has never lost its religious implications, and as a dramatic form it has its origins in the Muharram processions commemorating Husayn's martyrdom. Throughout the development of *ta'ziyeh*, the representation of the siege and carnage at Karbala has remained its central focus, with special attention placed on certain key episodes that correspond to each of the ten tragic days. Even though it is thoroughly Shi'ah in character and orientation, the performance tradition is heavily influenced by pre-Islamic Persian religion. The evidence for this influence does not come from Persian literature directly, because "dramatic" art was not an acknowledged medium of expression in Persia, but from the mourning rites for slain heroes that existed in eastern Iran before the advent of Islam.[7] The Persian writer Firdausi (ca. 935–1020 C.E.), for example, provides a late account of an Iranian prince named Siyavush, who, like Husayn, predicts his own tragic beheading. In the poet's national epic, the *Shāhnāmeh*, we read:

> They will strike off this guiltless head of mine,
> And lay my diadem in my heart's blood.
> For me no bier, shroud, grave, or weeping people,
> But like a stranger I shall lie in dust,
> A trunk beheaded by a scimitar.[8]

Veneration of deceased heroes had long been an important part of Persian culture; the theme of redemption through sacrifice found parallels in such pre-Islamic legends as the death of Siyavush cited above and in the ancient Mesopotamian rituals of renewal for Tammuz and Adonis.[9]

Perhaps because of their system of hereditary kingship and strong nationalistic sentiment, the people of the Iranian plateau were particularly hospitable to the Shi'i form of Islam.[10] According to legend, the daughter of the last Persian king of the Sasanid dynasty was taken captive during the Muslim invasion and was married to Husayn, merging indigenous ethos with foreign religion.[11] But even before the development of expressive ritualistic forms to reenact Husayn's passion in Persia, the earliest emotional remembrances for Husayn took shape in the Arabic world. From the beginning, the annual Muharram mourning ceremonies were observed with great emotion. Ayoub suggests that lamentation *(niyāḥah)* for Husayn started shortly after the battle of Karbala, when citizens of Kufah "met the captives of the Holy Family beating their heads and breasts and weeping in deep remorse for their own treachery."[12] Pageantry, however, was to be added later.

It seems likely that throughout the Ummayyad period (661–750 C.E.) the observance of Husayn's martyrdom was a private affair conducted in the homes of influential members of Husayn's clan, during which poets led lamentation sessions by reciting mournful verse.[13] As Shi'ism spread, however, so too did the mourning assemblies. By the tenth century, during the rule of the Persian Buyid dynasty (945–1055 C.E.) in Baghdad, impressive Muharram processions became well established. According to historians, the Buyid ruler Muizz al-Dawlah ordered the bazaars in

Baghdad to be closed down and draped in black cloth on 'āshūrā' of 352 A.H./963 C.E.[14] Yitzhak Nakash cites the historian ibn al-Athir, who writes that the ruler "forced the people to close the bazaars, suspend their business, to mourn, and to place cupolas covered with wool [in the markets]. Wailing women, their clothes torn, walked in the streets, slapping their faces and lamenting Husayn."[15] Chelkowski adds that ibn al-Athir "tells of great numbers of participants, with blackened faces and disheveled hair," repeatedly circumambulating the city while beating their chests and mournfully reciting dirges.[16] At that time the event was public and took shape as a procession, but during periods of non-Shi'i rule, the observance must have gone underground, continuing within the homes of the devout as a private observance, much as it did during the Ummayyad period. Evidence such as this suggests that the earliest mourning observances moved from predominantly Arab areas into Persian domains after 1500 C.E., when Shah Ismail I, the first king of the Safavid dynasty, declared Shi'i Islam the state religion of Persia and staged public performance gradually took shape.[17]

Persia's cultural influence in the region prior to the Safavids was substantial, but it again became a political power when Shi'i Islam was established as the state religion and was used to unify the country in opposition to the military campaigns of Sunni adherents such as the Ottomans and Uzbeks. It was at this time that the Karbala narrative was used to bolster a strong sense of national identity. Lincoln, for example, makes the following observation: "Invocation of the Husayn myth ever since has served, inter alia, to separate Shi'i from Sunni and Iranian from Arab."[18] It was at this time also that the Muharram observances received royal encouragement; commemoration of Husayn's martyrdom increasingly became a vehicle for patriotic sentiment even as it retained its soteriological function as a ritualistic act.

European eyewitness accounts of the processions are abundant, and they describe marching characters clothed in colorful regalia accompanied by mounted soldiers enacting the battle of Karbala. Chelkowski describes these early public displays as follows: "Living tableaux of butchered martyrs stained with blood, their bodies showing simulated amputations, were moved along on wheeled platforms. Mock battles were mimed by hundreds of uniformed mourners armed with bows, swords, and other weapons. The entire pageant was accompanied by funeral music and spectators, lined up along its path, beat their breasts, shouting 'Hussein, O Hussein, the King of Martyrs' as it passed by."[19] Such staged performance grew out of the processional observances held during the first ten days of Muharram.

As the Muharram ceremonies began to flourish and further develop under the Safavids, a second significant form of observance emerged as a genre of verbal and written poetry concerning the lives and actions of Shi'i martyrs. Belonging to the *maqtal* genre, these narratives in verse form were taken predominantly from a book written by Vaiz Kashifi titled *Rawḍat al-Shuhadā'* (Garden of Martyrs), and they were read to assemblies for the purpose of eliciting lamentation *(nawḥ)* from audience members.[20] The work, given an Arabic title but written in Persian, was widely circulated in Shi'i communities from the sixteenth century onward and had broad-based popular appeal. The text was later translated into Urdu in India to continue the narrative tradition there.[21] Originally, it was customary to recite or chant a chapter from the *Garden of Martyrs* in public each day during the first ten days of Muharram. Repeated in gatherings hosted by private patrons, the recitations came to be known as *rauẓeh khvānīs* (garden recitations). During these events a series of extended threnodies interspersed with exegetical digressions *(gurīz)* would occur to add secular color and allow the raconteur to display his skills at verbal art.[22] Other martyrology books were eventually written based on the model of Kashifi's classic text for use in such mourning assemblies *(majālis)*, and today they comprise a huge body of literature.

Traditionally, a *muraṣṣa' khvān*, someone with good recitation skills, would read elegies *(marṣīyahs)* embedded in the larger *rauẓeh* corpus or recite pithy ones from memory. The poet would recite while standing at a pulpit *(mimbar)* or sitting on a raised platform. From his elevated position, he would recite loudly in an oscillating timbre to insure that his tragic verses would be heard by all in the mourning assembly. Here is a powerful example of the genre from the opening lines of an elegy by the Persian poet Qaani (d. 1853 C.E.):

> What is raining? Blood.
> Who? The eyes.
> How? Day and Night.
> Why? From grief.
> Grief for whom? Grief for the King of Karbalā'.[23]

J. M. Unvala, who witnessed a number of Iranian *rauẓeh khvānīs* in the second decade of the previous century, described the poet and his effect on the audience as follows:

[He] sits and recites for about an hour an anecdote of the martyrdom in a sing-song manner, . . . He has such fluency of speech and such volubility, that he recites sometimes for hours together without stopping even to think. In order to dispel fatigue after every sentence or couplet he draws in his breath with a noise produced at the back of the throat. . . . His serious and grave features, his lachrymose voice, his gestures of helplessness and deep mourning, combined with the crescendo tempo, in which he reaches the climax of the tragic stuff of his recital, is sufficient to make even hard-hearted men cry dispairingly like babies and women beat their thighs hysterically, shed bitter tears and shriek incessantly *Husein, Husein*.[24]

It is important to emphasize again that such gatherings for lamentation were arranged to elicit emotional responses from audience members and to remind the pious of Husayn's suffering. Participation in these events offered the audience members the possibility of experiencing the martyr's pain vicariously through what I have been calling subjective apprehension. By subjective apprehension I mean a personal experience of Husayn's passion on the phenomenological level, a level on which individuals have direct access to the *imām*'s mediating powers within a larger social collective. This physical and psychological dimension of the ritual complex is the most central aspect of *muharram* praxis. But rather than generalizing about a phenomenon so richly variegated and complex, let us follow the historical progression of the narrative tradition's development to see how it dovetails with processional rituals to create a distinct ritual idiom.

Gradually, special elegies were developed for each of the days leading up to the tenth. By hearing these elegies recited on the proper days, participants made the past present, thereby actualizing their sacred history, even if in panegyric form. Through choice of episodes and voice modulation, the innovative narrator was able to excite and manipulate the emotions of his audience to produce an intense emotive unity, what Turner would call communitas. Because the occasions for reciting verses from the *Garden of Martyrs* were opportunities for the professional raconteur to display his own particular ability to innovate, the text became secondary to the bard's own creative prowess, thus giving rise to an oral canon of martyr narratives in flux. Digression and improvisation allowed the oral poets to engage in acerbic political and social commentary. The oral performances within stationary *rauẓeh khvānī*s were complemented by spectacular public events such as the special processions for ritual flagellation to participate in the *imām*'s suffering, a dual tradition that continues to the present day.[25] I will return to a contemporary example later, but for now let us see how the two traditions historically came together in ritual performance.

For nearly two and a half centuries, the two traditions—public processions and private recitations—existed side by side but separately, each becoming more complex and at the same time more refined and theatrical. In the middle of the eighteenth century, the two traditions fused to give birth to a new dramatic form known as *ta'zīyeh khvānī*, or more simply, *ta'zīyeh,* in which villains could be distinguished from heroes by their style of oration.[26] The master narrative still remained the Karbala tragedy, but scripts began to be composed about other martyred heroes who received the honor of having their own hagiographies come to life in performance. Since a number of figures from the beginning of time have participated in the cosmic drama of Husayn's passion, it is not surprising that dramas written in their honor should have emerged over time to complement Husayn's turmoil.

Pelly's 1879 translation of a *ta'zīyeh* manuscript serves as an excellent example of the expansion of the performance canon. His text comprises thirty-seven self-contained scenes ranging from the Old Testament "Joseph and his Brethren" (Scene 1) and the respective deaths of the members of the Holy Family (The Prophet [Scene 5]; Fatimah [Scene 7], Ali [Scene 8], Hasan [Scene 9], and Husayn [Scene 23]) to the culminating act, "The Resurrection" (Scene 37), with events leading up to the battle of Karbala sandwiched in between.[27] Writing some three decades later, Wilhelm Litten lists fifteen additional plays, beginning with Ismail's sacrifice and ending with a play about the sixth *imām*. This is followed by an act concerning the conqueror Timur, who figures prominently in legends relating the introduction of *muḥarram* observances into India later in the fourteenth century.[28] Thus we see that the repertoire expanded to include pre- and post-Husayn figures, allowing the whole of history to participate in the cosmic drama of the supreme martyr's passion. As Ayoub pointedly writes, "this long drama . . . has the entire universe for its stage and all creatures as members of its universal cast."[29]

Staged performances of such narratives grew out of the processional observances held during the first ten days of Muharram. As a compromise between public/moving processions and the private/stationary recitations, reactualizations first took place at socially marginal locations, such as crossroads, and in places like public squares where large numbers of people could gather. Soon, however, they moved into the courtyards of caravanserais, bazaars, and private houses. Naturally, the need for specially constructed sacred spaces to remember Husayn arose as the performative tradition developed. Ayoub documents the early emergence of *ḥusaynīyyāt*, buildings that were constructed for the sole purpose of mourning during the third century in Cairo, Baghdad, and Aleppo, which came to be departure points for public processions.[30] These specially constructed buildings have their South Asian parallels in the *imāmbāṛās* and *'āshūrkhānahs* of north and south India respectively. Chelkowski has also written extensively on the development of special performance arenas for Husayn in Iran, and I summarize his findings below.[31]

Chelkowski indicates that by the nineteenth century, nascent dramas found their homes in specially constructed buildings known as *takīyeh*s, an alternative term for *ḥusaynīyyāt*. Wealthy members of the aristocracy funded the construction and maintenance of these arenas in urban areas. Some of the buildings had the capacity to seat more than a thousand people. Considerably more modest ones began cropping up, however, in towns and villages. Many of the *takīyeh*s were temporarily constructed for the Muharram observances, and their architectural design allowed for dialogic interaction between the assembled audience and performers. The main action occurred on an elevated dais located at the center of the structure, a feature reminiscent of the raised platforms of the martyrdom narrators. Subplots could be performed in the space surrounding the central stage, creating intertextual frames of reference. Secondary stages on the periphery provided spaces from which actors could converse with those at the center. The overall effect was something akin to modern surround sound.

Corridors running outward from the center of the *takīyeh* were added to the central performing space. This arrangement allowed actors on horses and camels to come and go, as in a circus tent, rendering the entire building a performance space. Indeed, battles and other acts were enacted behind the audience, so that the feeling was one of being encircled by the dramatic action. This added effect enhanced audience participation. The *takīyeh*, in other words, became a microcosmic representation of Karbala that enabled spectators to participate in the historic events so central to their lives. The dynamics of the engagement of audience with performer through narrative enactment is one of the key features of events related to Muharram. Moreover, the theme of portable and temporary *karbalā*'s, the transposition of sacred space, is one to which I will return as the study proceeds to India and Trinidad in subsequent chapters.

In summary, *ta'zīyeh*s, like the *muḥarram* processions to be discussed at length below, developed historically as communal events, whether they were performed in houses, gardens, crossroads, or arenas, which makes them first and foremost social dramas. The important element in the observance was participation. An audience member could not just observe passively. The viewer had to show emotion by weeping in order to experience the suffering of Husayn, and only in this way could he or she completely identify with the martyr. Modern-day Muslim writers of polemical religious literature often even cite the physical benefits to be gained from weeping and wailing, just as New Age gurus, such as the laughing doctor of Mumbai, India, praise the healing effects of humor.[32]

In spite of the numerous historical transformations that contributed to the shaping of *ta'zïyeh* as we know it today, the soteriological purpose remained constant: participation in the performance helped an individual obtain salvation through the intercession of the martyr. The vicarious suffering and death of Husayn was an instrument of redemption for all believers, and belief was manifested best in performance participation. Staged *ta'zïyeh* has been central to the *muharram* observances in Iran for over four hundred years. It has also survived various political vicissitudes, such as the ban on *ta'zïyeh* performance by Mohammad Reza Shah Pahlavi, who, in 1932 decreed that mourning rites were incompatible with his program of modernization.[33] Despite his views about the rite's decadent and backward character, it has remained a creative force of religious and national expression, especially at times of weakness and oppression. At the same time, it has functioned as an agent of social change.[34]

In the next section, I want to shift to the contemporary situation and the material dimension of the Muharram ritual complex, for I wish to draw attention to some motifs that will recur as we move from Iran to the Indian subcontinent and then on to the Caribbean.

The Contemporary Phenomenon

I described above in historical fashion the interrelated phenomena of stationary and ambulatory performances pertaining to Husayn's passion. Now I wish to pay a bit more attention to the processional aspect of the rite. *Dasteh* (procession) is the term used most commonly in Iran for ambulatory rituals held during the months of Muharram and Safar.[35] That *dasteh* can also mean a "division of an army" should immediately alert us to the martial imagery intended by the use of this term, for the symbolism of battle is central to the occasion.[36] The most spectacular *dasteh*s take place on *'āshūrā'* and *arba'īn*, and their most salient feature in Iran, up until recently, has been ritual flagellation *(tatbīr)* performed by male members of the mourning community.

The flagellants, aged twelve and upward, are arranged according to height, the smallest preceding the tallest. Some of them who strip to the waist and strike their chests with the palm of their hands are called *sinezans* (chest beaters). Others wear black shirts cut away in the back so that the chains of their whips can fall directly on their flesh and are known as *zanjïrzans* (chain beaters). Another class of penitents known as the *shamshïrzans* (sword beaters) wear white burial shrouds symbolizing their readiness to sacrifice their lives, and they strike their foreheads with knives and swords, letting the blood drip down onto the shrouds. Yet another group, known as *sangzans* (stone beaters), scourge themselves with stones.[37] All these various penitential groups compete against one another to see who could draw the most blood. Nelly Caron writes that the flagellation processions "tried to outdo one another in the severity of their self mortifications, the least of which consisted of locking padlocks to the skin."[38]

Acts of self-mortification are accompanied with musical instruments. Cymbals *(sanj)* and large kettle and cylinder drums maintain the steady rhythm for striking blows. The leader of each subgroup, chanting dirges, follows the same rhythm. The entire *dasteh* will stop in front of a religious edifice or the tomb of a local saint, in front of the homes of prominent community members to receive donations, or in an open space. At such sites, the participants in one group beat themselves rhythmically while others join in the chanting of simple verses, such as the following:

> It is the eve of Ashura.
> Karbala is in commotion.
> How sandy is Karbala.
> It is the final evening.[39]

The tempo quickens until the excitement reaches an uncontrollable pitch. A sideshow may be performed, followed by more marching. The cries of the participants, who curse the villains while proclaiming sympathy for Husayn, are mingled with mournful songs. Canetti describes the communal nature of these processions as "an orchestra of grief . . . The pain they inflict on themselves is the pain of Husain, which, by being exhibited, becomes the pain of the whole community. The beating of their chests, which is taken up by the spectators, gives rise to a rhythmic crowd sustained by the emotion of lament. Husain has been torn away from all of them, and belongs to all of them together."[40]

The Shi'i *dasteh* is, by and large, the most common processional ritual performance, and it is a tradition that continues in many parts of South Asia today. Although it is one of the oldest forms of commemoration, more extensive accounts of the *dasteh*s begin appearing during the Safavid period. Resident foreigners in Safavid Iran left very rich but often contradictory accounts of what they saw.[41] One fairly typical account comes from Thomas Herbert, who wrote in 1698 C.E.: "Nine days they wander up and down, all the while shaving neither head nor beard nor seeming joyful, but incessantly beating their breasts; some tear their garments, and crying out Hussan, Hussan in a melancholy note, so long, so fiercely, that many can neither howl longer, nor for a month's space recover their voices. . . . The tenth day they find an imaginary Hussan, whom they echo forth in sentorian clamours, till they bring him to his grave; where they let him sleep quietly till the next year's zeal fetch him out and force him again to accompany their devotion."[42]

Although these accounts are fairly repetitive and stereotypical and focus on the sensational, they are a virtual year-by-year record of the development of the pageantry; they chronicle the steady increase in the number of *dasteh* participants costumed to represent various Karbala episodes. For example, floats of living tableaux on wheels eventually came to follow riders on camels and horses. Various attributes that symbolized the battle of Karbala were featured individually. These included standards, banners, martial clothing and instruments, and a variety of ancient and modern weapons.[43] Some of the weaponry (for example, firearms) may seem out of place to European observers, but the Shi'ah attempt to bridge the historical gap between Karbala and the present.

Fischer describes nine floats paraded in Yazd during the 1970s that accompanied the *dasteh*s in which many were performing self-mortification. The floats, which were located at both ends of the procession, included decorated camels and horses carrying Yazid, his men, and the blood-soaked corpse of Husayn; a green-clad Abbas attempting to get water; a large pan of water signifying thirst; and a man dressed as a lion mourning for the martyr. His earlier data from the 1960s adds the bridal chamber of Qasim and Fatimah, the cradle of Ali Asghar and his nurse singing wistfully, and a red-clad Harmala (the archer who killed the infant) shooting arrows into the grieving audience's midst.[44] Depicting such key episodes becomes the core of the exhibitionary complex and provides the central motifs for observances in India, where they take on new forms, while preserving the central ingredients of the master narrative.

It is clear that such massive displays were, and continue to be, an emotional and colorful spectacle for all concerned. Indeed, as the *dasteh*s pass by lines of spectators on either side, the spectators may be moved by emotion to join in the process. As the ambulatory rituals continued to evolve, numerous props were added to increase the spectacle's grandeur. Decorative items such as textiles, mirrors, lamps, and rugs donated by local participants were thus added to the *dasteh* out of devotion. The decorative items contributed by the devout once again reaffirm the communal nature of the event, reminding us that even though the event is primarily religious, it also functions as a social occasion for fostering a common group identity. Today some of the donated items are attached to biers, coffins, and standards. A lamp is often placed inside the replica of Husayn's coffin *(tābūt)* to symbolize the light emanating from his corpse.[45]

The *dastehs*, organized by guilds or special committees representing various districts of a town, follow a prescribed order of precedence, each carrying '*alams* (standards) inscribed with the name of the sponsoring organization. Sometimes a mobile passion play is performed as part of a mourning *dasteh*. In the past, all these elements added glamour and color to complement the crimson of the flagellants' flowing blood. In the present, all the elements described above are embellished with objects of modernity, such as villains wearing sunglasses. Although virtually everyone participates in the events on the level of popular practice, such forms of piety have not always gone without challenge and criticism from certain sectors of learned Shi'i society. William Beeman, for example, indicates that the performances were never popular with the clerical establishment, and we have already seen that the Shah had them officially banned, even though they were tolerated to a certain extent.[46]

Werner Ende has pointed out that flagellation rituals, as well as other aspects of the drama during Muharram, have been controversial throughout the 1900s.[47] He indicates that certain members of the Shi'i *'ulamā'* (clerical establishment) have over the years questioned the way that *muḥarram* is observed. The issue revolves primarily around the use of flagellation as a legitimate means of identification with the martyr. The great *fitnah* (struggle), as the debate came to be known in the twenties, was aroused by a pamphlet authored by a Lebanese Shi'i Muslim named Sayyid Muhsin (d. 1952), in which he declared flagellation, among other aspects of the processions, to be unlawful innovation *(bida')*. Although Ende's study is concerned with Shi'i communities in Iraq, Lebanon, and Syria, the same issue has been raised on occasion in Iran.[48]

Gustav Thaiss writes of the tense relationship between the ideal form of Islam propagated by the orthodox literary tradition and the concepts and practices of everyday life as follows: "In many instances they are often the same, but often there is a divergence between what the learned men of Islam believe and teach and what people believe and practice. Perhaps most outstanding here is the official attitude of disapproval of the majority of Shi'a 'ulema toward the self-mutilation and flagellation involved in the mourning processions during the month of Moharram, in contrast to the acceptance of such practices by a large number of believers in the bazaar as religiously praiseworthy behavior."[49] Most recently, there has been a ban placed on flagellation in Iran as a result of the tension Thaiss describes. The practice, however, continues in South Asia to the present day, especially in the form of breast-beating *(mātam)*. The tension between so-called high and low culture on the level of ideology and practice is a theme that runs through interpretations of Muharram wherever it is practiced. In Trinidad, where flagellation is ab-

Figure 1. An unadorned *nakhl* frame from Nain, located in central Iran, being constructed for *muḥarram* processions. Photograph courtesy of Peter J. Chelkowski, Sr.

Figure 2. A large *nakhl* from Mahriz in procession on the tenth. Photograph courtesy of Peter J. Chelkowski, Sr.

sent, the tension rests not in the mutilation of the body but in other practices with cognates in South Asia. For my purposes in this book, I thus
want to draw attention to another material feature of Iranian observances during Muharram, for it provides a useful point of comparison
with some of the objects used in processions both in India and Trinidad.

Perhaps the most outstanding structure to emerge out of this ceremony is the huge teardrop-shaped *nakhl*, which is constructed on a lat-
tice wooden frame (see Figure 1).[50] Virtually every town and village in
central Iran has one, and although there is a general uniformity in its
teardrop shape and design, each is built in proportion to the specific
community's financial prosperity. Some of them are as small as a baby's
cradle, while others are incredibly large, such as the one in Yazd, which
weighs, according to knowledgeable sources, three tons, requiring hundreds of men to carry it on their shoulders during the processions.[51] At
the height of approximately one meter, wooden beams set roughly a meter apart protrude around the bottom of the structure. Those who carry
the *nakhl* use these beams to lift the object in the manner of weight lifters.
There are additional beams along the length of the *nakhl* above these,
which rest upon the shoulders of those who carry it. These huge structures are focal points for the processions. The *nakhl* in Mahriz, for example, is a colossal structure that accommodates 156 people, 39 on each
side (see Figure 2).[52]

The word *nakhl* means date palm in Arabic. According to those directly
involved in the construction of Yazd's ritual objects, the *nakhl*'s structure,
with all of its decorations, symbolizes the *ma'fah* of Imam Husayn. *Ma'fah*
in the local dialect refers to the coffin of a holy person. Since it is said
that the bier of Husayn was covered with date palm leaves to protect his
corpse from the blazing sun of the desert, the structure symbolizing it
has come to be known as a *nakhl*. Others call this structure a *naql*, a term
that means "carrying from one location to another."[53] In Persian religious poetry, *nakhl* stands for "stature," especially of the martyred *imām*.
Edward Browne makes this point in his translation of Safavid-period
poet Muhtasham's (d. 1588) celebrated *haft-band* (poem of seven-verse
strophes). In the fifth verse, we read: "Many tall palm-trees from the
grove of the 'Family of the Cloak' [Holy Family] did the people of Kúfa
fell in that plain with the axe of malice." Then in verse eleven the term
appears again: "They cast to the ground his [Husayn's] tall palm-tree
even as the thorn bush; A deluge arose from the dust of the earth to
heaven."[54]

In eastern India, "stature" becomes translated into the "courage" of
Husayn. There Husayn's courage is embodied in an object taken out in
procession known as a *sipar* (shield) in Urdu and Hindi (see Figures 3

and 11). The shape and design of the *sipar* suggest strong parallels with the *nakhl*.

During the days preceding '*āshūrā*', the structure is covered from top to bottom with black cloth, which is the sign of mourning, and it is decorated with various objects made specifically for this purpose. Anyone can assist and participate in the ceremonial decoration of the *nakhl*, which is called *nakhl bastan*. Some do it because of a *nazar* (vow) and some out of sheer love for Imam Husayn. During the ceremony, people utter words of praise and greeting to the Prophet and his family. I describe the ornamentation here because it serves as a strong marker of continuity with the material culture of the tradition as it passes from Iran to India and onward to the Caribbean. Perhaps most noticeable on the black cover of the *nakhl* are the large and small decorative mirrors on its flat surfaces. The mirrors, often donated by people who have taken vows to perform some reciprocal act of exchange, are a gift of faith. These people believe that if they donate mirrors for the *nakhl*, Husayn will intervene on their behalf to have their *nazar* fulfilled. Others also donate mirrors, in addition to colored pieces of fabric or daggers with which to decorate the surface out of sheer love for the *imām*'s radiance. According to those involved in the ceremony, a popular folk belief is that the mirrors symbolize the light emanating from Husayn's body; this is the reason why lanterns are placed inside the coffin that often accompanies the larger structure in procession. Also, young women promise to donate mirrors for the *nakhl* if they find a good husband. This would symbolize the light of their destiny. Occasionally, lanterns are also hung from the *nakhl* to illuminate the entire structure in a symbolic way, reminding spectators that the structure's iconicity represents not only Husayn's bier but also his body. Moreover, because the *nakhl* also symbolically represents Karbala on another level, it serves as a microcosmic, multivocalic symbol of the overall event's master narrative, integrating as it does images of Husayn, his bier, and the plain upon which he was slain.

Daggers, along with swords, used to be hung on the covering of the *nakhl* to symbolize the weapons used by the enemy to assassinate Husayn. It is customary to attach a cypress tree made from a cross section of plywood to the front surface of the *nakhl*. Various designs made from cork and small pieces of arrow-shaped wood are placed on the wood's surface. In Persian literature, cypress has always symbolized a tall, straight figure in the shape of the beloved. The cypress attached to the *nakhl* stands for Husayn's erect body being riddled by enemy arrows like a porcupine on the tenth of Muharram. The pieces of cork symbolize the actual arrows that struck him.

At either end of the *nakhl*, extending from the top, is a *shaddeh*, a long

pole surmounted by a circular object festooned with colorful fringes, tas-
sels, and sashes. As an act of devotion, people donate garment-sized
pieces of cloth to be tied to the circular portion of the *shaddeh*. These fabrics can be of any color or even be multicolored. On the *shaddeh*s, the
pieces of donated fabric are so numerous that they have to be tied to
the circles in a very dense concentration. Recall that it is said that after the battle at Karbala, the members of Husayn's family were robbed of
their belongings. Ayoub corroborates this belief by citing the verses of an
unnamed poet:

[T]he womenfolk of Muḥammad were among the enemies, pillaged and their
goods divided amongst low and dissolute men.

They were pushed around like slave girls, mistreated and beaten with whips . . .
as though they were captives or even more lowly.

Their head covers and veils were forcibly torn off their heads and faces.

Behold a man, his limbs tied in stalks with no one to set him free, and a noble
woman taken captive and her earrings snatched away.[55]

The donation of these fabrics and tying them to the *shaddeh* is a symbolic
gesture in memory of Husayn's surviving family members. In addition,
flags adorn the structure on top. In Arabic, the word *al-ʿalam* can mean a
"distinguishing mark."[56] It can also mean a flag or banner, and that is
how it is used in Taft and Yazd to refer to a banner of distinction. *ʿAlam*s
often adorn the *nakhl* or are carried in procession with it to symbolize the
numerous standards carried by Husayn's party. On top of the *nakhl*,
between the *shaddeh*s, there is a horizontal wooden beam spanning the
structure. Several vertical sticks three to four meters high are attached to
the horizontal beam, so that people performing *naẓar*s may attach pieces
of cloth to them.

   According to Fischer, the *nakhl* is supposed to be taken out at noon on
the tenth. In his vivid description of the observance in Yazd, he notes
that the movement of the object represents a threefold desecration committed by Yazid's army under the command of ibn Sad and Shimr: "they
shed the blood of the Imam, they shed his blood during the time for Friday noon prayer, they shed blood during the holy month of Muharram
when fighting is supposed to be suspended."[57] These desecrations are
not to be forgotten by the pious, and they remind the faithful that there
is much tyranny and oppression in the world. As the *nakhl* moves about,
a special stew named in honor of the martyr is being prepared for later
communal consumption. Eventually, all of the *dasteh*s converge at a central mosque, while villagers gather in a nearby graveyard to march smaller

*nakhl*s to their own homes. At the conclusion of the evening events on the tenth, participants settle down to a communal meal, after a period of partial fasting. The meal provides closure to the mourning period.

Weeping and Laughing

Up until this point, I have been painting a rather pious and tragic picture of the observances during Muharram. There is, however, another dimension that needs to be acknowledged. Much of the literature on the event has focused precisely on the tragic, the melancholy, and the somber, but in this focus we run the risk of essentialism. Iranians—and for that matter, all Shi'ah—are not a morose lot, perpetually living in a darkened world within which an ethos of constant sorrow prevails. In fact, there is a festive and celebratory air engulfing the phenomenon of Muharram performances that demands our attention. Although the idea is controversial and is the subject of constant debate, we must recognize that there is room for joy and merriment within the Karbala paradigm. Browne, for example, mentions a genre of satirical poetry to be recited during the most serious occasion for weeping, the *majlis* assemblies created for this very purpose. He has translated a poem called "The Book of the Table, Censuring Hypocrisy," which is a work "in which the ostentation of the host and the greed of the guests are satirized with some pungency."[58] A few couplets from the poem will suffice for my purposes here:

> Of those who make mourning for Ḥusayn and sit in assemblies in
>   Frenzied excitement.
> . . . .
> A host of gluttonous men, all beside themselves and intoxicated with
>   the cup of greed,
> . . . .
> To sit in such an assembly is not meet, for without sugar and tea
>   It has no charm.
> God is not pleased with that servant in whose entertainment is
>   neither sherbet nor sugar.[59]

The image is one of a poet sitting in an assembly sarcastically commenting on the assembly itself. It is as if the poet is mocking the excesses of the aristocracy through biting social commentary, perhaps alluding to the feasting that occurred in Yazid's palace when Husayn's head was brought to him on a stick. The poetic license of the *rauẓeh khvān* allows him to address serious and self-reflexive issues in a comic way. Thus humor too has its function during the annual period of mourning.

To use another example, Beeman has surveyed the intertwined relationship between *ta'zīyeh* and *rū-ḥauzī*, a form of traditional Iranian *com-*

media dell'Arte that draws on indigenous folklore and even classical literature. Beeman sees the two, which at first seem almost diametrically opposed, as complementary because "they cannot be treated separately
within the context of Iranian society."[60] He suggests that both theater
forms project the same presentation of Iranian morals and ideologies but
do so from opposite ends of the performative spectrum: "Laughter and
tears, though seemingly opposite emotional expressions, may indicate alternate, but equivalent ways of dealing with similar emotional and social
situations."[61] The complementary emotions embodied in the acts of
laughing and crying resonate with the English expression "I laughed so
hard I almost cried," which reminds us that laughing and crying can
produce similar physiological effects and emotional states.

Another example comes from the sacred drama itself. Mehdi Abedi
reminisces about his childhood in an Iranian village, where he was recruited at a very young age to play the "barely nubile bride" of Qasim for
the wedding scene in a local *ta'ziyeh* production. When he was in the second grade, he finally refused to play the role of the bride. He recounts
the following: "What triggered the refusal I no longer exactly remember,
but I remember bursting into angry tears at either being pinched,
winked at, or obscenely teased as if I were a real girl."[62] He goes on to say
that "Such teasing and humor had a regular place: the man who played
Zeinab (sister of Husain, who led the women and children after the massacre . . .) always had a big mustache, and when someone would make a
rude comment to him, he would show his mustache from under his
chādor. Typically, he had an obscene tongue as well, and would respond
to propositioning with such retorts as, 'Yes, I'll sleep with you; bring your
mother too.'"[63] Abedi remarks that there was even "ribald mockery"
of the *ta'ziyeh* itself: "Shemr and Zeinab would replay their repartee from
the passion play in obscene variations, e.g., Shemr: . . . If you are Zeinab,
then what's that penis? Zeinab: . . . God knows it is an extra piece of
meat."[64] He finally notes that weeping was not always real but was sometimes pretend, but it nevertheless brought merit. Such reversals of the
somber mood associated with the sacred month must also be accounted
for in any discussion of Muharram rituals.[65]

Lastly, let me simply point out the testimony of Iranian friends who
have mentioned to me repeatedly that as young men and women they always looked forward excitedly to the advent of Muharram. They fondly
remember it as a time of festivity, food, family reunions, and occasions
for social intercourse. One male friend of mine, who had been a teenager
in prerevolution Iran, said many of the young men wanted to join *dasteh*s
not necessarily out of compassion for Husayn but because they wanted to
attract the admiring gazes of young women and prospective marriage

partners. Moreover, referring to the flagellation processions in Nabatiyya, located in southern Lebanon, Richard Norton and Ali Safa add that after the processions were over, "young men casually walked the street showing off their blood-spattered clothes as testimony to their fidelity to Shiism. Teenage girls enjoyed themselves, sometimes ogling their male contemporaries, sometimes giggling."[66] The flagellation therefore provided an opportunity for playful competition through a macho display of bloodletting. Muharram, in other words, offers the possibility of merging the sacred and the profane; it is profane social activity within a sacred frame of temporal reference.

The profane dimension is certainly found among the South Asian Shi'ah as well, and even more so among their Sunni brethren. In his brilliantly conceived 1966 Hindi novel titled *Ādhā Gāv* (Half a Village), which unfolds in ten chapters corresponding to the days leading up to *'āshūrā'*, Rahi Masoom Reza paints a picture of Muharram in a rural area of northern India as a time of excitement and celebration. For Reza, an avowed Marxist and secular Shi'ah, Muharram is filled with competition and sporting fun between neighborhoods. Concerning competitive breast-beating, for example, he recalls how "this matam used to be so powerful that the round and lotus-shaped candleshades and the crystal pieces of the chandeliers would tremble to its beat. And the silver-thread flowers embroidered on the hangings upon the platform where the tazi-ahs stood would melt into teardrops."[67] In his world the rituals are accompanied by swordplay as well as competitive attempts to faint during mourning assemblies to receive special attention and achieve elevated social status. Reza's *muḥarram* is an occasion for loud and colorful processions that attract merchants and vendors who set up stalls along the procession routes, giving the whole atmosphere a carnival-like feel.

The merger of the sacred and the secular, the happy and the sad, is a contested issue to which I should like to return in the following chapters. As we will see, the issue of praying or playing is a recurrent one. Although I do not want to ignore the pious and somber dimensions of Muharram, I also do not want to privilege them. My reason for doing so should become apparent as we proceed. I speculated earlier that as we move farther from the Shi'i core, the Muharram observances become increasingly localized, drawing on the indigenous customs and traditions of each geographic location where they take root to create something new. At the same time, I want to argue that the tradition remains to a large extent faithful to the underlying paradigmatic nature of the Shi'i master narrative.

In this chapter, we have seen that the material and visual dimensions of the public rituals combine with their verbal and dramatic dimensions to create a distinct ritualistic complex. Taken together, these multi-sensory events—stationary and processional, private and public, sacred and secular—comprise the observances for Husayn in Iran, telling a story that is relived each year by the faithful. Step by tedious step, the final ten days of Husayn's life are incorporated into each person's being through acts of bodily neglect and emotive upheaval. As a performance configuration, these events annually recreate a mood that keeps the historical master narrative of Husayn's passion alive in the hearts and minds of those who believe in the martyr's redemptive powers. So powerful is this narrative that it diffused along with the spread of Shi'i Islam to the Indian subcontinent, a topic to which I will turn in the next chapter.

Chapter 3

The Passage of Rites to South Asia

> *Mir Athar Husain Zaidi . . . spent the whole year eating opium and prepar-*
> *ing for Moharram. He had spent his whole life preparing for Moharram. The*
> *truth is that in those days the whole year was spent waiting for Moharram and*
> *the anniversary of the martyrdom of Imam Husain. . . . Moharram was noth-*
> *ing less than a spiritual celebration.*
>
> —*Rahi Masoom Reza,* The Feuding Families of Village Gangauli

Muḥarram in Comparative Perspective

Although *muḥarram* is observed throughout India and other countries of
the subcontinent with the great anticipation pointed out by Reza above,
the manner in which the observance is performed differs from place
to place. The ritual performances take on the vernacular character of
the regional environment within which they are practiced by building
on the concerns of local interest groups. This is the result of a number of factors. Many centuries of Hindu/Muslim interaction has led
to various degrees of cultural borrowing, resulting in great regional
variation. The ethnographic data suggest that some of the major reasons
are Hindu/Muslim ratios, urban versus rural practices, and Sunni/Shi'i
population distribution. Any of the above, or combinations of them, are
major factors in the formation of variation in Muslim ritual practice on
the popular level. A thorough comparative study of this phenomenon
has yet to be undertaken in South Asia. Indeed, A. R. Saiyid suggests that
it is a somewhat neglected field in Indological studies.[1]

An exhaustive survey of the sort Saiyid envisions is not attempted
here, because the secondary data available to me and my own observations can hardly do justice to the complexity of the rituals as practiced
throughout the entire subcontinent. Rather, the second section of this
chapter is based on a survey of the existing sources and my own occasional participation in *muḥarram* observances in northern India, with
some parenthetical information provided from the south of India. I fo-

cus on the north because this is the area from which the largest number
of Indians were uprooted and coerced to go to the Caribbean as indentured laborers from the mid-nineteenth century onward. The north Indian material is further supplemented by relevant literature about the
event in other parts of South Asia in an attempt to offer a mosaic
overview of the phenomenon that is the heart of this book. But my main
aim in this chapter is to bring to light certain aspects of *muḥarram* that figure prominently—or, conversely, do not appear at all—in Trinidad, the
geographic and ethnographic focus of the remaining chapters of this
study.

I realize that the congeries of beliefs and practices that I present does
not represent any specific tradition, thus making it difficult to study. But
if we accept Jim Masselos's proposition that rituals during the month of
Muharram must be viewed in the plural, then presenting a composite
can help us to flesh out some salient aspects of the phenomenon for comparative purposes. As he states, "Moharram is ambiguous, ambiguous in
situation, in interpretation and practice. In its ambiguity lay its strength,
popularity and its continuity."[2] Before proceeding with my ambiguous
survey, however, some general observations are in order.

There are some great differences concerning the manner in which
muḥarram is observed in predominantly Muslim countries and in India.
Perhaps the greatest and most significant difference between India and
Muslim nations lies in the use of the word *ta'zīyeh*. Whereas the term is
used in Persian to refer to the ritual drama, it has a different connotation
in South Asia. There it is the name given to the model cenotaphs, the focal point of the public processions that take place during the event in
many parts of northern India. Such differences notwithstanding, the historical consciousness instilled in believers by the Muharram narratives
continued to remain an integral part of the ritual complex as developed
and practiced in India. Indeed, I believe I can reasonably argue that it is
the historical narrative that has kept the tradition alive and vital in many
parts of the world. According to oral legend, *muḥarram* was known in India as early as 1398 C.E., when the conqueror from Samarqand, Timur
Lenk (1336–1405 C.E.), better known as Tamerlane in English, crossed
the Indus to implant Islam firmly in the subcontinent and to establish
political rule.[3]

Vernon Schubel provides an abbreviated account of the legend:

[W]hile in Iraq Timur converted to Shi'ism and became so deeply and emotionally attached to the area around Karbala that he would not move his troops from
that spot. In order to deal with this situation, the *'ulama* of the region built a
replica of the tomb which he could take with him out of the dust and clay of that
place. It is reported that nightly sounds of mourning and lamentation could be

heard arising from the model. It was this *ta'ziyah* which was brought to India by Timur during his invasion.[4]

Given that Timur visited Karbala only after his invasion of India, the historicity of the account is questionable. Nonetheless, it is a pious narrative still in circulation today that functions as an etiological justification for the ostentatious practice of building model tombs. These artistically rendered replicas of Husayn's actual tomb at Karbala came to be known as *ta'ziyah*s in Urdu and other north Indian languages. In South Asia, symbolic pilgrimage thus came to replace the arduous physical pilgrimage to Karbala.

Note that in India and elsewhere on the subcontinent the object of veneration is given the same name as the staged, dramatic renderings of Husayn's passion in Iran. This interesting terminological shift suggests something pervasive about Indian public display events—the importance of external displays and processions during communal rituals. In this sense, these rituals share much in common with Hindu religious processions. The similarity between Hindu and South Asian Muslim processional rituals has not gone unnoticed. Garcin de Tassy, for example, wrote in 1831 that "Muslim festivals, . . . appear to read like those of the Hindus." To illustrate, he compares *muharram* to the Durga *pūjā*: "Like the Durga Puja, the *ta'zia* is observed for ten days. On the final day the Hindus immerse the image of the goddess in a river amidst huge crowds and great pomp, while a thousand musical instruments are played. The same thing happened with the Muslim festival. Mourning is observed for ten days and the *ta'zia*, a replica of the tomb of Husain, is generally immersed in a river with the same pomp."[5] Juan Cole has pointed out more recently that Hindu participation in *muharram* has been fairly widespread for centuries. He also notes that Hindus introduced certain practices to the observance that were adopted by high-caste Muslims.[6] The observances during Muharram were thus transcommunal from early on in the encounter between Muslims and Hindus, allowing for public occasions during which actors could negotiate radically different cultural and sectarian worldviews. But as Saiyid rightly points out, Hindu influence alone is not enough to explain *muharram*'s development in South Asia.[7] In fact, even though rituals performed during the month of Muharram creatively adapted to Indian customs, very strong thematic ties to Iran remained.

In South Asia, the Iranian root concept of spatial separation between private and public aspects of the rite remained intact, even while localized rituals developed to express grief for Husayn by creatively incorporating indigenous customs (*'ādat*). In South Asia, the *ta'ziyah* procession (*julūs*) became the most popular display of public veneration or, alternatively, celebration during the month of Muharram, while the tradition of the *majlis* (mourning assembly) became a private expression of grief par excellence for the Shi'ah. Although they remain separate, the interrelated nature of private and public forms of observance is a central theme in South Asia as it is in Iran.

Muḥarram as a regular observance did not become widely established in precolonial India until Mughal times (beginning in 1526 C.E.).[8] But aside from Lucknow, the major Shi'i center in India, where an elaborate *muḥarram*-centered ritual complex developed in the eighteenth and nineteenth centuries under the royal patronage of the Navabs of Avadh, the observances never took a fixed form.[9] This is in part because aside from the Navabi period (1720–1856 C.E.) of Lucknow, there was never a strong Shi'i power base to facilitate fixed observance.[10] Further, a canonical source for the standardization of observances does not, to my knowledge, exist in Shi'i literature on jurisprudence produced in South Asia. This may be one reason why there is such a seemingly contradictory complex of practices associated with *muḥarram* in India, not to mention the fact that the Shi'ah are a relatively small minority throughout South Asia. In colonial times, for example, they did not exceed 4% of the total population in any of the provinces of British India, with the largest concentration being found in the former United Provinces, where they comprised over 31% of the total Muslim population.[11]

The numerical inferiority of the Indian Shi'ah should suggest that while theology may have been relatively fixed, local custom was grafted onto central aspects of the Shi'i observance to produce ritualistic forms not recognizable in Iran. Add to this the fact that Hindus and Sunnis also participate in various capacities, and we have an inevitable context for innovation, adaptation, and transformation. Nonetheless, a fairly strong core of motifs from the Shi'i master narrative, kept vivid through *marsī-yah* and other chanted traditions, has provided some continuity. The ritual traditions surrounding days seven through ten, the culmination of the observance marked with grand processions through the streets of cities, towns, and villages throughout South Asia, demonstrate the continuities quite well.

It is important to keep in mind that India was a religiously plural society during the Mughal period. The Muslim population in precolonial South Asia, though politically and economically powerful, was always a quantitative minority, and within this minority the Shi'ah constituted only a small percentage of the total population. Muslims thus had to cope with the Hindu majority and its overwhelming culture. As a result, a number of Hindu influences crept into *muḥarram*. This is only natural because social encounter inevitably results in cultural mixing to create innovative hybrid forms of local practice. The same process already seems to have been occurring in ancient Persia, where an earlier generation of scholars attempted to locate the origins of the lamentations for Husayn in pre-Islamic rites of renewal and eulogized mourning for fallen heroes. The process of religious and cultural mixing continues in the Indian subcontinent but with a unique twist. The Shi'ah of India had to cope with negotiating their forms of observance with Sunni varieties. Sunnis, it must be emphasized, also observe *muharram*, especially on the tenth, but do so for very different reasons. Ideological conflicts thus often erupt into physical violence between the numerous parties concerned.

To begin with, the concept of vicarious suffering, so prominent in Twelver Shi'ism, has been somewhat alien to Hindu thought, even though the idea is present in Mahayana Buddhist texts concerning the *bodhisattva* ideal. Hindus also do not observe or commemorate religious occasions; rather, they celebrate and play them out in accordance with the doctrine of *līlā* (divine play). The disputed issue of celebration versus observance is a pervasive one in South Asia, but the debate is not solely an Indic innovation, because we have already seen that similar discourses periodically took place at the Shi'i geographical core in Iran, as they do in many parts of the Muslim world. Concerning the proper way to observe and perform such rites, the eighth *imām*, however, provided very strict guidelines to observe *'āshūrā'* with grief and weeping, which would be rewarded with a blissful eternity in paradise. Those who did not observe in this manner would join Yazid in the "deepest pit of fire."[12]

Be that as it may, the idea of mourning as a measure of identification and devotion is not a major concept in the religious and philosophical speculations of the classical Hindu tradition. Nevertheless, on the level of devotional practice, female Hindu mourning groups are popularly found in south India, and cults of deified heroes and heroines are quite common on the folk level.[13] Public *pūjās* (ritual worship) are, however, characteristically engulfed by *melās* (fairs) that allow for the merger of sacred and profane activities.[14] It is indeed difficult to find any public religious service in South Asia being performed without the requisite merchants, vendors, acrobats, dancers, and performers. In this sense, the sacred and the profane are closely associated, if not inextricably enmeshed. It may not seem odd, therefore, to find elements of buffoonery, clowning, dancing, and sexual license associated with *muharram* observances in India. The clowning dimension is particularly true in the south, where the Muslim population is very much a minority even in so-called Muslim centers, which makes it difficult for it to exert control over external accretions to the rite. We must remember also that the Shi'ah remain a minority within a minority. One observer has noted, for example, that *muḥarram*, as performed in the Deccan, "is the biggest carnival of the year; observed more by Sunnis than Shi'as."[15] What this signifies is a gradual co-optation of the rite from the Shi'ah, which is the unavoidable consequence of coexisting in a religiously plural country.

By and large, the comic portions of the event are limited primarily to the Sunni sector of the Muslim community. This is probably the case because most of the Sunnis in India do not mourn the death of Husayn. T. Vedantam explains it as follows: "According to many Sunnis the festival signifies the triumph of virtue and truth over evil and that there is no place for mourning."[16] Learned Indo-Shi'i Muslims see comic behavior during Muharram as mockery, however, and such performances often lead to theological debates and physical clashes between Shi'i and Sunni Muslims.[17] But Sunnis make countercharges against the Shi'ah. Consider the following personal memoir by the well-known Indian Sunni scholar Khuda Bukhsh Khan (1842–1908 C.E.), whose father would never allow his children to view the Muharram processions because he regarded them as a "mockery" and a "travesty." Khan recalls how his father "thought it wicked to a degree to convert the anniversary of one of the greatest tragedies in the history of Islam into a day of carnival and festivity, instead of observing it scrupulously as one of veritable mourning."[18] Obviously, the learned *ustād*'s father was not aware of the private forms of worship held in the *majlis*.

For the Indian Shi'ah, however, *muḥarram* is still a predominantly sober event conforming to the Persian theological paradigm of identification with the supreme martyr through subjective apprehension. The manifest differences between Iranian and Indian Shi'i modes of observance are numerous nonetheless. First of all, in India there is very little staged reenactment of the historical events at Karbala, either privately or publicly.[19] Reenactments are limited mostly to martial displays with swords and sticks. Rather, the reenactment occurs as a gradual process unfolding over a ten-day period within a larger symbolic space. The arena of performance, be it the house, the neighborhood, the village, or the city, becomes a microcosm of Karbala. This is most vivid on the tenth of Muharram when the Indian Shi'ah symbolically "make a pilgrimage" (*ziyārat karnā*) to Karbala by visiting graveyards where the *ta'ziyah*s are buried.[20]

Instead of the ritual dramas, we find a greater emphasis on narrating the tragedy through the recitation of *marsiyah* (elegy), the singing of *nauḥah* (dirge), and other forms of chanted laments at numerous *majālis*. The *majālis* may be private or public gatherings for ritual mourning that are held both in homes and at specially constructed sites.[21] The development of *marsīyah* composition and recitation in India is obviously an in-novative continuation of the *rauzeh khvānī* tradition of Iran. Even though Kashifi's Persian classic was translated into South Asian languages, a separate and distinct poetic tradition emerged in the subcontinent. Based on their Perso-Arabic predecessors, new styles of elegy became prevalent in a number of Indian vernacular languages, and their recitation to in-duce weeping during mourning assemblies continued to preserve the memory of Husayn's passion.[22] The Indic tradition of *marsīyah* writing and recitation in Urdu goes back to sixteenth-century Golconda and Bi-japur in the Deccan, and the tradition flourished in nineteenth-century Lucknow.[23]

The *majlis* is the central focus of *muharram* observance in India, accord-ing to elite spokesmen of the Shiʻah. Keith Hjortshoj, working in Luc-know, has noted that the public processional rituals, fire walking, and states of possession that I survey below are virtually meaningless without the *majālis*. This may well be the case, but we cannot disregard ostenta-tious public events completely, for we have already seen that the private and public have been closely interrelated in Iran. Clearly, learned exege-sis serves as a guide for the normative behavior during the sacred month that is supposed to induce subjective apprehension of Imam Husayn's suffering, but the variety of activities found on the streets during the processions cannot be ignored either. It is precisely in these public are-nas that the non-Shiʻi sector of society participates most visibly and exu-berantly, leading to cultural encounter and gradual transformation of the observance through an ongoing process of cultural creolization. It is also in this public sphere that *muharram* becomes a contested phenome-non that needs to be negotiated between the numerous parties involved: Shiʻah, Sunni, and Hindu. But it is a sad truth that when the negotiating of ritual authority and practice fails on the peaceful level through what I call decreolization, violence ensues. Accounts from the colonial and mod-ern period amply demonstrate this fact. Communal violence between the Sunni and the Shiʻah or between Muslim and Hindu is often the case during Muharram. Some examples of this will be provided below, but to conclude this general discussion, let me return to the issue of the inter-action between public and private as the central ingredient of the obser-vances in India.

There is certainly a dialectical relationship between the private *majlis* and the public *julūs* that is not necessarily condoned by orthodoxy but is pragmatically maintained by the masses in popular practice. For example, during the ten days a participant may attend a number of *majālis*. While at a *majlis*, one may listen to the recitation of *marsīyah* corresponding to the historic events commemorated on that day. There will be intense ritualized weeping and *mātam* (breast-beating), followed by a period of silence. After the *majlis* disperses, the individual may participate in one of numerous public processions for a while and then attend yet other *majālis*. This pattern continues for the duration of the observance. There is no incongruity here. The individual can still experience the suffering of the martyr through participation in both types of events. The drama, in other words, is not acted out on a stage in India but is nevertheless reenacted and experienced through the varied actions of the community of believers, even if other public activities surrounding the event verge on the carnivalesque. The *marsiyah* recitations during the *majālis* and the communal processions that occur in varying degrees of intensity throughout the first ten days of Muharram are two central aspects of such performative action, and there is an oscillating tension between them.

Let us now move on to a brief survey of various *muharram* activities. By using specific ethnographic examples and travelers' accounts, I wish to underscore the interaction of public and private domains of observance as well as the multisectarian nature of the phenomenon in India. The literature upon which I draw is both historical and modern, but I focus on accounts from the mid-nineteenth century to the third decade of the twentieth century because this is the period when Indian indentured laborers were uprooted to various islands under British control.

A South Asian *Muḥarram* Montage

Throughout most of the Indian subcontinent, the observances begin with the sighting of the new moon on the evening before the first of Muharram. In many areas they continue until the eighth of Rabi al-awwal, which is said to be the day when survivors of the carnage were released by Yazid.[24] Most of the important activities, however, occur during the first ten days of Muharram, on the twelfth of the month, and on the fortieth *(cahallum)*, which falls on the twentieth of Safar.[25] There does not seem to be a set date to begin work on the *ta'ziyah*s.[26] In some regions, work on them continues throughout the year, whereas those with inner bamboo frames that are reused year after year need only to have the outer wrapping replaced, which is normally made of layers of colored paper, mica, and tinsel. In the latter scenario, communities can afford to wait until the last days to complete their *ta'ziyah*s. The length of time devoted to the construction depends on the complexity of design and the object's size. It is believed that the spirits of Hasan and Husayn enter into the *ta'ziyah*s as they are being built, infusing the structures with significant curative powers.[27] The spirits remain in the objects until the symbolic time of Husayn's death, after which the spirits leave the objects. From this time onward, they are no longer considered sacred and "may be kicked about and anything done with them."[28] In fact, in some areas, small coffins (tābūts) are placed inside of the ta'ziyahs to symbolize the spirits, and in Baluchistan, Pakistan, women even make small effigies representing the two martyrs out of cloth to place inside the coffins.[29]

The size and shape of the ta'ziyahs vary from place to place, but they all consist of a wooden or bamboo base and frame, a tomb chamber, and in some places a central dome representing the one on Husayn's actual tomb in Karbala. They are essentially three-tiered structures, but occasionally they can be as high as six tiers. John Hollister records one being twenty-seven feet tall.[30] I will provide fairly elaborate descriptions of the Trinidadian structures and the process of their construction in Chapter 5 but quote here from Ja'far Sharīf's 1920s account to give the reader a sense of their form and design: "It is usually covered with a network of paper neatly cut, and it is sometimes decorated on the back with plates of mica (talq). It is also ornamented with coloured paper formed into various devices and has tinsel fringes, the whole structure surmounted by a dome which is often contrived so as to move around at the slightest breath of air. Its beauty appears when lighted up within and without. In shape it is square, its sides varying in height. . . . Some instead of covering it with a paper network make strings of glass bangles (bangrī), with white paper flowers, and behind they tie saffron-coloured cloth or paste red paper."[31]

John Oman provides another impressionistic description from the Panjab in the following early twentieth-century account, in which he freely imposes his European aesthetic sensibilities Elaborating on the imaginary nature of the designs inspired by Husayn's actual tomb, he states:

"[T]here were many of considerable size, others quite diminutive; but all bright and glittering with tinsel, mica, and coloured paper; some were quaint, some pretty, and some decidedly grotesque. . . . One of these tazias might be merely a tower of four or five stories built on a light bamboo framework. Another more elaborate and bizarre in form would have the appearance of a strange composite being, with a woman's face and the body of a peacock, bearing a house on its back. Some tazias were supported upon winged horses with long ostrich-like necks, surmounted with human faces of feminine type. One was borne on the head of a winged angel, who, by means of a simple contrivance manipulated from behind, was made to beat his breast in a rather ridiculous fashion.[32]

Obvious biases aside, Oman's description gives us a flavor of the variety of structures built for this occasion. His description implies that the ta'ziyahs are not identical replicas of Husayn's tomb, but rather artistic

Figure 3. A reverse mica painting (c. 1850–60) by an anonymous artist from Patna, Bihar, depicting a *muḥarram* procession with a variety of *taʿzīyah*s, *ʿalam*s, and *sipar*s. By permission of the British Library. Add. Or. 401.

renderings constructed in competition with other builders' creations (see Figure 3).

Since all Muslims observe the death of Husayn, both the Sunni and Shiʻah construct cenotaphs in many parts of India, as in the city of Banaras. This is not to say that everyone agrees on the manners and methods to be employed in observing the occasion correctly. Nevertheless, even Hindus venerate the structures because of their healing powers, and some go so far as to view Husayn himself as a *deva* (deity).[33] There is even mention of Husayni Brahmins in the ethnographic record.[34] A difference, however, exists in the reasons why the Shiʻah and the Sunni observe the death, as well as in the manner of observance. Many members of the Shiʻi community, for instance, hold that the Sunni are directly responsible for the murder, and it is common practice among them to curse *(tabarra')* the first three caliphs ritually as an integral part of the observances. On the other hand, there is a popular Sunni belief that it was actually the Shiʻah themselves who carried out the deed.[35] Thus, in many locations, Sunnis counter the curses by performing daily *bayān* (declaration) each evening from the first through the tenth, praising the good qualities of the first three caliphs in order to assert and justify the Sunni position on the interpretation of the historical events.

Other disagreements that are aired during *khutbah*s (sermons) conducted in both camps focus on the construction of *ta'zīyah*s, the use of martial drumming, and the performance of *mātam*. Many Sunnis claim that the construction of *ta'zīyah*s borders on anthropomorphism, which is forbidden in Islam. With regard to drumming, they argue that the use of military instrumentation is appropriate to remind people that Husayn died for a religious cause. Lastly, on *mātam*, they claim that the practice was forbidden by the Prophet in one of his sayings *(hadis)*. Shi'i clerics, on the other hand, disagree on each of these points.[36] In consequence, both have their own reasons for participating in these rites. But such differences and disagreements are voiced mostly on the ideological level. Upon closer investigation we find that there is not a strict ritual division between the two factions in practice, even though there were times in the past when the rite was performed separately. There is, in reality, a certain degree of interaction and free play between the two sectarian groups on the public level today. Doctrine and practice thus coexist in creative tension with one another. Some Sunnis do, in fact, lament and bring out *ta'zīyah*s, while some Shi'ah use drum accompaniment during their processions.[37] Another example from Banaras based on my own inquiries is that people say the Sunni are supposed to wear green during the month of Muharram and that the Shi'ah should wear black.[38] But during times of interaction between the two groups on the street, Sunnis could be found wearing black, and the Shi'ah wearing green. While there are no absolute rules of behavior during Muharram, I will consider some of the salient differences in ritual observance below and then proceed in the next section to discuss the celebratory element in the public rites.

On the private level, however, the story is quite different. It is relatively rare for Sunnis to attend Shi'i *majālis*, partly out of philosophical reasons and partly out of practical fear of physical retribution by fervent Shi'ah who may hold them responsible for Husayn's death. In Iran, for example, people have reported that the villainous characters in the dramas have often been attacked and, in some cases, even killed out of an emotional frenzy. This may be an urban legend, but Abedi reminisces that "Shemr would gallop into the center calling Husain to show himself, and announcing to the audience, 'I'm not Shemr, nor is this the land of Karbala; I'm just playing a role.' This formula was partly used to fend off the danger that onlookers would become so enraged at his killing of their beloved Imām that they would kill him."[39] So, for reasons such as these, there are usually public prayers held in Sunni mosques, readings from the *Qur'ān*, and *khutbah*s acknowledging the Karbala tragedy as an unfortunate incident in which members of the Prophet's family were killed, but nothing more.

Hindus and foreigners, on the other hand, are most welcome at the private gatherings organized by the Sh'iah because the historical events are seen as universal tragedies and opportunities to convert those moved by the elegies.[40] Hindu intellectuals such as Jawaharlal Nehru are drawn to the observance precisely because of its universally tragic nature. As Nehru wrote in 1939, "sacrifice for a noble cause can never be in vain. And though we may sorrow for it, it is more fitting that we should derive inspiration from it. The fact that countless generations have been powerfully affected by the sacrifice and tragedy of Kerbala is in itself significant of its abiding value. . . . We shall have to forget our petty selves and minor complaints and think in terms of the larger good. That is the lesson of Kerbala and it is in this spirit that I hope all of us will pay homage to that sacrifice."[41]

Essentially, the recitations in formal settings follow the historical events day by day and are relatively uniform across India because of a standard publication distributed by the All-India Shia Congress, in which canonical narratives for each specific day are printed.[42] The two Indian census volumes on the observances in Lucknow and Delhi in the north and Hyderabad in the south both contain the following serialization of the daily narrative recitals for the Shi'i *majlis*:

first day: demands by Yazid's men for Husain to give allegiance to Yazid or to accept death
second day: departure of Husain for Karbala
third day: arrival of Husain in Karbala
fourth day: account of Hazrat al-Hurr
fifth day: account of Abad, one of the sons of Imam Husain who had fallen sick at Karbala
sixth day: account of the martyrdom of Hazrat Ali Akbar
seventh day: account of the martyrdom of Hazrat Qasim
eighth day: account of the martyrdom of Hazrat Abbas
ninth day: account of the martyrdom of Hazrat Ali Asghar
tenth day: account of the martyrdom of Hazrat Imam Husain[43]

Each formal *majlis* also follows a standard pattern of observance and is led by a *zākir* (one who praises God). According to Regula Qureshi, the format progresses in a specific sequence. First, *sauz* (short lament) is performed to express "one emotion intensely and concisely," followed by *salām* (salutation), which is often "reflective or didactic in character."

There then follows the *marṣīyah*, "chanted usually by group in unison," which "may be followed by a *marsiyā* poem in the style of formal oratory." This is followed by *nauḥah*, which is a "dirge, simple, highly expressive and lyrical in character." After *nauḥah* is complete, *mātam* is performed. In the assembly, this term stands for an expressive and passionate dirge as well as the breast-beating performed by the participants. The *majlis* closes with a "salutation of the martyrs and imāms in Arabic, a type of litany chanted by the leader of the *majlis*," which is referred to by the term *zīyārat*.[44] Perhaps this last practice alludes to a kind of internal or mental pilgrimage to the shrine of the martyr being eulogized on that particular day. Whatever the case may be, the formal *majālis* are complemented by private ones, which can be arranged by anyone with adequate financial means (see Figure 4). Due to gender segregation, women often conduct their own *majālis*.[45]

Regardless of how raucous *muharram* may become as the tenth approaches, many early accounts describe the solemnity of the first day of Muharram. Mrs. Meer Hassan Ali, for example, refers to Lucknow on this occasion as "the Deserted Village." She comments still further: "The profound quiet and solemn stillness of an extensively populated native city, contrasted with the incessant bustle usual at all other times, are too striking to Europeans to pass by unheeded."[46] The first day's solemnity is marked by ritual purification of the body and by cleaning the home and the place of worship. The pious cut their nails at this time, whitewash their homes, and clean sacred sites, while women untie their normally braided hair and break their glass bangles as a signal that the official period of mourning is starting. In rural areas of India, even in villages lacking a Shi'i population, *cauks* (squares) are demarcated to serve as sacred space on which to place the model tombs. Nadeem Hasnain and Sheikh Abrar Husain suggest that in such non-Shi'i villages "a large number of Sunni Muslims and a considerable section of Hindus . . . keep *Tazias* and observe mourning in one form or another" (see Figure 5).[47] When asked why Sunnis participate, an Indo-Shi'ah responded to John Hollister that "the Sunnis recognize Hasan and Husain as grandsons of the Prophet whom he greatly loved, and that they were killed. Some too have found prayers answered, and so continue to pray."[48]

The first day is devoted to final arrangements for processions and for setting up platforms throughout Muslim sectors of the city. From these platforms the story of Husayn is transmitted in numerous but less formal ways than in the ritualized *majlis* liturgy. The most common form of transmission, however, is the *marṣīyah*. At other times, there are exegetical lectures given by Shi'i clerics pertaining to the event, which combine fervent piety and political content, as in Iran. Cole mentions that "Some

Figure 4. A watercolor by an anonymous Murshidabad artist (c. 1812) depicting a *majlis* in the royal *imāmbāṛā* of the Navab of Lucknow. By permission of the British Library. Add. Or. 2595.

notable-class Shīʿis depicted the encroaching British as the evil Yazīd in the 1857–58 rebellion. Among laboring-class devotees of the Imām the tax collectors and police of the Shīʿī government itself may have been seen at times as the real Yazīd."[49]

Many groups of all religious persuasions engage in processions to indicate the inauguration of the rite. The Shiʿah also set up *sabīl* tents and stands to distribute water or sherbet to travelers in memory of the thirst suffered by the martyrs. This day is also marked in some parts of India by a rite called *koḍālī mārnā* (adze digging), during which the *fātiḥah*, the exordium of the *Qurʾān*, is read over sugar candy representing the martyrs. The neighborhood group then goes to a predetermined spot where the digging instrument is used to strike the ground and turn over one clod of dirt. A day or two later a fire pit *(alāvā)* is dug in which fires are lit every night. Each evening stick and sword dances are performed around the fire, and some people who have taken vows walk across the glowing embers barefoot or throw the coals into the air with their hands. This activity occurs in numerous neighborhoods in Banaras and other locations

Figure 5. A reverse mica painting (c. 1850–60) depicting an attendant fanning a *ta'ziyah* with a fly flapper. The *ta'ziyah* rests on a *cauk*. By permission of the British Library. Add. Or. 413.

throughout India, and the *alāvā* is said to represent the fiery trench dug for protection by Husayn's party on one side of their encampment at Karbala. In some places, the *alāvā* is dug in front of permanent or temporary *imāmbāṛā*s.[50]

In Banaras, as throughout most of India, temporary shelters known as *imāmbāṛā*s in the north are set up near masjids in many Muslim neighborhoods on this day.[51] These serve as resting places for the *ta'zīyah*s and other ritual objects, such as the special *'alam*s (standards) relating to the character in the tragedy mourned that day (see Figure 6). Permanent *imāmbāṛā*s containing nonephemeral *ta'zīyah*s known as *zarīḥ*, which are made of precious metals and jewels, are also decorated throughout India from this day onward. The Muslim population of Banaras is not isolated to one area of the city. Sunni and Shi'i *muhallā*s are often interspersed with Hindu residential areas, even though there are some large concentrations of Muslims scattered about in clusters. Some of the neighborhoods are not strictly segregated. One can find both Sunni and Shi'i populations, as well as some Hindus on the periphery, living in a given area. A number of such neighborhoods are oriented around small *masjid*s. Each *muhallā* that can afford to have its own *ta'zīyah* constructed

Figure 6. A watercolor (c. 1795–1800) depicting the inside of an *imāmbāṛā*, with a *ta'zīyah* in the foreground and a *rauẓeh khvān* seated at the rear. By permission of the British Library. Add. Or. 938.

Figure 7. A reverse mica painting (c. 1850–60) from the Banaras region depicting a standard bearer. By permission of the British Library. Add. Or. 412.

does so. Others that are in close proximity to one another may combine efforts on the cenotaph construction. But in a number of places, especially in urban areas, many people purchase disposable *ta'ziyah*s of various size, design, and execution, depending on their financial means, from professional builders who may be Hindu or Sunni.[52] The *imāmbāṛā*s also serve as gathering places for the ritual recitations of the day's events at Karbala. Each *imāmbāṛā* is marked by another *'alam*, a three-sided flag hung from a banner staff that represents the one carried by Abbas, the standard bearer for Husayn's party. The banner staffs are fastened into the ground on either the first, fourth, or fifth day (see Figure 7).[53] Participants and spectators believe that these flags are imbued with the power to bestow miracles during the month of Muharram.[54] Similar to Iranian custom, it is for this reason that barren women in the Panjab who take vows offer cloth for the standards (see Figure 8).[55] The power invested in this temporary sacred space is transferred to all objects within its precincts. Especially powerful is the *ta'ziyah* itself. Because of the immense power within these sacred hot spots, the complete environment surrounding it must be kept ritually pure at all times. In other words, the *imāmbāṛā*, as well as the objects within it, are loci of *barakat*, the grace of God. It is a common sight during Muharram processions to see people touching the objects or passing underneath them to avail themselves of the healing power. An account from the early twentieth century makes note of the transactions that occur:

Some were Hindu women, probably unfortunate mothers, who thus paid respect to these effigies of the martyrs' tombs, in the fond hope that Imam Husain would graciously extend his protection to their surviving children and grant them long life. . . . From time to time some persons, for the most part women with babies in their arms, approached the *tazias*, and made trifling offerings of flowers, sweetmeats, and money, which gifts were formally accepted by the attendants, and some trifling return, generally a garland of small flowers, given in exchange by way of acknowledgement to the pious and now happy oblationer, who, beaming with satisfaction and hope, would place it without delay about her infant's neck.[56]

The following days are filled with prayer and *marsiyah* recitation both in private and in public gatherings. Once the *'alam*s are posted in front of the *imāmbāṛā*s, offerings of food are placed in their presence, censers for burning frankincense *(lobān)* are lit, and the *fātihah* is recited over them every night. After these evening prayers, the food placed in front of the banners is distributed to all in attendance. This special food, known as *tabarruk*, is considered to be a blessing and parallels the Hindu practice of distributing *prasād*. Hindus who observe *muharram* distribute *malīdah*, a cake made of pounded meal, butter, and sugar.[57] These social acts of prayer and commensality are followed nightly by verbal reenactments of

Figure 8. A Panjabi *muḥarram 'alam* topped with a *panjah* being taken out in procession during the month of Muharram in 1973. Notice the various cloth offerings for vow fulfillment tied to the standard. Photograph by Richard Kurin. Courtesy of the Smithsonian Institution's Folkways Archive.

episodes from the tragedy corresponding to that particular day.[58] They can take the form of poetry, song, lectures, and personal petitionary prayer *(du'ā')*. People from outside of the cities often visit the *imāmbāṛās* and ask Husayn, or the specific martyr being remembered on that given day, for favors and they frequently make vows *(mannats)*. They may ask her or him to heal a sick kinsman, insure the wealth of the family, or to pray for the dead. In Banaras, devotees who have relatives living in the city will remain there until the tenth of Muharram, the climax of the observances. Others return to their respective villages feeling confident that Husayn will aid them in life as well as in death.

Although *muḥarram* is intensely religious for the Shi'ah, there is also a strong social dimension associated with it. Saiyid, for example, reports that residents of the Sunni-dominated town of Chanorba, Uttar Pradesh, who live and work elsewhere try to return home each year during the period to "celebrate" the holiday.[59] Sharīf adds that in south Gujarat, merriment and masquerade replace grief from the fourth until the tenth.[60] Although marriages cannot be performed during the contiguous months of Muharram and Safar, this social occasion provides opportunities to make matches and arrange for future unions. The kind of celebratory atmosphere that the occasion encourages is an issue to which I will return below.

On the morning of the fifth, Shi'i processions move throughout various sectors of the city.[61] In Lucknow, the standard of Abbas is taken out for the first time in memory of his courageous action to bring water for camp members.[62] This event marks the beginning of a series of processions that reach a peak on the tenth but continue sporadically until the eighth of Rabi al-Awwal. Each group begins its own procession at the neighborhood *masjid* or at the nearby *imāmbāṛā*. The *'alam*s that mark the *imāmbāṛā*s are disengaged from their places of rest to be carried in the procession. Hired low-caste Hindu drummers noted for their musical expertise playing *tāsā*s (clay kettledrums), *ḍhol*s (wooden cylinder drums), and often cymbals, sometimes coming from as far away as Calcutta, walk at the front of the crowd (see Figures 9 and 10).[63] Drummers are also sometimes recruited from the Sunni community, and less frequently they may be Shi'ah. The musicians pound out a rhythm to which all Shi'i men respond by beating their chests with an open or closed fist. This first procession is done in verbal silence.

Some Sunnis also march in the processions, but they generally remain aloof from the main procession and do not perform *mātam*. This may in part be because Sunnis in Banaras, as in many places in India, do not condone *mātam* or any other kind of self-mortification, whereas for Shi'i males it is the most ostentatious and courageous performative act of re-

Figure 9. A *tassa* player from the Banaras region (c. 1850–60). By permission of the British Library. Add. Or. 407.

Figure 10. A bass player from the Banaras region (c. 1850–60). By permission of the British Library. Add. Or. 408.

membrance and subjective apprehension. The Sunni perceive the act as a form of self-mortification not condoned by Islam, as noted above. One Sunni bystander told me that "if one beats himself while on earth, he will be cut in half by a sword and cast into hell (*jahannum*) on *qiyāmat*," the Day of Judgment. In Bengal, however, Sunnis do perform chest beating, as we will see later. But many Sunnis, like Hindus and curious tourists, join the processions to watch the spectacle (*tamāshā dekhnā*) and enjoy a festive holiday out on the streets because it is, in one nineteenth-century observer's opinion, "this festival which is observed with the greatest pomp and show."[64] In other words, the entertainment value alone is enough to entice non-Shi'ah to participate.

On the evening of the fifth day, groups of Sunni men belonging to specific *akhāṛā*s (clubs) assemble in predetermined, semi-secret places throughout the city. Each year a few men attempt on this evening to become possessed by Qasim, Hasan's young son, who is said to have been wed to one of Husayn's daughters, Fatimah Kubra, on the battlefield. The one who is chosen to be the club's *dulhā* (bridegroom) leads the fire-walking and -running on the tenth. This is a predominantly Sunni phenomenon. Theoretically, no Shi'ah participate in the possession rituals in Banaras. In fact, some Shi'ah with whom I spoke told me that this performance is a mockery of the whole event. It is, however, normally tolerated, but occasionally tempers flare. During such times small-scale riots have been reported that have led to injuries and occasional death. Elsewhere, however, such as in Lucknow, the Shi'ah do walk on glowing coals as a form of "*mātam* on fire."[65]

Legend has it that an Indian pilgrim from Bijapur in the Deccan went to Karbala and found the horseshoe that was lost by Qasim's horse on the morning of the tenth. The pilgrim brought the horseshoe, or *na'l ṣāhib*, back to Bijapur in order to display it as a relic of the highest order.[66] After the demise of Bijapur's power, the *na'l ṣāhib* (venerable horseshoe) was transferred to Hyderabad. The custom may have diffused to other parts of India from there. Although orthodox Muslims, Sunni and Shi'ah alike, may not necessarily acknowledge that such a marriage was ever performed, since Qasim was quite young at the time of the massacre, the belief is widespread on the folk level in India, and Qasim plays an important role in the observances. The venerable horseshoe, being the annual locus of Qasim's *dulhā* spirit, is imbued with great powers. Possessions that are a result of this practice in Banaras reinforce the vitality of this custom. The description I supply below pertains to one neighborhood in Banaras, but the practice occurs in numerous locations on the fifth and sixth throughout the city.

The room in which possession occurs is empty except for the wall facing Mecca. This wall is smeared with *sindūr* (vermilion paste), representing the blood of those who died at Karbala. There is a *panjah* at the center of the wall. The open hand is flanked above and on each side by a horseshoe with a lemon placed in the middle of each one. The ornamental props serve the function of clearing all malevolent *jinns* (spirits) from the immediate vicinity and warding off the evil eye.[67] Incense is burned to purify the room while the spectators (all male) enter and crowd around a central space that has been demarcated for the upcoming ritual. A prayer rug is rolled out in front of the *panjah*, and when all the preparatory work is completed, the first nominee is led in. He kneels down facing Mecca and touches his head to the floor. A cleric reads the *fātiḥah* in order to invoke the spirit or essence (*ḥāl*) of Qasim. This process does not take long, and in a few minutes the *ḥāl* of Qasim enters the gently swaying candidate, who immediately becomes possessed and begins to snort like a horse. His pupils turn upward as he goes into violent convulsions. At this point in the proceedings, the bystanders wrestle the possessed person to the floor. Once the possessed man is calm, he is lifted up in the air and tossed around the room while everyone shouts "*dulhā, dulhā*" in metrical unison. The candidate is then revived and taken from the room. Preparations for the next potential groom are made, and he is then brought in to undergo the same ordeal. This process continues until all the contenders have had their try.

After the meeting ends, a committee of learned elders decides who among the possessed ones shall be chosen to lead the fire-walking and -running. The man is chosen on the basis of both spiritual strength and physical agility.[68] Once the meeting dismisses and the neighborhood *dulhā* is chosen, he may visit other similar *dulhā*s throughout the city. The origins of walking on fire during Muharram are obscure but may have been influenced by similar Hindu practices. Hjortshoj, citing data from Mirjhar Jain, suggests that in Lucknow, where the Shi'ah do practice it as a form of *mātam*, this rite was introduced by Burmese Shi'ah in the 1940s.[69] Whatever the case may be, the practice is both penance and amusement at the same time. No one with whom I spoke afterward showed any evidence of pain or blistering.

Another ostentatious procession that occurs at various times involves a horse covered with a *sindūr*-stained white shroud, often with a turban placed on the saddle to represent the missing rider. The horse procession also includes a bloodstained coffin. The horse has a special meaning for the Shi'ah, a meaning that differs considerably from that for the Sunni. As noted earlier, not only mankind, but all earthly creatures partake in the passion of Husayn. Ayoub has suggested that animals are even able to express a greater degree of empathy and loyalty to the suffering martyr than humans because of their utter innocence and irrationality, which provides them with a kind of "mysterious knowledge."[70]

In the Arab world, aside from the camel, the horse stands unrivaled among all the animals in the domesticated realm. It is viewed as the most intelligent animal on earth and as an extension of the rider in some cases. Moreover, it is often seen as the critical factor for a warrior's success or failure in battle. It is no small wonder, then, that the "empty stirrup" is viewed as a powerful symbol of grief for the fallen *imām*. Shi'i literature written in Arabic and Persian, as well as oral tradition in India, holds that Zuljanah *(duldul)*, Husayn's bereaved steed, wandered aimlessly through the corpse-ridden battlefield searching for its rider. It is purported that the horse neighed constantly and wept profusely while rolling in pools of blood on the plains of Karbala. One source claims that after having killed forty enemy soldiers, it ran to the women's tent and beat its head on the earth until its own demise.[71] The horse's mournful action set the example for the women's laments that followed. The horse's role in the cosmic drama is thus characteristically reenacted as a regular feature of the Shi'i performance of *muharram* processions in north India.[72]

One neighborhood usually provides the horse for the duration of the event in Banaras. These dusk-till-dawn processions focus on the horse and the bloodstained coffin. The marches are usually led by *shahnāī* bands that play *nauḥah* melodies as the small groups wind their way through the various neighborhoods during the last watch of the night.[73] The number of people multiplies as these small groups join into a united whole. It is said that strength is added every time a new group joins. Everyone weeps and performs *mātam* for many hours. People passing by reach out to touch the coffin with their right hand. The hand is then passed through one's hair, allowing for a transference of *barakat*. These evening processions are, in one sense, for the horse's benefit. He is led out through the plains of Karbala in search of his rider. It is a symbolic journey in which all participate in the grief and agony of the original event, which is coterminous to the present. Every hour or so, the horse is led to prominent Shi'i homes. The woman of the house comes out and asks the horse where its rider is. Certain learned men of the community watch the horse's response. If the horse signals a direction, the crowd will follow, and after the gesture is read, the woman who asked the question gives the horse milk to drink. The procession often continues in this manner until daybreak. These processions are emotion-laden events; movement is often halted in midstride for intense weeping by the participants.

The climax of the observance begins on the seventh. In many places the day begins with a *mehndī* (henna) procession in honor of Qasim and his would-be bride, Fatimah Kubra. *Mehndī* is the South Asian custom of dying the bride's hands and feet with henna in anticipation of the wedding. This procession is accompanied in some places—such as Delhi, Lucknow, and Hyderabad—by small, one-story *ta'zīyahs* termed *menhdis*.[74] These objects are quite often accompanied by a standard bearer carrying a spear with a lemon impaled on the blade. The spear and lemon symbolize the legend of Husayn's decapitated head being transported to the enemy camp on the tip of a spear.[75] Mushirul Hasan cites the following verse on this:

> When the caravan of Medina, having lost all
> Arrived in captivity in the vicinity of Sham
> Foremost came the head of Husain, borne aloft on a spear
> And in its wake, a band of women, with heads bared.[76]

On the evening of the seventh, other processions embark with the standards of Fatimah, Husayn, the *na'l ṣāḥib*, and the "sword of Ali," which last until the early hours of the morning. The eighth is somewhat quiet in private, but devoted to Abbas in public. Then on the ninth, known as *qatal kī rāt* (night of murder), the standards for Abbas and Husayn are taken out.[77] If two separate processions should happen to meet on the road, the standards from each group are made to embrace.[78] All these processions are merely preludes to the tenth day, when in many places, as in Hyderabad, all the standards, except Qasim's, and all of the *ta'zīyahs* are taken out "in great pomp" and with "every kind of revelry."[79]

One of the many interesting items taken out in the past during the culminating Hyderabad procession is the *āftābgīr*, a royal parasol or fan said to be shaped like the leaf of the sacred pipal tree *(ficus religiosa)*. The fig leaf's shape is similar to the teardrop shape of the *nakhl* discussed in the last chapter and may have some sort of structural parallel. In any case, the leaf-shaped fan is suspended from a long vertical pole, and often two swords are suspended from each side of the parasol section of the object (see Figure 3). The swords are said to represent those of Hasan and Husayn. The earliest account I have read that describes these objects comes from the 1798 diary of Charlotte Florentina Clive (1787–1866). In her entry for June 25, she writes:

This morning we went into the city of Hyderabad to see the procession of the *Tazia*, on account of *Mohurrum*, or great Mussulman festival in honor of the sons of Ali . . . The *Tabout* is accompanied by the *Pimja* (which is also carried separately by the poorer sort,) and both by crowds of youths, and little boys, with Chattries and Aftabgeeries, (Umbrellas) some made of cloth, but the greater number of paper, of various colours, on the top of long thin bamboos, to the summit of which a rope is fastened, which enables those little devotees to balance and direct their poles.[80]

Sharīf rounds out Mrs. Clive's account by explaining how one such umbrella is "carried by a man who rests the pole on his waistcloth while others hold it up with ropes. Whenever the bearer halts they lower the parasol and shake it over his head, but in their excitement they often knock one parasol against another and break them. Many do this in fulfillment of a vow."[81]

Contemporary accounts of the event in Hyderabad do not make mention of this object, and I have personally never seen one. The reason I mention this particular local practice, however, is because of the way the parasol is carried "in the waistcloth." Although there may be no demonstrable parallel between the *nakhl* and the *āftābgīr*, the similarity in shape is tantalizing as a morphological feature for comparison. I do not re-

Figure 11. An 1850s depiction of a *sipar* from the Bihar region resting on a *cauk*. By permission of the British Library. Add. Or. 416.

hearse such a comparison here, however. Instead, I want to use the parasol's mode of conveyance to link it to what I believe is a stronger object for comparison, namely, the *sipar* of Bihar mentioned briefly in the last chapter.[82] These cloth-covered objects, in the shape of a semi-circle mounted on a vertical wooden pole, represent shields and symbolize Husayn's courage. In modern times they are often black and are decorated with five or six round shields, swords, and other ornamentation, including mirrors.

Nineteenth-century illustrations of the *sipar*s from Patna, where the largest Muharram ceremony in Bihar takes place, show them to be red (for blood) and green (for poison), the colors of Husayn and Hasan respectively (see Figure 11). The *sipar*s, as depicted in the illustrations, bear a resemblance to the *āftābgīr*s and could very well be a regional variation. Moreover, the shields of Bihar are carried in the same manner as the parasols; that is, they are hoisted up and rested in a waistcloth, with spotters all around to guide the one carrying the object. My concern here is not to make a firm connection between the parasol and the shield, but to demonstrate some conceptual continuity between the *nakhl* of Iran, the *sipar* of north India, and the "moon" of Trinidad. I believe the *sipar*s are Indian variants of the *nakhl* for reasons that will become clear in Chapter 5. I bring these objects to the reader's attention now because I am attempting to flesh out certain ritual objects and practices that resonate with my Trinidadian data.

The *muḥarram* observance culminates on the tenth for all observers. On the evening of the ninth, Sunnis dig pits much larger than the *alāvā* fires in various neighborhoods throughout the city of Banaras. Huge fires are built in these pits, and they are tended until there is nothing remaining but glowing embers. Then, a short while after midnight, men and boys dressed in green run barefoot through the glowing embers. This begins as a localized phenomenon in each separate neighborhood and then grows into one large group as those walking on fire converge. The sense of intensified ecstasy experienced by the groups consisting mostly of young men increases as the night progresses. The running and converging continues until the fires are completely stamped out, and the groups then proceed to run in a circular route along the main roads of the city shouting Husayn's name. The running continues until daybreak, at which time everyone returns home for some rest. Some of the very enthusiastic participants join up with the Shi'i crowds that begin forming near the *imāmbāṛā*s at daybreak for the *ta'ziyah* processions.[83]

The procession on '*āshūrā*', the tenth, is truly the culmination of the observance. All Muslims fast on this day until the *ta'ziyah*s are laid to rest, and a more pervading sense of brotherhood and *communitas* emerges from this common practice. Sectarian conflict is slightly alleviated on this day, but tensions still remain an ever-present reality. On this day all *ta'ziyah*s are brought out and paraded through the streets of the city. Once again, the procession begins in a localized fashion but builds up as the day progresses. The *ta'ziyah*s are thought to be especially powerful on this day; lending a shoulder to carry the platforms upon which they rest is said to be meritorious. As the *ta'ziyah*s pass, mothers carry their ill children underneath them. It is held that this action has the power to cure an individual of all illness. The procession is accompanied by more *mātam* being performed to the beat of the drums at the head of the procession, the continual chanting of "*yā Ḥasan, yā Ḥusayn*," the occasional *marsiyah* recitation, and periodic fits of hysterical weeping. The more severe male participants pierce their skin and cut themselves with knives to show that they too are willing to suffer the pain to which the victims at Karbala were subjected. This procession lasts most of the morning. Toward noon the procession divides and each group proceeds to a graveyard in or around the city, often passing through hostile neighborhoods to arrive at their destination. Now the *ta'ziyah*s are considered dead, so the symbolic burial can take place.[84] The disposable *ta'ziyah*s are buried at this time, and those who choose to keep their frame for the following year bury only the outside wrapping of the cenotaph.[85] The remainder of the structure is then stored in a *masjid* or a permanent *imāmbāṛā* for the following year. The burial marks the end of the fasting. All participants may now return home to partake in a solemn meal. In some parts of India, the *ta'ziyah*s are placed on display for people to see, as if lying in state during a wake, and they are not disposed of until *tījā*, the third day after a death on which offerings are made.

Another tradition worth mentioning here is the rituals performed on the tenth for the closure of the *alāvā*s because they bear strong parallels to similar practices performed in Trinidad. Sharīf provides a succinct description:

Fire is lighted in the fire-pits round which they walk thrice and recite the Fātiha facing Mecca. Then they put a small coin with some milk and sherbet into an earthen pot, cover it, and lay it in the fire-pit which they fill up with earth, and fix a pomegranate branch on the mound. Next year the pot is dug up and some women for a consideration get the coins from the superintendent, bore holes in them, and hang them from the necks of their children to protect them from evil spirits. Some people after the fire-pit is closed pour sherbet over it and burn a lamp there for three or four days, as they do in the case of a real grave.[86]

Although this day is the climax of the event, it is not the end. The Sunni and Shi'ah alike continue the observance in various ways. For the Sunni, it is a matter of extra prayer and listening to *marsiyah*s, activities that generally prolong the event until the end of the month. The Shi'ah, however, continue with smaller processions throughout the next two months. As was suggested above, the Shi'i observance begins achieving closure on the twentieth of Safar, when processions similar to those on the tenth are performed in accordance with the Islamic day of mourning that takes place forty days after the death of a loved one. The last procession is held on the eighth of Rabi al-Awwal to commemorate the release of the surviving captives of Husayn's party and their return to Medina, when *cup* (silent) *ta'zīyah* is performed.[87] These silent processions seem to be unique to the areas in north India influenced by Lucknow's Shi'i culture. According to B. K. Roy Burman, the custom originated in this way:

In the latter half of the 19th century there was a nobleman in Lucknow, known as Nawab Agghan. One morning, a few days before 10th Moharram a dead body was found lying just in front of the door of the Nawab and he was held on the charge of murder. On 10th Moharram when the *tazia* of the Nawab's family was due for burial, he was in police custody and the burial could not take place. Nawab Agghan was ultimately cleared of the charge of murder and was released on 7th Rabi-ul-Awwal. He took his *tazia* for burial on 8th Rabi-ul-Awwal. But 8th Rabi-ul-Awwal marked the termination of mourning; so he took out the *tazia* procession in the early hours of the day very silently without performing any *matam*. In the subsequent years, he followed the same practice, and now it has become the custom in his family.[88]

The final journey on *'āshūrā'* is a symbolic pilgrimage, a spatial rite of passage that all mourners for Husayn must complete. It is the penultimate show of subjective apprehension of the historical incident in an eternally present situation. For subjective apprehension to be realized absolutely, some of the historical conflicts between the Shi'i imamate and the Umayyad caliphate should be experienced communally in some representational fashion. This is accomplished by the physical movement of Shi'i processions through foreign turf in this microcosmic, symbolic landscape. The passing of Shi'i processions through Sunni and Hindu neighborhoods is a threat, a physical danger, and a potentially volatile situation. Echoing Turner's sentiments, Hjortshoj suggests that in Lucknow: "Muharram is a time ('both in and out of time') in which people cross boundaries, structural divisions within the city and within Islām that they would otherwise not cross. . . . Ritual expressions of opposition are pushed to the limits of implication."[89] But it is precisely during the *'āshūrā'* procession that potential conflict and opposition can be mediated and temporarily overcome when Muslims are in the minority position because both the Sunni and the Shi'ah participate in the processions, albeit for their own specific reasons. More often, however, disparate modes of practice lead to ideological disputes and communal violence. The reasons for ideological dispute have to do with the issue of observance versus celebration, a crucial issue to which I wish to turn in the next section.

To Pray or to Play?

In the preceding discussion I alluded occasionally to the celebratory mood that leaks into the mournful nature of Muharram observances. European accounts from the colonial period most often focus on this spectacular dimension of the rite's public portion. Clive's eighteenth-century account of the procession in Hyderabad is characteristic of the attitude conveyed in many such descriptions by travelers:

The procession in Hyderabad this year, commenced at 9, and lasted till 4 o'clock of the evening of the 25th of June, presenting such a mixture of pomp and meanness, pride and humility, devotion and fanaticism, as it is hardly possible to reconcile the imagination, and still less to describe. The *Tabout*s were numerous, and beautiful, and the Shiah Omrahs to whom they belonged, and by whom they were accompanied, displayed much state, and magnificence on this occasion. I am sure I am within bounds in saying, that 200 elephants, some of them painted and decorated in a pretty manner, and from one, to two hundred thousand people passed in the procession. Each Omrah, was preceded by a party of Mons. –de Perron's (late Raymond's) and his own troops—his standard borne on an elephant, a Nobut, or band of music, and followed by his relations and dependants, some on elephants, others on horses and camels. The predominant colors were white, green, and red, but the *Omrah*'s, and probably all those of the Shiah sect who could afford it, were dressed in green; these were a variety of castes, as a great number of Gentoos, particularly women, *Sunni*s, etc. entered in the crowd, no doubt to see the procession, and partake of the amusements of the day.

  A variety of curious figures preceded the *Tabout*s, and *Pimjas*—here, a champion in armour, with a mask, and there, another with a head-piece (resembling Mambrino's helmet in Don Quixote with the exception of being polished iron, instead of brass.) In one place, a party beating their breasts with violence, and exclaiming "*ya Hussein, ya Hussein;*" another, chanting a doleful ditty; and a third, marching with solemn pace, and downcast look. In another situation, a set of devotees—cutting no doubt from the appearance of their countenances, a good joke in *their* way—and refreshing their exhausted frames by a hearty whiff from a well dressed hookah; another, of frantic wretches dealing in imagination only, death and destruction to the enemies of *Ali*,–and each man by his gestures, and actions, apparently combating a host of foes, while a set of funny fellows—one in particular with his *body* and *hair*, dyed blue—were dispersing in a most bountiful manner, and by way of encouragement, filling the eyes of the champion, and the mouths of the chanters, with a handful of sweet *Abeere*,—one man was riding a sham camel, which was very unruly in his motions; another represented an enormous tiger, and a third, a beast I never saw, viz: a tiger-man, with a long tail, and his legs chained, to prevent from getting loose. These, and a thousand other antics, joined to the noise occasioned by drums, and fifes; collery horns, and trumpets; nobuts, and cymbals; produced such a confusion of sounds, as it is impossible to describe, and contrasted with the solemn dignity of the Omrahs, the hollow sound of the Naggar (or large drum,) and the anxiety of the Tabout,

Figure 12. A watercolor by a Murshidabad artist (c. 1800) depicting a *muḥarram* procession, with large and small *ta'zīyah*s and bare-chested men performing *mātam*. By permission of the British Library. Add. Or. 4394.

Pimja, and Aftabgeery bearers, and followers, excited no small degree of pleasure, from contemplation of human nature, in all its different stages and situations.[90]

Loud music in a cacophony of sounds, parades of animals, humans in masquerade, throwing perfumed scent on bystanders, singing, and dancing, all in the midst of a somber occasion to weep for Husayn (see Figure 12). It is no wonder, then, that some observers have likened the rite to the Hindu festival of Holi.[91] Elsewhere in her somewhat fanciful account, Clive contrasted the somber mood of the Shi'ah with the carnivalesque atmosphere generated by the Sunnis and the Hindus. It almost seems as if two or more separate *muḥarram*s were occurring simultaneously. This is certainly a plausible and optional way of interpreting the event. But we can also see it as the inevitable convergence of religious, sectarian, political, and economic interests. The mixing of the sacred and profane in the cosmopolitan atmosphere of Hyderabad is a familiar scene in other parts of India as well.

Oman, for example, describes how the illuminated tombs accompanied by "deafening tom-toms" and surrounded by patrons and supporters arrived at a final destination in the Panjabi city of Lahore under constant surveillance by the police. "This marshalling of the *tazias*," he writes, "is a moment of intense feeling and keen rivalry. Whose *tazia* is the best, the biggest, the most elaborate, the most costly? These are the questions that occupy the minds of all the participators in the show, and each year the Muharram brings its triumphs and its disappointments to some or the other of the *tazia* builders and their friends." The element of competition is a theme to which I should like to return, but for the moment I want to draw attention to Oman's observation that a festival or *melā* was taking place at the local *karbalā'*. After describing the variety of structures on display, he writes that "amidst this collection of 'tombs' I was surprised to come upon what was virtually a fair with the usual merry-go-rounds, bustling groups of people—mostly women and children—and itinerant vendors of sweetmeats. Under awnings the savory *Kabábs* were being cooked and sold to appreciative customers."[92]

I mentioned above that *melā*s virtually always accompany public religious processions in South Asia, so it should not surprise us to find them associated with Muharram observances as well. They are also common occurrences throughout South Asia on *'urs* days, the death anniversaries of Sufi saints.[93] Naturally, any public event is going to draw in vendors to exploit the financial opportunity. By and large, however, the carnival atmosphere surrounding the Shi'i forms of observance is generated by the non-Shi'i sectors of the population. But even this is not always the case. As I have suggested, sacred activities go hand in hand with secular ones during public displays.

I ended the previous chapter by suggesting that even in Iran a festive mood provides a backdrop to the mournful posture of the religious community participating in Muharram-related activities. The Iranian atmosphere in no way, however, resembles the carnivalesque dimension we encounter in India. As mentioned above, the latter is inevitable in a multireligious nation because people of different faiths participate in the rituals for their own ideological and spiritual purposes. Moreover, they may not necessarily believe or even know the esoteric meanings attributed to the event by the Shi'ah. Yet all, to some extent, know portions of the master narrative and believe in Husayn's miraculous ability to intervene in human and divine affairs. As we have seen, both Sunnis and Hindus take out *ta'ziyah*s for Husayn, but as a general rule neither religious community performs *mātam* because they do not see the occasion as a time for mourning. Some Sunnis do, however, perform *mātam*, especially in rural areas. To get a sense of how the event is celebrated by non-Shi'i communities, I shall close this section by exploring two ethnographic descriptions of three different geographical locations where *muharram* is performed by Sunnis in India.[94]

Saiyid provides a detailed account of Sunni *muharram* performances in two rural areas: Fatehpur village in Maharashtra and Chanorba town in

Uttar Pradesh.[95] Saiyid stresses the "localizing" factors involved in the rituals. Although I disagree with his statement that they "do not have the remotest relationship with Islam," his point that the rituals are thoroughly "Indian" innovations is well taken.[96] He sees in them "collective participation" that generates widespread public "celebration" on a scale not comparable with other Islamic holidays. Saiyid also points out that most of the people who participate and enjoy the "festival" are from the lower socioeconomic groups whose ancestors may have been Hindus prior to conversion. His observation on the low socioeconomic class of the revelers resonates with virtually every account I have read. Saiyid refers to the result as "syncretism," a term I avoid in favor of creolization. Aside from this slight terminological disagreement, I essentially concur with him that the accretions to *muharram* he documents are strategies of adaptation to life among a non-Muslim majority.

In the seaside village of Fatehpur, the new moon of Muharram is marked by bringing out kettledrums that have been stored in rooms next to the local *masjid*s of each neighborhood. The drums are sounded to signal the start of the holiday, and kettle drumming continues during each of the ten nights but is most pronounced on the seventh, eighth, and ninth. The villagers of Fatehpur also dig an *alāvā* pit in front of the *masjid* located in each respective *muhallā*, and men and children dance around this pit to the sound of drums until midnight every evening. The fervor of the dances increases from the seventh evening onward. While men dance, women recite vernacular *marsīyah*s around the fire. As a general rule, these performances are oriented around neighborhoods, and people from each neighborhood gather at their own fire pit. Saiyid does point out, however, that inter-*muhallā* masquerades and visitations take place throughout the period of celebration. This neighborhood organization leads to a "spirit of healthy competition."[97] Tents are also set up in each neighborhood to house *ta'zīyah*s built by the men of each sector. Women bring sweets and sherbet to the tent every evening, and after the dancing is completed, prayers are said over the offerings. The blessing is followed by shared food and drink distributed to everyone in attendance. This pattern continues through the evening of the eighth, but on the ninth the dancing moves away from the tents and pits and onto the lanes of each neighborhood.

Unlike urban areas such as Banaras, where many people purchase *ta'zīyah*s from professional craftsmen in bazaars, men of each neighborhood in Fatehpur build their own from the sixth onward. They can complete the structures so quickly because the frames are recycled and kept in storage for annual reuse. Constructing the tombs is a group effort in terms of both labor and finances, which makes them representative of a specific group's own neighborhood. Neighborhoods thus compete to see who can make the most decorated *ta'ziyah*s. When the structures are complete, many people make *mannat*s (vows) to them, and Hindus from surrounding villages visit to receive the *darśan*(auspicious site) of the objects. On the ninth evening, the fire pits are filled in and the *ta'ziyah*s are taken out in procession to the beating of drums, dancing, and liquor consumption. On the tenth, the tombs are destroyed. The domes of the structures are taken off and cast into the water, and the bases of the structures are taken back to their neighborhood *masjid*s, where they remain until *tījā*. In Fatehpur, *mātam* is performed by the Sunni participants, but Saiyid explains that it is replaced by drumming in Chanorba, even though the practice is still referred to as *mātam*.[98]

In Chanorba, work on the *ta'ziyah*s takes place throughout the year, and a *mehndī* for Qasim and Fatimah Kubra is performed on the seventh day of Muharram. In contrast to the practice in Fatehpur, the Chanorba tombs are based on occupational groups and are not necessarily oriented around specific neighborhoods. Elites do not participate directly, but they do contribute funds for constructing the cenotaphs and they preside over competitive *marsiyah* singing and stick fighting. Masquerade also occurs. Men dress up as monkeys and do comic performances during the processions. On the tenth, a *melā* is organized by Hindu shopkeepers, who contribute money to the festival in order to stimulate sales. During this final procession, the *ta'ziyah*s are arranged hierarchically to reflect the town's social order, and each structure is said to be a reflection of group pride and team spirit. Once again we notice a healthy sense of competition that can foster inter- and intragroup unity. But competition can also lead to divisiveness under certain circumstances, an issue to be analyzed in the next section. For the moment, let us move on to consider one last Sunni example from West Bengal.

Lina Fruzzetti provides ethnographic data on the provincial town of Bishnupur. She indicates that the Sunni refer to the occasion by the Bengali term *utsab* (festival), which is essentially the equivalent of *melā*. The dynamics here are somewhat different than in either Chanorba or Fatehpur because the Sunnis are in a minority position compared to the Hindus in Bishnupur. Fruzzetti points out that because of this position, Muslims use the occasion to foster Islamic solidarity among the thirteen Sunni quarters in the town. Thus they minimize the ideological splits between the Shi'ah and themselves and emphasize Islam vis-à-vis Hindu others. Fruzzetti also describes a festive atmosphere with much mock fighting and other physical feats of strength. There is also liquor consumption, *mātam*, and the purchase of new clothes to be worn in the procession. While each of the thirteen neighborhoods collects donations to build the model cenotaphs, not all neighborhoods build their own. Some combine their efforts, beginning work on the structures from the first day of the month. *'Alam*s are posted near the graves of the town's saints on this same day to mark the occasion.

In Bishnupur the actual festival takes place on the seventh and ninth. On the seventh, low-caste Hindu drummers are hired to accompany the processions and there are displays of stick fighting. The eighth is quiet; then on the ninth the *ta'ziyah*s are taken out to the accompaniment of drumming and *mātam* performance. In the past, the local *rāj* (king) would award prizes for the best *ta'ziyah*, but this practice has declined along with the power of the royal family. Nonetheless, each group vies to build the best. As elsewhere in India, the structures contain bouquets of flowers symbolizing Hasan and Husayn. The flowers are buried after the procession in the local *karbalā'*, which is the town's Muslim grave-yard. Sometimes, but not regularly, the whole structures are buried. Because the participants are mostly from the lower economic classes, as in Chanorba and Fatehpur, the structures are usually saved and redecorated each year. Fruzzetti, echoing Saiyid, sees the festival as fostering group pride and unity in the face of the majority Hindu population, stating that it symbolically actualizes the ideal model of a universal body of believers.[99]

As I indicated at the beginning of this chapter, population ratios and cultural mixing of local custom with religious practice can lead to an enormous amount of variation. By now it should be clear to the reader that it is extremely difficult to generalize about *muharram* on any pan-Indian level and hopelessly impossible to demarcate practices in a quest to identify definitively which practices are strictly Hindu, Sunni, or Shi'ah. On the other hand, I have also conveyed that there is a core stock of symbols and images taken from the Shi'i master narrative that can be drawn upon in the creative production of local traditions. The question that naturally arises from my discussion is whether there is a correct way to observe the martyrdom. Another question that immediately comes to mind is who owns the ritual complex? A useful way to think about these problems is to use the indigenous classification of internal and external interpretations and practices that correspond to the theological terms I introduced in Chapter 1. I refer here again to the esoteric *bātin* and the exoteric *zāhir*, which I also wish to parallel with conceptions of private and public observances.

The Shi'ah, we can say, control the interior and exterior domain in Iran, where they are the majority population. In India, however, the Shi'ah, being a minority within a minority, have had no alternative but to adapt their rituals to a religiously foreign environment, even if the practices are contested from time to time. Moreover, because of the ostentatious nature of the public display and the miraculous power of the martyrs, *muḥarram* has drawn in participants from other faiths who have created their own forms of worship that are more in line with a celebratory mode of behavior. As John Hollister states about Shahjahanpur in the former United Provinces, "Sunni participation . . . has transformed it until the element of mourning has almost been completely eliminated, and the time for the procession has been changed to night, getting under way about ten o'clock, and reaching Karbala in the morn."[100] Because of this transformation, the Sunni and Hindu versions of the rite are naturally less reminiscent of the mournful mood of the Shi'i form. Even though the lines of demarcation were rather rigid from time to time in the past, the boundary lines of praxis are, for the most part, permeable and fluid. The Muharram rituals in South Asia thus have become dislodged from their solely Shi'i moorings to create an interreligious form of practice that combines solemnity with celebration, fusing the sacred and the profane. This is how I understand the development of the rite in Trinidad as well, and although the demographics are incredibly different, the strategies for survival there are reminiscent of the Indian scenario. What then can be said in general about contemporary *muḥarram* observances in South Asia?

The contemporary force of the historical incident is most vital, permanent, and everlasting for individual and community in the ritual performance of the event in its many local manifestations. Subjective apprehension is realized in the performance of participatory rituals for the Shi'ah and public celebration for many members of the Sunni and Hindu populations. Further, "this ritual idiom serves as a bridge across time and space, upon which a paradigmatic statement of a universal human tragedy is carried out to, and enacted in, a specific context in the present."[101] It is the specific contexts of *muḥarram* that add local variation and color to a universal experience of tragic suffering for the global Shi'i community. But it is also local variation that allows for the creative expansion of the rite to other sectarian segments of the community. Divergences run parallel to continuities in the specific case examples I surveyed above. It is also in specific local contexts that the public portions of the rite provide the possibility for political protest, social divisiveness, sectarian violence, and government intervention, as we have already seen to be the case in Iran. Although Saiyid and Fruzzetti both emphasize the unifying nature of *muḥarram* in their respective studies of relatively rural areas, there is ample historical evidence to show the opposite in many urban centers.[102] Before making the transatlantic journey to the Caribbean, I want to close this chapter by looking briefly at the important social dimension of conflict during *muḥarram*, for it is an issue that emerges again in Trinidad.

Public Observances as Stages for Political and Sectarian Agitation

In previous chapters, I have alluded to the numerous ways in which the month of Muharram has afforded the Shi'ah a symbolic and theological means to protest and rebel against oppression and tyranny. It should be clear to the reader at this point that resistance to ruling forces is a major Muharram theme around the world, and we will encounter more political examples in the Caribbean. Ideological conflicts leading to protests that result in government intervention may often lead to violence, as they have on numerous occasions in India. Communal violence during the sacred period has occurred between the Shi'ah and the Sunni on the one hand and between Muslims and Hindus on the other. In more isolated cases, disputes have arisen within the Shi'i fold itself. As Oman notes:

> For the maintenance of order in the streets, the police, having ascertained the localities where several *tazias* of the year have been built, prescribe the precise route which one must follow in order to reach the appointed meeting-place. On these occasions the resources of the guardians of the public of the peace are, in large cities, often taxed to the utmost, for the spirit of fanaticism is in the air, and the hostility of the rival sects of the Sunnis and the Shiahs, inflamed to the highest degree, often leads to serious trouble. Muslims and Hindus also occasionally come into collision at Muharram time; and even between different bands of Shiahs affrays sometimes take place owing to the eagerness of each party to be early at the meeting-place, as there is merit to be gained from precedence in this respect.[103]

I begin with a few colonial examples of Muslim/Hindu discord and then turn my attention to Shi'i/Sunni conflict, with passing reference to intra-Shi'i disputes. In the entry to her diary cited above, dated June 4, 1800, Clive rather bluntly writes that at "twelve o'clock we went to see the ceremony at the Tank, all the little Mosques were pulled to pieces and washed, and then put together again; they are presented to the Tank by the people, who join in singing and dancing as if they were mad. When the ceremony is over, the shrines are covered with a cloth and carried home without any procession. The boys continued singing, in their dresses of yesterday, and were by this time very hoarse. As usual there was a fight and a man was killed."[104] Clive matter-of-factly throws in at the conclusion of her description something that every European seemed to take for granted, namely, that Muharram would lead to violence. Oman also makes note of potential violence in Lahore at the beginning of the twentieth century: "Occasionally there was a great deal of rushing about amongst the men, as something that promised to lead to a fight occurred anywhere. The native police seemed to be having a lively time of it to keep the peace and ensure order."[105]

In his survey of fictional accounts of India written for a British audience, David Pinault argues that English writers viewed rituals practiced during Muharram as "anti-English treachery among the natives" and considered "the holyday part of a threat to the very borders of the Empire."[106] He concludes by stating suggestively that certain writers of fiction often chose Muharram as their context because it matched a set of presuppositions among their European reading audiences that everyone, including children, shared collectively. I tend to agree with him, but even though colonial accounts may be highly exaggerated to play on the expectations of the intended reader, this is not to deny that rioting and violence did in fact frequently occur during the ritual period. Two consistent problem centers in the past have been Bombay and Lucknow. There were riots in Lucknow in 1908, which accelerated in the 1930s and continue today, while similar occurrences seem to have subsided in present-day Bombay.[107]

Confrontations have the greatest potential to occur when *muḥarram* coincides with Hindu lunar festivals such as Durga *pūjā*. The oldest account I have been able to find comes from Louis de Grandpré's 1789–90 log of his visit to Bengal. While in Calcutta during the month of Muharram, he wrote:

The Moors celebrate also an annual festival, which is called *Jamsey*. I did not obtain any accurate information about the nature of this ceremony, but it appeared to me to be of the mournful kind. A sort of funeral exhibition is carried through the streets, accompanied with banners, resembling standards. There was a great concourse of people, and every individual had a stick in his hand, with a small flag at the end of it. They walked in ranks on the different sides of the street with great regularity. In the middle of the procession were some who performed feats of strength, and showed their activity by the most hazardous leaps, bawling out all the time as loud as they were able. As neither the period of this festival, nor that of madam Dourga is determined by astronomical returns, they vary, and sometimes happen together: in that case, the government is obliged to use the utmost vigilance and precaution, to prevent the most serious accidents. Whenever the processions meet, neither of them will give way to the other, and the ancient enmity of the two casts revives in all its rancour: the parties attack each other like furies; the remembrance of the ancient victory of the Mahometans rouses a courage and inspires a confidence on one side, which on the part of the Indians are equally supplied by enthusiasm, and they both fight with the most inveterate malice. Jamsey and madam Dourga are broken to pieces in the confusion, while their followers murder one another on their remains, and the battle is only terminated by the destruction or rout of one of the parties. A spirit of revenge produces a repetition of these battles on the following days, and it is impossible to foresee the length to which the massacres will extend, if the government does not possess an armed force sufficient to restrain combatants.[108]

Grandpré is obviously basing his fanciful account on secondhand information, but his detailed description suggests that such incidents did transpire when sectarian festivals coincided. Evidence for such conflict over right of way also comes from the Reverend M. A. Sherring, who reports that in the 1860s a riot occurred in Banaras for a similar reason, although it had been aggravated by earlier incidents. Writing about the Muslim desecration of the Hindu deity Shiva's venerated *lāṭ* (pillar), Sherring relates with an obvious bias how a conflict developed

during the Mohurram festival, a season when the fanaticism which is inherent in the disposition of a Mohammedan reaches its boiling point. It so happened, that, in that year, the popular Hindu festival of Holí took place at the same time. The processions of both classes of religionists were traversing the streets together; and it was, consequently, almost impossible for the violent passions of either section not to display themselves, when the processions passed one another. And so it turned out; for, on occasion of two large processions coming near each other, the one refused to give place to the other, imagining that the honour of the religion which it advocated would be sacrificed by so doing. As neither party would yield, the altercation proceeded to blows, each struggling to force a passage through the ranks of the other.[109]

The Muslims apparently lost the fight, so to seek revenge they entered the Aurangzeb mosque in the city and toppled the *lāṭ*. Sherring goes on to say that the incident led to other altercations, during which *masjid*s were razed by Hindus. These destructions resulted in a final heinous act of retaliation by the Muslim population. Quoting Reverend William Buyers's *Recollections*, Sherring states that the "Mussalmans, in order to be revenged on the Hindus for the defeat they had sustained, had taken a cow, and killed it on one of the holiest gháts [bathing steps], and mingled its blood with the sacred water of the Gangá [Ganges]."[110]

Unfortunately, Sherring does not provide us with the adequate contextual information needed to understand which Hindu and Muslim parties were involved in the confrontation. Rather, he presents us with generic versions of both faiths, leaving us very little to go by for the formation of a viable interpretation of the occurrences. This is the danger with using such pedestrian accounts culled from colonial memoirs. While they may provide useful, if checkered, descriptions of indigenous practices and events, they need to be used with caution. Sandria Freitag reminds us that conflict was not so dichotomous before the 1930s, and much rioting was intragroup. She states that "more often than not, the original competition so often labeled 'Hindu-Muslim' was not between coherently defined communities seeing themselves as 'Hindus' and as 'Muslims,' but between subgroups."[111] In other words, communal violence between members of different religious communities often resulted as a byproduct of disagreements among different competing groups of the same religion. Freitag argues that the Sunni and the Shi'ah of Lucknow, for example, used to practice Muharram observances together, and Sunnis even attended Shi'i *majālis* regularly before 1906. But after the practice of cursing the first three caliphs was introduced into the city by Shi'i leader Maqbul Ahmad in 1904, legislation was passed to keep the two communities apart during the month of Muharram to avoid sectarian confrontations. Thus whereas all Muslims shared the same *karbalā*'s prior to 1906, two distinct and separate *muharrams* emerged after 1906.[112]

Masselos provides an example of intragroup conflict from Bombay to support Freitag's statement. Here two *imāmbāṛā*s were established, one to cater to Shi'ah of Arabic descent and the other to Shi'ah of Persian descent. The rivalry between the two *imambāṛā*s ultimately led to violence in 1846.[113] By extension, such rivalries spilled over into the Sunni community, whose processions focused on the construction, display, and procession of *ta'zīyah*s. Masselos notes that because the innovations introduced by the minority Shi'ah were seen as repugnant, tension resulted, especially from the practice of cursing the first three caliphs. The Sunni eventually urged the British government to intervene, which led to restrictions against Shi'i forms of observance. In 1836, the British banned the public procession of the Zuljanah and thus took the side of the majority in this instance, favoring Sunni *ta'zīyah* processions over Shi'i *mātam*. In this way, the Sunni *ta'zīyah muharram* became the standard form of public observance, while the Shi'ah continued their private forms of worship.[114] Colonial legislation in favor of predominantly Sunni practices may be part of the reason why the tomb processions became such an ostentatious display throughout much of South Asia and still remain the most vital public tradition in the contemporary scene among all participating groups. Whatever the case may be, more important for the argument I wish to make in the following chapters is Masselos's other emphasis on the social and organizational role of the neighborhood in the formation of local identity.

In two illuminating articles analyzing Bombay's *muharram* in the eighteenth through the twentieth centuries, Masselos argues that the rivalry and competition was not so much between different sectarian communities— although that was certainly one dimension of the conflicts—but was rather between different *muhallā*s of the city. We have already seen how important the neighborhood unit has been in the social organization of *muḥarram* in many locations. In Bombay it is the same. As in Chanorba, the Bombay *muḥallā* was the locus of the occupational group in colonial India and was the basis for Muslim social organization. Consequently, the structure of authority and power operated within the neighborhood. Different neighborhoods, mostly consisting of lower-class Sunnis, built their own tomb replicas that were sponsored by wealthy Jain and Hindu patrons. These neighborhood groups would gather support for their competing processions by recruiting people on the streets, which led to the incorporation of *badmāsh* (rabble rouser) elements of the population who had "little to do with" the religious dimension of the processions. Masselos cites a report from 1838 written by the superintendent of police to this effect. The superintendent notes that the "punjias of boys and lads enjoy it [the Moharram] as a means of riot and dissipation which is anything but good for the morals, while it has nothing whatever to do with the Religion of the people."[115]

Neighborhood rivalry and enmity, with the aid of ruffians, led to clashes when different processions converged and fought over right-of-way privileges to assert territorial control. Violence in 1904 and 1908 forced the British to intervene officially in 1911, despite a policy of non-intervention into the religious affairs of the "natives" reinforced by the Queen's Proclamation of 1858.[116] The superintendant's phrase "nothing whatever to do with the Religion of the people" was a common and clever ploy used by colonial authorities to skirt the law prohibiting them from intervening in religious matters. British perceptions of what may have been "religious" were often at odds with indigenous conceptions.

What Masselos suggests is that while earlier conflict was directed at other *muḥallā*s, after 1911 it was aimed at the British in retaliation for their intervention. This exacerbated the situation, and the British took measures to suppress the processions altogether. As these suppressions were implemented, Masselos notes an increase in *majālis*, and one Sunni group even brought out a *fatvā* (edict) in 1912 to justify this, stating that the *ta'ziyah*s really had very little to do with Islam. Here we notice the official opinion of the British influencing the decisions of elite members of the indigenous community responsible for setting neighborhood policy. The suppression of public processions led to peace for a few years following the intervention, but not without heightening tension between the different sectors of the city that were involved in the observances. All the above themes—neighborhood rivalries, intersectarian and interreligious discourses, debates over the correct way to perform, assertion of local power and authority, and colonial government intervention—are important ones to which I will return in the next chapter as we cross the Atlantic to the Caribbean to explore the *muḥarram* phenomenon in much greater historical and ethnographic depth.

We have seen in earlier chapters that Muharram can be used to justify protest or even to legitimize revolution and warfare in Iran due to the heightened state of emotion induced by the rituals. In colonial India that kind of battlefield mentality could be fueled by the zealousness of other religious communities, local pride, or government intervention. While such incidents of communal violence reported by Grandpré and Sherring generally occurred in urban areas, they were not unheard of on the village level. Pinault cites a British officer's account of a confrontation in a rural area over passage along a route shaded by pipal trees sacred to Hindus: "Either the gilded tower or the pipal tree has grown since last year; the image will not pass unless a branch is cut. The Hindus of the village with their six-foot bamboo quarter staffs have collected and wait grimly for the first insult to the sacred tree. The Muslim escort of the image will not agree to deviation by a yard from the usual route, still less that the tower should bow its head or be carried aslant."[117] I myself have witnessed young Hindu men armed with *lāṭhīs* (bamboo bludgeons) guarding a grove sacred to their village deity during Muharram in West Bengal to keep Muslim processions from defiling the site. Although I never witnessed any physical altercations myself during the two years I spent in Birbhum District in the early 1990s, many of the youths recounted in heroic detail numerous incidents of past clashes.

The variety of contexts and events described above should make it clear that Muharram-related rituals and performances, whether sacred, secular, or both, are plural in practice and multivocalic on the symbolic level. They mean different things to different people. And while the master narrative provides the central motifs from which to create innovative new modes of observance, it becomes clear in the South Asian context that the ritual complex is no longer the sole property of the minority Shi'i community. Moreover, it is also the case that while Turnerian *communitas* might manifest itself in certain situations of emotive unity, the public portions of the procession have provided a long history of conflict and discord. Thus, although I am compelled to acknowledge the conclusion of Saiyid and Fruzzetti concerning the congealing nature of *muḥarram* on the less complex organizational level of the village or small town, their observations do not seem to hold true in cosmopolitan arenas such as Bombay, Calcutta, Delhi, or Lucknow. This is especially true in the aftermath of the tearing down of the Babri Masjid in Ayodhya on a fateful day in the early 1990s. Instead, I am more inclined to accept Masselos's conclusions that *muḥarram* is an "occasion for the display of tension through both play and violence."[118] I also thoroughly agree with Cole's discussion of the tension that exists between Turnerian structure and antistructure. As he writes about *muḥarram* in colonial Lucknow, "social distinctions temporarily broke down into liminality and a generalized feeling of leveled community *(communitas)*. . . . But in important ways mourners intensified structure, emphasizing distinctions of class and status in the exclusivity of the mourning sessions at *imāmbāṛahs* and in the primacy of notable pageants during the Muḥarram processions. . . . Moreover, at the same time that ceremonies drew together the participants from various classes and religious communities, they often sparked communal violence because some Sunnīs and Hindus objected so strongly to them."[119]

It is, perhaps, the display of tension during Muharram that allows for relative calm in its aftermath. As I intend to suggest in the next chapter, violent altercations also occurred at times in colonial Trinidad, leading to similar problems even today. I now turn my attention to an area that has firm roots in the *muḥarram* experiences of north India, drawing as it does on traditions we have seen to be pervasive in many parts of India as well as in Iran. In Trinidad, however, the observance developed a distinctive style of performance all its own.

Chapter 4
Onward to the Caribbean

> *The day was very unpropitious for the exhibition of the paper decorated coolie castles . . . , the number of castles was not inferior to that of former years, neither was it possible to mark any difference in the multitude of Indian and creole labourers whose creed, or whose love of novelty led them to join in the tumultuous HOSEM. It may certainly be presumed that the state of the weather added to the mirth of the coolies who appear to have fenced, paraded, and even fought amongst themselves with a degree of vigour and liveliness of spirit.*
>
> —*Trinidad Sentinel, 1857*[1]

Coming to Trinidad *Incognito*

From 1845 to 1917, with a short break between 1848 and 1851, East Indians were brought to the Caribbean basin as indentured laborers and carried the spirit of Muharram rituals with them. With the abolition of slavery in 1833, the British freed the African slaves on the sugarcane and other plantations of their Caribbean colonies. At that time, before the introduction of the European sugar beet on a commercial scale, sugar was still a precious commodity and its manufacture an important source of income. Much previous scholarship suggests that because the former slaves identified working on the cane plantations with slavery, they refused to work the menial estate jobs as free laborers and migrated to cities and towns in search of other means of employment in factories or skilled jobs of other sorts. This stereotype of what Douglas Hall calls "memories of misery" needs to be somewhat modified in light of the fact that the plantocracy wished to expand production but keep wages down, a policy that discouraged Afro-Creoles from returning if they had left or remaining if they had stayed.[2] Moreover, there is abundant evidence to suggest that ex-slaves were being treated unfairly by the suspension of allowances such as free medical attention and housing, which forced them to seek shelter off the plantations while continuing to work irregularly as wage laborers on the estates.[3]

In order to avert financial ruin, plantation owners, albeit reluctantly, had no choice but ultimately to accept the British Crown's scheme to bring indentured laborers from India.[4] A large number of these laborers hailed from economically depressed regions of what are today's modern Indian provinces of Uttar Pradesh (former United Provinces) and Bihar in north India. The laborers were given passage and initially a three-year contract (changed to five years after 1862) to work for wages. According to their contracts, they were to eventually receive a free return ticket to India.[5] The return ticket, however, could not be secured until after a residence of ten years.[6] Indians thus had to settle off the plantations for at least five more years before they could even consider returning to India. Alternatively, they could re-indenture themselves for another five-year term. The majority of East Indians, however, stayed on the island and came to influence local culture through the maintenance and preservation of their own religious and cultural traditions. Conversely, indigenous culture also had an effect on Indic practices as a strategic consequence of adaptation.

Among all the cultural practices brought by the East Indians, the Muharram rite came to eclipse all others in many parts of the Caribbean basin where Indians settled after their period of indenture (for example, Surinam, British Guiana, Trinidad, Jamaica). This does not mean that other public displays performed by Hindus (for example, Divali, Phagwa) were completely overshadowed by *Hosay*, but the latter provided a more flexible arena for interracial and interreligious participation. Muharram rituals allowed East Indians, at least in principle, to participate equally in a public show of ethnic identity, regardless of their religious persuasion, a point to which I want to return in more detail below. But first I need to say a bit more about Indian indenture and the early years of settlement to provide the reader with the necessary historical context for understanding the multidimensional role that Muharram rituals have played over time in Trinidad.

East Indians arrived in Trinidad after successive colonial infrastructures already had been firmly developed. The Spanish legacy in Trinidad from 1520 to 1797 allowed colonists from the French Caribbean to establish an estate or plantation system after 1783, which ultimately offered the British the opportunity to exploit the system after 1797.[7] For the first four decades of British rule, African slaves provided the necessary labor force to keep the large agricultural complex in good and profitable working order, but after the full emancipation of slaves in 1838 a dire need for laborers arose. Indentured Indians filled this gap. Laborers from the subcontinent had already started arriving in other regions of the Caribbean rim as early as 1838,[8] but the first did not arrive in Trinidad until

1845, when, on May 3, the *Fatel Rozack* arrived from Calcutta carrying 217 passengers.[9] Figures compiled for the period between 1851 and 1908 suggest that a total of 129,224 contracted Indians landed in Trinidad. By 1917, the year indentured Indian immigration officially ended in the British Empire, a total of 143,939 Indian immigrants had entered the island.[10] Add to this number the native births on the island, and Indians gradually came to be a significant physical and economic presence. Due to the increasing number of locally born Indians, the Indian population grew to 25% of the total in 1871 and 33% in 1901.[11] The statistics suggest that "Creole Indians"—those born on the island—began to outnumber the indentured Indian population by the century's end, which circumstantially fostered the development of a permanent Indian society in Trinidad.

Only a negligible percentage of the Indian population returned to British India. Bridget Brereton estimates that between 1870 and 1899 only 21.2% returned home, and Robert Smith's figures suggest that by the end of the indenture period less than 12% had returned to the homeland.[12] Most chose to remain on the island after their period of indenture, and on the eve of the Republic of Trinidad and Tobago's independence on August 30, 1962, Indo-Trinidadians were the second largest ethnic group on the island, comprising roughly 36% of the total population.[13] Of this group, approximately 70% were Hindu, 15% were said to belong to various Christian denominations, and the remaining 15% were Muslim, all being subsumed under a general category of Sunni. According to the 1960 *Census of Trinidad and Tobago*, Hindus made up 23% and Muslims 6% of the total population.[14] The 1990 *Census* lists 15% of the 40% total of Indo-Trinidadians under the category of Muslim, and the latter still comprised approximately 6% of the entire nation's numbers.[15] Today, the percentage of Indians in the population is rapidly approaching that of their Afro-Trinidadian fellow citizens. Smaller ethnic communities that round out what Donald Wood calls a "rich *pot-pourri* of immigrants" include Chinese, Lebanese, Syrian, Spanish, Portuguese, French, British, American, and only a very few indigenous Carib.[16]

The Shi'ah, on the other hand, have not received separate mention in the historical record as a distinct sectarian group. Based on a perusal of numerous official documents, Smith, for example, misleadingly claims that there are no Shi'ah on the island.[17] Given that many Shi'ah practice *taqīyyah*, dissimulation to guard against religious persecution or discrimination, it is easy to see how Smith could have fallen into this oversight. In fact, it is virtually impossible to know what percentage of Trinidad's Indo-Muslims adhere to Shi'i doctrine. We do know, however, that Sunnis were among the earliest immigrants, and a number of Shi'i adherents must have been among them, even though passenger records do not mention sectarian affiliation. My working assumption is that some Indian Shi'ah were recruited along with people of other faiths early on, arriving as generic Muslims who only later asserted their sectarian religious identity, and even then only in subtle ways, if and when it suited their collective aspirations.

I base this assumption on the fact that the largest majority of indentured laborers (approximately 90%) were recruited from the Gangetic plain of north India.[18] Wood adds that "the overwhelming majority came from the poor central regions; from Bihar, from Oudh [Avadh]."[19] Recall from the previous chapter that the Shi'ah are most concentrated in the former United Provinces, which roughly corresponds to contemporary Uttar Pradesh. It is in U.P. that Lucknow's vital Shi'i culture continues to thrive today. The city had a great religious and cultural impact on "the satellite townships, where the imambaras and mosques stood as reminders of Shia domination under the Nawabs" at the time when recruiting was taking place.[20] During 1867–68, 1877–78, and 1878–79, the three recruiting seasons for which there is the best and most reliable evidence, emigration records from Calcutta show that 27.9% of the total came from Avadh and 16.2% came from Bihar.[21] These statistics are important indicators to suggest that there must have been some Shi'ah on board during the early years of indenture, but perhaps because of their prerogative to practice taqiyyah, their religious affiliation remained obscure. Moreover, these numbers should also alert us to the fact that muharram practices as performed in Trinidad should bear a strong resemblance to some of the customs and rituals from that area outlined in the previous chapter.

Even though we can never be certain, a Shi'i oral historian, the late Shair Ali of St. James, suggests that a male ancestor in his family mentally carried the muharram ideals with him from Calcutta. Shortly after arrival, he quickly took steps to establish the emotive expression of sorrow for Husayn by introducing the construction of cenotaphs and the beating of drums. Ali's view is consonant with Smith's contention that Islamic culture was initially carried in the "hearts and memories" of the transportees.[22] Although the exigencies of life on the plantations did not allow for the easy maintenance of cultural norms and religious praxis, such inward preservation allowed Muslims to reestablish their own sociocultural patterns in a timely fashion once their period of indenture had expired. While many other religious and cultural practices seemed subdued under the constraints of indenture, Hosay continued to be observed persistently on a number of plantations.

Finding the overwhelming popularity of Hosay to be a curiosity, Wood states that "it is by no means clear why Hosein should have become so popular not only in Trinidad but in other colonies as well."[23] This fact should not surprise us, however, because we have already seen that the event attracts people from all walks of life in South Asia due to its healing power and its colorful splendor. We must also bear in mind from my discussion in the previous chapter that the majority of people who participate outwardly in South Asian *muḥarram* on the public level belong to the poorer subaltern classes, be they Hindu or Muslim. If we remember that most of the indentured laborers who came to Trinidad from British India were forced to make the journey due to economic circumstances, famine, and disease in rural areas, then it should seem less strange that *Hosay* would continue vibrantly in plantation colonies. Indeed, Muharram rituals did thrive in Trinidad as well as in other places where the indenture system was implemented because the largest number of recruits came from the core areas of the rite's performance. In addition, Wood indicates that a large majority of the indentured laborers came from the lower and untouchable castes. Chamars, from the outcast leather-working community, seem to have been among the largest caste groups on the island.[24] The fact that Hindu Chamars traditionally were hired to play drums during *muḥarram* processions in India allows us the viable possibility of assuming that their continued role as drummers on the island added to the vigor with which the observances developed during the plantation period. By all accounts, the drumming was loud and outstanding, being one of the defining characteristics of the event that drew participants from different racial and religious backgrounds into it.

To understand the strong forces behind the transplantation of Muharram rituals to Trinidad, we must turn our attention to plantation life, which was was difficult for the Indians. It was nothing more than, as Hugh Tinker calls it, a "new system of slavery."[25] Brereton notes that "indentureship was merely slavery with the jail substituted for the whip."[26] It is not surprising, then, that even today East Indians in Trinidad often say that unscrupulous recruiters tricked or lured them into coming to Trinidad to work by promising them unprecedented wealth. As the personal experience narrative of Fazal, a former laborer from greater Bengal, poetically asserts:

> i come to wuk for money
> an go back
> i been wukking in de ship
>   i come calcutta
> dem muslim fellar fool me
>   bring me dis country
> e say

> e ha plenty money
> e axe me
>   how much you getting every month
> i say
>   three rupee
> e say
>   you chupid
> over dey sara bara anna rogh
>   every day[27]

After the indentured laborers arrived in the nineteenth century, they found that life on the plantations was not as they had been led to believe. The terms of indenture greatly restricted their freedom of movement, and transgressing the rules often led to harsh fines or jail sentences. Because Indian social life was restricted initially to the estates, "free" Trinidadians (that is, non-Indians) considered the Indians to be transients and exotic others, stereotypically not to be trusted to invest anything in the island's cultural heritage or economy. The early Indians, pejoratively known as "coolies" on the island, continued to dress in native costume and speak their own language. The predominant language spoken among the early Indians was Bhojpuri, a dialect of Hindi spoken in eastern U.P. and Bihar, the regions from which, as we have just seen, the majority of the recruits came.[28] Also perceived as an economic threat because they were taking away valuable jobs, the Indian indentured laborers were not regarded favorably by the local Afro-Creole population. The European plantocracy, too, did not look favorably upon them, even though the East Indian laborers made possible through their toils the recovery of the sugar industry after 1848, which led to a remarkable expansion in production during the decades between 1850 and 1870.[29] But this expansion did not occur without a cost.

Unfair wage and labor practices by estate owners and overseers, as well as deteriorating physical conditions on the plantations, led to numerous strikes between 1870 and 1900, which peaked between 1882 and 1884. The period of strikes that accompanied harsher conditions on the estates was no doubt linked to the decline of the sugar industry between 1870 and 1890 brought about by the falling prices resulting from free trade.[30] It is significant that the so-called *Hosay* riots occurred during this peak period, a point to which I devote a lengthier discussion below. Suffice it to say for now that Muharram rituals continued to provide a public platform for airing grievances against the oppressive forces of the plantocracy's hegemonic power. We have already seen similar cases in Iran and India with regard to excessive exertion of governmental force against the subjugated people's collective will. Most of the strikes and protests on the island's estates were stimulated by increases in tasks that had to be performed on the plantations by laborers without adequate monetary compensation, the result essentially being lower wages for more work performed.[31] Naturally, laborers saw such unfair practices as legitimate excuses for sociopolitical agitation.

As the early Indians on the island secured freedom after their indenture period, they became fairly successful and achieved financial independence. Brereton notes that by the end of the nineteenth century there were Indian settlements cropping up away from, but near, estates as Indians cashed in their return tickets for Crown lands. This resulted in a permanent and significant Indian peasantry by 1900.[32] From 1869 onward, Indians took to rice cultivation in the wetland areas around the Caroni Swampland and Oropuche Lagoon because a majority came from agrarian backgrounds in India.[33] They also became involved in cane farming, outnumbering Afro-Creoles in this sphere by the second decade of the twentieth century. Later, between 1880 and 1900, with the decline of the sugar industry, many gradually moved into the interior of the island to engage in cocoa planting, which led to significant financial success in many cases, the most celebrated being the fortune accrued by the Partap family.[34] The broader implication of freedom and economic autonomy is that Indians could exploit their success to begin establishing their own Indic forms of culture on the island within the larger framework of colonial Creole society.

During and after the plantation period, Muslims and Hindus alike began to nucleate, founding permanent villages and giving them Indian names, often after the town or village from which a founder came. Living together in ethnic communities based on common languages and customs, coupled with more economic freedom brought about by the adoption of wet rice cultivation, allowed for more cultural autonomy, which, in turn, produced the appropriate conditions for an attempted replication of Indian culture on Trinidadian soil.[35] But this is not to say that living in a new land had no effect on the immigrants. In fact, Indian village social institutions had to be greatly modified as a strategy of adaptation. Although the village *pañcāyat* (governing body) was reintroduced, caste hierarchy suffered, as did the extended family.[36] By all accounts, however, new innovations such as intermarriage between Muslims and Hindus were quite common during the early years and continue, albeit less frequently, to the present day. Despite the rifts between the two religious communities that developed in the 1940s over the delicate issue of political alliances, intermarriage continues today, especially in urban areas. In fact, Wood notes that the major distinction during the Trinidadian colonial period was not between Hindu and Muslim but between north (Calcutta) and south (Madras) as cultural and linguistic markers indicating points of departure.[37] Although Indians may have made the linguistic distinction, colonists made a distinction based on work capacity, stereotypically perceiving those from the south to be less fit for the task of plantation labor.

The trend toward intermarriage further marked the cross-fertilization of religious customs. Inhabiting less accessible rural areas also allowed Indians to minimize their contact with non-Indians. Thus East Indians began to reassert their cultural and ethnic identities through an informal policy of isolationism by the establishment of their own villages. Having stated this, however, I should note that not all East Indians lived in a rural and isolated environment after their period of indenture. A small proportion was also urban, and a significant number of free East Indians were mobile by the 1890s, which allowed for the free flow of ideas and the oral transmission of accounts of current events. In his geographical study of two Indo-Trinidadian villages between 1890 and 1910, Bonham Richardson, for example, corrects the traditional interpretation of a peasant/plantation dichotomy. He asserts that free East Indians of the period engaged in a variety of subsistence activities, moving daily and seasonally to engage in cash cropping and wage labor, thereby maintaining a balance between village activity and plantation labor.[38] Such a symbiotic relationship between central estates and peripheral villages should caution us against overemphasizing isolationism as the root causal factor to explain East Indian cultural and religious retentions.

Although customs may have been nurtured in an insular fashion within the ethnic communities' peripheral villages, the mobility required for subsistence and economic prosperity demanded a certain amount of interaction with external agents. Aisha Khan convincingly suggests that the factors pointed out by Richardson enabled religious and cultural variation as much as possibly homogenizing practice. Moreover, she indicates that itinerant preachers moved about to spread news and religious ideas, which led to revitalization.[39] Revitalization must thus be seen as contributing to the revival of Indian culture just as much, if not more so, than retentionism. I think it is therefore fair to say that an extreme form of isolationism was never a possibility for any of Trinidad's residents, but strategies for managing diversity and cultural encounter need to be addressed. Using the inside/outside model to manage internal and external practice is useful in this respect, for living in semiautonomous villages certainly aided attempts to perpetuate or revive Indic practices on Caribbean soil.

Informal isolationism seems to have been even truer of Muslims when we compare their behavioral patterns with Hindus and Christians of East Indian descent. Aside from the minimally required economic and political interaction necessary for survival, Muslims did not mix very much with non-Indians because they were especially concerned about religious conversion and acculturation by the Canadian Presbyterian Mission, whose sole target was the island's Indian community.[40] In fact, missionary accounts frequently remark with frustration that Muslims are the most difficult people to convert because they dogmatically refuse to bow down to missionary pressure. The Reverend Kenneth J. Grant, for example, writes of the island's Indo-Muslims: "Their zeal is commendable. . . .The Hindu abroad is much more approachable and amenable to Christian instruction."[41] Furthermore, during the years immediately following the end of the indenture period, Indo-Muslims rarely lived in urban centers. Again, I must stress that there were exceptions to the rule, but living "in the bush" aided Muslims in forestalling the impact of external forces that potentially could have influenced the realms of belief and ritual practice. Muslims thus lived in a distinct culturally isolated, but economically interrelated, social milieu, having extensive cultural contact only with other East Indians. As a result of early Muslim xenophobia and the self-imposed insularity in which most East Indians chose to live generally, the *Hosay* observance slowly began to acquire an ethnic and cultural flavor that reflected coexistence and transcended Muslim/Hindu communal differences.[42] This seems to have been the case from the plantation period onward. At the same time, however, I want to argue that the process of integrating Afro-Trinidadians into the observance of *Hosay* was already beginning to occur on the plantations.

Because the first-generation Indians living in Trinidad were cut off from the homeland in a diasporic situation, however, through a process of what we might call "cultural amnesia" time slowly eroded their early experiential memories. This gradual decline of collective memory results from a number of complicated and interrelated factors that range from the constant pressure for Christianization prior to independence in 1962 and absorption into the majority Afro-Trinidadian community afterward to a lack of formal religious education.[43] These pressures, combined with the intensification of change brought about by modernity and growing religious factionalism in all communities after World War I, gave rise to a renewed sense of political weakness and uncertainty of belief among East Indians. Uncertainty, in turn, led to further indigenous interrogation of an Indian identity, which was already being reconstructed from earlier fragments. The postwar years and an oil boom also created new jobs, resulting in an even more mobile East Indian community.[44] Increased mobility then led to more fluid interaction with non-Indians, allowing for a heightened degree of ideological and ritual cross-fertilization, especially in cities. Simultaneously, urban ideas were penetrating deeper into the bush as communication channels became more efficient with the increased availability of electronic media.

The processes mentioned above gave rise to the need for a reasonable amount of free play in interpretation to reconcile the incongruity between self-perceived notions of unchanging tradition and the growing need for innovation as a strategy for cultural adaptation. While cultural adaptation took place in virtually every sector of public life, it was clearly visible in outward religious practices. Thus even as the pious imaginings of East Indian Muslims continued to transform aspects of ritual and belief, the need to come to terms with being citizens of an emerging nation-state grew into an important concern. Indeed, the Young Indian party, formed as early as the 1920s, placed great emphasis on the unity of all subjugated races and religions. Khan suggests that members of the party were "Western" educated and openly valued the benefits of being "creolized," even while advocating Indian social and religious customs as part of the island's budding national culture. Furthermore, on the authority of Brinsley Samaroo, she argues that the Young Indian party urged Indo-Trinidadians to stop looking at India as the motherland and accept Trinidad as their permanent home.[45] The struggle over being Indian or Trinidadian is quite apparent in the history of Muharram rituals on the island, to which I now turn.

Hosay in Trinidad Past

A very short time after the East Indians landed on Caribbean soil, *Hosay* (derived from the name Husayn) became a symbol of ethnic unity.[46] But this is not the whole picture. As had been the case in South Asia, indentured immigrants often used the rite as a collective act of defiance against colonial rule. It also served as a public occasion for fights and riots to break out between competing groups, as will become clear below. For the moment, however, let me pursue the integrating thread of the argument. John Morton, an early Presbyterian missionary in Trinidad, points out that *Hosay* was an occasion during which "Indians joined to remember the old country."[47] By contrast, in a letter to the *Trinidad Chronicle* dated April 11, 1871, he calls the event a "creolism."[48] Morton's colonial musings concerning *Hosay*, although tainted with a Christian bias, are certainly correct on two levels of analysis when read in their wider context, that is, *Hosay* represented in part a nostalgia for India stimulated by a diasporic consciousness and was also a by-product of taking root in

Trinidad. But his view is a simplistic one at best, and I wish to enrich it as my argument progresses. Nonetheless, on one basic level of analysis *Hosay* continues to this day as a set of rituals identifying the East Indians of Trinidad with their imagined homeland. In this sense, it does allow for a nominal display of ethnic unity, as Wood points out.[49]

A unified ethnic identification during the observances results from the innovative combination of both Hindu and Muslim components in the rituals as well as the assertion of a shared experience of servitude and a common longing for an Indian past. Because *Hosay* has been infused with the practices of many indigenous cultures over the years, a number of those who participate in building the *tadjah*s today are not necessarily Shi'i Muslims nor even generic Muslims.[50] Many are, in fact, Hindu and Christian, sometimes belonging to diverse ethnic groups. Interreligious participation is a process that had already started in India and continued on the plantations of Trinidad, where Indians were forced to live in close quarters, as they did on the ships during passage. Let me leave this strand of thought for the moment, however, and turn my attention to a closer look at the historical development of the rite on the island.

The first notice of the commemoration on the island comes from Morton's Presbyterian missionary colleague, Kenneth Grant, whose 1923 memoir includes mention of *Hosay*. He writes about what he calls an Indian fête that took place in the 1850s at an estate near the town of Couva: "The first estate in Trinidad to make a Tazzia was Phillipine, the property of Sir Norman Lamont; this gave that estate the right of precedence, but other estates in subsequent years entered the list and from their extent of acreage, the number of men at work, the output of sugar, and the grandeur of display disputed the claims of Phillipine."[51] Earlier in his account, Grant notes counting eighty-three *tadjah*s passing by his door.[52] These presumably represented different estates whose processions would converge in a grand parade leading to the water, where the structures would be immersed. Wood confirms this assumption when he writes: "it is the rival *taziyas* that compete for admiration, and to be first in the procession or first at the edge of the water. The rivalry of Hosein was between estates and it was the working group and not religion or the same home district [in India] which determined the allegiance of those who took part."[53] As in India, we notice the element of competition between groups and social organization based around occupation or spatial location.

What the above information suggests is that during the plantation period, loyalty to the neighborhood that we saw to be a critical feature of social organization in India was replaced by loyalty to the estate—during *Hosay*, at least. The importance of the neighborhood, however, reemerged after the plantation period and reasserted itself as the primary node of organization and social activity. Just as neighborhoods competed against one another in India, so too did estates enact rivalries with each other in Trinidad. Wood sees the competitive nature of the processions as a unifying force on the most local level because, in his words, "loyalties to the estate transcended those of race."[54] As the Bombay example in the last chapter should suggest, what may be perceived as unity on the most local level—the neighborhood or the estate—can also lead to divisiveness within the community as a whole. The tension between structure and antistructure engendered by competition can provide a milieu in which certain divisive factors within society can be enacted, interrogated, negotiated, and temporarily resolved through public ritual performance. The kind of symbolic negotiation to which I refer becomes a crucial strategic factor for navigating the complexitiess of cultural creolization in a polyethnic nation such as Trinidad, whose Afro-Trinidadian sector of the population has been becoming involved in *Hosay* gradually over time.

Afro-Trinidadians probably began participating in *Hosay* enthusiastically from the very beginning of its observance on the island, but their involvement waned after 1885 for reasons to be explained in the next section.[55] At first, during the 1850s, rowdier elements of the Creole working class joined in the celebration of *Hosay* as a public event, much as they would have in the better-known Carnival. As time passed, however, the same Afro-Trinidadians became involved as paid drummers; sometimes they were even hired to carry the *tadjahs*.[56] We see in their participation a pattern that I first mentioned in the last chapter, noting that Hindus and Sunnis either participated simply out of fun or for hire to beat drums or carry the cenotaphs, and sometimes simply for a good fight. In Trinidad, we see a strong parallel. In the past, the Afro-Creole participants did not necessarily share in the religious sentiment of the event, but joined in for their own purposes. The process of co-opting *Hosay* for numerous agendas thus began quite early in the fête's history on the island and continued to develop over time, and it crystallized most visibly in St. James, the ethnographic focus of my subsequent discussion.

Although Wood ideally views the fête as a congealing agent fostering "a ray of hope in race relations," he himself admits that fights and riots often broke out during *Hosay* time as a result of competition, which eventually led to government intervention.[57] He notes that newspapers frequently reported disturbances during the first few years of the celebration and in 1859 there was a riot in St. Joseph, a "hotbed" of rowdy behavior at Indian fêting time. In 1865 a ruthless riot broke out over precedence between the Indians of Woodford Lodge and Endeavor Estate located in

Chaguanas. Afro-Creoles and Chinese joined in the fracas, which resulted in the murder of a Chinese worker. Here we notice yet another ethnic minority group, miniscule in numbers, being incorporated into the *Hosay* milieu. The *Port of Spain Gazette* reported on June 14, 1865:

> After some time, when the parties had moved about three hundred yards eastwards, they halted at the gate at the entrance to Woodford Lodge Estate where one of the emigrant bodies reside—the way home for the second procession being about six hundred yards more east to the Endeavour Estate. . . . A band of chinese were seen advancing, summoned it is thought, by a curia of visible signals preconcerted or not, and joined by their Endeavour friends. Now the Woodford Lodge party, disregarding all the efforts of Oxley [a corporal], and backed by creoles, rushed at the chinese and their neighboring combatant coolies and completely repulsed them. One man, a chinese, was killed and his body thrown into the canal parallel with the road.[58]

The year 1872 also marked the outbreak of vicious fighting during *Hosay*.[59] This scenario should remind us of similar conflicts replayed during *muḥarram* in India, and colonial authorities responded in a like manner by attempting to heavily curtail the public processions. The chain of violent events surrounding *Hosay* in Trinidad came to a climax in 1884, the year of the infamous *Hosay* riots in San Fernando.

Fêting and Fighting

I have been suggesting throughout this work that one of the subthemes of the commemoration is ritual as a mode of defiance to counteract, if only symbolically, the abuse of official authority. This is one of the ritual complex's hidden transcripts. We have seen that the month of Muharram and its ideological underpinnings gave rise to revolutions and wars in Iran, street protests and communal violence in India, and similar conflicts in Trinidad during the plantation period. Elsewhere in the Caribbean world, the potentially dangerous nature of *Hosay* led to it being banned by colonial rulers. This was the case in Surinam, and in British Guiana much popular pressure was put on colonial authorities to have *Hosay* banned or at least restricted to within the plantations themselves or to designated roads to limit movement and to avoid public confrontations between competing processions. In British Guiana in particular the *tadjah* became a symbol of defiance for sugarcane plantation laborers against their British overlords. Before returning to Trinidad, I wish to explore this theme in British Guiana because legislation there most probably led to the initiation of similar policies in Trinidad.

Chandra Jayawardena was one of the first contemporary scholars to indicate the potentially explosive nature of *Hosay* in British Guiana. In his view, however, the violence tended to be "expressive rather than instrumental." As he states, "Thus while the coolies declared their resolve to 'make great war' and kill 'everybody' they restrained any individual attempting violence."[60] Basdeo Mangru focuses more specifically on *tadjah* processions in his analysis, so it is to his work and a related government document I turn. Mangru cites a vast array of historical sources that paint the Guyanese variant of *Hosay* during the plantation period in a manner reminiscent of India: stick fighting, dancing, masquerade, doleful chanting, intoxication, and, of course, parading the model tombs.[61]

Official colonial sources such as Dennis Comins's 1893 *Note* familiarly but stereotypically present the observance as an unruly affair, which "has degenerated into a period of dissipation."[62] Citing the Commissioners of 1870 report, Comins quotes: "Except as an excuse for holidays and excesses, it has nothing to commend it in this county. . . . The anomalous character of the festival may be appreciated when it is remembered that the Muharram is a strictly Muhammaden anniversary which is here professedly celebrated by all East Indians, among whom the Hindus predominate. If it be impossible to make the collection orderly, it would probably be found that it could be put down without much difficulty."[63] Again, as in India, the colonial authorities emphasized the supposed nonreligious nature of the observance to justify eliminating it.[64]

Why did the colonial government find *Hosay* such an annoyance and why did it want it banned? Mangru explains that the processions, which were often sponsored by grog shops, would halt at these watering holes for participants to have a hardy draught. Fighting inevitably would break out under the influence of rum and *ganja* (marijuana), especially when rival *tadjah* processions—armed with knives, cutlasses (machetes), and sometimes even guns—would meet on the road and demand right-of-way privileges, as he notes: "Violence became more widespread when rival Tadjah processions clashed in the middle of the road, each refusing to give way to the other. . . . it was not uncommon for rival Tadjah factions to hire Chinese immigrants, reputed to be 'the best and strongest fighters' to spearhead their encounter. Frequently the procession blocked the road completely and the participants in their excited and inebriated state would assault estate personnel and travellers who refused to show reverence."[65]

The violent and insolent nature of these processions came under attack as early as 1865 in the indigenous press. Nevertheless, the plantocracy, for its own financial self-interest and against popular opinion, supported the processions as a way to manipulate laborers, which added yet another agenda to the contested performance. For them, *Hosay* functioned as the proverbial "steam valve" that offered Indians an occasion for periodic freedom to vent their frustration. By their endorsement of *Hosay*, plantation owners thought they could control the laborers by keeping them complacent. As for the Indians who participated, Mangru sees their actions as a method of resistance against the "feeling of helplessness and dependence" brought about by the indenture experience.[66] In other words, whereas the plantocracy saw in the rite a safety valve to keep the Indians under control by allowing them to blow off steam, laborers understood it as a vehicle for empowerment. Seeing the event as an opportunity to assert power and another excuse for rowdy behavior, Afro-Creoles also joined in the processions and even started their own Good Friday version called Black Tadjah. It is not clear what their motivations for doing so were, but as in Trinidad, Afro-Creoles were often hired to carry the objects or provide chorus and music. Others were attracted simply because of the spectacle and loudness of the event. Fear of the unification of laborers from different ethnic backgrounds as a result of *Hosay* was one of the factors that ultimately led to legislation to have it controlled.

By 1869, under pressure from the popular press, the colonial administration took strict measures to curtail the processions and prevent *tadjah*s from confronting one another in public. To this effect, Ordinance No. 16 of 1869 was ratified. After stating that each *tadjah* group must have a headman responsible for its orderliness and movement along officially specified routes, the ordinance continued with these rules:

No "Tadjah" processions will be permitted to enter the precincts either of the city of Georgetown or of the town of New Amsterdam.
 In case any Tadjah procession shall pass along any public road, it will be the duty of the headmen to regulate the march of the procession so that no obstruction be caused to the general public; and in order to ensure this as far as possible, no such procession must be permitted to occupy more than half of the width of the road, and must confine its march to the left half of the road, or to form itself in group so as to obstruct the free passage of the public.
 During the march of any Tadjah procession along a public road, it will be the duty of the headmen, in case of its meeting with, or overtaking, any carriage, waggon, cart or other vehicle drawn by any horse or other animal, or any person riding on any horse or mule, or any animals being led or driven, to cause all noises to cease, whether arising from the beating of drums, the playing of musical instruments, the singing or shouting of the persons forming the procession, or from any other cause under the control of the headmen, during such time as any portion of the procession shall be within a distance of 50 yards from any such vehicle or animals as before mentioned.
 Every headman and every immigrant . . . who shall willfully disregard any of the above regulations . . . will be liable to be imprisoned with or without hard labour for any term not exceeding six months, or to pay a penalty not exceeding 96 dollars.[67]

The government legislation to restrict the movement of the *tadjah*s to one side of the road and to force them to remain on designated routes led to a period of calm. But in 1879, twenty people were injured, including police, when a confrontation occurred between an Afro-Creole youth of one plantation and an Indian youth of another. Their brawl led to a major confrontation between the laborers of the two estates that resulted in court trials for twenty-five participants. Soon thereafter four people were killed during *Hosay* at Zorlen in neighboring Surinam. Although such incidents were isolated, colonial injunctions against the observance continued. That the restrictions had their desired effect is attested as early as 1893. Writing about the laws controlling the movement of *tadjah*s, Comins could state confidently that "forbidding the procession to leave the estate, and having no opportunity for display, the processions have died a natural death, and the coolies have lost to a great extent their interest in the anniversary."[68]

Mangru further points out that with increasing missionary pressure—not only from Christians but from Hindus and Muslims as well—the *tadjah* processions fell into ill repute. By the time of Guyana's independence in May 1966, the processions all but disappeared in favor of more "respectable" religious festivals among Hindus and Muslims. As in India, the issue was whether the processions manifested any religious meaning and whether they posed a threat to the ruling powers. Apparently, under the influence of missionaries who thought that *Hosay* was irreligious and a colonial regime that supported this claim, Indians began to turn to more "authentic" religious festivals imported from the homeland. Mangru, like a number of other authors cited above, understands *Hosay* as a unifying factor that bridged Hindus and Muslims in a collective effort to resist the humiliating situation and powerlessness of being an indentured worker.[69] Certainly, this is partly the case, but it cannot be the whole story because the government successfully wielded its power to quash the observance in its efforts to weaken any presumed unity among laborers.

About the same time that legislation to curtail the observance severely was being considered in British Guiana, the most unfortunate incident to occur in the history of *Hosay* in the Caribbean was beginning to take shape back in Trinidad. Again, the issues tended to foment around government intervention, which ultimately led to defiance. That defiance, however, sadly brought about catastrophe in Trinidad, for on October 30, 1884, the most traumatic incident in Indo-Trinidadian history occurred. On that day colonial police and British soldiers killed a number of *Hosay* participants. Kelvin Singh writes that the "causes of the tragedy must be sought in a number of interrelated economic, cultural, and political factors."[70] This is my task in the remainder of this section.[71]

The so-called *Hosay* riots, which some individuals sympathetic to the Indians refer to as a massacre, took place in San Fernando, the capital of the vast sugar districts of the Naparimas. Singh points out that *Hosay* was usually a relatively peaceful observance, and only twice before 1884 had violence led to a fatality.[72] We must thus search for other reasons to explain the events that occurred on that fateful day. As mentioned above, sugar prices were declining in the 1880s, which led plantation owners to take out their own economic woes on the Indian laborers working on their estates by creating strategies to extract more work from them for less pay. This was mainly accomplished by increasing tasks for which a lump sum would be paid to the individual laborer. As Fazal, an East Indian indentured laborer working during the period at the turn of the century, stated:

> one time plenty task
>   five row have to wuk
> dat have to finish before we go
>   o tomorrow have to finish it
> for same money[73]

Thus the worker in actuality would be receiving the same amount of money for more work performed. As tasks began to increase, local newspapers that supported the plantocracy bolstered an anti-Indian sentiment by creating "alarmist campaigns" against Indians and *Hosay*.[74]

Social unrest on the plantations continued to mount as tensions in Trinidadian society at large increased because of the sugar industry's crisis. Everyone was looking for someone else to blame for economic misfortune, and it seemed that the Indian laborers were the easiest target because they were regarded for the most part as transient foreigners. Then during the 1881 *Hosay*, a man named Harracksingh who was an Indo-Christian *sirdār* (headman) from an estate was killed under obscure circumstances. Headmen were not very well regarded by their fellow indentures because of their exploitative tactics, but they did often arbitrate with plantation bosses on behalf of workers. Be this as it may, Anthony de Verteuil, echoing other similar accounts, believes that the murder was committed over precedence rights. As he explains, Harracksingh was the headman of Palmyra estate. Like many estate headmen, Harracksingh organized his estate's procession during *Hosay*. His attempt to force the Palmyra procession into the lead position in front of Phillipine, which, as the oldest estate, took precedence over other estates, compelled the members of Phillipine to attack, leading to Harracksingh's death.[75] The murder came in the wake of another disturbance, known as the Canboulay riots, which occurred during the celebrated Trinidad Carnival of 1881 when colonial police attempted to control the dancing and stick fighting that were regular features of the event. The rioting lasted a few days, and several people were reported dead. The encounter between colonial forces and Afro-Creole revelers led to the stick fighting practice of Cannes Brulées (Canboulay) being outlawed that same year.[76]

The same year as the Canboulay riots, worrying that the violence surrounding Harracksingh's death would give orthodox Sunnis a bad name, over one hundred leaders of the orthodox community petitioned Governor Sandford Freeling. With the aid of Reverend Grant of the Canadian Presbyterian Mission, they requested the governor to ban *Hosay* on "religious grounds."[77] Fears of similar disturbances during 1882, most likely fueled by a prolonged angst over the so-called Indian mutiny of 1857, prompted the Trinidad Legislative Council to pass an ordinance to curtail the processions, which was supposedly based on the model of the restrictions on *Hosay* imposed in neighboring British Guiana.[78] Thus in July of 1882, a government decree called Ordinance No. 9 was issued, and it contained much the same language as the British Guiana proclamation cited above, but provided much greater detail. Sections three, four, six, and seven read as follows:

[3] No such procession will be allowed to enter the precincts of the towns of Port-of-Spain or San Fernando, nor will any such procession be allowed to use or cross any high road or public road except on the express permission in writing of the stipendiary magistrate of the district in which the procession shall pass.

[4] Immigrants not residing on plantations may, with the consent of the proprietor or manager of any plantation and on the written authority of the stipendiary magistrate of the district, be permitted to join the immigrants residing on any plantation in the celebration of the festival, but they will not be permitted to bring any Tadjah from without on to such plantation.

[6] No other than an immigrant or the descendants of immigrants shall take part in any procession or in any way interfere with such processions.

[7] Stipendiary magistrates are hereby empowered to grant licenses to the Mahommedan "headmen" of any plantation or village and to others being Mahomedans, as shall be necessary for the burial of the sacred earth representing the body of the martyrs, or for carrying out any religious rites connected with the festival of Mohurrum.[79]

The full text was published in Port of Spain's *Royal Gazette* that same year and in the *San Fernando Gazette* on August 23, 1884. It is clear that the ordinance's aim was to segregate Hindus, Muslims, and Afro-Creoles into fragmented groups by limiting the number of participants in these rituals and by heavily curtailing the movement of the *tadjahs*. As in British Guiana, the measures seemed to work for the first few years.

The processions passed peacefully in 1882, but there was more industrial unrest marked by frequent strikes among plantation workers in 1883.[80] Then there were again street confrontations between reveling Afro-Creoles and police during Carnival in 1884. As early as 1859, journalists had complained that East Indians were allowed to practice their fête unrestrained and without molestation even though restrictions were imposed on the Afro-Creole carnival.[81] Although such rhetorical comments were directed at the lack of restraint against the Indians, no doubt the jealousy aroused by such pronouncements provided a reason for Afro-Creoles to rebel during Carnival in the 1880s. The Hamilton Report on the 1881 Canboulay disturbances lends credence to this view, as it urged that measures be taken against *Hosay* so that it also would not become an unruly affair like Carnival.[82] But, in addition, there was a divide-and-rule policy in effect to keep Afro- and Indo-Trinidadians apart and therefore not united, which more than likely motivated the decision to place severe restrictions on *Hosay* in the 1882 ordinance.[83] This whole chain of events led to a prohibition established on July 30, 1884 that prevented the *tadjahs* from entering the towns.[84]

Naturally, the Indian community thought the measures imposed by the colonial government were unjust. In response, a group of thirty-two Indians led by one Sookhoo, who was the *sirdār* of Phillipine estate and a native of Shahjahanpur in the former United Provinces, petitioned to have the ordinance revoked. I mention Sookhoo's provenance here only because Shahjahanpur was mentioned in the previous chapter as one of the locations where Sunnis had all but usurped Muharram performances from the Shi'ah. This fact should provide further support for my claim that control of *Hosay* was largely in the hands of non-Shi'ah in Trinidad. Although it is impossible to determine population statistics based on religious or sectarian affiliation, it is clear that important administrative positions having to do with the structure and organization of *Hosay* were in the hands of Indian Hindus, Sunnis, and Christians.

To return to Sookhoo's plea, his party's grounds for the petition were that "your petitioners consider to prohibit them from observing their religious rites when the moon calls your petitioners to do so [and such a prohibition] would be detrimental to them, and would consequently tend to embitter your petitioners' existence." He and his fellow petitioners appeared in the San Fernando Police Court only to hear accusations that they were under a "misapprehension" of the intentions of the government's regulations, which the administrator claimed were carefully framed to ensure order throughout the colony. The administrator went on to say that the government was not infringing on religious rights, and he insisted that the regulations "do not in any way interfere with the religious rites connected with the festival." But he stated that "no procession can possibly on the ground of religion claim to enter the Town of Port of Spain or San Fernando, or to proceed along the high roads of the Colony without the permission of the magistrate of the district."[85]

It seems that the government was bent on provoking a confrontation, regardless of the cost, by emphasizing social order over religious observance. Thus, as the 1884 *Hosay* approached, an Executive Council meeting was held at which it was decided that military troops would be called in to assist the local police.[86] Twenty-five marines were to be sent to the St. James Barracks, Port of Spain, fifteen to Couva, fifteen to St. Joseph, and twenty to San Fernando.[87] Indians could not believe that the soldiers and police would "shoot people like fowls" and continued their preparation for the processions under the assumption that the defenders of the law would load their weapons with harmless powder as a physical but symbolic deterrent to violence.[88] Unfortunately, they were wrong. As Singh points out, "The evidence, both official and unofficial is confusing and sometimes conflicting."[89] What we know for certain is that on the evening of October 30, the Riot Act was read to processions entering San Fernando from at least three locations, after which the police detachments opened fire on the crowd. As the dust cleared, it became evident that there were 107 casualties, with 16 dead.[90]

Singh, who has done the most extensive research on the topic, believes that the *Hosay* participants acted more or less in innocence, but Wood suggests that if the Indians behaved riotously it was due to tension over increased tasks on the plantations.[91] Others speculate that Indian laborers were protesting against the British as a form of latent nationalism in response to the 1857 uprising. Yet another observer suspects that Afro-Trinidadians in the crowd may have instigated a confrontation with the police by coercing Indians to take out the *tadjah*s as retaliation for the ban on Canboulay a few years earlier.[92] Moreover, as I have noted, boisterous elements among the Afro-Creoles had been joining in the procession from the 1850s onward, and one of the hidden intentions of the 1884 regulations was to curb their participation in the event to keep the subaltern masses divided along ethnic and racial lines.[93] It seems likely at least that the rowdier elements in the crowd, whether they were Indian or Afro-Creole, may have provoked a confrontation to some degree because of their resentment of suppressive government actions. Singh mentions that "Some Indians were alleged to have made threats of retaliation if they were attacked, others were said to have shown indifference to the prospect of death."[94] Here again, we see *Hosay*, like Carnival for Afro-Creoles, serving as a form of resistance against the hegemony of the plantocracy and against government intervention, which most often supported the interests of the plantations' aristocracy. Strategies of government intervention during *Hosay* in the British Caribbean must thus be seen in the broader transnational context of similar policies implemented to control *muḥarram* in British India if we are to make overall sense of the controversial events surrounding the rite in the colonies.[95]

The effect of the 1884 incident on the performance of *Hosay* on a grand scale was, to a certain extent, a death knell. After 1885, Afro-Creole participation in the San Fernando event declined, and the processions gradually faded away there and in many other locations due to pressure from orthodox Sunni groups, such as the Anjuman Sunnat-ul-Jamaat Association (ASJA), which was influential after 1935.[96] Moreover, the Presbyterian Mission harbored "an uncompromising hostility" toward the rite.[97] Such missionary pressure, combined with the small size of the Shi'i population in central and south Trinidad, gradually led to the virtual extinction of Muharram rituals in all but one location on the southern tip of the island. An exception to this scenario of suppression comes from St. James in the north, where *Hosay* rose in prominence as it declined elsewhere. No shots were fired in St. James on October 30, 1884, because participants were able to reach the adjacent waters of Peru Bay without entering the city of Port of Spain, of which St. James is now a suburb. But why should the rite survive there after it has all but died out in most other locations on the island?

For one thing, St. James, which had evolved from abandoned estates (Peru lands) and was known as "Coolie Town" in the nineteenth century, had a large concentration of urbanized Indians to keep the tradition alive. By 1919, tramcars linked St. James to Port of Spain, enabling people of all ethnic groups to attend and participate. This broader participation was an economic benefit for the area as well, which may be part of the reason why St. James became incorporated into the Port of Spain municipality in 1938. Becoming part of the major metropolis on the island resulted in St. James losing its plantation character, and Indians were drawn into urban Creole culture. This process allowed for much closer interaction between Indians and other members of Trinidadian society, which gradually led to the breakdown of ethnic boundaries and a cross-fertilization of traditions, something that did not happen to the same extent in San Fernando.[98] Also, because the Shi'i element in central and south Trinidad was always negligible, it allowed orthodox Sunni organizations to continue pushing for the abandonment of *Hosay*, with little resistance from those who wished to continue performing the rite.[99]

Lack of resistance was not the case in St. James, as we will soon see, for there a core of Shi'i families defied criticisms and continued to practice the tradition wholeheartedly and with innovation. Even though a large urban crowd could provide many opportunities for protests and riots, Singh speculates that by the time St. James became incorporated, the creolized tradition already was too deeply rooted in local urban culture for any official action to be taken against it.[100] The result is that today St. James has the most spectacular *Hosay* performance on the island, although it is also performed in the rural area of Cedros, south Trinidad. Let us now move on to some further considerations about *muḥarram* in the Caribbean before turning to an overview of the rituals in the last section of this chapter.

Hosay as Multicultural Phenomenon and Tradition

In the Caribbean basin, particularly in Trinidad, the *Hosay* observances were, as adumbrated above, influenced to some extent by certain African rituals. In turn, *Hosay* had an impact on Carnival, one of the most spectacular public display events held in Trinidad, for which it has become famous worldwide.[101] A *Hosay* float was even incorporated during Carnival. As early as 1878, there are journalistic reports of the "Coolie Hosé" (that is, *tadjah*) being depicted in Carnival processions.[102] Borrowing elements of culture, in other words, went both ways in a dialogical fashion. The development, evolution, and transformation of the Muharram observances from their origins in Iraq to their contemporary manifestations in the Caribbean is thus the result of intercultural factors that produce a multidimensional and polyethnic set of traditions. We have already seen this to be the case in India, where the rituals adapted to Indian life by incorporating elements of the local cultures into which they were transplanted. In the case of the Caribbean form, however, the most interesting development is that the mourning dimension has been transformed on one popular level of interpretation into a kind of public celebration largely due to the creolization process. But this view also needs to be tempered by pointing out the deep solemnity of the active participants on the private level. It is this dynamic tension between private and public meanings that will be explored in subsequent chapters. Nonetheless, the discourse on the transformation of *Hosay* is one that remains in the spotlight down to the present day.

The hotly contested issue of "carnivalization" is a constant point of tension in Trinidad. As I have suggested earlier, the debate over celebration versus piety also occurred in India, where the colonial government used such distinctions to rule whether a particular practice was religious. In contemporary Trinidad, journalistic debates occur each year concerning the most appropriate way to observe or celebrate *Hosay*.[103] While I have been arguing in previous chapters that similar debates took place in Iran and India, the Trinidadian mode of discourse is the one that I wish to explore in the greatest depth in the remainder of this study. If *Hosay* has been going through a long and gradual period of co-optation by Sunnis and Hindus in India and by Hindus, Christians, and Afro-Creoles in Trinidad, what of the Shi'ah? Although the occasion for taking out *ta'ziyah*s is central to Shi'i theology in many parts of the world, other Muslims and non-Muslims also participate in the event, albeit for different reasons, as we have already seen. In countries like India, where Shi'ism is a minority religion, the process of absorbing alien ritual practices has inevitably developed as a mechanism of survival. This has been the case in Trinidad as well, where the observance has been adapting to Caribbean ways of life for over a century and a half. Prior to the arrival of Indians, the observance was unknown on the island. Despite claims by some Afro-Trinidadian popular and revisionist historians that a number of their enslaved ancestors from West Africa may have been Muslims prior to their conversion to other faiths in the New World, there is no evidence to suggest that *muḥarram* observances predate the arrival of East Indians.[104]

The tradition of *Hosay*, as many Indo-Trinidadian Muslims of the Shi'i persuasion are quick to point out, has been going on annually ever since shortly after the first indentured laborers arrived from India. From Grant's account cited above, we know that the observance began to be practiced on the island within a decade of the arrival of the first indentured laborers. Indeed, descriptions of the ritual portions of the event, even in more contemporary times, seem very familiar to those who have witnessed the phenomenon in South Asia. In Joan Koss's 1959 testimony, she "watched a seemingly endless procession of women light lamps and murmur prayers while throwing rice and flowers to paper gilt tomb effigies (*tazias*) that were later carried in the processions. Those afflicted with an illness were thought to obtain blessings which could restore their health."[105] Her description easily could have been describing the parallel event anywhere in north India.

Continuities, however, exist side by side with changes. Some practices are noticeably missing; breast beating, flagellation, horse processions, eulogy recitation, and stick fighting do not figure prominently in contemporary manifestations of *Hosay*.[106] In fact, only one historical account that I have read makes even the slightest suggestion that self-mortification has played any role whatsoever in *Hosay*.[107] Because many of the East Indians who were brought to Trinidad came from what is now Uttar Pradesh and Bihar, it is fairly clear that their traditions of *Hosay* are cognates of earlier forms practiced in north India. What this implies is that a heavy dose of Sunni and Hindu accretions to the observances found promi- nence in Trinidad, while distinct Shi'i forms of piety, such as *mātam*, were downplayed significantly.

Hosay in Trinidad was and still is characterized by familiar Indian events such as the mass *tadjah* processions, drumming, prayer meetings in mosques, and, less frequently today, eulogy recitation and martial dance displays. But in addition, we also find less orthodox modes of action such as the consumption of alcohol, sensuous dancing (jumping up), and other forms of carefree abandon, which do not conform to the sober and mournful experience that characterizes the Shi'i observance in other parts of the world. Ironically, these unorthodox modes of behavior are viewed by many of the island's Sunnis as not being Islamic, even though the Sunni were the ones who significantly contributed to the celebratory mode of the phenomenon in India, which subsequently took root in Trinidad. I must note, however, that the excessive claims about the prac- tice of "jumping up" are polemical, exaggerated by the Sunni to further their cause of eradicating *Hosay*. Although dancing and partying do oc- cur, I have seen both activities decrease over the past decade. Jumping up notwithstanding, many of those spiritually and physically involved in the construction of *tadjah*s and the performance of *muḥarram* in St. James continue to insist that they are practicing something that adheres faith- fully to the Indian way: tradition as taught to them by their forefathers. Tradition becomes an authoritative trope in legitimizing the *Hosay* enter- prise. In short, the past is used as a "scarce resource" to authenticate the present.[108]

It is historically accurate to say that the observance has continued more or less uninterrupted since the first landing.[109] To assert, however, that no performative change has occurred in the observance suggests a strong tendency on the part of the Indo-Trinidadian Shi'ah to question the forces of change by describing the ritualistic *Hosay* tradition as a set of practices not affected by time or space. By taking such a conservative po- sition on the central event of their religious calendar, the Shi'ah maintain a distinctive feature of their sectarian position, while simultaneously con- necting mentally with a shared, albeit imagined, Indian past. The contin- ual reification of self-perceived cultural and spiritual continuity has served to establish a cognitive link with a homeland known more through imagination than by means of historical or genealogical facts.[110] Gradu- ally, the few Shi'ah who have practiced the tradition have come to down- play creolization in favor of "authentic" Indian practice.

Although the St. James *Hosay* is organized by Shi'i families, it should be evident to the reader by now that more than this small minority is involved in its outward performance. True, they are the guardians of secret theological doctrines concerning the original meaning of the event, but we have already seen that accounts going back to the plantation period suggest that this was an event shared by all East Indians and other ethnic groups. The development of *Hosay*, however, remains undocumented and uncertain. Even though oral family histories of those Shi'ah involved in the organization of *Hosay* and the construction of *tadjah*s claim that their ancestors began the practice shortly after their arrival on the first boatload of indentured workers, the original list of passengers does not contain their names. They may have used fictitious names to sign in at the time of recruitment or changed their names after their arrival in an attempt to employ *taqīyyah*, a concealment of identity permitted to the Shi'ah so they may avoid persecution. Whatever the case may be, aside from incomplete oral histories, we do not know precisely how *Hosay* began on the plantations. What is clear, however, is that not just Shi'ah have been taking part in the spectacle, for others, as I have been arguing, have enjoyed it in a secular way as well. Even though I cannot state this definitively, my best guess is that *Hosay* grew as a phenomenon that was simultaneously an expression of Indian identity, a pious act of religious expression, and a mode of resistance both to government control and to the forces of acculturation.

Today non-Shi'i participants of East Indian origin participate in imagining a tenuous link with the motherland through the *muḥarram* observances, but many de-emphasize its spirituality. For them, the religious dimension of *Hosay* is respected by observing some of the taboos related to the construction of *tadjah*s. Even while non-Shi'i East Indians may believe in the healing powers of the *tadjah*s and make vows to them, this religious aspect is downplayed in favor of the event's Indianness.[111] For many, it is simply a way of identifying with the homeland in a purely secular fashion, and even the observance of taboos is currently considered to be a nonreligious custom by non-Muslims of East Indian descent. Whether Indo-Trinidadians have over the years performed *Hosay* out of a firm religious commitment or out of nostalgia for the homeland, they have all identified in one way or another with being Indian. In this sense, *Hosay* was already an ethnic pageant that transcended religious affiliations in the premodern period, even while it allowed some Muslims to retain sectarian beliefs about the observance's nature and significance. *Hosay* can thus be understood on at least two levels, as far as East Indians are concerned: religious rite and cultural tradition. Acknowledging this, we must then also account for Afro-Trinidadian perspectives, which brings us to the discourse on the making of "national tradition."

Within the intermingling spheres of religiosity and ethnicity, the Shi'ah remained a very small and secretive minority within a minority, guarding the esoteric meanings of the rite. Notwithstanding the participation of Trinidadian citizens from all walks of life, including Afro-Trinidadians, Chinese, and others, Indo-Trinidadians have continued to express their Indianness through *Hosay* over the generations on the exoteric level. The categories of interior and exterior understandings allow us to flesh out different levels of discourse and meaning, levels that become discernible when the rituals become public. Given the above scenario, I want to reiterate what should by now seem fairly obvious to the reader. *Hosay* has resulted in what is today one of the most spectacular cultural performances on the island, and even though it is not as well known as the famous Trinidad Carnival, the observance is certainly one of the most visible East Indian public display events found in St. James. Because of the media exposure it has received, *Hosay* has been elevated in popular consciousness to the status of a definitive Indian event throughout the island. Through *Hosay*, the homeland is imagined and presented in an encapsulated display of religion and culture to an audience knowing very little about India. The display itself then gives rise to other imaginings by non-Indians, which leads to further contention and negotiation of meaning on different levels of analysis.

As might be surmised from the brief overview given above, *Hosay*, as observed today, is most likely rooted in Muslim interaction with East Indian Hindus and Christians during and immediately after the plantation period. This is not surprising in and of itself because we have seen that Hindus and Sunnis often participate exuberantly in South Asian *muharram* observances. But this tradition of participation, with a long, complex, and global history, continued to develop in Trinidad by grafting elements of Afro-Trinidadian expressive culture onto the tradition or, minimally, modifying preexisting practices, artifacts, and terminology to suit Caribbean sensibilities.[112] To make matters even more complicated, the postcolonial government has become involved in the propagation of *Hosay* as an item of national culture. This was highlighted in 1971 when the former prime minister, Dr. Eric Williams, visited the four *tadjah*-building yards in St. James in an attempt to convince the craftsmen that entering into commercial ventures would boost the economy by creating a festive atmosphere appealing to tourists. His effort was aided by the government's Tourism Development Authority, which attempted to lure foreigners to the island with advertisements for special fares to fly with

British West Indian Airlines during *Hosay*.[113] So it is not surprising that when the month of Muharram falls after the Christmas holidays or after Carnival, a period of national celebration is often extended to include *Hosay*. Governmental validation resulting from the attempted fusion of ethnic and national identity has thus also contributed to the construction of multiple understandings and representations of *Hosay*, which are at the heart of local discourses pertaining to cultural borrowing and creolization. To conclude this chapter, I provide a brief overview of the *Hosay* tradition as it is practiced today in order to provide the reader with a fitting context for the extended ethnographic and theoretical discussions that follow in subsequent chapters.

Hosay Today: An Overview

There are two major centers of Muharram observance in Trinidad today. One is the northern town of St. James, the suburb of Port of Spain discussed above, and the other is the Cedros district in the southwest of the island.[114] Although one could speak of a "unified" *Hosay* tradition in Trinidad, variation resulting from rural/urban differentiation, ethnic and religious affiliation, and other elements has shaped the observance in subtle ways. Further, some participants from St. James in the north emphatically state such differences by saying, for instance, "we have nothing to do with them" (that is, the southern customs). In fact, many of the people involved in the construction of the tomb replicas in the north have never witnessed the observance as practiced in the south. The reluctance of northerners to relate to the southerners has to do with lingering stereotypes of the southerners being backward and uneducated, whereas northerners like to think of themselves as modern and cosmopolitan. Parallel traditions have therefore developed out of one imagined parent tradition. Some of the similarities and divergences are discussed below.

In St. James, the four yards organizing the Muharram observances are family-based operations, while in the south, the yards have only loose family associations and are primarily organized around community networks derived from plantation estate antecedents. In addition to the construction and parading of the *tadjah*s, two huge green and red moons that strongly resemble the *sipar*s of Bihar (see Figure 11) are constructed and paraded by yet two more family-based yards in St. James. The moons are corporeal representations of Hasan (green for poison) and Husayn (red for blood), who remain the focal point for the contemporary observance.

In the north, the core of the observance is drawn from the Muslim community, especially from the Shi'i sector. It must, however, be underlined that although the sectarian distinctions in Trinidad are downplayed for most of the year, during *Hosay* the distinction becomes more pronounced because of debates over correct practice and doctrine. Among Trinidadian Muslims, those who belong to the more orthodox or fundamental groups stand apart from the others, regarding themselves as staunch Sunnis, defenders of the purity of Islam. Such groups are often highly political and are very critical of the Muharram observances in Trinidad. As a result, those who orchestrate Muharram activities, particularly the Shi'i organizers, must always be on their guard against being criticized by such groups.

The Muslim population involved in the southern observance is relatively small. The rituals are thus organized, controlled, and performed mainly by Hindus and Christians. This is partly because there are fewer Muslims in the south, but also because there has been such a strong anti-*Hosay* lobby there since the events surrounding the 1884 massacre. It would be incorrect to consider the conspicuous absence of a significant Muslim population in the south to be a new development because it seems that their minuscule population in the region has been a persistent factor in the maintenance and transformation of the tradition in that part of the country. When one of the main organizers of the event in southern Trinidad was asked if he saw a contradiction in being a Hindu who participated in the Muslim rite and believed in its power, he simply responded, "I presume I am a Muslim one month each year." Such religious oscillation reflects the amalgam of many different cultural influences that have gone into making *Hosay* what it is in Trinidad.[115] Moreover, those Trinidadians who are passive participants still regard the event as an East Indian fête, perhaps because of the colonial legacy of representing it as such. But, again, this should not surprise us because we have seen the same to be true in India. Some non-Muslims who are involved in the construction of the *tadjah*s even go so far as to suggest that the observance is more a cultural performance than a religious one, which hints at the way the rite has been shaped by economic factors in addition to social ones.

A significant socioeconomic aspect of *Hosay* is that the southern version has not been subjected to any great amount of commercial exposure because media coverage of it has been severely limited. This is partially a result of the rural nature of the Cedros area. Having once been coastal sugarcane and coconut plantations, the surrounding villages have retained their rural flavor as stereotypical sleepy fishing villages in the deep south. Consequentially, the *Hosay* observance has not attracted many spectators from beyond the immediate area. In contrast, the St. James *Hosay* is an urban phenomenon that has received a great amount of attention in the press, on television, and by word-of-mouth, resulting in more extravagant and lavish productions. This is especially true in the light of the encroachment by government organizations upon the observance to promote it as a tourist attraction—an Indian carnival. The latter factor has influenced popular perceptions of the event to some degree and needs to be considered when discussing the variety of meanings embedded in *Hosay*. To complete my brief overview, let me continue with the essentials of the observance as performed in both the north and the south.

In both areas, *Hosay* consists of building replicas of Husayn's tomb, which in reality are not replicas but rather, like those of India, imaginative renderings of the original structure located at Karbala. Small *tadjah*s devoted to Husayn's older brother Hasan are also built in both areas. Worthy of note in this regard is that some of the active participants firmly believe Hasan died together with Husayn at Karbala. Hasan and Husayn are known in much of the Muslim world by the Arabic dual form of *ḥasanayn*, and in many countries Hasan is also remembered during Muharram. The coalescence of the two brothers in Trinidad, however, could be the result of the influence of Hindu epics regarding the heroic exploits of twin brothers.[116] In Bengal, for instance, the tragic saga of Hasan and Husayn is included in a vernacular rendering of the pan-Hindu epic *Mahābhārata*. Whatever the case may be, it is clear that the community's sacred history has been reformulated to suit local sensibilities. The Karbala paradigm's master narrative continues to undergo change as the creative process of imagining the past produces ever-newer versions of religious and ethnic identities but nevertheless provides some semblance of continuity with an imagined Indian past. Preparations in both locations also involve the making of flags that parallel the *'alam*s of Iran and South Asia, the cooking of special foods during ten days of partial abstinence, the construction of new *tassa* and bass drums, reskinning older ones, and beating special rhythms performed exclusively during Muharram.

The process of building the large *tadjah* used to take forty days, but now, due to modern construction methods using power tools and materials like styrotex, the length of time spent on construction has become more variable. The minimum required, however, is to begin at least by the first day of Muharram, as is common in many places in the south. In the north, work on the *tadjah*s usually begins after the holiday feast called Baqra Eid, which is celebrated on the tenth day of Zul Hijja, the last month of the Islamic calendar.[117] Although participants in both locations loosely adhere to the temporal framework of the Islamic lunar calendar, many differences in structure, technique, and design exist between northern and southern *tadjah*s. The north, for example, is more "traditional" in building the base and internal frame, which is made primarily of a reed called *roseau*.[118] Three of the four crews currently building *tadjah*s in St. James employ *roseau* to bind the base and strengthen the frame. Otherwise, they have departed quite significantly from tradition in the scheme of color, shape, and external décor, making the *tadjah*s more colorful and glitzy, like the costumes and floats of Carnival. The northern *tadjah*s exemplify what Regina Bendix calls "material creolization," which visually reflects the multicultural and cosmopolitan nature of the event in St. James.[119]

In the south, the frame is now made solely of wood. The exterior is more traditional, however, being constructed in what is sometimes referred to locally as the old style. The structure of the *tadjah* is angular, the color is predominantly white, and the external decoration is based on white crêpe paper flowers called "knot roses."[120] In both north and south, the height of the *tadjah* is currently limited to 15.6 feet due to the height of electrical and telephone wires in the streets. Earlier *tadjah*s, however, resembled Indians ones described in the previous chapter that in the past were twenty or more feet high, with as many as six tiers. In both areas, each *imambara* has a headman whose function is similar to that of the *sirdār* of the plantation period. The headmen collectively are responsible for making financial arrangements, securing parade permits from the police, and, theoretically, for maintaining the orderly behavior of the crowd during the processional rituals and drumming. The latter, however, is the task of the police in reality. Each camp also includes a master builder, the builders themselves, drummers, and the men in charge of maintaining the drums.

Although the whole event, beginning with the cutting of the *roseau*, can be construed as a ritual process, the most intense ritualistic portions of *Hosay* begin to increase from the first of the month of Muharram. Those who are involved in *tadjah* preparation abstain from the intake of meat, fried foods, alcohol, and salt and from sexual intercourse. In the past, the prohibition applied to the whole duration of the forty days. Some individuals engaged in building the *tadjah*s at present follow the proscriptions as a form of sacrifice, but it is more a matter of personal volition than a general rule. The key to a successful observance here is adaptability and tolerance because many of the proscriptions serve more as ideal types, reflecting reality, not replicating it. Shoes must be removed while working in the *imambara*, which is technically off-limits to women. In reality, however, postpubescent girls may work inside as long as they are not menstruating. Thus whoever works on the structures is supposed to remain ritually pure. Acts of abstinence, long hours of hard work during the evening hours, and financial investment are all viewed as ongoing sacrifices made by community members throughout the first ten days of Muharram. Participants give up much during the ritual period in order to show grief and austerity for the prototypical martyr who died on the plains of Karbala, thereby experientially identifying with his suffering. In this way, they participate locally on the esoteric level in the global Shiʻi master narrative and paradigm of Husayn's suffering.

In general, precept and practice are consonant in the urban north and rural south. Yet much creative variety is to be found on both the individual and community levels. In the next chapter, I will present a thicker description of *Hosay* in St. James as I experienced it through participant observation intermittently between the years 1991 and 1997. I will follow the general sequence of events in chronological fashion, pointing out certain southern variables where appropriate.[121]

Chapter 5
Building the *Tadjah*,
Constructing Community

> *What I knew about Islam was what was known to everyone on the outside. . . .*
> *They had their own martyrs. Once a year mimic mausolea were wheeled*
> *through the streets; men "danced" with heavy crescent moons, swinging the*
> *moons now one way, now the other; drums beat, and sometimes there were*
> *ritual stick fights. . . . Islam, going by what I saw of it from the outside, was*
> *less metaphysical and more direct.*
>
> —*V. S. Naipaul,* Among the Believers: An Islamic Journey

Outside In

V. S. Naipaul speaks to us as a liminar from the margins of the *Hosay* community. Being Indo-Trinidadian, he is squarely situated on the inside of the community of worshippers he witnesses, but being a nonparticipating Hindu, he is on the outside looking in. Although he lacks the necessary interpretive skills needed to comprehend the event fully from the inside perspective of a participant, he shares something with those he observes, even though he is not completely cognizant of the experiential directness at which he so acutely points. The writer's epistemological dilemma concerning his nation's major Islamic public performance demonstrates a basic idea to which I wish to return at the close of this chapter, namely, that things may not always be what they appear to be on the surface. Hermeneutic activity by spectator and believer alike thus provides layers of contextually embedded meaning that is multivocalic in nature, offering different modes of understanding based on an individual's level of awareness and closeness to the ritualistic tradition.

It is clear that performances embody multiple meanings for all the communities involved in the event, meanings that may not be the same for all involved. But the creation of meaning becomes even more complex and diverse as we move from the yard to the street, when the private productions of the yards' activities enter the public sphere. It is on the street that artisans, performers, and audience members come together in creative acts of interpretive expression. Moreover, in heterogeneous, polyethnic cultures such as Trinidad, where many ethnic and religious communities coexist, if not always peacefully, each representative group brings its own preconceived notions to bear on the events being performed and observed. Interpretations and understandings therefore may not always correspond to a prototypical set of historically derived assumptions about the phenomenon performed, and meanings may often vary to such a degree that they become contested and mutually exclusive. In this chapter, I wish to illustrate this point by describing explicitly different sets of interpretations pertaining to *Hosay*. To do so, however, I must first provide a fairly extensive description of the processes, both symbolic and actual, leading up to the great processions that are the center of the annual event in Trinidad. My logic for doing so is to provide the reader with the appropriate contextual backdrop for my subsequent theoretical discussions of negotiating and debating creolization, identity, tradition, and the pros and cons of transnationalism in Chapter 6.

Social Organization and Socialization in the Yards

As I briefly described in the previous chapter, the activities during Muharram are centered in six specific family-based yards—four building *tadjah*s and two building moons. The *tadjah*-building yards are named either after their neighborhood location or after the founder: Bay Road Yard and Cocorite Yard are named after their geographic locations, while Ghulam Hussein Yard and Balma Yard are named after their respective founders. The moon-building yards are named after the color (red, green/blue) of the creations produced there.[1] Each *tadjah*-building yard, sometimes called a "camp," after the Carnival term "*mas* camp," attracts its members from the neighborhood in which it is located.[2] The esoteric moon yards, however, resemble men's guilds in the sense that one must be secretly initiated into the mysteries of the specific moon before one can participate actively in constructing it and dancing or playing it during the processions. Each yard, as previously stated, has a headman, a master builder, and a master drum maker. Further, the headmen all belong to an organizing committee that is responsible for public relations, financing, and other activities.[3] In 1992 the committee was formally institutionalized as the St. James/Cocorite *Hosay* Association, with Bunny Emamali, headman of Balma Yard, as its chairman. There is thus a sense of cooperation among the yards, but there is also a healthy sense of playful competition. The theme of competition that runs through the long history of the development of the rite's passage from Iran to South Asia to the Caribbean crystallizes in Trinidad.

We saw in Chapter 3 that in India the locus for the social organization and mobilization of the *ta'ziyah* processions was the *muḥallā*. Similarly, the yard is the focus of a neighborhood unit in St. James. During the plantation period, the estate served a similar function because it was to one's fellow laborers one pledged allegiance, regardless of race, ethnicity, or religious affiliation. With the decline of indentureship, however, the organization of *Hosay* became the domain of the yard. All the yards are spatially aligned within walking distance along an axis known as Western Main Road, the street running through the center of St. James along which processions take place on the evenings of the eighth through the tenth and on the tenth day of Muharram.[4] But the yard is much more than just a temporary place of gathering during the month of Muharram. It is within the yard that neighborhood children grow, play, learn, fall in love, marry, and die. As one female *Hosay* participant put it, "we grow in it, we love in it, we have children in it, we die in it." It is also from the neighborhood within which a yard is situated that people are attracted to the *Hosay*, quite often at a young age. One Afro-Trinidadian Christian member of Balma Yard, for example, told me that he has known Noble Bisnath, the master builder, since childhood and said, "we play cricket together, we do everything together. So this is also a group activity, not limited to Muslims, especially in the area of drumming."

It is thus through liming (loafing) together in the yards that one eventually enters into the tradition of *Hosay*. Liming, an ever-present activity in Trinidad, provides the communicative context within which much informal knowledge of *Hosay* traditions and practices is transmitted. Indeed, a considerable portion of my own understanding of the phenomenon was conveyed to me during such sessions. While liming one day, Raiez Ali, headman of the Ghulam Hussein Yard and descendant of the yard's founder, related to me how he became involved. He said that when he was very young, he used to watch the others in the yard quietly, without interfering, during *Hosay*. He also visited all the other yards in St. James but always returned home to his own. Then when he felt he was ready, he went out to nearby Curepe town to try his hand at building a small *tadjah* for the forty-day procession on the twentieth of Safar. Some of the masters of the time started seeing his creations and urged him to get involved with the big ones. After a few years of practice, he began to help "the guys" in his own yard, eventually moving up in the ranks to become a designer. The first year of my fieldwork in St. James, 1991, was his second year in that position, and today he is the headman of his yard. His experience is fairly typical of how one achieves status and moves up in the hierarchy of activities in preparation for the event.

Raiez's father, the late Ibrahim Ali, who was the previous headman and master drummer of the Ghulam Hussein Yard during the early years of my research, remarked to me that children grow into the *Hosay*.[5] "The boys," he said, "start on the junk pile, move to skinning, then drum-making, and finally *tadjah* building," the central male activities involved in preparing for *Hosay*. When a boy begins working on a *tadjah*, he does menial tasks at first, such as mixing flour paste for gluing paper onto the frame, running errands, or buying materials. But as the child gains experience, he moves up to more skilled tasks in ascending order: cutting cardboard, carving styrotex (styrofoam), and working on ornamentation. Ibrahim's statement seems to suggest that the construction of the model tombs is the most important activity in the yard's work hierarchy during *Hosay*. When I inquired if he thought the building of the *tadjah* was the most essential task, he took off his baseball cap, scratched his head, and replied simply, "Not really. When it all gets started, it's a combination." His idea of the relationship between the parts and the whole is one that was stressed over and over again to me by people involved and is an indigenous conceptual theme that will arise several times throughout this chapter. The point I want to make here, however, is that people who pledge allegiance to a particular yard organize their life around it and around *Hosay*. Later in life, as one marries, further kinship bonds reinforce one's social relationship to a particular yard. But because members socialized in one yard might marry into another, there is also a fluidity of affiliation created through kinship bonds. Marriage partnerships also often lead to conversion. Conversion, as both local residents and scholars have pointed out, is also fluid and more a matter of convenience than religious belief.[6] A few examples will help to illustrate this point.

The late Sookran Ghassie, who worked on *tadjah*s in Ghulam Hussein Yard for twelve years while he was courting one of Ibrahim Ali's sisters, was born a Hindu and converted to Catholicism in high school, at which time he changed his name to James. When James finally married into the yard, he converted to Islam, but he kept his Christian name for the rest of his life. Similarly, another of Ibrahim's brothers-in-law, Albert "Aloh" Dookuwa, met his future wife while he was a master builder in the Ghulam Hussein Yard. He too converted from Christianity to Islam in order to marry into the yard. Noble also converted from Hinduism to Islam when he joined Balma Yard as a result of his marriage to Rasheeda. In these examples we see people marrying into yards and changing their religion in accommodation to the yard. But there are also examples of marrying out of a yard, as in the case of one of Noble's younger brothers, who married out of Balma Yard and into Ghulam Hussein Yard but continues to participate at Balma. Rasheeda herself is from Balma Yard but married into the Ghulam Husayn Yard. She subsequently returned to

Balma when her now-deceased first husband left Ghulam Hussein to join Balma. The issue at stake leading to his decision concerned certain ideological disputes over the most appropriate way to build the *tadjah*. These examples, which could be multiplied many times over, should serve to demonstrate the fluidity of both religious choice and social affiliations between the different yards.

On one level, intermarriage serves as an integrative factor leading to cooperation among the camps. On another, however, it can cause divisiveness when a family member leaves his or her extended family to join another family's yard after marriage, as we will see in Chapter 6. There are no absolute rules of patri- or matrilineality here because choices are often made depending on numerous factors ranging from economics and space considerations to jealousy and personality issues. The key, however, to successful yard relations as well as a successful *Hosay* is flexibility, tolerance, and cooperation, as participants repeatedly stressed. One participant, for instance, told me, "not everyone goes by rules; whatever is convenient." And another chimed in that while "we try to stick to the rules, we are only human." This sense of "being human" is what leads to a considerable amount of fluidity within yard structure and allegiance. And while it may sometimes lead to tensions between yards, it also contributes to the dynamics and creativity of *Hosay*. The circulation of members from one yard to another, especially among the bass drum players, allows the tradition to remain vibrant and alive, even though some members seem to think that it is in decline due to economic and ideological factors.[7] These are points that will resurface later in my argument when I discuss in the epilogue current debates about proper practice and the authenticity of the event or whether *Hosay* should continue at all. For now, let us return to the conceptual space of the yard.

The concept of the yard also bears great importance in Afro-Caribbean culture to demarcate in a complementary fashion private space from public space, which we can dichotomize as inside/domestic versus outside/public. Donald Hill traces this inside/outside pattern back to the days of slavery on the plantations during which the focal point of the slave's life oscillated between activities in the yard, the plantation, and the garden plot. He convincingly argues that this pattern was easily adapted to free life after emancipation. As he states, the Afro-Trinidadian peasant's "progeny were to be found in the yards whenever a fete, game, or ritual transformed the yard from a woman's mundane work place to an ideal world of song, dance, or communication with the dead. Yards were the hub of the everyday life for rural Creole families and the center of local activity. . . . People lived in the yard; they only retreated indoors to sleep or when it rained. Yards were for chores, socializing, and other diversions and for ritual."[8] His description applies equally well to the Indo-Trinidadian yard.

Peter Wilson, in his classic work *Crab Antics*, developed the well-taken point that certain kinds of sociability take place in the Caribbean yard and on the road that generate interrelated value systems. The two systems to which he refers have been conditioned by colonialism. The system referring to the yard he terms "respectability," which is derived in large part from the values imposed on subaltern subjects by British and Christian missionaries, while the other, "reputation," is largely a subversive response to colonialism's hegemony enacted by men on the road.[9] Although Wilson's theory of sociability in the anglophonic Caribbean is based on gender, with women reinforcing the respectable values of the yard system (such as marriage, home, education, self-restraint, work, and family) and men upholding the values of the road (such as drinking, gambling, carousing, braggadocio, and competing), Abrahams has extended the model on St. Vincent to less sex-specific behavior. Abrahams writes that the "two worlds coexist in easy complementarity, conflicting with each other only in regard to the distribution of the men's resources or when a man insists on bringing crossroads behavior into the world of the yard. In such cases, the canons of order and respectability are challenged."[10] Building on Wilson's distinction between inside (yard) and outside (road), Abrahams brilliantly demonstrates, by way of numerous performance traditions, that West Indian life is based largely on a pattern he terms "competitive interaction."[11]

Most of the literature on this play element in Caribbean culture comes from research on the Afro-Creole sectors of the population, but I think it is fruitful to think of the Indo-Trinidadian use of social space, at least in the urban context of St. James, within this same framework.[12] To make this point, I draw on the Islamic terminology of *bāṭin* and *ẓāhir* with reference to inside and outside respectively. One could argue that common Afro- and Indo-Caribbean conceptions of space are part of the creolization process. I also want to temper the argument somewhat by pointing out that the distinction between inside and outside, the home and the world, is one that is observed in India as well, especially with regard to *muḥarram*. Recall from earlier chapters that during the sacred month private/stationary practices are demarcated from, yet interrelated with, public/processional ones. Although the Indic dual value system of inside and outside does not quite fit Wilson's model, there are close enough correspondences to make an argument for cultural and social analogy.

What I seek in the remainder of my analysis is a middle ground between a retentionist position (cultural survivals from India) and one based on acculturation (creolized adaptation). By "middle ground," I do

not mean a homeostatic space; instead, I see it as the place where elements of retention, acculturation, and accommodation converge, a place
where the rituals are negotiated in subtle and complex ways. To understand the complexities of the middle ground, I want to suggest a dialogic
strategy by which *Hosay* participants in St. James seek to find parallel
concepts in Afro-Trinidadian culture to serve as analogies and cultural
synonyms for their own Indic-based practices. This can occur on the linguistic, the material, and the conceptual level. In essence, then, I wish
to suggest a kind of "reverse creolization" that we might also refer to as
"decreolization."

I want to argue that in terms of *Hosay*, the expressive grammar is Indic
and the vocabulary is in some cases borrowed from Afro-Creole culture.
Although I do not want to suggest a rigid either/or binary in making this
assertion, my perspective is inspired by more recent developments in creole sociolinguistics and makes more sense in discussing *Hosay*. In many
instances, lexical borrowing, or lexification, is simply a process to refer to
the creation of cultural or linguistic equivalents, not a movement toward
standardization in favor of the dominant culture. The process of lexification becomes more salient as my argument continues to unfold. To allow
it to unfold, I first need to provide the reader with a fairly close description of the event as I witnessed and experienced it in 1991. Let me thus
shift to the ethnographic present tense to provide a close reading of
Hosay from the time that preparations began that summer.

In and Out of *Imambaras*, 1991

I walk into an open garage attached to a house in the Balma Yard compound, just two minutes off Western Main Road. It is June 12 in Noble's
imambara, and he and his crew are already three weeks under way with
construction. Down the road at Cocorite, just outside St. James, the crew
started work about two months ago in order to get ahead of the others.
Ghulam Hussein and Bay Road have yet to begin because there are some
funding problems at Ghulam Hussein and Anthony "Muggy" Millette,
the master builder at Bay Road, has not arrived yet from his home in
New York (he returns every year for *Hosay*). Noble, who has by now been
making *tadjah*s for ten or twelve years, has a reputation for making pretty
*tadjah*s. Some say he is the best among the current generation of builders,
but every year each yard tries to outdo the others. For some it is fierce
competition, but for others like Sammy "Junior" Ali of Cocorite, it is simply
a matter of style. "Some look more like a mosque," he says, "but ours is
like a castle." Muggy later added that his *tadjah* is always more "church-
like." Hence each yard has a distinctive style.

Noble's *tadjah* this year will be the same as last year's since that one could not be paraded due to a government curfew imposed after an Afro-Muslim faction led by Abu Bakr staged a preemptive coup d'état during Muharram.[13] But even so, Noble later took his unparaded *tadjah* to the bay for immersion, for as he tells me, "*Hosay* wouldn't be finished if I didn't."[14] This sense of closure is essential to the completion and success of the event, for without bringing out the *tadjah*s and eventually immersing them on Teejah Day, the ritual would remain meaningless and no efficacy would be derived from it. Noble's structure, like the others, is built on a wheeled-base platform called a *katheeyah*, which is made of metal and 2" × 4" timbers crisscrossed with lengths of *roseau* cut from the nearby Caroni Swamp some weeks ago.

As Noble explains to me how the base is constructed, others on the crew begin reminiscing about the great lime they had when they went out to cut the reeds a few weeks earlier. Later Junior from Cocorite tells me how his yard's crew used to go down the Caroni River by boat to cut *roseau*, but he says that nowadays there are so many drug smugglers out on the water that it is risky business to be cutting *roseau*. Since those days, his yard has been using all wood and no reed. The cutting of the *roseau*, occurring as it does weeks before the ritual period actually begins, is the first group activity performed by each yard's crew. Everyone involved sees it as a wonderful opportunity to get out of the house and yard, gossip, and perhaps have a few drinks afterward. The *roseau* reeds are nailed and tied together with twine to provide a firm foundation for the structure that will be placed on it. At the corners of the *katheeyah* are square inserts into which the *tadjah* is dovetailed. The base of the *tadjah* itself, often referred to as the *chowk*, is 8'8 1/2" front and back, and 7'5" on the sides. Ghulam Hussein's base will be slightly larger this year, measuring 9' front and back, and 7' on each side.[15] Cocorite and Bay Road fall roughly in between. But "biggest don't mean best," as Noble once commented.

The *tadjah* itself is constructed of wood and reed. Each of the corners has a minaret with an onion dome reminiscent of a Russian Orthodox church. The largest dome will be in the center of the structure, with another one fused on top of it. The skeleton of the domes, like most of the *tadjah* itself, is made out of carefully cut cardboard that is often recycled but is sometimes bought in sheets for the occasion. Noble, being a skilled carpenter by profession, has a good eye for detail. Normally, he does not sketch out a design but sees it in his mind's eye.[16] On the evening I visit, the other members of the crew in the *imambara*, including six to eight regulars, respond intuitively to Noble's cues in an almost synergistic fashion. It seems quite remarkable that in such a small space, which is virtually filled by the base and *tadjah* frame, the crew's members work in an organic fashion, each intuitively knowing from years of experience what to do and when. Other less experienced volunteers come and go, helping out how and when they can, or just stop by to lime. So long as they are "pure" and take off their shoes, all male friends are welcome inside. Liming plays an important part in the *Hosay* as a social event. Since all the men in each yard are friends or relatives, constructing *tadjah*s or drums gives them a good reason to get together and talk about politics, sports, music, and other current events. In Noble's *imambara* most of the men are either relatives or have known each other since childhood, having grown up together in the yard.

The atmosphere in the *imambara* is somber but friendly as everyone jokes and talks to kill the hours of the early morning. Work normally commences at approximately ten o'clock in the evening and often continues until dawn, especially as the sacred ten days of Muharram approach. Meanwhile, wives, young girls, and female relatives—some visiting from as far away as Boston, Toronto, and London—are in the kitchen preparing *saada roti* (plain flat bread), roasted tomatoes stuffed with garlic, eggplant, and other vegetarian dishes to feed the crew as the wee hours of the morning push on. All these foodstuffs have to be roasted because "chonking" (frying) is not allowed during the period of abstinence.[17] The work in the kitchen is all conducted under the watchful eye of Noble's wife, Rasheeda, the matron of the household. To refresh the crew as the night drags on, Noble's youngest son, Jameel, from time to time brings in thermoses of hot tea and coffee prepared by his mother.

On the back side of the yard behind the kitchen is the drum room, where Noble's stepson Shazzad, a cousin named Brian (known to his friends as "Shabby") and their Afro-Trinidadian friends Calvin and Tom, who both beat drums, are preparing the *tassa* and bass drums for this year's event. The intense amount of labor and the economic burden, not to mention the partial fasting and celibacy, are understood by all involved as a sincere form of sacrifice for the event. Sacrifices of this sort can be viewed as a form of *mātam*, as can the drumming, and they serve as a replacement for the *mātam* performed in Iran and India. No *Hosay* participant performs any physical act of violence against his or her body in the sense that blood is shed as in India and Iran. Junior once mentioned to me that he had seen a television documentary about Muharram activities in Iran. He was amazed to see people beating themselves in the name of Islam. Although Junior is now a Seventh Day Adventist after his marriage conversion, he comes from a Shi'i family at Cocorite. Even so he still could not believe that participants would be practicing flagellation. "What kinda celebration is that?" he asked in astonishment.

But blood is shed, if only inadvertently. Narine Manmohansingh of Bonasse, a Hindu *tadjah* builder in the south, better known as the "Shark," a few days later related to me a local belief that blood must always be shed during the construction period. A builder might cut his finger or get scraped on the head, but some blood must flow. When I eventually told this to Junior, he raised his eyebrows and conceded that he had already pierced his finger by accident earlier that week. He also told me a story about how a drug dealer hit him with a beer bottle on the street a few years earlier during the procession; he still bears the scar today over an eyebrow. "Yeah," he said, "I guess blood does flow."

Balma Yard's *Hosay* is sponsored by Mohammed "Hamdoo" Emamali, a self-made man of modest education who currently owns and operates an import shop located on a nearby commercial road. Hamdoo made his fortune in construction and investing in real estate. Nowadays he is semiretired and spends much of his time in the shop or with his family. Hamdoo has for quite a long time been a spokesman for the *Hosay* organizing committee and is thought by many in the St. James community to be very knowledgeable about cultural things. Knowing him to be a generous man with his time, I always sought him out when I was confused or puzzled about something for which I could find no answer elsewhere. Hamdoo, like so many others in the *Hosay* yards, entered into the tradition through his family. In his case, it was through his father, Popo "Balma" Emamali.

As Hamdoo tells it, when his father was a young man, perhaps sixteen or seventeen, he was very tall and handsome. Then suddenly one day he developed warts all over his body. He became scornful and stayed indoors most of the time at his mother's house on Vidal Street in St. James and cried over his condition. Nearby there lived an old Indian couple in a hut with an earthen floor. Sometimes the afflicted young man would go to them for solace. So one day the old man told him that he must make a promise (that is, take a vow) to build a *tadjah* for five years.[18] "But you must believe in it," the old man said. Hamdoo's grandfather had built *tadjah*s during his lifetime, and the old man suspected that because the continuity had been interrupted Hamdoo's father was now suffering from warts. Popo then made a promise to build for five years. The first year passed, and there was no change in his condition. The second year passed without any change as well. But then during the third year, when Popo was taking his *tadjah* to the ocean for the throwaway on Teejah Day, all his warts fell off. But the result was even worse. Now he was pockmarked from head to toe. By the time they immersed the *tadjah*, however, his skin had miraculously healed. According to Hamdoo, the marks never reappeared. Hamdoo's father died in 1983 at age 82, which would

mean that he started building *tadjah*s about 1918. Numerous other people tell similar stories of miraculous cures that occurred following a
promise, and this reason in large part is why so many people continue to
participate each year.[19] Even many outsiders who do not know the esoteric lore associated with the model tombs believe in their power. It is
thus quite common to see pregnant Afro-Trinidadian women reveren-
tially touch the structures to guarantee a successful childbirth without
any complications.[20]

Hamdoo's father continued to build the structures annually until he
became very ill one year. By this time Hamdoo was a young man, and his
mother told him that she thought his father was going to die. She then
asked him to make a promise that he would build *tadjah*s if his father re-
covered. Hamdoo says he was trembling in fear but made the promise at
his father's deathbed to honor his mother's request. His father survived
after an Indian doctor performed a home surgery without anesthesia,
and he went on to live in good health for many more years. From that
incident onward, Hamdoo took over the *Hosay* responsibilities and built
*tadjah*s, according to his reckoning, for about twenty years. Immediately
after him, his brother-in-law Noble continued the tradition, and Hamdoo's younger brother Bunny took over as headman of Balma Yard. Today Hamdoo provides much of the financing, which can mean quite a
sum of money. In 1991, the Balma *tadjah* cost roughly TT$15,000, which
would have been equivalent to about U.S.$3,300 at that time. The cost of
the *tadjah*s is the responsibility and burden of each respective family
yard, except in the case of the Bay Road Yard, whose structure is called
variously the community *tadjah* or the *pancchaiti tadjah*.[21]

The community *tadjah* has its origins back in the plantation period,
when most families could not afford to build their own.[22] Thus donations
would be gathered from all the Indians in St. James to bring out one
common community structure.[23] The hereditary family in charge of this
tadjah still controls it today. The current master builder, Muggy, is a de-
scendent of the *pancchaiti tadjah* lineage (see Figure 13). Although he is
now a Christian, his mother is still a practicing Shi'ah. Muggy lives in
New York, near the garment district, but returns home every year to
build the *tadjah*. His artistic impulses earlier compelled him to design
floats and costumes for a well-known Carnival panyard known as the
Amoco Renegades.[24] The Renegades occasionally bring out a small *mas*
band (masquerade group) during Carnival, and Muggy brings that carnivalesque aesthetic sensibility to bear on his own colorful *tadjah*s. Although each yard competes to build a different and unique *tadjah* every
year, Muggy's are always distinct because each year he brings materials
such as velvet, polyester, belly dancing beads, Christmas lights, sequins,

Figure 13. Master *tadjah* builder Anthony "Muggy" Millette cutting styrofoam to be applied to the exterior of his 1991 creation. Photograph by Guha Shankar. Courtesy of the Smithsonian Institution's Folkways Archive.

tinsel, and ornaments with him from New York, where he buys these items at after-Christmas sales.

One of the reasons that the cost is so great for the builders is that much of the material is imported. Each family has its own overseas connections to bring materials home for this central familial holiday. The Balma Yard, for example, has family in Boston and Toronto. The Boston portion of the family brings tinfoil to cover the *tadjah* each year. Duty charges, however, make the prices very high by local standards. This extra spending, like all the other hard work that goes into making the structures, is considered to be a sacrifice. As Hamdoo once told me, the *tadjah* by itself is meaningless.[25] Its construction involves hard work, perseverance, and endurance, and this sacrifice of time, labor, and finances, coupled with a belief in the *tadjah*'s healing power and grace, is what really matters to participants within the inner circle. The general public, however, is little aware of this.

It is the evening of June 23, just a day shy of the tenth day of the month preceding Muharram, and as the great feast known as Baqra Eid comes to an end on the tenth of Zul-Hijja, the four *imambaras* are closed off from public view. Yard crews erect a fourth wall of cardboard leading into the rooms to create an air of secrecy and to demarcate sacred space.[26] Work has already begun much earlier, but starting times vary from yard to yard because there is no fixed rule on when to begin. As the pace of work quickens in the *imambaras*, work is simultaneously progressing in the drum rooms. Baqra Eid is a turning point in the preparations. Now that all four yards have closed off their *imambaras* to the gaze of the public, they become sacred spaces. To enter, men must take off their shoes, as if entering a mosque, and must be pure. Being pure means abstaining from meat, salt, fried foods, alcohol, smoking, and sex from this day onward until the tenth.[27] Also, no leather can be worn in the *imambara*. From this point onward as well, women are forbidden to enter the *imambaras*. Their domain is the household and the kitchen, and it is there that women make their integral contribution to the preparations. After all, the men say, "we couldn't work if the women didn't feed us every evening." Besides cooking, women also contribute by preparing the special sweets for consecration during the first ten to twelve days of Muharram. They also prepare the various accoutrements needed for communal prayers, such as lamps and incense, and they sew the flags that are taken out on the eighth night.

Figure 14. Kirk "Purple" Rodriguez working on the internal frame of the Ghulam Hussein *tadjah*. Photograph by Guha Shankar. Courtesy of the Smithsonian Institution's Folkways Archive.

At this stage in the building process, the framework of the *tadjah*s has been built on the *chowk*s in all four yards. The frames are a combination of wood and *roseau* (see Figure 14). *Roseau* is preferred by three yards, but is not used by Cocorite, as Junior mentioned above. Builders say that *roseau* is preferred because it is resilient and pliable. When the *tadjah*s are taken onto the streets, there is much jostling, and the road can be bumpy because there are no shock absorbers attached to the wheels of the platform. Wood, being harder, does not bend and sway as gracefully with the force of the bumps, and this can lead to cracks or tears in the structure. In the past the frames were made without nails. During Hamdoo's days as a builder at Balma, each junction was tied together with threads retrieved by unraveling burlap sacks. Today both nails and string are used to bind the frame together. The custom of binding the framework with tied knots has been carried out traditionally by family members to symbolize their unity; after this work has been done, the rest of the yard crew can join earnestly in the activity. Some participants, especially women, told me that the beginning stage is an opportunity for family members to reaffirm their kinship relations, for it is the tradition of building and bringing out the *tadjah* that protects the well-being of a family. (As noted above, Popo Balma's malady was associated with a break in the continuity of the tradition after his father died.) Hence the inaugural ritual of building the *tadjah* is a private family event to guarantee the health and prosperity of kith and kin during the coming year.

By now, however, the *tadjah* crews have increased to eight to ten permanent members in each *imambara*. Cocorite started the earliest and at this stage in the process is considerably ahead of the others. Its structure is already covered with the mandatory white butcher paper that engulfs the entire frame in each of the four yards. The butcher paper can be thought of as the plywood of a building's exterior, which is then covered by siding, shingles, or other more ornamental trappings. In the case of the *tadjah*s, the white paper will be covered with an assortment of delicately crafted shapes of colored paper, tinfoil, tinsel, styrotex, or other materials. The traditional adhesive used to paper the *tadjah* is flour paste (*laie*), a simple mixture of regular white cooking flour and water stirred to a smooth and creamy consistency. Some, such as Muggy, prefer commercial adhesives, especially for the second layer of colored papers, because they are less prone to dissolve if it rains during the processions. I have seen *tadjah*s whose paper was peeling after a full day of continuous rain, so each yard is careful to apply the glue mixture evenly in the proper quantities to avoid such catastrophe on the streets. The papering of the frame occurs simultaneously with the construction of numerous small onion domes (*gumjees*) made of cardboard to be placed on top of the minarets. At the center will be a large cupola called the *gummadge (gummaj)*.

Each member of the crew is assigned specific tasks that are performed year after year in an assembly line fashion. The master builder oversees the others, troubleshooting where necessary or coming to the rescue when a major mistake in design occurs. The master also pencils out the cardboard and paper designs that are cut in quantity by designated cardboard and paper cutters. As Ibrahim mentioned above, boys entering into the tradition usually begin with minor tasks such as mixing flour paste, fetching tools, and doing simple cutting until they achieve a certain status in the yard based on both age and artistic ability. No one is ever turned away, and one of the major tasks of the master is to tease out the talent in a newcomer. Noble has always been especially good about finding things for younger members to do. In later years, he even tolerantly put me to good use, apprenticing me off to anyone who needed extra assistance.

As in India, all the yards build three-tiered structures. In the past, again following an Indic pattern, they could be as high as six tiers, gradually decreasing in size from base to crown. But because of the introduction of telephone wires, which some say occurred in the same year as the 1884 *Hosay* massacre, the size must be limited to 15 1/2'. The base of the structure is the wheeled platform termed a *katheeyah*, a word most likely derived from the Hindi word for wood *(kāṭh)*. Upon this base is built the previously mentioned foundational *chowk*, on which is built up the *barka tor (baṛe kā tor)*, called the "big gate," which serves as the "entrance" of the structure's body. Towering minarets are placed at the corners and the crown or *gummadge* is placed at the center of the structure, being connected to the body by a "little gate," the *chotka tor (choṭe kā tor)*. Usually the pinnacle of the *gummadge* is the highest point of the structure. This is the basic formula followed by each of the yards.

The ingenuity lies in how each master builder uses the basic formula to give birth to a unique design each year. Sometimes interesting innovations occur out of a sense of artistic competition. In 1992, for example, Noble built a *gummadge* with a lid on top that moved up and down on a cantilever, so that he could build higher than the wires and have the tallest *tadjah*. The same year, knowing that Noble was experimenting with something special, Raiez of Ghulam Hussein Yard had his crew make two central *gummadge*s, while Muggy of Bay Road used stained glass windows brought from New York for his alcoves. This healthy sense of competition keeps the artistic dimension of the tradition fresh and alive. Cocorite's *tadjah* is always distinctively castlelike in shape. During the 1992 *Hosay*, Cocorite's builders installed an auto battery in the base of their *tadjah* and put flashing lights on it, so that people from St. James could see a brilliant, flashing structure coming up over the horizon as the *tadjah* crossed the bridge on Western Main Road leading into St. James.

Such competition between builders is a major reason for the secrecy in the *imambara*s, but I should stress that there is also a great amount of cooperation. Headmen work together on the *Hosay* organizing committee, while builders share materials and tools. For example, a recent innovation introduced by Noble is the use of a manual meat slicer to cut thin strips of styrotex that can be bent easily around corners and curves. After his innovation became collective yard knowledge, others often came to Balma to use the slicer. Similarly, if one yard runs out of a particular decoration and another has an ample stock in store, the latter will share. Materials such as glue are also sometimes bought together in bulk and then divided.

The financial cost of the *tadjah*s is the burden of the extended family in each yard, with the exception of the community *tadjah* at Bay Road. In reality, however, there are exceptions at Ghulam Hussein Yard, where a Roman Catholic Afro-Trinidadian who works at a bank in St. James has served as financier in years past. Raiez once told me that the rule is that the actual cost of building the *tadjah* must come from the family, but donations may be used for buying food, drink, and other perishables for the members of the crew. My contribution in 1997 to Noble's yard, for example, was giving money to buy meat for breaking the abstinence and lending my rented car to enable crew members to move around the island to cut *roseau* and buy clay shells and skins for the *tassa* drums. Each person provides what he or she can to make the event a successful one. People in all the yards speak fondly of the days during the oil boom in the seventies when "money flowed like water." In those days much was spent on building the prettiest *tadjah*s, but today financial insecurity threatens the tradition.

Ibrahim Ali often mentioned to me in 1991 that there was no guarantee that his yard would bring one out the next year. And if the *tadjah* is not built, the drums remain silent also. Here is the double bind that the yards face. On the one hand, they rely on the patronage of outsiders to a certain degree, which means they have to meet the expectations of those patrons. On the other, they hesitate to commercialize and secularize the event. So what does one do when a rum shop offers to sponsor the building of a *tadjah*?[28] The dilemma is one that must always be negotiated delicately today by members of the community, and it is reminiscent of the scenario during the nineteenth century. Yard members are aware that if they accept donations from bars they might run the risk of having their creations labeled "rum *tadjah*s," as they were called in British Guiana.[29]

An accusation such as this would place practitioners at a greater risk of criticism from orthodox Sunni Muslims who already see the event as a mockery of Islam. Journalists do not help the image and reputation of the *Hosay* participants either. As one Hindu journalist of Indian descent wrote of the event in 1987, "Late in the afternoon of the third day, frenzied Trinidadians will follow the drummers dancing and wailing in the year's second carnival."[30]

A number of people involved voiced the pervasive concern about criticism to me year after year, and even urged me, as an "expert," to speak out in their defense.[31] Aside from external pressure to have the observance banned, there is the cost factor. Imported material is expensive. Using imported material, which might seem to the untrained eye to be nothing more than kitsch, is considered traditional among the families. And because there is a strong adherence to tradition, no one wants to break with it and use more local materials. "It is somewhat ironic," I wrote in my field notes, "that 'tradition' as conceived here means imported paper, tinsel, etc." This does not mean, however, that the *tadjah* construction lacks innovation. *Roseau* is being replaced by 2" x 4" planks and ¼" plywood, cardboard has been used for about forty years, and Shark has introduced cross-sections of plastic PVC tubing to bind the columns of the minarets (see Figure 14); all these changes are suggestive evidence for material adaptation. Adaptation is conditioned by the exigencies of the availability of materials. And as older *tadjah* designers retire and move aside for younger ones, some fear that the tradition might wane. Nonetheless, there is still a sincere effort among most concerned to keep *Hosay* alive and well.

On June 27, I spend the evening at Ghulam Hussein Yard. Crew members are slightly behind in their schedule and are just completing the wallpapering of their *tadjah*. Rain is pouring down outside, so everyone is huddled under an eave or in the drum room/*imambara*. Ibrahim Ali, always the yard's trickster and philosopher, pulls me aside when he observes me asking the workers too many questions. In a frustrated fit, he says, "You can't understand *Hosay* without experiencing it. You can't understand or experience the drumming without building them and beating them." Ibrahim thinks (incorrectly) that I am a journalist and is initially skeptical of my presence. His experience with journalists has been that they misrepresent and distort in their attempts to sensationalize, and thereby publicize, the event for the sake of tourist consumption. He thinks at first that I am just another one of them. Like a Zen master, what he is telling me is that simply asking questions will get me nowhere on the road to understanding. But this evening is a breakthrough in our relationship, for he is finally speaking to me more openly and honestly about the tradition.

My first field recording of me talking with Ibrahim dates from this rainy evening. Like a student at the master's feet I sit there and listen patiently as he explains some of the lesser-known aspects of *Hosay*. As he speaks and I listen, his wife Mona brings us *rotis* stuffed with potato, freshly made at her roadside shop. The conversation ends temporarily as we eat. In the distance through the rain, I can hear his brother Aziz tuning a bass, while others are tapping the *tassas* to see if the skins are tight enough to beat. All the yards are supposed to beat during individual practice sessions tonight, but the rain is coming down in sheets and there is little hope of starting the fires needed to heat the skins. Tonight there will be no practice sessions, but work on the *tadjahs* will continue until the early hours of the morning. I return to the sacred room in which everyone is continuing to paper. In my absence, the crew has decided that they need a second layer of butcher paper to get the crinkles out. This indeed will be a long night. The gentle strains of Islamic devotional music coming from a boom box, however, mix with the sound of the rain and the scent of fragrant incense burning to purify the sacred precincts and provide a serene atmosphere for passing the hours in conversation with "the boys."

Because their previous master builder Aloh Dookuwa retired some years ago, Ghulam Hussein's *tadjah* cannot rival Balma's, but there is great agreement in St. James that their drum room is by far the best. Everyone on the streets, of course, has his or her own favorites, but there is general popular consensus that Ghulam Hussein has the most powerful and talented drummers as a collective unit. Because Ghulam Hussein's relative, Yussuf Ali, is said to have brought the first *tassa* from India, it is widely held that he started the drumming tradition in St. James. It is also widely accepted that drummers from that yard taught the other yards how to make and play drums. In earlier days, before they had their own drum rooms, Balma and Cocorite Yards had to hire drummers to accompany their *tadjahs* on the streets. This is still the case with Bay Road. It hires a small band from a nearby village and pays them in *rotis*, according to Muggy, but this band pales in comparison to the sheer power and brute force of Ghulam Hussein's drummers. Ghulam Hussein Yard is known for bringing out anywhere from eight to ten basses and thirteen to fifteen *tassas*, by far the most. This is why bass players from all the yards desire to "take a knock" in Ghulam Hussein Yard. During evening practice sessions, bass drummers often move from yard to yard not only to preview the competition but also to step in and try their hand. Usually by midnight some, if not most, of the best bass men end up at Ghulam Hussein. Yet each yard has its followers based on neighborhood loyalties. The fluidity and reciprocity, jealousies notwithstanding, allow for the social circulation of persons and goods. *Hosay* is a time of tension but also one of spirited cooperation and conspicuous display.

The rain not only makes it difficult to beat the drums, it also hinders the construction of the *tadjah*s because the flour paste will not dry. I am back at Ghulam Hussein's the next morning, but everyone is sleeping because the paste is not dry from the night before. I wander down the road to see how Muggy is doing with the Bay Road *tadjah*. He recently arrived from New York to begin construction, freshly stocked with boxes of materials for his community *tadjah*. But his crew suffered a flood in the *imambara* a few nights ago and were forced to delay the start of construction. Muggy is not worried, however, because his *tadjah* will progress at a quicker pace once they get moving. Sitting at his master's table, what he once jokingly referred to as his throne, he shouts orders to his relatives and friends, while further refining his design as I enter, somewhat wet from the rain that persists outside.

According to his family's tradition, his ancestor Noor Mohammed brought *Hosay* to St. James. This same claim is, of course, also made by the descendants of Ghulam Hussein, who assert that he was the great granduncle of Ibrahim Ali and his siblings. Raiez believes that Noor Mohammed and Ghulam Hussein came over on the same ship, so they were *jahājī bhāīs*, boat brothers. Boat brothers often formed strong bonds that lasted a lifetime during indentureship, and in some cases these bonds still continue between boat-related families. Muggy cannot tell me, however, much more than he has already said. "This year," he says in his usual jolly manner, "mine is gonna be a 'New York state-o-mind.' " This refers not only to the fact that he now resides in New York and that the materials are from the famous garment district but also to the design, which he says is "New Yorkish."

Muggy also cooperates in building a secular *tadjah* for a West Indian Labor Day Carnival in Brooklyn, and he says that this year's structure looks like his New York ones from the previous years.[32] Unlike the others, Muggy's is one solid structure rising up from the *katheeyah*. I complement him on his unique op-art minarets, and he responds by saying that his will be different from all the others because of the elastic and the red satin cloth he has brought from the garment district. The elastic is frilled and seems to me to resemble an exotic form of a female garter belt. The effect is certainly unique enough to attract the comments of anyone who will be out on the streets in less than a month. Muggy is sometimes envied by others for the wealth of materials to which he has access in New York, but they also have their own family connections abroad, so they may secure materials to make their respective *tadjah*s distinctive rivals.

I bid Muggy and his crew adieu and move on up the Western Main Road, where I turn down a side street to visit with Aloh and Feroza Dookuwa. Feroza is a daughter of the Ghulam Hussein Yard, and Aloh is the previous master builder. He is said to have introduced the use of cardboard and styrotex about 45 years ago, and his work is still well known in the community. On our first visit together, we limed on his front porch as he showed me his photo album of previous *tadjah*s that he had built at Ghulam Hussein. His range of styles is extremely impressive, but nowadays he refrains from going to the yard. His sons and sons-in-law, however, continue to beat bass at Ghulam Hussein, and he himself lends advice to Raiez whenever the latter requests it. Perhaps more than anyone Aloh and Feroza embody the spiritual nature of the event. Once when I was speaking with them, Aloh cried as he said, "Yeah, man, it brings tears to your eyes." On another occasion, he said that when he was serving as a master builder, it was "like you see God in it." Feroza is equally pious about the event, stating that one is supposed to mutter Husayn's name constantly under one's breath when doing anything related to the preparation for *Hosay*. The word she used was the Arabic Sufi term *dhikar* (recitation), as if the very act of performing *Hosay* was a recitative meditation in praise of God. This kind of deep religious respect for the tradition is fairly common among the eldest generation of the community. Their sincere sense of piety is not as apparent, however, among the younger participants. The latter respect the tradition, even if they are not Shi'i in orientation, but they lack the sense of extreme devotion and belief of Feroza's generation.

It is now July 2, and I am back in Noble's compound in the evening. His friend Johnny's mother just died, and Johnny will have to stop working on the *tadjah* to prepare for the funeral. There is a kind of saddened atmosphere in the sacred room, but work continues unabated. This is, no doubt, a setback, but the remainder of the gang pushes ahead to make steady progress. Noble is working on the *gummadge* and has created an extremely interesting design. He is using styrofoam coffee cups to inlay into the walls, domes, and minarets of the structure (see Figure 28). These will be spray painted and dusted with golden glitter to give a sense of depth to his *tadjah* when lights shine on it in the streets. Noble is very innovative in choosing new materials to use for his creations. Nevertheless, for him, tradition means staying within the confines of what has been mandated in the past and working within that framework to make each year's *tadjah* better. A few years ago Noble designed the first-ever round *tadjah*. No one had thought it was possible because of the angular materials traditionally used for the frame. He was successful, however, and achieved fame and recognition for his creation.

After a long night spent making the rounds to all the yards, I sit under a ceiling fan in a vain attempt to escape the oppressive heat and humidity of my room. I write the following in my notebook on July 9:

The community *tadjah* is coming along quickly because they have nine people working away in assembly line-like fashion like Santa's helpers struggling to make the Christmas deadline. As a result of their rapid pace, the quality of their work seems to be lacking a bit. But Muggy assures me that the creases and crinkles will be covered by the finer ornamentation that will go on top. The gang was listening to a pop station on the radio while drinking coffee, liming, and working in haste. Rock and roll, reggae, and *Hosay*. What a combination! Meanwhile, at Ghulam Hussein's there is a much more subdued air. Islamic religious music is playing on the tape deck and everything is much quieter. Perhaps because of this somber mood, a knowledgeable member of the camp confided in me that many Shi'ah have become Sunni under pressure. The person remarked that because they are small in number they have been forced to become Sunni at least on the surface. Everyone with the surname Ali or Hussein was, at least once upon a time, Shi'i in orientation. But when I asked him if the change was just on the surface or in belief and praxis also, he replied that it is unfortunate that the "change" (i.e., conversion) is both on the surface and in belief. He stressed that the change was forced due to majority pressure.[33]

There is no doubt, however, that some members of the *Hosay* community are practicing Shi'ah, even though they do not have their own mosque and are forced to pray with the Sunni majority for the mandatory Friday communal prayers.

Although some of the local Shi'ah of Indian descent might appear to be Sunni on the surface, their firm resolve to continue the *Hosay* tradition does not decrease over time. Indeed, there are devout Sunnis who participate as well. One stellar example is a young boy from across the street who comes to Ghulam Hussein Yard every evening during Muharram to play *tassa* drums. Somewhat of a child prodigy, he is acknowledged to be the best adolescent drummer. But he is also training to be a *Qur'ān* chanter and wants to go to Saudi Arabia for higher religious studies. He proudly recites to me verses from the holy book in Arabic each time I see him but equally proudly displays his prowess on the drum. He is the only boy who has thus far received the privilege of being a "cutter," or lead player. For him, the ideology underlining *Hosay* does not agree with his own theological training, but in his own mind he separates theology from custom. For him, *Hosay* is about heritage, about being Muslim, and about being Indian. This is why when the new moon is sighted on the evening before Muharram he rushes to the yard. His parents do not discourage him either, saying it is better for him to be in the yard than on the street.

According to the local almanac, the new moon will appear this year at 12:06 a.m. on July 13 and the month of Muharram will begin. From this moment onward, abstinence must be observed strictly, and not even leather belts are to be worn in the *imambara*s. As midnight approaches, everyone in the yards is playing it by ear. Those weaker in discipline may sneak off to indulge in forbidden pleasures one last time, but work continues steadfastly as those who remain behind turn a blind eye to the brief disappearance of their comrades. Workers at Ghulam Hussein are having difficulty getting the multibond glue they need for their styrotex, and Balma's workers are out searching for last-minute materials for their *tadjah*. There is a sense of tense excitement and nervousness in the air as midnight approaches, but all seem to feel confident that everything is on schedule. Only the community *tadjah*, which was already off to a late start, seems to be lagging behind. With bags under his eyes from many long nights of working round the clock, Muggy forges ahead heroically. At Balma some members have stayed behind to apply crinkled tinfoil to

Figure 15. A youth practice session for *tassa* and bass at Balma Yard. Photograph by Guha Shankar. Courtesy of the Smithsonian Institution's Folkways Archive.

the outer surface of their creation. Cocorite is still in the lead, having started weeks earlier than all of the others.

It is the opinion of some that there seems to be more cooperation these days than in the past, but the metaphor of "war" between the yards in the form of competition is not uncommon. Jameel, Noble's youngest son, often remarks, for example, that as things progress during the ten days the competition becomes "really like a battle." Jameel and an Afro-Trinidadian yard mate named Tom painted the *chowk* in front of the house yesterday in anticipation of the first, at which time an itinerant *imam* will begin visiting the yards each evening to say communal prayers for the family in front of the *chowk*, which is an inconspicuous square in front of the *imambara*. But from the beginning of its creation, the *chowk* becomes sacred space. The first step is to give it a fresh coat of white-wash, after which it is decorated. Each yard, including the ones building the two moons, has a *chowk*, and each has similar objects placed on it for the prayers. Yet each is also distinctive in its own way. Balma places halved coconut shells painted green and white around the border, with metal wagon or bicycle wheels interspersed in the design. The whole

Figure 16. The ornamented Balma *chowk*, with *tassa* drums awaiting consecration on the first of Muharram, 1991. Photograph by the author. Courtesy of the Smithsonian Institution's Folkways Archive.

area is fenced off, and potted palms in freshly painted green and white pots are placed around it.[34] Ghulam Hussein's *chowk* is somewhat special and has a history behind it. It will be painted tomorrow, as will those of Bay Road and Cocorite. As midnight approaches, people stare up at the sky to sight the moon, for from that moment onward the preparations will take on a heightened sense of urgency.

It is now July 13, the first of Muharram. Everyone seems tired and overworked, but the pace quickens nonetheless. The two moon yards begin building their structures today, and the drum practice sessions out in front of the *chowk* will go on later into the night, perhaps until one in the morning (see Figure 15). The increase in drumming attracts what Hamdoo calls "Mr. John Public," the "onlookers looking on." Most stand out on the street, while some more familiar with the yard's personnel enter the compound but stay clear of the *imambara*. They move from yard to yard to get a preview of the coming attractions, now only a week away. This year the evening prayers are being performed by Abdul Mandal, a Sunni from Bengal who came over to the island after indentureship had ended; he receives a fee from each of the yards for his services.[35] His driver is also rented to ferry him from one site to the next. Some years certain yards hire their own exclusive *imam*, but this year Imam Mandal is making the rounds for all in his capacity as an itinerant *imam* not associated with any particular mosque.

Prayers are normally between seven and eight. Prior to the *imam*'s arrival, offerings of *maleedah*, a sweet made from shredded *roti (bus up shut)*, sugar, butter, nuts, and raisins; a glass of water and sweet milk representing the thirst of Husayn's party; and bowls of candy and toffees are placed on the *chowk*, along with vials of perfume. This perfume will be sprinkled on the sacred objects in a manner similar to the throwing of *abīr* (colored powder) and *'iṭar* (perfume) in South Asia. On the first night the drums are also placed on the *chowk*; they are consecrated on this evening and considered sacred thereafter (see Figure 16). In addition, several small earthen wick lamps *(deeyas)* are placed on the *chowk*. The number varies from yard to yard, but the standard is five, to represent the members of the Prophet's holy family. Bay Road uses only two, however, one for Hasan and one for Husayn. There is also what is known as a *chiraaghie* (lamp) bowl, in which monetary offerings for the itinerant *imam* are placed. Lastly, an incense burner filled with *lohban* (frankincense) is lit and placed on the *chowk*. With these preparations made, everyone in attendance waits patiently for the cleric to arrive and evening prayers to begin.

When the *imam* arrives, everyone gathers behind him facing the *chowk*. Men remove their shoes and women cover their heads with scarves, but there is no segregation according to gender. Many non-Muslims are among those gathered at the *chowk*, and all the men, Muslim or not, wear the obligatory skullcap. The *imam* begins with an Arabic recitation of the opening verse of the *Qur'ān*. He then continues with the verses named Yasin and Rahman. The prayers are relatively brief, after which each person in attendance walks up to the incense burner, bows, and draws the purifying smoke toward his or her face with a sweeping motion of the hands. After the praying and ritual purification are completed, one of the young women of the yard takes the tray of *maleedah* to distribute some to all in attendance. Another follows her with the candy offerings. Noble's stepson Shazzad then takes the burner around the yard, into the drum room, the kitchen, and the *imambara* to purify the precincts within which the sacred work is being done. The builders then return to the *imambara* to continue their construction work, and the drummers return to the drum room to prepare for the evening rehearsal. One drummer tends the fire lit near the drum room to heat the *tassa*s for tuning later in the evening. This procedure is replayed each night and in each yard for the next ten nights.

The Ghulam Hussein *chowk* plays a special role during the observance,

Figure 17. Noble Bisnath, master *tadjah* builder, plays his bass on the streets during Flag Night, 1991. Photograph by Guha Shankar. Courtesy of the Smithsonian Institution's Folkways Archive.

and secret rituals are performed there during each of the three last nights after the processions. Although it is not common knowledge, family patriarchs say that the Ghulam Hussein *chowk* is the local *karbalā'*, not the Queen's Royal College (QRC) grounds as most people think. Although the point is disputed, some say that only the funeral prayers (*janaaza*) are said at the QRC grounds and that the actual *karbalā'* is now at Ghulam Hussein's. Earlier, the *karbalā'* was at the community *tadjah*'s *chowk*, but when that property was sold about fifty years ago, it was transferred to Ghulam Hussein's *chowk*, which itself was once moved when the extended family compound was expanded to house one of Ibrahim's sisters after her marriage.[36] The present Ghulam Hussein *chowk* lies in front of the yard's *imambara* and has a hole dug in the center, which is covered by a large, hollow lead object shaped like a bulb and painted green and white. The hole serves as a functional counterpart to the *alāvā* pit dug in many parts of India. For this reason, Ghulam Hussein's yard bears a special importance as a locus of esoteric rituals not allowed to be observed by outsiders. An interesting, but probably circumstantial fact is that the Ghulam Hussein Yard sits at the spatial center of the yards, making it an axis mundi of sorts. It thus seems only appropriate that it should be designated as the local *karbalā'*. One senior Hindu *Hosay* participant from San Fernando, Balchand Rampaul, once poetically described the *karbalā'* to me as "the place where all good things come to an end."

As the first of Muharram passes, the pace of work in the *imambara*s quickens in anticipation of the evenings of procession and drumming. The two moon yards also begin constructing their creations from the first onward. By now the fine work on the *tadjah*s is well under way. In Ghulam Hussein's camp, a Venezuelan yard member of Portuguese descent nicknamed "Purple," who is a nonpracticing "Christian Catholic" as he puts it, is assigned to cut intricate designs onto the face of sheets of styrotex to be used as windows on the *tadjah*. Purple is philosophical about his work. He says that his inspiration is not conscious but comes to him like a blessing, one that cannot be consciously felt. "You don't see it by receiving. That is not the blessing." He continues, "You don't feel it like a breeze. It will just automatically happen. And it will happen when you don't even know it." His work in the yard began when he was taken in as a wandering youngster. Like so many others, he grew up in the tradition, and when he showed signs of talent in cutting styrotex, he was given that job. He also joins the drummers to play *jainch* (cymbals), used to make the drum hands sadder or "deader." Although it is rare for drummers to work on the *tadjah*s, it is quite common for *tadjah* builders to beat drums or take turns playing the cymbals during the processions. Noble, for example, has his own personal bass drum that he made. Occasionally, he will play it on the streets, but he rarely plays it during the practice sessions (see Figure 17).

At Balma, a number of specialists also crank out quantities of items in their own line of expertise. Duck, an Afro-Trinidadian yard member, has the sole task of making "worms," hollow tubes of crimped tinfoil created in various hues. He does this by rolling a sheet of tinfoil around a thin metal rod. Then he pushes inward from the two ends to create a crimped effect. The rod is then removed, and the worm is stretched to the appropriate length. These hollow tubes of crimped foil are pliable and bend easily around arches, gateways, and windows. Similarly, others mass-produce numerous kinds of ornamentation needed in quantity to decorate the *tadjah*. One traditional item hung from the *tadjah* in quantity is the *paan*. *Paans* are so called because they are shaped like the betal leaf *(pān)*, which in India is used as the casing for a combination of spices, lime, and tobacco that is chewed as a mildly stimulating digestive aid after a meal. These small items are cut from delicate silver foil into four separate segments that are glued together to create the image of two interpenetrating *pān* leaves. In India, it was customary in the nineteenth century for women to distribute *pān* to the men to chew at *majālis*. Although it is also customary to abstain from *pān* during Muharram in India, not many people observe this taboo, just as Trinidadian builders do not observe fully the ban against smoking. The two work a similar effect in controlling the craving to eat.

Older women involved in the tradition told me about how in days gone by, a wife or sister had to give a certain number of *pān*s to her male relatives. With the decrease in *pān* chewing in Trinidad, however, that custom has also ceased to exist. Nonetheless, it now is represented in the twinkling silver *paans* on the *tadjah*. Normally, young girls of the yard make the *paans*. Their work symbolically recreates earlier offerings to male relatives. Sitting in the living room watching television or listening to the radio, they lime and cut hundreds of the *paan* quarters, which are then glued together and hung to dry from strings in the yard. When the *tadjahs* go out on the road, the *paans* flitter about on threads, refracting light to create a dazzling effect. Muggy this year brought from New York sequins that are hung from the waist belt of belly-dancers' costumes, and he used these sequins to replace the traditional *paans*. By incorporating such untraditional elements into the making of his *tadjah*, he cuts down on the amount of time and labor needed to complete his creation. Thus, while he got off to a late start in comparison to the other three yards, it is during the last days leading up to the tenth, when fine ornamentation is applied, that he catches up.

The designing and building of the *tadjahs* is an ongoing, emergent process. Noble emphasizes on more than one occasion that "the *tadjah* is never done." His brother Terry, who has been working with Noble for many years, chimes in that the design is always being altered to suit their needs, even while it is in progress. Now, for example, because it is July 16 and the processions are only four nights away, they have decided to stretch the worms a bit longer so that six worms can cover the same surface area as seven. There is thus less crimp in a worm, which, according to Terry, is "not as nice," and the worm is also more difficult to work with because it is thinner. Traditionally, the worms were fixed to the surface of the *tadjah* using pins and flour paste. The pins were needed because the flour paste took longer than synthetic glue to dry. But using commercial glue now eliminates the need for pins. Essentially, these modern materials make the work easier and quicker, but they are "not as nice." As the years pass, many more recent innovations will be added to the tool kits of the builders.

On the prior evening Noble's youngest son Jameel and his cousin Barry started making the small *tadjah*, which is taken out on the second night of procession. The small *tadjah*, representative of Husayn's older brother Hasan, is simpler in design and execution, but it is a way for younger members of the yard to acquire the necessary skills to one day succeed the current master builder when he retires. Noble lovingly provides advice when necessary, but this is Jameel's opportunity to demonstrate his budding skills as a builder. As we watch Jameel and Barry at work on the small *tadjah*, Noble mentions that people who make promises commission him to build very small *tadjah*s to place on the *chowk* during prayer. They may also offer flags that then become the property of the yard to which they are offered. The idea behind this seems to be very similar to Indian, primarily Hindu, traditions of *vrat* or *mānasik* (vows) during which an individual makes a small offering of a handcrafted or purchased item in the hope that some favor or miracle will be granted.[37]

As work continues in the *imambara*s, many of the yards make a second trip to the Caroni swamp to cut *roseau* to use as flag poles on the evening of the eighth. As designated male yard members return to the swamp with their machetes in hand, women sew the borders of the flags to be placed on the poles. The flags are of various colors in the different yards, ranging from the traditional red, green, and white cotton to blue, yellow, and multicolored sequined polyester.[38] More and more relatives begin arriving from throughout the island and abroad as Flag Night approaches. As in India, *Hosay* is an occasion for family reunions. The rite remains an ethnoreligious anchor in a community dispersed by multiple diasporas and transnationalism. All the families involved have relatives living abroad, and the observance provides them with an appropriate

Figure 18. Drummers of the Ghulam Hussein Yard perform in unison during the procession on Big *Hosay* Night, 1991. The noted bass player, Devil, beats his bass in the foreground. Photograph by Guha Shankar. Courtesy of the Smithsonian Institution's Folkways Archive.

Figure 19. Named *tassa* drums hanging in the Ghulam Hussein drum room. Photograph by the author. Courtesy of the Smithsonian Institution's Folkways Archive.

occasion to reunite annually, just as many Afro-Trinidadians do during Carnival.

The familial dimension of the event is most often stressed by the women of the yards, who see it as not only an occasion to exchange gossip with kin from faraway places but also an opportunity to reconfirm marital bonds with their husbands. Celibacy for the period of building is, no doubt, difficult for both genders, and there is much bawdy joking about this both during the preparations and afterward during the limes that occur once the *tadjah*s are immersed.[39] Female group activity, such as the cooking and flag sewing, brings women of the yards closer together through their own communal chores. They drink tea, joke, talk about their husbands and boyfriends, discuss what they will wear for the processions, and essentially "hang out" together. The occasion also provides the opportunity for young girls to learn how to cook in general and how to prepare the special foods more specifically. There is no question that the task of preparing meals for all "the guys" is burdensome and requires round-the-clock attention. It is as exhausting as the male work and is appreciated as an integral part of the preparations by all concerned. Sometimes meals are taken by as many as thirty male yard members as late as two or three in the morning. Thus the matron of the yard also must make great personal sacrifices to guarantee the event's success. If the men do not eat, the work does not get finished on schedule, which would be detrimental to the well-being of all concerned.

As Flag Night approaches, the *tadjah*s and moons are nearing completion. Let us wander into the world of the drums to see how things are taking shape there and then proceed to the moon yards to get a glimpse of how the moon men go about preparing for the event.

Drumming *Hosay*

While building the *tadjah* requires artistic skill and the ability to work with finely textured materials, the making of drums requires not only a special skill but also sheer strength. Many of the drummers, especially the bass men, are well built and muscular. Carrying a heavy drum through the streets for six or seven hours in humid temperatures ranging from 80 to 90 degrees while beating it constantly is a sacrifice in and of itself. The famed bass drummer "Devil," an Afro-Trinidadian in Ghulam Hussein Yard who was with the yard until his death a few years ago, was respected throughout the community for his bass power. His authority in drumming matters and abiding by the rules was obeyed by all. I once saw him physically eject two young men from the yard when he smelled rum on their breath. A soft-spoken man with a massive torso even into his sixties, he commanded the admiration of drummers in all yards, and many people on the streets used to crowd around the Ghulam Hussein Yard to hear him play his bass (see Figure 18). Paralleling players of steel drums in the past, many *tassa* drummers fondly name their instruments, drawing inspiration from both pop culture and the Shi'i master narrative. Drums may thus carry titles such as "martyrdom" and "Karbala," but also "poison," "passion," and "lover," which are painted on the surface of the drum skin (see Figure 19).

As emphasized earlier, the drum "rooms" are comprised of separate crews. The crews are diverse, consisting of people from various religious denominations and ethnic backgrounds, all of whom pledge loyalty to a specific yard. Many of those who beat the drums have made promises to do so, and it is rare for drummers to contribute to *tadjah* building. Instead, they focus all their energy on getting the drums in tune for the processions. Drumming and building are equally important domains of activity, however, as Ibrahim Ali suggested above. The holistic nature of the event cannot be overemphasized because each activity goes hand in hand with the others. In other words, the parts do not equal the whole. Recall that there are basically two types of drums: the *tassa* and the bass

Figure 20. Brian, a bass maker from Balma Yard, bores out the inside of a mango tree trunk. Photograph by Guha Shankar. Courtesy of the Smithsonian Institution's Folkways Archive.

(sometimes onomatopoeically called a *boom*). *Tassa*s are clay kettle drums capped with goatskin hides, while the bass drums are cylindrical, being made out of either cedar or mango stumps. Balma's Calvin, a muscular bass maker and player, tells me that most of the guys prefer mango because it is stronger. There is an assortment of handmade tools used to build the drums. All the tools and the various parts of the drums apparently once had Indian names, but these have been, for the most part, forgotten. English names are now used because very few Indians in St. James have retained any vernacular Indian language. Some Indian terminology is still used, however, to refer to certain parts of the drums.

The making of a bass drum begins with cutting a tree trunk. Once cut and dried, the solid stump is bored at the center and hot metal pokers are inserted to burn out as much of the wood as possible. Once the solid structure takes on a semihollow appearance, the internal wall is further refined by shaving it with long, semihollow tubes of metal sharpened to a point at one end. Some bass makers like Shabby prefer standard carpenter chisels to complete the task (see Figure 20). These are hammered along the inner wall to chisel out excess wood until the desired thickness is achieved. Some sanding occurs, but the inner walls have a coarse texture when the chiseling is finished. Each drum takes approximately one full day's labor to complete. After the body is entirely bored, a secret resin, sometimes referred to by the Indian word for spice, *masaalah*, is applied to the walls. This retards cracking and provides a richer and deeper tone to the sound. The resin is made of five ingredients mixed in differing quantities. Each yard has a secret mixture that is jealously guarded by its members.[40] Like the *tadjah* builders, drum makers compete with one another to produce the best sound. Their competition is most apparent during the processions when yards face off in a "clash," during which the loudest and fastest rhythm, the "war hand," is played simultaneously by two opposing yards. Jameel, Noble's youngest son, tells me that "it is like a real battle." Martial terminology is often invoked in the yards to refer to different aspects of the observance. The clashes and martial terminology employed for *Hosay* parallel similar phenomena enacted by steel bands during Carnival but are not without historical precedent in India.[41]

The resin mixture is also applied to specially prepared deerskins purchased from hunters in the central hills. Deerskins are preferred because they are thicker and tougher and can withstand the constant beating with a stick. While the skin is still soft and wet, a round, double-rimmed slip of bamboo the size of the drum's circumference is used to frame the skin. The skin is then smoothed along the edges to avoid punctures or tears. But before the skin is attached to the bass drum, a coat of resin is smeared on the inside of the skin, again to produce the desired deep tone. Once the skin is framed, smooth, and taut, and the resin has been applied, the bamboo frame is placed on the open head of the drum and ten bore holes are punched evenly around the surface. The skins are attached to the basses using strong rope that is threaded through holes punched along the periphery of the skins, where the skin curls around the edge of the drum's head. Ideally, the tension should be even across the heads on both ends of the drum. The drum's tension, and thereby its tuning, is controlled by tightening brass rings that pull the rope together into plaits. After the skin is tightened, the excess skin is cut off as close to the frame as possible. If the excess skin is in good condition, it can be used to thread the *tassa* drums.

When this process is finished, the bass is left in the drum room for a few days to get seasoned. It cannot be in direct sunlight because that would make it pop when played. The drying process has to occur gradually, and it can take three to four days. Basses are played by hitting one end of the drum with a stick that is made of guava wood and wrapped with cloth to muffle the sound, while the other end is beaten alternately with an open palm. According to Bachu Bhagwandeen, an old Hindu drum maker from Fullerton in the south, the stick side is made of a male skin because it takes more pressure and has to be louder. The hand side is from a female skin. The function of the bass is to provide a steady back beat rhythm for the cutter, the *tassa* player who provides the lead. Each of the five "hands," or rhythms, played has a corresponding bass rhythm.

The production of the *tassas* takes shape in a different fashion, although the shells are not made in the yards. Instead, they are commissioned from a Hindu potter in the nearby village of Chaguaramas to the south. Mr. Goolcharan and his brother supply drummers from both St. James and Cedros with *tassa* shells, and because the demand is high at *Hosay* time, they often make them continuously throughout the year to avoid a last minute rush. Baking them to a "fire red," he tells me, is essential to avoid cracks when the drums are later capped. A small hole is also poked through the bottom of the shell with a stick or nail when it is still wet before firing. This hole allows heat to escape when the drums are heated near an open fire to tighten the skin before the drum is played. Aziz Ali, master drummer and drum maker in the Ghulam Hussein Yard explained to me in rather humorous but logical fashion that the *tassa* is like a human body. It has to have an orifice to release gas so it does not explode. Sometimes an extra pinhole is later inserted on the periphery of the skin to allow a free flow of heat from top to bottom. Aziz refers to these two orifices as the mouth and the anus. The anus is the hole at the bottom of the shell and the mouth is the one on the surface of the skin. According to oral legend, the first *tassa* drum in Trinidad was made of metal and was brought to the island by a relative of Ghulam Hussein. The metal drum still hangs in the Ghulam Hussein drum room, which is adjacent to its *imambara*. When I asked if the drum was still being used, I was told by Raiez that it was not in use because it did not sound as crisp as the clay ones. It still hangs majestically in the room, however, as a reminder of their founder and the homeland from whence their ancestors came.

The goatskins used for capping the *tassa*s are purchased at the Sunday goat market in Debe to the south.[42] The quality of the skin is said to depend on the diet and grazing range of the animal. The gamier the animal, the tougher the hide, according to Aziz. Ibrahim added that goats from Venezuela are preferred because they have a greater ranging distance; hence they have a better diet and are stronger. After the skins are purchased with much haggling, they are brought back to the yards and stretched onto a pallet to dry in the sun. Once they are dry they are conditioned by rubbing off excess fat and hair with a soft wooden scraper. After the curing process is completed, they are removed from the pallets and cut to size. The *tassa* drums are capped by vertically aligning the center of the skin, marked by a stripe caused by the spinal cord, with the "hangman," sometimes referred to as the *kān* (ear) or the *bandhnā* (tie) by older people who remember Indic terminology. The hangman is the leather loop at the top of the drum through which cloth is placed to harness the drum around the player's neck.

The threading on the *tassa* is much more ornate than on the bass because more precision is required. Hence there are a greater number of holes punched along the border. The term used for this threaded section on the border is *boddhi*; it is called "housing" in Trinidadian English.[43]

The threading for the *tassa*s is not done with rope, as for the bass, but with strips of deer hide purchased from hunters in the central hills. These strips are referred to as *ḍorī*, the Hindi word for string. Whereas the goatskin has to be male, the deer hide cord can be of either sex. As new drums are being made, old ones are also being reconditioned, or recapped. The drumsticks used to strike the *tassa*s are called chops and are made from thin strips of *roseau*, with waxed cloth tips. *Roseau* is preferred because of its spring. Because the drums are only used during Muharram, they fall out of tune and require much labor to prepare them for *Hosay*. As the other crews construct their respective *tadjah*s, the drum men prepare for the musical accompaniment through construction of the drums and drumming practice sessions. Children who wish to

Figure 21. Women of Balma Yard carry flags behind the Balma flag platform on Flag Night, 1991. Photograph by Guha Shankar. Courtesy of the Smithsonian Institution's Folkways Archive.

enter the drumming tradition are provided with "baby *tassas*" made of plastic shells and artificial hides.

Drummers often emphasize the communicative quality of the drums. "The drums tell the story," Jaffar "Jim" Ali of Icacus in the south told me. During a conversation held while he was lying in his hammock one day, he further noted that everyone (meaning active participants) knows what phase the procession is in by the hand that is being played at any given moment. Ibrahim confirmed this when he said to me, "It's just like what you call the talking drums. We start this drumming here and people way down the street there, they just get the sound of the drum. You know, it tells them something. There's some message there. The drum tells such a large story that no one can explain it." An Afro-Trinidadian *tassa* drummer and practitioner of Orisha listening in on our conversation added that the "drums help enlighten the soul, help to awaken the soul to the true feeling of participation." I earlier speculated that the drum hands became speech surrogates as they replaced the singing of *maseeha*s (elegies), but I now believe that the two existed side-by-side to accompany the singing of sad songs.[44] The late Shair Ali, one of Ibrahim's brothers, once mentioned that the sad songs used to be sung in accompaniment with the drum of sorrow, one of the hands to be discussed below. But as the tradition of singing died out along with the use of Bhojpuri, the dialect of Hindi originally spoken by a majority of the indentured laborers in the nineteenth and early twentieth centuries, the drums came to grow in communicative importance.

Unfortunately, the history of the sad songs is not documented, nor is the history of the drums. Fragments are still sung in the south, but very few people even remember what they mean. From oral accounts and written memoirs coming from the plantation period, however, we know that elegies were indeed sung in the Caribbean wherever *Hosay* was observed. Martha Beckwith, writing about the early 1920s in Jamaica, writes of women's mourning songs lamenting the loss of the martyr: "the songs are not written down in books but are taught by the priest . . . and thirty or forty may be known in one district, all sung to variations of the same tune."[45] This is quite a large repertoire considering the songs were preserved by memory and passed on orally. In Jamaica these songs were sung on the evening of the ninth and during processions on the tenth. The performance of these songs, along with the accompaniment of musical instruments, occurred in conjunction with a number of other events. Among the instruments were *tassa* and bass drums, accompanied by *jainch*, the local rendering of the Persian *sanj* (cymbal).

It is truly unfortunate that we have no reliable written accounts from Trinidad of singing from the period of the turn of the twentieth century, aside from passing mention in travelers' accounts and official records. Again relying on oral sources, however, we see that songs were in fact sung in Bhojpuri in the past.[46] When the *tadjah*s were brought out on the tenth, women would walk behind them and sing sad songs. As Rasheeda explained to me, "My mother told me that it used to be sad. All of the older women would follow along singing and crying, you know." Today they simply carry flags (see Figure 21). What has remained pervasive in Trinidad down to the present has been the beating of drums. Although the use of drums, often accompanied by cymbals, is a common phenomenon during the observance in Iran and India, the percussive instruments had a limited function in the Iranian context, serving as a backdrop for the performance of bodily mutilation. To a large extent, it is a function that was maintained in South Asia. This fact notwithstanding, the specific utilization of *tassa*s during the month of Muharram became associated with India and the places where Indians eventually settled in the diasporas brought about by trade and indenture.[47] Based on what scant information is available, it seems safe to say that bass drums and cymbals were used to accompany *tassa*s in India during the nineteenth century at the time when indentured laborers first came to the island. This conjecture is supported by drummers in Trinidad who insist that they play the same style brought to the island by their forefathers, as the testimonies given above should attest.

Although *tassa*s and basses were being used during the plantation period, when the sad songs were still being sung regularly and with vigor, they seem to have acquired a greater communicative role as the singing tradition gradually declined. In response to this development, drumming rhythms become more elaborate, taking on metaphorical and esoteric intricacies whose meanings in earlier times were, at best, incipient. A greater amount of theological prestige was thus attributed to the communicative role of the drum hands as a nonverbal medium to convey the master narrative of Husayn's passion. The elevated communicative status of the drums allowed the tradition to remain squarely within the Karbala paradigm. The hands played during the processions in Trinidad provide the central motifs of the more elaborate verbal narratives of Iran and India. That is, they convey the notions of marching or journey, war, death, sorrow and lamentation, and burial. Let us look, then, at the progression of hands played in St. James.

There are five "natural" hands that participants believe were passed down orally to the present through the drumming families, creating continuity between India and Trinidad. Although there is much disagreement on how to define the hands among the drummers, especially between those residing in the north and in the south, all agree that *mahatam* is the

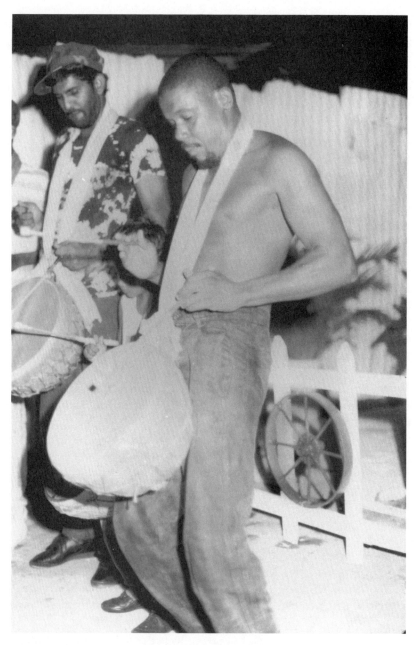

Figure 22. Calvin, a drummer from Balma Yard, in the role of cutter
performing in front of the Balma *chowk*. Photograph by the author.
Courtesy of the Smithsonian Institution's Folkways Archive.

war hand.[48] I provide two alternate listings of the sequence for performance based on the consensus of numerous drummers in the north and in the south:

First Consensus	Second Consensus
kabulkana: the marching hand or drum of peace	*teen chropa:* peace hand
mahatam: the war hand or war drum	*kabulkana:* marching/fine hand
nubie salbat: the burial hand or burial drum	*mahatam:* war hand
teen chropa: the sorrow hand or drum of sorrow	*chalta kabulkana:* burial/dead hand
chalta kabulkana: the walking kabulkana	*nubie salbat:* lamentation hand[49]

Shair Ali adds a sixth hand called *dingolie*, which is a hybrid hand influenced by indigenous soca rhythms that is played during the return after the burial prayers are said, when sorrow gives way to happiness.[50] Not everyone agrees on this practice, however, perhaps because people are reluctant to admit to "creole" rhythms influencing *Hosay* hands. Soca is, after all, associated with Carnival and is therefore seen in a negative light by many less cosmopolitan Indo-Trinidadians. On the other hand, because it can be argued that the rhythm is only played after the proceedings are more or less concluded, there should be no argument that this purported sixth hand violates the canonized form of drumming.

The hands are played in a loosely conceived chronological order that corresponds to temporal and spatial clues along the processional route, all part of drummers' lore in St. James. Usually, however, ordering the rhythms is up to the cutter, the lead *tassa* player. He stands at the center of the horizontal line of foulé- or fuller-men (filler-men), the chorus that provides the ostinato (fill) for his lead playing (see Figure 22).[51] The bass men move in front of the *tassa* row, also in a horizontal arrangement, while the *jainch* players move about between them, or walk to the side (see Figure 18).[52] Like the numerous *rasas* (flavors) of classical Indian music that conjure up specific moods or emotions, the rhythms of the *Hosay* hands produce intuitive responses in individuals who have been initiated into the esoteric meanings of the tradition.[53] The peace hand represents Husayn's original intention simply to meet his followers, while the marching hand suggests movement and solitude. Then as the conflict with his enemies ensues, there is a shift to the war hand. Later,

Figure 23. A bass player from Ghulam Hussein Yard plays pensively during processions on Small *Hosay* Night. Photograph by Guha Shankar. Courtesy of the Smithsonian Institution's Folkways Archive.

battle gives way to grief as the funeral procession and burial occurs. At this somber time, the *chalta* (moving) *kabulkana*, by slowing down the rhythm of the *kabulkana* to a crawl, centers attention on the sadness of Husayn's burial.[54] Finally, the realization that Husayn is no more leads to a feeling of lamentation. The drums thus are supposed to evoke a mournful mood. Aziz Ali, moreover, stressed on more than one occasion that *jainch* accompaniment makes the sound "deader" or sadder.[55]

The five hands evoke moods similar to those associated with the earlier sad songs, and they distantly echo the progression of the ten days' events narrated in India and Iran.[56] The above discussion suggests that—at least for participants initiated into the esoteric level of understanding— the drum hands play a quintessential role in the transmission of religious knowledge and act as a catalyst for subjective apprehension. The symbolic language of the drums acoustically enhances the experience of re-membering Husayn's passion. When the Shi'ah of Trinidad hear them, many believe that they are participating in a shrouded but global com-memoration of a tragedy that transcends time and space by linking all believers, past and present. Indeed, as one drummer stated in a philo-sophical vein, "When the drums speak, we know who we are."

It is remarkable that so little research has been conducted on *muharram* drumming in South Asia, given that virtually every colonial account pro-vides ample mention of its pervasive and ostentatious presence in the rituals. We are thus fortunate that Richard Wolf has provided us with a nuanced study. Wolf suggests that the *tāsā*, *dhol* (bass), *jhānjh* (cymbals) combination was first brought together to create a genre of military mu-sic performed during the rite in nineteenth-century Lucknow. This in-sight lends added credence to my earlier assertion that the core practices of the Trinidadian variant were brought from eastern Uttar Pradesh and Bihar, where the same drum types were in use at the time when inden-ture began (see Figures 9 and 10).

In Lucknow, drumming contests were staged during the first ten days of Muharram, when challenges were issued to all. During these chal-lenges, "the beats should fall (*zarb paren*) with such rapidity that one stroke (*qur'ah*) cannot be distinguished from another."[57] This description could very well fit the Indo-Trinidadian war hand and very much resem-bles the clashes to be discussed below. Moreover, although Wolf's data suggest an overall ambiguity between language and rhythm in South Asia, I think he would agree that rhythms do elicit emotional responses. In the case of drumming performances during the month of Muharram, the mood evoked would be somber and mournful for those participants familiar with the esoteric master narrative, but celebratory and joyous for those who do not know the inner meaning. The acoustic celebratory tone of the drums is what compels spectators to jump up, yet the emotion evoked is pensive for those in the know (see Figure 23).

Another material dimension of the observance that embodies esoteric knowledge known only to an inner circle of initiates is the construction and dancing of the moons. I turn my attention to them now before proceeding with a description of the processions.

Moonlighting

One significant aspect of the performance that has not been so prone to creolization is the esoteric moon phenomenon. I would like to suggest that while some aspects of the performance have undergone a certain amount of cultural convergence resulting from strategic adaptation, the traditions of building and dancing the moons, as well as their esoteric body symbolism, have been compartmentalized due to secrecy among participants. Compartmentalization of the moons has offered participants the possibility of retaining the strongest resemblance to their Indic, and by extension Iranian, precursors. By doing so, Shi'i East Indians have kept alive a vibrant tradition of religious folk art, a performance tradition, and its esoteric significance. One might wish to rely on Sufi terminology here to describe the secret meanings that I will be discussing shortly by utilizing the Arabic term *bāṭin* introduced earlier, which is used in mystical practice to refer to the hidden meanings of things. These would be diametrically opposed, but complementary, to their exoteric meanings. I return to this idea here to discuss participant versus audience knowledge of the event. But the theology of the term *bāṭin* itself might be one element responsible for the preservation of the moons' meaning among those who bring them out in procession.

Scholarly opinions and popular understandings in Trinidad suggest that the *Hosay* moons are an entirely indigenous phenomenon, having sprung up out of Caribbean soil in an autochthonous fashion. I myself held this opinion as recently as 1992. The following winter, however, I stumbled upon some very interesting mid-nineteenth-century paintings housed in the prints section of the India Office Library in London (see Figures 3 and 11). Suddenly I had evidence of moons in India that temporally and spatially connected Trinidadian moons with cognate traditions back home across the "black waters." This evidence forced me to reevaluate my data and come up with a more viable explanation. Discussions with scholars of Persian culture provided the impetus to posit a further link between India and Iran, thus taking the tradition of moons back to the vicinity of the historical narrative's point of origin.[58]

Recall that in Iran huge symbolic funeral biers called *nakhl*s are carried

by the devout and are paraded back and forth. The *nakhl*s are covered
with mirrors on the surface to reflect the mourning images of the participants in the procession (see Figure 2). Further, they are believed to
embody Husayn's great stature. It is thus said that the shape of the *nakhl*
is in the form of a teardrop to remind mourners constantly that one must
weep for Husayn each year during the special time of Muharram. Now
what we notice here is not a bodily representation per se but a representation of a body fluid derived from the eye. The eye, of course, is in the
head, which is one of the central visual and poetic images of Husayn
found in Persian and Urdu elegies. I do not think that this is a coincidence and would like to suggest that the symbolism of Husayn's head is
at the root of this abstract form of bodily representation. It is my opinion
that the *nakhl* is the latent prototype for the much more ornate and styl-
ized moons that we find first embodied in the Indian *sipar* and then later
in the Trinidadian moons.

We do not know when the first moons appeared in India, and their
history is very obscure. While I have gone through a number of eighteenth-
and nineteenth-century travelers' accounts and diaries, I have found no
descriptions of the moons, even though very fanciful descriptions of the
*ta'ziyah*s abound.[59] The pictorial representations of *sipar*s that I have
found, however, are dated approximately 1850 and originate from the
area around Patna in Bihar (see Figure 11). This point is important because the Bihar and U.P. areas served as the major arenas for the recruitment of indentured laborers during the peak of the period. These points
suggest that moons were being used in the area of recruitment during
the middle part of the nineteenth century, and it seems plausible that
knowledge of their meaning and construction were brought along early
in the indenture process. The moons reappear in missionary accounts
written during the plantation period in Trinidad, and oral history further tells us that they have been used in an unending annual cycle ever
since the first arrival. Since I lack written accounts of the moons from India and have been unable to speak with "moon men" in Bihar, I do not
know anything about their representational meaning, short of what I
suggested in Chapters 2 and 3. All I know for certain is that they are
literally shields standing for the courage of Husayn that are carried
in Sunni *muharram* processions. My contemporary Trinidadian material
provides me, however, with ample interpretive data.

The moon tradition was compartmentalized because one had to be initiated into two special men's guilds—one red, one green—in order to
participate in the construction and dancing of the moons.[60] Only initiates
were indoctrinated into the *bāṭin* meanings of the moons. Now whether it
is intentional or coincidental that only East Indians were initiated, the

fact remains that no Afro-Trinidadians belong to the so-called moon yards. Thus it is not common knowledge that the moons represent the bodies of the two brothers. The concealment of knowledge due to restricted access has led to a much greater retention of original style, form, and, possibly, meaning.

I cannot, of course, be certain about meaning because I have been able to attain only scant evidence from India, but in Trinidad, the moons are clear symbolic representations of Hasan and Husayn on at least two levels of interpretation. On one level, the large structures are believed to represent only the heads of the brothers: green for Hasan, who historians believe was poisoned, and red for Husayn, who was tragically decapitated during the battle on the plains of Karbala.[61] This, based on the *nakhl* prototype, is most probably the original meaning. But on yet another level, the moons are completed bodies, replete with martial symbolism, clothing, and other body parts, such as the *panjah*s. The moons are also spoken of as embodying and exuding human emotions such as fear, longing, and joy. This is most aptly depicted during the evening procession on the tenth, when the two moons embrace and kiss prior to the departure for battle. The kissing of the moon is similar to the em-

Figure 24. The green moon resting on its *chowk* prior to consecration on Big *Hosay* Night, 1992. Photograph by the author. Courtesy of the Smithsonian Institution's Folkways Archive.

bracing of the *'alam*s in India. Emotions raised by this moment are mixed. Most of the nonparticipating members of the audience applaud and yell in joy, yet those who are initiated know that this is the "kiss of death" and it evokes sadness in their hearts.

Aside from their differences in color and size (the green is 6'2" x 6'2", and the red is 5'8" x 5'8") as well as a few minor variations that I will point out in the course of my description, both moons are ornamented in the same fashion.[62] The back side is plain, decorated only with a styrotex symbol of Islam—the crescent moon and star, often draped with a garland, against a solid field of red or green (blue).[63] The ornamentation is more elaborate on the front side. Here we find the martial symbols to which I alluded above. Let me continue, then, with a description of the more ornate sides of the objects.

The construction of the two moons begins when the guilds cut bamboo and *roseau* at the Caroni.[64] The first thing that is done when building begins is the attachment of the "merry bamboo" to a bamboo cross that gives the objects their semicircular shape. The merry bamboo is the bowed, crescent-shaped slip of bamboo that is extended from one horizontal end of the cross over the vertical post's apex and then attached at the other horizontal end. The basic frame provides a hollow enclosure that is later stuffed and ornamented. The horizontal bar of the moon has a "window" at the center where the vertical and horizontal bars of the cross intersect. This is so that the moon dancer will be able to see where he is going as he twirls the moon on the street. Strips of *roseau* are then attached to the interior in a crisscross pattern resembling the latticed hollow frame of the Iranian *nakhl* (see Figure 1). A series of vertical strips are attached to the outside with a horizontal series running on the inside. These are then nailed together to complete the skeleton. Once the skeleton is formed, it is covered with integument consisting of straw. This is, if I may beg the reader's indulgence, the straw man that will be clothed in armor. I use the words "skeleton" and "integument" here intentionally because the moons are clearly corporeal representations of the brothers on two levels.

After the skeletons are stuffed, the reusable objects that adorn the inside and outside of the moons are ceremoniously brought out from the crates in which they have been stored in both yards. As is the case with the Iranian *nakhl* and the Indian *sipar*, knives are then stuck blade first in an even distribution along the merry bamboo's perimeter.[65] The largest knife, almost the length of a sword, is stuck vertically at the top in alignment with the central vertical post, and two midsized knives, larger than the perimeter series but smaller than the central one, are stuck at the bottom of each corner.[66] The weight of the knives must be evenly distributed

to create a perfectly balanced moon. After the knives are inserted carefully, a white funeral shroud is sewn over the frame. Large woolen blankets in red or blue/green are then sewn over the entire structure to cover
it. These blankets are referred to as the *pagrīs* (turbans) of the brothers,
again suggesting head symbolism. Then five long bolts of cotton cloth,
one mauve (the color of mourning in Trinidad), two white, and two red
or blue/green, are gathered along the external perimeter of the merry
bamboo. Once the cloth has been fixed in place around the periphery of
the crescent, a frilled border known as the *jaral* or *jalar* is created.[67] Each
bolt of cloth is 20" wide and 120' long. When gathered, they together
provide enough loft to conceal the knives and swords inserted into the
merry bamboo. I provide these details to give the reader a sense of how
heavy the moons are when completely decorated. Indeed, one must have
great stamina and strength to carry them, for allowing a moon to touch
the ground once it is lifted off the *chowk* is extremely inauspicious and
could lead to danger or harm. I have been told that in bygone days anyone who allowed the moon to fall would be beaten. Some said they might
even be killed, but no one could recall this ever having happened. These
stories are probably an exaggeration, but the intensity and sincerity of
the practice should nonetheless suggest its importance to the overall
event, for on the tenth day, the focus is solely on the moons.

Once the cloth work is completed, the external ornamentation of the
decorated face is applied. The whole surface is first covered with approximately one hundred small round silver discs that are polished and
sometimes covered with tinfoil. The discs are called *aini*s, the local variant of Hindi/Urdu *āīnā* (mirror).[68] On top of these "mirrors" on the red
moon are placed five evenly balanced, round *tawa*s (*tāuvā*s), griddles
used for cooking *roti*s, one for each member of the Holy Family. The
green moon has six, one representing each of the six yards involved
(see Figure 24).[69] Although the *tawa*s are physically cooking griddles,
the last generation of retired dancers who had a better knowledge of
Hindi referred to them as *ḍhāl*, which means shield. Two *panjah*s are
placed on top of each of the moons, and six bells are hung horizontally
along the bottom, three on each side of the window. Finally, peacock
feathers are inserted into the top of the red moon, and another cap
ornament is added to the green moon. I raise all this Indian terminology here to make the point that the moons are exactly the same as
Husayn's *sipar*s (shields) that are paraded in Bihar (see Figure 11). I will
expand this analysis below, but first I must identify the most important, if
inconspicuous, object on the ornamental side of the moons. At the very
top hangs a 12" x 16" cloth bag called the *makna*, a finely embroidered
sacred sack within which are placed red and white frangipani flowers

to be buried later during secret rituals performed at Ghulam Hussein's *chowk*.[70]

The corporeal symbolism can be interpreted on two levels. On one level, the moons represent the heads of the brothers. The fact that the red and blue blankets covering the skeletons are called turbans indicates the head, as does the fact that the mirrors are associated with the eyes. On the other level, the moons represent their whole bodies. One member of the green yard explained to me that the inner white shroud represents the brother's "pantaloons." We also have their torsos covered with armor and shields. Finally, we have their hands stretched up in prayer. Body symbolism is, as we have already seen, an important aspect of the observance's development in both Iran and India. Here in Trinidad it is preserved as the *bāṭin* lore nurtured orally by members of the tradition's inner circle and literally unknown to others in the public sphere.

In this section, I have attempted to show that there is a clear precedent for the construction of the moons that links Trinidadian Shi'i ritual practice to Iran via India. I would thus argue that the presentation of the moons as the bodies of the slain heroes is not a unique adaptation or creolization suited only to the sensibilities of the Shi'i community of St. James, but is instead a continuation of a tradition that still flourishes in rural Bihar today. It is equally important, however, to stress that the Indian *sipar* is a Sunni innovation and that there are Sunnis among the men who carry the moons in Trinidad. It is not clear where, when, why, and how Sunnis creatively usurped the Iranian *nakhl*'s shape and design for their own purposes. This usurpation does reinforce, however, one of the central points of this book, which is that Sunni and Hindu elements pervaded the rituals prior to the advent of East Indians in the Caribbean. From this point of view, we must admit that the rite was already a shared, creolized tradition on the public level well before the rite's introduction in Trinidad.

What does the body symbolism of the moons say about esoteric knowledge of the rite? Presenting the moons as bodies of the brothers provides a visual counterpart to the historical narrative concerning the tragedy of Hasan and Husayn. When this presentation of the moons is combined with the acoustic counterpart of the drumming ensembles, a multisensorial experience of the master narrative is conveyed to participants knowledgeable in the esoteric lore of the tradition. For the audience, these may just be moons paraded in public, but they are much more for the moon men. The moons can be read from a semiotic point of view as part of a larger cultural text that conveys basic religious tenets and morals embodied in the Karbala paradigm to those who understand the implicit meanings of the moons' body symbolism. But because the moons are only revealed once annually, I would suggest that the crescents cannot be understood and fully appreciated without viewing them in relation to all the other aspects of the procession, such as drumming, praying, and parading *tadjah*s. Indeed, moon men say that without the drums to provide the rhythm, they could not dance the moons. By linking all these multisensorial images together, we place ourselves in a good position to comprehend how Indo-Trinidadian *Hosay* participants internalize the Shi'i master narrative through a variety of sights and sounds in a manner that makes good sense to them. I now turn my attention to a description of the ritual performances in which the moons achieve their meaning for participants.

Performing *Hosay*

Up until the eighth, the activities in the yards have been primarily yard-based, that is, performed in private by and for family members and people who comprise the collective yard groups. Aside from the drumming, which is performed for anyone who wishes to listen, the ritual activities in the yards are an insider phenomenon. These activities socially bond the various groups together in ways unknown to outsiders. But the last three nights of the *Hosay* open up the observance to the general public because the central rituals performed on the eighth, ninth, and tenth of Muharram are processional rituals performed outside the yards. It cannot be stressed enough that in both Cedros and St. James, participants insist that the *tadjah*s must be brought out onto the streets in order to complete the event successfully. This was demonstrated poignantly in 1972, when government medical authorities wanted to postpone *Hosay* due to a polio outbreak. *Hosay* organizers, however, reacted to the quarantine by stressing that it was a religious observance that had to be done at the proper time and in the appropriate context.[71] Making the observance public by bringing the ritual items outside not only allows for spectacle but also enables a large audience to experience the aesthetic beauty of the *tadjah*s while simultaneously creating new sets of meanings concerning the significance of the event. The essential notion of inside/outside perspectives is a recurring point of tension in the community at large. As the understandings of various groups shape and influence opinions about the observance, the event itself subtly changes in response to vying opinions. Being mindful of the contested nature of the rite's public portion, let us continue with a description of the event.

On the evening of the eighth of Muharram, called Flag Night, the rituals become public when each yard brings out a wheeled platform covered with flags that is reminiscent of the *'alam*s (standards) paraded in parts of India and Iran. The flags not only represent the standards of Imam Husayn's party, but also visually signify the promises (vows) made by individuals. In Cedros the flags are mostly red and some are green, colors signifying Islam in general and the brothers specifically. In St. James one finds a plethora of colors, each signifying a particular sort of promise. Some of the standards in both places are topped with *panjah*s made of pounded gold and silver metal. Not all the flags, however, represent promises. Some are brought out as supplementary ornamentation and are recycled after the rituals to be used as neck straps for *tassa* drums in future years.

During the day of July 20, yard members, both male and female, are busy attaching the flags to the *roseau* poles, and a male member of each of the six yards paints the *chowk* of the yard once again. In some yards, such as Ghulam Hussein, the flagpoles are painted, and in others crêpe paper strips of various colors are wrapped around them to give the appearance of a flowing stripe from top to bottom. Simultaneously, work continues on the small and large *tadjah*s to be brought out on the next two evenings, while the men of the drum rooms make final preparations to get the instruments ready for the evening's performance. The moon yards also construct small *tadjah*s to be brought out the next evening. But by and large the center of activity revolves around preparing the wheeled platform *(katheeyah)* on which the flags are placed. The platforms are draped first with cloth, and then the flags are fastened to the platform. The platform now rests on the yard's *chowk*, and an empty space is left at the center. Here a tray of food offerings called *zirnee*, consisting of *maleedah* and other specially prepared sweetmeats, is placed on a small stand erected at the center of the platform. There is also a small pile of flour placed on the tray to represent the dirt or sand of Karbala, which is later deposited in the pit at the center of the *chowk* at Ghulam Hussein's yard. The tray is covered with a white cloth, which is also referred to as a *makna*, and it is then bound shut. The contents of the *zirnee* are later distributed to participants as another communal food offering.

Participants believe that the spirits of the two brothers enter into the large *tadjah*s on midnight of Flag Night. This is said to make them come alive, and to prove their presence, a drop of blood is believed to appear under each of the *tadjah*s.[72] They are also believed to shake violently as the spirits are entering. A Balma member told me that he remembers once being in the *imambara* alone at midnight on this evening many years ago. Suddenly, the entire *tadjah* started quivering. He wanted to run or yell for help, but he became temporarily paralyzed and dumbfounded. Experiences like these reinforce the local belief in the power of *Hosay*, regardless of race or creed. One Afro-Trinidadian now living in New York, who returns each year for the event, told me he does so because he "worships" the *Hosay*, even though he is not a Muslim. Similarly, Miller, an Afro-Trinidadian mechanic, told me after prayers on Flag Night in 1991 that he was once on crutches after an accident when he decided to make a promise. When he did, he was able to walk again. But the greatest miracle of which I have heard involved a man at Balma who recounted how his daughter's heart had stopped. Technically she was dead, but he claims that the *tadjah* brought her back to life again. Personal experience narratives such as these and those recounted earlier echo the words of the old Indian man who told Hamdoo's father that one must believe in it for it to be efficacious. As Ibrahim Ali stated, "you can't understand it without experiencing it."

Before the standards are taken out onto the street, they are consecrated on the *chowks* of the yards with communal prayer recited by the *imam*. As a method of purification, the flags are sprinkled after the prayers with water and the perfumes that were placed on the *chowk* on the first night.[73] The flags of each yard are then brought out to the sound of drumming at approximately the same time. Drumming begins in the yards at about ten in the evening, an hour before the flags are taken out onto the streets. First the boys with lesser experience begin to play in front of the flags; then roughly fifteen minutes before the flags depart, the most experienced drummers step in to accompany the yard's platform to the street. Marching ahead of the platforms, they begin by playing the drum of peace, which signals the beginning of the procession and the emergence of the flags. Behind each platform, women of the respective yards, dressed in their finest clothing and with heads veiled, carry flagpoles in their hands (see Figure 21). Wheeling the platforms about is primarily the duty of men.

When the crews turn onto Western Main Road, where they are met by large crowds waiting in anticipation, all the yards line up at an equal distance from one another. The cutter of each yard then signals a shift to the marching hand, which continues to play while the flag platforms slowly begin moving along the main road. For the community of believers, this portion is a reenactment of the peace march of Husayn's party but the bystanders who surround the platforms use this occasion as an opportunity for a fête. The bars along the road are packed, and numerous food vendors, mostly Hindu, have set up booths along the procession route. Although a somber mood is secretly harbored within the esoteric circles of yard participants, the public mood is festive and people are ready to "jump up" as they would during Carnival. *Hosay* processions have been relatively peaceful in modern times, but drunken brawls do occasionally flare up. To avoid or contain such minor altercations, mounted police are stationed at different points along the road. Usually, there is one policeman moving alongside each yard's crew. As the standards solemnly move along the road, audience members dance and sway rhythmically to the sound of the drums and cymbals.

The procession moves in the direction of the Haji Gokool mosque at the far end of the Western Main Road nearest to Cocorite, where the platforms turn and move to the other end of the road, then turn again for the return to the yards. Although the Green Moon Yard makes two flags in the memory of Hasan and Husayn, it does not bring out its own platform. Instead, it places its flags on one of the other platforms, usually Cocorite's, as it will do with its small *tadjah* on the next night. Significantly, there are five platforms, symbolically representing the five members of the Holy Family. Although local oral tradition holds that the platforms are lined up in a hierarchical fashion based on the length of years participating, it is also a matter of spatial convenience. Balma, for example, is located the farthest from the mosque and Bay Road the closest, while Ghulam Hussein is halfway in between. Cocorite has to enter

Figure 25. Crowds hovering around the Balma *katheeyah* on Small *Hosay* Night, 1991. A small *tadjah* in honor of Imam Hasan rests at the center, surrounded by flags. Photograph by Guha Shankar. Courtesy of the Smithsonian Institution's Folkways Archive.

onto the road from the bridge into St. James on the far side of the mosque. Thus, while tradition says that this spatial arrangement is based on seniority, it also represents the physical location of each yard. In any case, the order as the platforms move toward the mosque is as follows: Cocorite, Bay Road, Red Moon, Ghulam Hussein, and Balma.

The platforms are not in constant motion. As with most Indian religious processions, the movement is punctuated by periods of stillness. The drums, however, never cease to play until all the platforms have returned to the yards. The marching hand is played continuously when in motion. But when the platforms occasionally halt, the other hands are played, acoustically retelling the story of Husayn's passion. As the platforms near the mosque, they end up closer together and the drumming gets louder and faster. Two yards turn at the same time, so as they are turning, the pair faces each other. This is when the clash occurs. The preferred hand for the clash is the war hand. The drummers of each yard, turning closely, face off in opposing rows between their two platforms and beat at a frantic pace, each attempting to outdo the other. Crowds form around them and cheer for their home team. Clashes can last anywhere from a few minutes to ten or fifteen, largely depending on the rivalry between the two camps involved and the enthusiasm of the audience. When the clash is finished, the hand immediately changes and the two platforms slowly begin heading toward the other end of the road, making room for the next two to turn and clash. This friendly competition to win the crowd's approval is also a symbolic battle. It is simultaneously a reenactment of the historic Karbala battle and a confrontation between the neighborhoods in which the yards are situated, the latter being similar to the pattern in Bombay that I discussed in Chapter 3. Yet whereas in India the standoffs often led to communal violence, here in Trinidad tensions are diffused through this symbolic means of warfare. In addition, because the war hand is an expression of *mātam*, it conjures up remembrances of Husayn's passion through which active participants subjectively apprehend the martyr's sacrifice.

By the time all the platforms have turned, the order of procession is reversed, with the exception of Cocorite, which is now sandwiched in the middle. Balma is in the lead, with Bay Road at the rear.[74] Each platform is surrounded by its respective yard members and other familiar people from the yard's neighborhood, but occasionally a drummer or cymbal player may leave his own group to play with another.[75] As I mentioned earlier, yard allegiances are somewhat fluid. But when the platforms are ready to reenter the yards, the original ensembles are reunited for the return. Thus as the platforms approach the other end of the road, the point most distant from the mosque, the ensembles close in for another

Figure 26. Noble Bisnath crowning his *tadjah* on the uppermost tier on the afternoon preceding Big *Hosay* Night, 1991. Photograph by Guha Shankar. Courtesy of the Smithsonian Institution's Folkways Archive.

Figure 27. Noble Bisnath fixing the upper portion in place on the second tier of his *tadjah*. Photograph by Guha Shankar. Courtesy of the Smithsonian Institution's Folkways Archive.

Figure 28. The completed 1991 *tadjah* rests on the Balma *chowk* prior to processions on the tenth. Photograph by Guha Shankar. Courtesy of the Smithsonian Institution's Folkways Archive.

series of clashes. After this encounter, they turn again for the return. The procession is now closest to Balma's yard, and Balma is still in the lead and the first to reenter its yard. The procession gradually winds down as each platform reenters its yard, and by four in the morning, the official curfew for the event, the platforms have all been put to rest again on their respective *chowk*s and the drums have been silenced. The crowds on the street gradually die down, but bars remain open twenty-four hours a day. Many revelers are still liming on the streets, not at all aware of the solemn ritual about to take place at Ghulam Hussein's *chowk*.

Once the flags are back on the *chowk*, the headman of each yard takes his yard's *zirnee* tray and proceeds to Ghulam Hussein's yard, where communal prayers are once again recited by the *imam*. Prior to the prayers, each headman places his tray on the *chowk*. People who have made promises are also allowed to attend, but the gates to the yard are shut to keep out the general public. In an air of secrecy, a ritual reaffirming the social and kinship bonds between the *Hosay* yards occurs. I mentioned above that Ghulam Hussein's square is currently considered by most participants to be the local *karbalā'*. It is thus mandatory for each yard's headman to attend these prayers before distributing the *zirnee* for consumption.[76] After these private rituals are completed, the headmen return to their own yards for some rest before the next day's activities.

In earlier years the processions were accompanied by other Indic practices such as a *jharoo* (*jhāṛū*) broom dance to sweep away any negative forces impeding the procession and purify the route. Stick fighters wielding *lāṭhī*s also demonstrated their martial skills in the *gatka* battles so reminiscent of the north Indian village context. *Banaithi* (fire stick twirling) was performed to woo the audience.[77] It is difficult to say when these practices ceased in St. James, but older members still recall them from their youth. One toothless *tadjah* crewmember reminisced how he lost his teeth when the blows became too severe during a *gatka* bout. Although the event is less sensational today, it is still as spectacular and continues to draw large crowds.

The following evening, the ninth of Muharram, is dedicated to Husayn's older brother, Hasan. This night is locally known as Small *Tadjah* (or *Hosay*) Night.[78] The sequence of prayer, drumming, and procession continues in the same manner as the night before, but this time a smaller *tadjah* measuring anywhere from two to three feet in height is placed on each yard's platform along with some of the flags. Before the small *tadjah*s leave the yards, the young men who built them circumambulate the *chowk* in their respective yards three or seven times before the drumming begins. Once again, some hours after the evening prayers, the platforms move onto the streets to the accompaniment of drumming (see Figure 25). As the small *tadjah*s leave the yards, the *tadjah* builders bid them farewell. Some, exhausted from more than a month of long and sleepless nights, remain behind to complete their structures for the next evening's performance. The crowd is larger on this evening, even though the largest audience will gather the next night for the processional display of the big *tadjah*s and moons. As on the previous evening, the green moon's ritual object is being carried by Cocorite to maintain the symbolism of five. Again, the processions follow the same prescribed route as described above for Flag Night, returning to the yards by four in the morning.

The small *tadjah*s are also immersed at the conclusion of the observance on Teejah Day along with the promised flags and large *tadjah*s. But Bay Road takes its down to the bay even before returning to its yard on this same night. Once back in the yards, participants prepare to break the fast by killing a goat in the *ḥalāl* style.[79] The meat will be used for making curry to be shared by everyone in the yards on the following evening. These two evenings are really only preludes to the big night. Although the importance of doing everything according to sequence is emphasized as part of the entire event's holism, even yard members admit that the final evening is the most tense and exciting.

After the goat is slaughtered, the sun is starting to rise. There is very little time for sleep because the large *tadjah*s must be brought out and "crowned" by the men, and women must prepare for the great feast that will take place after evening prayers (see Figures 26 and 27). The previously mentioned "Shark," a Hindu builder from the south, says that every year when he enters the *Hosay* house at six in the morning on this day, he weeps profusely. "It is spontaneous and uncontrollable," he says. "I cry my eyes out." Although no one in the St. James yards is weeping, at least not publicly, the atmosphere is still somewhat pensive. During the day the builders in each yard tear down the temporary fourth wall to bring out their structures. The *tadjah*s are then brought out of the *imambara*s and crowned with the large domes that complete the structures. Once the *gummadge* has been fixed in place, each completed *tadjah* is placed on its yard's *chowk* (see Figure 28). Because the *tadjah* is no longer inside the *imambara*, the room once again becomes profane space and people of both genders can enter, even with their shoes on. The space now becomes a dining room for the sacrificial meal that will follow evening prayers. If there is time remaining after the crowning, everyone bathes and puts on clean clothes for the evening prayers. As in *mas* camps during Carnival time, men usually wear matching jerseys with the name of the yard on the front and the imprint of a sponsor on the back. Yard members reassemble in the compound at prayer time, which is slightly

Figure 29. The Bay Road *tadjah* being kissed by the red moon on Karbala Day, 1991. Photograph by Guha Shankar. Courtesy of the Smithsonian Institution's Folkways Archive.

Figure 30. A line of Ghulam Hussein *tassa* drummers heading to the Queen's Royal College grounds on Karbala Day, 1991, with *tadjah*s in the background. Photograph by Guha Shankar. Courtesy of the Smithsonian Institution's Folkways Archive.

longer on this evening because the *tadjah*s will not leave the yards until about midnight. As in India, this evening is also referred to as *qatal kī rāt* (night of murder).

Many participants believe that the *tadjah*s are dead after midnight on this evening, but Noble says that for him, the *tadjah* is no longer fresh after evening prayers. After the prayers are completed, everyone involved breaks their partial fast with a meal of goat curry and *roti*. Some yards, such as Ghulam Hussein, however, do not feast until Teejah Day. Prior to leaving the yards, family members circumambulate the structure seven times and throw rice mixed with cloves or cinnamon onto the *tadjah*. This practice is called *baksh*ing (blessing).[80] At the same time, the two moon yards are also preparing to bring out their moons. Each of the two yards has approximately twenty-five participating members. Dressed in red or blue (green) shirts and white pants, but wearing no shoes, they also perform evening prayers at their respective *chowk*s, where the moons now rest, positioned to face Mecca (see Figure 23). This gesture is said to represent the brothers saying their final prayers before going into heated battle. The yards also *baksh* their sacred objects. But when they circum-

Figure 31. The two St. James moons resting on the Queen's Royal College grounds prior to the *janaaza* prayers in 1991. Photograph by the author. Courtesy of the Smithsonian Institution's Folkways Archive.

ambulate counterclockwise, they chant "I say, *Hosay*" over and over again until the consecration rite is complete after five revolutions of the *chowk*.

The big night is an exciting time for participants and audience alike, and the drumming is considered to be the best and fiercest on this evening. When the *tadjahs* and moons move onto the street, the spectacle begins. The multitude of people is overwhelming, and the excitement is akin to a great festival. The spectators openly admire and comment on the shape and decoration of the *tadjahs*, and they enjoy the sight of the well-dressed, beautifully madeup teenage girls who follow the procession. The competition among the various camps concerning who has built the finest *tadjah* is openly discussed by the crowd as well as by participants. There is competition among the drummers also in the form of more clashes at the turnarounds. But for all this rivalry, there are no judges and no awarding of prizes for the best, as occurs in Carnival. Rather, everyone appreciates the aesthetic beauty of the colorful *tadjahs* and the artistic skill of their makers. In St. James, the two moons add an extra dimension to the spectacle.

The moon men enter Western Main Road from opposite sides of the streets. Each moon man wears a *chomatee* (leather suspender harness) attached to a *kamarband* (belt) around the waist, at the center of which is a metal cup in which the bottom of the moon's vertical post is placed when he is dancing. This allows the dancer to twirl the moon easily as he moves it from one shoulder to the other. Because of the immense weight of the moons, the bearer trades off every few minutes with someone else from his team, allowing each member of the yard to carry the moon at least once before the evening is over. Most of the moon men go barefoot to have better traction when twirling the moons, but others wear socks to protect their feet. As they twirl the moons, a spotter stands on each side watching attentively just in case the moons should tip and fall. The two moons meet at a roughly predetermined spot in front of the local mosque, at which time they kiss, or touch, symbolizing the last meeting of the brothers.[81] As the kissing of the moons is performed, the crowd applauds joyously, reversing the somber, mournful, and esoteric meaning embedded in this act for the community of builders and their families. For the crowd of onlookers, this is a joyous occasion, a celebration. At this point, it is very difficult to contain the crowd, which is more interested in the profane dimension of the event, the carnival-like atmosphere.

Drinking of rum and beer by the spectators increases with the steady progression of drumming and the graceful twirling of the moons. The crowds party, while the participants beat drums and internally mourn until roughly four in the morning. The moons also kiss each *tadjah* when they first pass them (see Figure 29). As everyone shouts "*Hosay!*" some of the older female members of the Indo-Trinidadian community throw rice and cloves at the structures when the moons kiss the *tadjah*s. Once the moons have passed and kissed all the *tadjah*s, they spin ahead of the pack in the direction away from the mosque, out of audible hearing range of the drums. Because the rhythms are essential for patterning their movements, they must chant the rhythms to themselves as they dance. At the turnaround, they are once again within earshot of the drummers as they prepare for the return. As the hour of four steadily approaches, each *tadjah* and moon is moved back to its own yard, where it rests until late in the morning. As I mentioned above, although opinions vary from yard to yard, local tradition holds that the *tadjah*s are dead from the end of this evening's performance.

After their rest, the *tadjah*s are moved once again in procession about noontime. The order of the *tadjah*s is now consonant with the ideal hierarchical pattern, with Bay Road in the lead, followed by Cocorite, Ghulam Hussein, and Balma. In Cedros, the daytime procession on the tenth does not follow any prearranged plan. In St. James, however, the *tadjah*s and moons move along the same route and beyond to the grounds of

Queen's Royal College (QRC), where land was granted by the queen of England in 1863 for the purpose of serving as a local *karbalā'* (see Figure 30). Since the *tadjah*s are now considered dead, the focal point of attention shifts to the moons in St. James. The moon yards twirl ahead of the *tadjah*s and reach the QRC grounds first. The *tadjah*s slow to a crawl as Ibrahim Ali signals the start of his special drum hand designed for this purpose: the dead hand or *chalta kabulkana*. Once they have arrived, the moons are erected upright, facing each other, and the members of each moon yard, now donning prayer caps, line up behind their respective moons (see Figure 31). They place their *chomatee*s in a pile on a white shroud spread at the base of each moon. Then an *imam* recites the *janaaza* (funeral prayers) at 3:30 in the afternoon. This, according to local tradition, corresponds to the time when Husayn was actually killed on the plains of Karbala. Curt Ali, of the Blue Moon Yard, says that by the time the prayers are said, the time of day has passed when the two brothers are believed to have been beheaded, but rather than getting lighter, the moons become heavier because of the tragic burden they now bear. The *imam* follows the funeral prayers with a petitionary prayer requesting Allah to bless and save each individual who has participated in the observance.

By the time that the *janaaza* service is completed, the *tadjah*s begin arriving at QRC, but they do not enter. The moons then depart the area and begin their return journey to St. James. Now there is less twirling, and the moons are simply carried back into St. James. As each of the *tadjah*s passes QRC, they also begin their return to the sound of the more upbeat soca tempo *dingolie*. As this activity attracts crowds, the moons secretly rush off to Ghulam Hussein Yard. The green moon enters the yard first and is placed facing Mecca, while the red moon twirls outside the gate. Inside the yard, a white shroud is erected over the *chowk*, and another secret rite is performed to empty the contents of the *makna* into the central pit.[82] Once the green moon's ritual is finished, it returns to its yard, and the same series of acts is performed for the red moon. The red moon then returns to its own yard, and the shroud is removed. By seven in the evening, all the moons and *tadjah*s are once again resting on their respective *chowk*s. There are then communal prayers at Ghulam Hussein's *chowk*, after which everyone partakes in a meal. Later in the evening, when the commotion of the day's activities has died down, the headmen return to Ghulam Hussein's yard to deposit the full contents of their *makna*s in the pit.

In St. James, a complete day of rest follows before Teejah Day, the occasion for destroying and immersing the structures.[83] During this day of rest, the *tadjah*s remain in plain view on the *chowk*s for the entire period.

Passersby can stop to admire the structures, and families use the day of rest to lime one last time before the objects are finally destroyed. Group photos are taken in front of the *tadjah*s for family albums, and sumptuous meals are consumed by everyone in attendance. Feasting occurs throughout the day, and plans are made for the next day's throwaway as well as for a postobservance beach lime.

When Teejah Day begins, different yards follow specific customs unique to their own families. The day begins in all yards with prayers at about ten in the morning. At Ghulam Hussein Yard, plates of rice pudding and *maleedah* prepared by the women of the household have been placed on a dining table in the former *imambara* along with two swords in memory of the brothers.[84] All the men of the yard sit around the table, with the *imam* at the head. As he recites Qur'anic verses, the men pick up chick peas from a bowl one by one and blow on them while reciting "God is great." Each bean is then thrown onto a plate. The meaning of this ritual is uncertain, but one person has suggested that it represents those gallant men who perished along with Husayn during the Karbala massacre. When this ritual is completed, the sweets are distributed to all in attendance, and the men move outside to begin destroying the *tadjah* unceremoniously.

Armed with crowbars, hacksaws, and hammers, the men, minus the master builder, take apart the structure and place the pieces in burlap sacks for transport to the ocean. Two bouquets of flowers representing the brothers are also stuffed into the sacks, to be immersed with the remains. All of the other yards use the closest route from their homes to wheel their entire *tadjah*s to the water, where they are "drowned" with the small *tadjah*s, flagpoles, and promised flags. One yard member, however, commented that "you can't drown a dead man!" Nonetheless, the moment is a sad one for the builders, so they rarely accompany the crew to the water. For them, this is the real sacrifice of the event. Destroying something that they have lovingly created is a test of faith and belief. They know it has to be done, but it saddens them to witness it, even as it reminds them of life's impermanence. As the *tadjah*s move toward the water, children with sticks are attracted. They accompany the objects to the shoreline, where they wait enthusiastically for a chance to whack the objects with their weapons. When the cupolas are removed and thrown unceremoniously in the water, the children beat them and the rest of the structures furiously with their sticks.

When the *tadjah*s or parts of them wash up on shore the next day, the people of the camps gather the remains and bury them. So what was the labor of many days and the aesthetic creation of many artisans is annihilated within a short span after its completion. It is a sad moment, no doubt a catharsis for many, and there are more than a few damp eyes in the crowd.[85] Even though local meanings have been shaped by contextual exigencies, the ceremony's final moments hint at its somber beginnings, and the crowd unknowingly reacts with appropriate solemnity. Each year new *tadjah*s will be built, and after their very short life span, they will also meet their end in the tranquil waters of the Caribbean, far removed from the harsh desert plains of Karbala.

Liming in the Aftermath

After the intensity and discipline of *Hosay* is over, a period of cathartic release and absolute freedom from social rules provides a much-needed break to wind down before total reentry into everyday life. To this end, each yard plans some sort of daylong picnic or extended vacation. In 1991 all the yards planned a "beach lime" at nearby Maracas. A successful lime, defined by Thomas Eriksen as "the art of doing nothing," entails proper preparation.[86] After Teejah Day, guys from the yards make lists of essentials. Noble's brother Terry, a member of Balma Yard, stresses that the following are needed for a successful beach lime: duck for the curryque (the Indo-Trini equivalent of an American barbeque), lots of beer and rum, cricket bats and balls, and bathing trunks for the obligatory sea bath. Everyone chips in to buy the necessary items.

The day after Teejah Day is spent organizing the excursion and buying the food and drink. Discussions are held to determine the logistics of transportation. How many cars will be necessary? How many guys will be bringing their wives or girlfriends? How many cases of beer do we need? Do we have enough ice chests? Should we bring mangoes and which variety is best this year? What time should we leave? Once there is a consensus, the food and drink are purchased, the duck is marinated for the next day's trip, *roti*s are made, and the beer is put on ice. The next day we gather early at Balma to load the cars. At the same time, the other yards are also getting ready. After the supplies are packed, everyone hops into the vehicles and heads up the road.

Maracas is a short drive up the coast from St. James. A lovely sandy beach partially shaded by swaying coconut palms appears after a thirty-minute drive along a hilly and winding coastal road. The beach, targeted for tourism development by the Trinidad and Tobago Tourism Development Authority, is a favorite with locals, so the strategy is to get there and stake out a nice shady spot before the crowds appear. When we arrive, it is about eight in the morning. We find a spot near a freshwater stream, unpack our supplies, and prepare the grill for the curryque. Some are already setting up a cricket field, marking the perimeter with stones and coconut shells. Although in the home, the kitchen is the women's do-main, here in the outdoors food preparation is left to the men. The women, mostly the younger females of the yard, are here with their hus-bands and boyfriends, and their company is appreciated after more than forty days of separation. The mood is happy and festive as some of the guys prepare a fire and guzzle their drinks. Some members of the crew wander over to the creek to get wet, while others head for the waves of the ocean. A short way off we spy the other yards making similar prepa-rations for their own limes. Each yard uses the occasion as a public dis-play of solidarity. As Eriksen points out, "[P]eople who lime together tend to belong to the same age group, to the same rank category with re-gards to occupation, and the same ethnic group. Usually, they live in the same neighborhood."[87] Although some of Eriksen's criteria apply, the post-*Hosay* lime is not racially segregated, and people from different class and occupational backgrounds do participate. The effect is essentially the same, however: absolute freedom from the respectability of the yard.

As the food is being prepared, some are playing cricket, while others engage in gossip, joke, tease, talk big, and discuss the recent *Hosay*. Of course, the hubris of each yard is great, so each naturally thinks its *tadjah* was the prettiest. As the day progresses and people loosen up, the yards start mixing to a certain extent. People from one crew who are related to those of another may visit each other's sites and exchange pleasantries, have a beer, and eat some food before returning to their own spot on the beach. The whole idea of the lime is to just let the world slip away tem-porarily and reaffirm one's social network and yard allegiance. But *Hosay* is still on everyone's minds. Noble is already talking about design schemes and color plans for next year, and others talk about their own future contributions to making the next event a successful one. Although, as I stressed in several places above, there is competition and rivalry during *Hosay*, this beach lime affords the possibility of reintegrating the solidarity of all the yards. It offers the opportunity to balance the tension between structure and antistructure. Because allegiance is somewhat fluid, the yards, though all distinct, share a common heritage and experience. This heritage is not only Islamic, or Indo-, or Afro-Trinidadian, but "*Hosay*ian," as one member of the crew put it. Everyone is united in a common pur-pose, but the understandings and meanings attributed to the event vary considerably. Any public event is, of course, bound to give rise to multi-ple interpretations, but because of the esoteric and veiled character of *Hosay*, the field is wide open for public interpretation and opinions vary greatly.

Newspapers and electronic media that have been covering the event from about the first of Muharram will lose interest gradually over the next few days and turn their attention to other major cultural events, most notably Carnival, the greatest fête celebrated on the island. As this year's *Hosay* fades into history and into the collective psyches of the St. James public, dreams of new *Hosays* begin to take root in the minds of participants. Another year will pass before the new Muharram moon appears to signal the start of yet another period of observance. In the meantime, profane celebration is the order of the day. We eat, drink, play, and swim throughout the day and into the early hours of the evening. By nine, everyone is ready for the return to St. James. We douse the fire, pack up the gear, load everything into the vehicles, and head as a train back into St. James along the same winding road that brought us to Maracas. The end of the lime marks a complete return to mundane life after a lengthy period of separation from normal life in the society at large.

Closing Remarks

The explication of *Hosay* in Trinidad provided above should suggest not only the theme of continuity and change with regard to theology and symbolism but also community process in religious performance. *Hosay* is certainly religious and ritualistic on the most esoteric level, but it is also cultural and national on more widely engulfing levels. More specifically, the notion of multiple meanings to which I alluded at the outset of this chapter takes center stage, so to speak, because the event functions differently for performers/artisans and audience members. It conjures up variegated images drawn from a long history of Shi'i observance on the one hand and the Trinidadian experience on the other. For the small community of believers, two or three hundred at most, the religious and mystical dimension, familial activity, and East Indian identity are highlighted through the inside, esoteric activities that occur during the private forty days leading up to the processions. The experiences of active participants who are steeped in *Hosay* lore are not felt and comprehended in the same manner by the general public.

The general public interprets the three nights and one day of procession as a celebration performed in a festive atmosphere. As many bystanders say, "It is just another excuse for a fête," or "It is like a little Indian carnival." For them it is also a community experience, but a profane one, celebrating sensuality and excess. They do not understand the sacred dimension of *Hosay*, nor are they very interested in it. But as in so many other public display religious events, the sacred and profane are intertwined, for as participants emphatically state, "The *tadjahs* must be taken out. The building of the *tadjah* is not enough." An appropriate context thus determines the completeness and efficacy of the event by providing access to closure. Like every cyclical event, there must be a beginning and an end. Otherwise, the efficacy of the sacrifice would be nullified. Recall that this point was tragically punctuated in 1990 when, as a result of the aborted coup d'état mentioned earlier, the *tadjah*s were not paraded entirely, even though the objects of veneration were completed and were eventually immersed in St. James. Participants lamented that the event fell short of completion because the objects of veneration were not brought out.

Audience/performer interaction in a public space imbued with an aura of both sacred and profane meanings defines this event and opens up the possibility of many levels of interpretation. By opening it up, the event becomes what we might call a double performance that simultaneously exemplifies what I have identified as *bāṭin* and *ẓāhir* understandings. The event from this perspective is esoteric, sacred, and ethnic on the inside, while exoteric, profane, and national on the outside. But on both sides of the yards' fences, *Hosay* offers the opportunity for various sorts of boundary crossings that merge and transform religious, ethnic, and cultural factors into new Trinidadian configurations. *Hosay* in Trinidad, as an arena of multicultural performance, thus exemplifies the process of cultural creolization noticeable in the grafting of indigenous ethnic elements onto an imported substratum of religious observance. In allowing this to happen, the *Hosay* observance has not only survived; through celebrating diversity, it has also creatively responded to the various needs of a nation-state constituted by a polyethnic citizenry. As I have been stressing, however, the above points are all subject to negotiation and heated debate in Trinidad. In the next chapter, I will turn to the theoretical issues that have been raised in this study.

Chapter 6
Conclusion
Maintenance and Transformation via Cultural Creolization

> *[T]hose who are directly connected with building our* taziahs . . . *will not make it a carnivalish or bacchanalish affair because we know the significance of it, and we know the reason for doing it, right? . . . In Trinidad, especially, people will get frenzied the moment you start beating* tassa *drumming. And so they start dancing right away and whatnot. And so you really cannot contain them, you cannot prevent them. The police is helpless to prevent anyone from dancing, or jumping, or drinking. You couldn't very well go and tell people, "Don't drink beer tonight," or to have them lock up their liquor shops and whatnot and so. No, it would be impossible to do something like that because we live in a cosmopolitan population! This is not an Islamic state. We are not only Indians, you see. This is a small United Nations. Trinidad is likened to a small United Nations.*

—Hamdoo Emamali, 1992[1]

Creolization in a Polyethnic Context

In the previous chapters, I traced the multifaceted development of *muḥarram* through time and across space in order to understand what the rite means today within a global context for the citizens of Trinidad. Central to this exercise has been an interest in noting cultural convergence as a creative agent of ritual change. We have seen that the process of mixing is not just limited to Trinidad, but has been occurring gradually throughout the rite's developmental history. A note of caution is necessary here, for I do not use *mixing* in any pejorative sense. I am in agreement with David DeCamp when he writes that in sociolinguistics the term does not suggest that "a pidgin or creole is only a potpourri with no uniform coherent structure of its own." He continues, "These are genuine languages in their own right, not just macaronic blends or interlingual corruptions of standard languages."[2] So too is *Hosay* not a cultural corruption, even though some may believe that it is. I use the term *mixing* here as synonymous with the less evaluative term *convergence*. Because *mixing* is used locally to refer to convergence, I use the two terms interchangeably.

Be that as it may, in Chapter 2 we saw that the practices associated with Husayn's passion may have originated in Iran and Iraq as a result of grafting earlier pre-Islamic beliefs and practices onto the Shi'i master narrative. Then in Chapter 3 we noticed that the rituals continued to grow and change as a result of cultural encounters between religious and ethnic groups in the Indian subcontinent. It is therefore not surprising that transformations should have continued to occur as the rite passed from South Asia to the Caribbean. In each of the three cases, a process of indigenization has occurred, or what sociolinguists refer to as nativization. We have also seen, however, that a number of persistent themes have remained constant during the long passage from Karbala to St. James. In this chapter, I explore some key issues for understanding the dynamics of what I have been referring to as cultural creolization. During our journey we have seen that Trinidadian practitioners had to adapt the rituals to local circumstances to secure their survival and allow them to flourish. It is my contention that the Indo-Trinidadian Shi'iah allowed the rite to indigenize through the successful deployment of *taqīyyah*. Had they not done so, the rite would have fallen into obscurity, as it did in both British Guiana and Surinam. Strategies of adaptation included a healthy amount of cultural accommodation and reinterpretation, which I see as central to the creolization process.

Creolization as a concept to speak of the convergence of distinct cultural practices perpetuated by different ethnic groups sharing the same geographic, economic, and political landscapes within a context of unequal power relationships was borrowed originally from linguistics. In linguistics, the concept took shape within a discourse concerning encounters between indigenous populations and colonial rulers, and the issue of power relationships between the colonizers and the colonized informed the study of linguistic change under such circumstances. Until the late 1960s, the "pidgins" and "creoles" resulting from such uneven encounters were seen as corrupted and not even worthy of study.[3] Corruption suggested degeneration to simpler forms of basic communication. As the study of linguistic creolization progressed, however, this value-laden idea was discarded in favor of more complicated interactive models. Peter Mühlhäusler, for example, points out that the most significant change in creole studies has been the shift from static, descriptive studies to dynamic ones that account for temporal and social change.[4] For Mühlhäusler, as for most scholars working in this field today, creolization as an antistatic phenomenon involves expansion rather than retraction and increasing complexity over simplification.

My task here is to point out one basic premise shared by most, if not all, students of the field. Creolization essentially involves the grafting of two or more languages together to create something new. Although it is subject to debate, many believe that the socially dominant language, the superstrate, provides the lexical labels, while the grammatical structure is provided by the subordinate languages, the substrates spoken by the creole makers.[5] By extension I wish to argue that this model can be used to talk about religious and cultural phenomena such as rituals. In the case of *Hosay*, the cultural substrate, or grammar, would be Indic in nature, while the cultural superstrate, or lexifier, would be Afro-Trinidadian. But as I have already stated earlier in my study, I do not see this linguistic model as an absolute either/or proposition. The model is, however, a useful way to conceptualize the dynamics of ritual change in a cultural context of contentious encounter conditioned by power relationships. DeCamp has pointed out that "creoles are capable of sudden and massive changes, especially in vocabulary. . . . Their variability is the result of social forces, however, not their inherent structures or their mixed origins."[6] I believe that such massive changes in the ritual vocabulary of *Hosay* began to occur as a result of social forces at play on the estates during the plantation period and have continued down to the present. The linguistic creole metaphor is therefore a useful way to engage in an analysis of the dynamics of how such accretions occur through intercultural transactions to shape the event in the present.

In the early 1970s, the historian Edward Brathwaite provided a richly textured analysis of cultural creolization in Jamaica. For him it is a locally produced phenomenon influenced by external factors. He understands cultural creolization as a distinct kind of "cultural action" that is material, psychological, and spiritual in nature.[7] Brathwaite also discusses the process as being based on a historically affected sociocultural continuum.[8] In 1980, Lee Drummond proposed a similar creolization continuum in his theory of intersystemically connected local culture in the Caribbean. Drummond also agrees that due to a lengthy period of ethnic interaction Caribbean culture has developed along a continuum, the boundaries of which are fluid and permeable. From his perspective, a locally bounded expressive system based on discrete ethnic customs is only a subsystem that undergoes constant transformation within the larger system of the cultural continuum.[9] Although some sociolinguists have critiqued the continuum model as being too diachronic, and therefore unable to explain changes in linguistic praxis, I still find the concept useful and have described the sociopolitical and economic factors historically involved in resultant ritual change.[10] This point of view allows us to free ourselves from the restrictive notion of bounded culture. It offers us the possibility to admit that adaptability and the reinterpretation of a culture's symbolic universe are essential strategies for understanding how meanings emerge anew as social contexts continue to shift in response to human encounters in the domains of work, worship, and play.

Building on Drummond's foundational lead, Ulf Hannerz has more recently discussed the contemporary transnational world of movement and mixture as a world in creolization.[11] He sees the negotiation of creolization and the social organization of any complex culture as a "network of perspectives" requiring the "management of meaning" because the division of labor in any society also entails the "division of knowledge."[12] Hannerz viably argues that precisely because not all people in a multicultural scenario share the same understandings the collective cultural inventory of a society expands, remains vital, and leads to increased diversity. Distinct ethnic cultures thus have less cultural autonomy and rely more on interrelations and conversations between distinct segments of the population in question. As a result, numerous streams of ethnic culture actively engage one another in the creolization process to shape newly emergent forms of social practice.[13]

Hannerz's points are well taken. Creole culture is a dynamic and creative process of blending different streams of distinct cultures into something new, but linguists have pointed out that "decreolization" also comes into play as part of the convergence continuum.[14] Decreolization involves reanalysis or reinterpretation of preexisting forms to suit contemporary needs. This is what I see happening in *Hosay* on one level of interpretation. In applying the concept of decreolization, however, I do not accept, as some of the literature argues, that the superstrate (Afro-Trinidadian) is the target destination of the item being creolized. Instead, I use it in conjunction with the concept of "streamlining," which suggests that "new forms are taken from a pool of existing possibilities and used to fill new syntactic and discursive functions within a paradigm."[15] Fusing the two concepts together forces us to admit that superstrate and substrate influences are not mutually exclusive; rather, they are complementary and interactive. In Jourdan's opinion, "speakers in the course of negotiating communication use whatever linguistic and sociolinguistic resources they have at their disposal, until shared meaning is established and conventionalized."[16] If we replace "linguistic resources" with "cultural resources" in the above quotation, we place ourselves in a good position to understand how certain shared meanings emerge out of *Hosay*. But the phrase "shared meanings" does not always translate comfortably as "accepted meanings."

I have been arguing that those Indo-Trinidadian Shi'ah who are involved in the production and performance of the rite allow spontaneous change to occur by drawing on Afro-Trinidadian lexical labels that parallel preexisting ones in their own cultural grammar. In this sense, we notice a resistance to creolization on the esoteric level. There is no doubt, however, that creolization is visible on the exoteric level. From my perspective, it is this negotiated reality that marks what Hannerz would call the "conversation of cultures."[17] The creative tension between the esoteric and exoteric dimensions of the rite thus allows for the continued cultural vitality of its localized form. I want to return to the creolized and decreolized elements of *Hosay* in the concluding section of this chapter, but first I need to pursue some other salient themes in the discourse on creole culture that have emerged repeatedly in this study. In the following section, I discuss the contentious nature of ethnic identity formation. Then I proceed with a section on the local negotiation of tradition before pursuing a discussion on the local/global dialectic that must be addressed before determining to what extent *Hosay* can be identified as religious, ethnic, national, or transnational in the final section.

Ethnicity, Contested Practices, and the Question of Ownership

Ethnicity has been studied from a number of different perspectives by a variety of scholars.[18] Most recently, Marcus Banks, in reevaluating the analytical value of the concept, has warned that ethnicity is "a collection of rather simplistic and obvious statements about boundaries, otherness, goals and achievements, being and identity, descent and classification, that has been constructed as much by the anthropologist as by the subject."[19] Even so, I see no reason not to pursue the idea as one node of analysis, for ethnicity is, as Banks would agree, one aspect of social identity that needs to be mapped in the "constantly changing terrain of human relations."[20] Thus, while mindful that ethnicity is as much an anthropological construction as it is a social reality, I nonetheless believe that the maintenance of ethnic identity is an important concern for Trinidadians in the ongoing debate over the politics of representation.

Public events centered on religious displays and cultural performances contribute a great deal to the maintenance of a sense of ethnic identity. Here I would like to explore the dialectic between religiosity and ethnicity, and also the effect of innovation on notions of unchanging tradition, by looking at *Hosay* in the light of the data presented in earlier chapters.

Like many other cultural events practiced by diasporic people throughout the world, *Hosay* is the creative result of a transnational phenomenon passing through densely layered local circumstances. As we have seen, while many participants understand it as a traditional event—canonized in a frozen form in the past and preserved through performance in the present—the rite has changed a great deal due to the skillful innovations employed by participating community members. This is most readily apparent in the presentation and exegesis of the spectacle by Shi'i Muslims residing in the area.

The Shi'ah of St. James, one very small Islamic community within the Trinidadian East Indian population, are primarily responsible for keeping this urban ritual complex intact in a form that they think is unaltered by the passage of time or movement through space, as I suggested in Chapter 4. Their view is a minority opinion challenged by virtually every other cultural and ethnic group on the island. Needless to say, the issue at stake is not whose opinion is correct, but how exegetical arguments about a large-scale performance form a public matrix for the assertion of various identities and raise questions concerning cultural ownership and authenticity. As I intend to make clear below, the interpretations posed by majority groups have led to numerous discourses of contention concerning not only the freedom of religious expression, but also the important issues of cultural rights and autonomy in a polyethnic society.

This section will address some ideas that have become commonplace but not moot in the study of ethnic identity. For example, Fredrik Barth's classic formulation of ethnic boundary construction as a process consisting of maintaining differences is still an important consideration for understanding how certain communities may perceive their own sociocultural role to be static and continuous in a heterogeneous nation-state.[21] Although the Barthian paradigm is critical for understanding in-group and subjective attitudes concerning ethnic identity, it must also be complemented with thick accounts of cultural interaction. When cultures interact, ethnicity becomes "situational" and "creative,"[22] or what I am calling "emergent."[23] The assertion of ethnicity often occurs at the margins of sociological boundaries, such as public venues, where interaction occurs most frequently.[24] Here, in these places of intense interaction, the possibility of transgressing boundaries presents itself most fully, resulting in the emergence of multiple identities as a strategy for coping with cultural encounter and change. The processes leading to the inevitable mixture of cultures created through encounter and change have been referred to variously by resorting to linguistic and biological metaphors such as creolization and hybridization. Being aware that concepts borrowed from the sciences have their limitations for describing cultural realities, I use the term *creolization* nonetheless because it is used regularly by urban Trinidadians themselves to depict the dynamics of their present situation.

Hosay is an occasion during which both the maintenance and change of ethnic identity can be documented as a process of creolization. In what follows, I intend to present some of the relevant discourses about *Hosay* in an effort to show how a multicultural and public display event can shape opinions and memories, identities and lives. The discourses with which I am concerned here interweave ethnicity, race, and nationalism through a process of heated negotiation that affects not only the self-perceptions of individuals living in diasporic conditions but also the larger cultural and religious ideologies that shape local experience and belief.

The contemporary processions that occur during the annual event have, to a limited extent, become nationalized and are a regular feature of Trinidad's cultural landscape. As a result, *Hosay* cannot be perpetuated by Muslims alone, for they are no longer the sole custodians of the tradition. Given that these rites have developed historically as various local phenomena grafted onto a core master narrative, it is useful to discuss the event in its contemporary Trinidadian context as a multicultural and polyethnic phenomenon lending itself to many different levels of interpretation. As various ethnic and sectarian groups claim the right to include themselves in the *Hosay* milieu, interpretations often compete for authenticity and authority in the hermeneutic arena, acting as discourse strategies for the assertion of various identities. *Hosay* is, in this light, a contested practice that is debated each year as the observance approaches. I would like to explore now some of the controversies surrounding *Hosay* that have been raised steadily as the event has gained notoriety and popular attention over the years. I focus on the rhetorical and apologetic statements repeatedly appearing in the press, on the radio, and on the television screen.

Much of the controversy focuses on the way that *Hosay* is practiced in Trinidad, or even whether it should be practiced at all. Although, as I stressed in Chapter 3, Sunnis had participated in Indian *muḥarram* observances for quite a long time, there has always been a degree of difference in ritual practice and a conflict of interpretations in theory as to why one should mourn the death of Husayn. For the Sunnis, it is more a matter of respecting the death anniversary of a member of the Prophet's family. Further, they do not believe in the redemptive qualities associated with Husayn's actions in the same intense way as Shi'i theology expounds. The Shi'ah, on the other hand, understand Husayn's martyrdom within the Karbala paradigm as both a theological and political issue. Unfortunately for them, they are not able to dictate how others outside of their

sectarian fold participate, as the lengthy quotation from Hamdoo Emamali that begins this chapter suggests. The large, drunken, and unruly
crowds present on the streets during the processions have given Sunnis
more reasons to stigmatize *Hosay*, and by extension, the Shi'ah. Because
most Sunnis on the island have observed the event passively from a distance throughout the past, they used to be content with simply trying to
control interpretations of *Hosay*. Public drinking and dancing, however,
have forced them to act more severely in modern times, calling for bans
of the observance in St. James. We have seen in Chapter 4 that this kind
of orthodox activism in part led to *Hosay*'s demise on much of the island
after the 1884 riots, and similar courses of action continue to this day in
St. James.

Although an attempt by Sunnis to ban *Hosay* was made as early as
1881, a concerted effort in modern times was not made until 1974, when
the Islamic Youth Organization (IYM) orchestrated the mobilization of
three larger governing bodies (the Tackveeyatul Islamic Association [TIA],
the Anjuman-Sunnat-ul-Jamaat Association [ASJA], and the Trinidad Muslim League [TML]). Leaders of all the groups met at the Nur-e-Islam
Mosque in San Juan, Trinidad, to draw up a resolution.[25] Their main
objection was the age-old theme that *Hosay* should not be celebrated.
Because the observance has deteriorated into a mockery, the argument
goes, it is un-Islamic and should not be practiced at all. As one spokesman of the IYM later wrote to the *Express* in 1985:

On the martyrdom of Hosein, it is said there was great rejoicing and revelry
by the Kharjees. After beheading him, his head was stuck on the tip of a spear
and they danced around shouting "Hosein! Hosein!" no doubt in glorification of
their victory. Gradually, as time elapsed, it was perhaps conveniently changed to
"Hosay," in an obvious attempt to distort the mockery of the celebration of the
martyrdom of Hosein. How could a sacred and great feast of martyrdom of a
Muslim be turned into a celebration? Of course, such a celebration can only be
done by enemies of the Muslims.[26]

Under pressure, even some Shi'i adherents have begun to take this position. In the following statement issued by Imtiaz Ali just a few years later,
the sentiments echoed above are repeated almost verbatim: "It is indeed
sad to state that his death on this blessed day of Ashura or 10th of
Muharram is observed in Trinidad as the festival of *Hosay*. . . . So jubilant
were the apostates at his death that they paraded in the streets carrying
his head and shouting, 'Hussein! Hussein!' and this has lost all its original flavour and has been replaced by merry-making, fêting and drinking
with all its attendant evils."[27]

Ali causally links celebration and alcohol to discredit the observance.
To alleviate the issue of alcohol consumption, Junior Ali recently pointed

out to journalists that drinking is a nuisance and should at least be curtailed, if not stopped altogether, during *Hosay*.[28] But he, like all the other family members participating, would not like to see the tradition come to a halt. Due to the economic benefits of the observance, neither would their sponsors, some of whom happen to be tavern owners of East Indian and African descent who cater to the insatiable thirst of the audience members. Because their establishments are ideally located along the main road where the processions take place, they would not like to lose the business generated during the three long nights of the spectacle. Both Junior and the rum peddlers would like to see *Hosay* continue, but obviously for different reasons.

Leaders of Trinidad's orthodox Muslim bodies realize that it would be extremely difficult to have *Hosay* totally abolished because it is so firmly rooted in the Creole culture of St. James, as indicated in Chapter 4. But because they believe that it "is a deviation of misguided Muslims and some who are not Muslims," as Abdool Latie suggests, they think the observance should at least be contained within the four yards where the *tadjahs* are built.[29] Latie's logic resonates with earlier colonial interventions that led up to the *Hosay* riots explored in Chapter 4. By eliminating the processions, there would be no revelry, and the Islamic nature of the observance would be restored. In 1983, Imam Hassan Karimullah, the public relations officer of ASJA, voiced this opinion when he stated that "the holding of parades is not a practice of Islam. . . . Pious Muslims strongly condemn the display of festivity and rejoicing which creates an entirely unworthy notion of this day."[30] Latie, linking the event with alien practices, then dogmatically suggests that the event is even an assault against the normative opinion held by practitioners of Muslim faith: "the carnival-type celebration is totally out of keeping with the practice of Islam."[31] In short, Sunni leaders would like to agree on a compromise that would eliminate processions during *Hosay* while allowing the Shi'ah to continue their unique mode of worship within the privacy of their own yards. *Tadjah* builders, however, will not agree to this because they believe that the processions are an integral part of the overall context of *Hosay*. Without the public display and later immersion of the structures, the event as a sacred enactment would be incomplete, providing no spiritual benefit to the community.

Even though many *Hosay* participants go so far as to agree that the observance is not a time for celebration, they are forced to provide constant rejoinders in defense of their right to observe the occasion. For example, Hamdoo Emamali, long-time spokesman for the *Hosay* organizing committee, states that the "Hoosay Festival is an occasion for lamenting and not, as onlookers make it, a time for fêting. Here in Trinidad we take

everything and make it a fête."[32] Emamali places the blame on the audience, who cannot be excluded by the organizers but can be criticized to
take the pressure off those actually involved in the ritual acts. Although
he views this process of carnivalization in a negative light, he does hint at
an alternative and positive way of understanding the processional phenomenon as one of cultural creolization and homogenization: "Mixing is
a very good thing. We should not have any differences: there ought not
to be differences."[33]

So far we have seen a number of polemical statements at play: the issue
of celebration versus commemoration, intoxication and wild abandon
versus sober piety, and carnivalization versus creolization. It is fairly clear
that the Trinidadian Sunni and Shi'ah basically take opposing views
on these contested issues, with some give and take on both sides. Shair
Ali, however, has attempted to justify festivity by linking it to piety. He
advocates both commemoration and festival. In an influential editorial
published in 1990, he states that "the atmosphere of elation which is generated by those Muslims who participate in the Hosein festival is defi-
nitely justifiable [because] Hosein gave his life for Islam. To live was the
death of Islam, to die was its preservation, so he died to protect Islam
and his death should be marked both by sorrow and happiness."[34] This
overtly Shi'i point of view has not been able, however, to silence the opponents of the event. The following year an unidentified spokesman of
ASJA spoke out in opposition to *Hosay* even more forcefully, sealing the
verdict earlier imposed by Latie. He writes that *Hosay* "undermines the
true nature and concepts and the moral, social and religious values of
the Islamic religion" because it is "a bacchanalian event and the revelry
and anti-Islamic practices connected with it are against the tenets and
fundamental principles of Islam."[35]

Sunni Muslims of Indian descent are not the only ones opposed to
Hosay in its festive form. On July 23, 1991, the year after an aborted coup
attempt led by Abu Bakr, who was the American-trained spiritual and
political head of a Black Muslim community in Trinidad, another Black
Muslim faction, known as the Saifud-din Tijani (SDT) or the Sword of
Religion Group, brought out an anti-*Hosay* procession. Boldly walking
toward the oncoming *tadjah*s, a small group of SDT members wore sand-
wich signs to remind the crowd that "everyday is Karbala" and carried a
black coffin while chanting in Arabic, "There is no God but Allah [and]
Muhammad is the Prophet of Allah."[36] Such sentiments resonate with
the examples provided from Iran in Chapter 2.

Yet other Afro-Trinidadians, who wish to co-opt the observance for the
purpose of both hedonism and nationalism, downplay the religious dimension even more than secular participants of Indian descent. Carl Ja-

cobs, an Afro-Trinidadian journalist and lover of *Hosay*, took this position nearly four decades ago when he argued that aside from the tradition of *tadjah*-building, there is very little religiosity involved. Instead, he claimed that *Hosay* is a unique Trinidadian phenomenon, more social than religious: "So please," he wrote, "let us have no more talk about 'religious significance.' Who say? I say, Hosay!"[37] Jacobs questions the rights of ownership, arguing that the spectacle is an integral part of Trinidadian patrimony. His position has not gone unheeded. The *tadjah* builder Muggy Millette once mentioned to me in the early 1990s that *Hosay* "is an Indian thing. It is more cultural than religious." His statement rings even truer when we consider that he and a group of other Trinidadians still build and parade a *tadjah* annually on Labor Day in Brooklyn. As the Indian diaspora via the Caribbean continues, the cultural facet of the event will eventually come to overshadow the religious dimension, according to Muggy.

Polyphony and the Negotiation of Identity

What are we to make of this polyphony of voices? Certainly the rhetorical strategies employed above serve as vehicles for the assertion of multiple identities. I have attempted to illustrate that religious identity is the central rallying point for Trinidadian Muslims during *Hosay*—albeit for opposing sectarian reasons—while Afro-Trinidadians of other faiths perceive it to be a period for the articulation of nationalist sentiment. East Indian Hindus and Christians, on the other hand, emphasize secular Indian culture in this same context. Broadly speaking, these three categories become polarized at *Hosay* time. Now if we look further at the processes leading up to the processions, even more categories must be added to the list.

As I discussed in the previous chapter, *tadjah* construction is a family affair. Although these families intermarry and socially interact throughout the rest of the year, each group unofficially competes to build the prettiest *tadjah*. Furthermore, the four groups also provide percussive accompaniment for their floats during the processions, each hoping to outdo the other by playing more loudly and better. Thus normal, everyday social interaction is curtailed as the liminal month of Muharram approaches, leading into yard-based affiliations that supercede the nation-state, religion, and culture. Since peer pressure is exerted on individuals to remain faithful to one yard only, conflict necessarily arises when new microallegiances temporarily become the social order of the day. In extreme cases, this may lead to actual physical brawls, but usually it amounts to simple pejorative gossip during the construction period prior to the processions and symbolic clashes, when the yard-based groups face off on the street to vie for the audience's enthusiastic response and support. Not only is yard identity at stake here, but personal identity as well, for the individual participants must reflexively ask themselves questions of consequence: "Who am I? What am I? How am I?" Let me illustrate this point with an example from my field notes.

Harry Ramcharan (a pseudonym) is a middle-aged Hindu whose older brother is a master *tadjah* builder in St. James. Harry has been assisting his Muslim sibling in building the model cenotaphs at one of the *Hosay* yards since he was a young man. As a result, he has developed a style of building based on his brother's designs. Eventually, Harry married into another one of the *Hosay* yards, which has always been Shi'i in orientation. He began spending more social time with his wife's family, even though he continued to build *tadjah*s with his brother. But in 1991 Harry was asked, actually contracted, to design and oversee the building of the *tadjah* associated with his wife's family because this yard lacked a designer at the time. The result that year was two very similar-looking *tadjah*s. In an environment where secrecy, innovation, and creativity of design is a criterion for aesthetic value, Harry's *tadjah* angered his brother and the other members of his familial yard to such a degree that he was temporarily ostracized. So serious was the dispute that his brother did not speak to him for the whole year. From the brother's point of view, Harry had sold out to the in-laws' natal yard in two ways. He had accepted money to perform the job—which goes against the pious and sacrificial nature of the creative act—and he revealed secret construction techniques that had previously given his brother's *tadjah*s their distinctive mark. On the night of the *tadjah* procession that year, I overheard one audience member say in an intentionally sarcastic tone that "this year there are two *tadjah*s from the same yard." Needless to say, such an admonition damages the pride of the yard in a cultural environment that traditionally values competition.

Harry's social dilemma was quite complex. On the one hand, he needed to satisfy his wife's family by complying with their request for artistic assistance. It was his well-intentioned way of showing support and trying to fit into a different religious environment in which he needs to confirm his kin solidarity. On the other, he needed to remain faithful to his hereditary yard by assisting his brother. His problem was that he did not succeed in properly negotiating these two roles, and as a result, he failed to play out with competence his two kinship positions of husband and brother. It is not that Harry did not try, for he did insist that his two sons, both of whom practice the faith of their mother, beat drums in his hereditary yard. This was Harry's way of attempting to participate in the activities of both groups. The attempt failed, however, and Harry's familial prestige suffered as a result. The following year the issue was resolved after the post-*Hosay* lime and Harry was back building with his brother again, while continuing to guide and instruct future master builders in the yard of his in-laws.

The central question that must be asked here by the participant is if one should remain faithful to the nuclear or to the extended family. Ideally, one should do both, but intermarriage makes this an improbable achievement. Harry's miniature drama is one example of factionalism among many that surface at *Hosay* time. Tensions thus flare as the three nights and one day of procession approach. By the time the *tadjah*s hit the street on the first night, the atmosphere is thick with divisiveness. Once the processions are over, however, a period of social realliance takes place during the great feasts that occur after the tenth of Muharram and on Teejah Day, the time when the drums are put away for another year and the *tadjah*s are broken up and immersed in the ocean. Participants, who have been performing abstinence up until this point, also use the occasion for a beach lime, as we saw in the previous chapter, where various yard members meet each other again, share food, and gossip to rekindle enduring friendships and family ties. The lime thus functions as an occasion for reintegration and social solidarity. To return briefly to Harry, he could be seen liming with members of both groups after the 1991 processions, and this bid for normalcy eventually led to his reincorporation into his brother's yard.

The analysis presented above suggests that ethnic identity is not simply a question of maintaining strict demarcations between social groups. Rather, events surrounding *Hosay* reconfirm that ethnicity is situated, being contextually formulated on both the social and individual levels.[38] In the case of East Indians living in Trinidad, ethnicity is often an emergent vehicle of empowerment used in different ways and at different times to achieve various political and economic objectives by a community that is economically stable but often socially stigmatized by the Afro-Trinidadian portion of the population. Moreover, Indo-Trinidadians feel marginalized from the mainstream of society because of their South Asian origins. As I argued in Chapter 4, such feelings are largely the inherited legacy of earlier colonial interventions. As a strategy for adaptation and a device for coping with cultural change, ethnicity must be multivalent, for it is not possible always to wear the same ethnic hat if one wants to be an Indo-Trinidadian Shi'i Muslim, a reliable friend, and a morally responsible family member. Rather, these "differential identities" must interact constantly so that the individual can function normally in society.[39] The trick to achieving a harmony of identities rests, of course, in the successful management of these identities: knowing when, where, how, and to what degree they must be asserted.[40] Herein lies the importance of studying expressive culture in relation to ethnicity and nationhood. Through the competent negotiation and enactment of performance—in this instance *Hosay*—participants have the opportunity to display simultaneously their fluid identities while preserving in an innovative way a central religious observance that has been a paradigmatic feature of the Shi'i worldview for over a millennium.

The way that Indians strategically deploy the concept of tradition also demonstrates the multivalent nature of the community's social world. I turn to it now to further the argument that culture and identity are in a constant state of negotiation in the creolization continuum.

Debating Tradition and Authenticity

The concept of tradition has been going through a significant amount of revision over the past few decades.[41] Scholars have moved from lauding the term as the congealing agent of little communities to deconstructing it, inventing it, inverting it, and reinscribing it with a new dynamism that is culturally constructed and thought to be operative in all societies.[42] Dan Ben-Amos has unraveled the term more recently to point out its pluralistic uses in the context of American folklore studies, suggesting that it is used in at least seven distinct analytical senses, however subtle they may be.[43] Some critics have even argued that the term has outlived its usefulness with "the passing of traditional society" and have called for its abandonment.[44]

Yet even though the term does not translate comfortably into many languages, the concept of a phenomenon that is passed on without change over time through various communicative media does, in fact, exist in most cultures to some degree or another. This, as we have seen, is the case among the Indo-Trinidadians of St. James.[45] The term is also used readily in popular discourse in the same sense that earlier scholars understood it, that is, as a superorganic principle that boldly operates to defy change by maintaining cultural practices perceived to be transmitted in an unaltered fashion over lengthy periods of time and through space. In this sense, the past is used to make authoritative claims about the present, or as Susan Stewart writes about the function of a souvenir, "to envelop the present in the past."[46] In the transnational arena in which we currently situate ourselves, it is, of course, necessary to interrogate the premise of tradition as a "frozen" or "stagnant" body of cultural beliefs and practices in the face of debates concerning modernity.[47] But is it really necessary to throw the baby out with the bath water? I do not think so. As Richard Handler and Jocelyn Linnekin point out, the " 'traditional' and the 'new' are interpretive rather than descriptive terms: since all cultures change ceaselessly, there can only be what is new, although what is new can take on symbolic value as 'traditional.' "[48]

It is thus important to explain why some people cling to the notion of tradition as a viable trope for modern life. The reason may have something to do with strategies pertaining to the construction of identity. For when people resort to invoking the notion of the traditional, they often do so to validate the authenticity of some custom or belief that remains central to a group's collective social identity, be it local, ethnic, religious, political, regional, or national.[49] Quite often it is used when an individual or group is under pressure to conform to the normative behavior and opinions of the dominant group, as is the case with South Asians living in the Caribbean.[50] In this section, I would like to explore further the sometimes ambiguous, and always controversial, relationship between ethnic identity construction and tradition invention by looking more closely at how the term is used rhetorically among the East Indian population of St. James.

As we have seen from my earlier discussions in this book, until fairly recently Indo-Trinidadians have always thought that they have been somewhat slighted on the political and cultural fronts. Indeed, until the 1995 election of Basdeo Pandey as the first Indo-Trinidadian prime minister, the government of the Republic of Trinidad and Tobago had been continuously controlled by Afro-Trinidadians since independence. One of the long-standing postcolonial issues resulting from political autonomy, economic self-determination, and sociocultural freedom has been an ongoing and conscious process to create a Trinidadian "national culture" firmly grounded in African based practices.[51] Moreover, the stereotypical argument goes, unique ethnic social institutions such as the caste system are not visible any longer because of the emergence of a national mentality.

Much of the discourse on Indo-Trinidadian culture, despite many hints to the contrary, pejoratively suggests that Indian religion and culture in Trinidad, as well as language, have all "deteriorated" into an amalgam of syncretistic forms. In other words, they have become "creolized." As with creole languages, creole culture often lacks social legitimacy from the lexifier's point of view.[52] That Indo-Trinidadian culture lacks authenticity is obviously not my position, but it is one that constantly echoes in the popular imagination. Cultural performances, for example, such as the *chutney wine* phenomenon that I will discuss briefly below, are criticized for either being too ethnic or too mixed. The natural question that begs to be asked is who owns such practices if they are the result of cultural and ethnic mixing. With the notable exception of Indo-Trinidadian religious revivalism on the island, the mixing phenomenon is certainly true on one level of objective analysis, as we have already seen.[53] The larger social context within which the national drama of Trinidadian culture takes place, however, defies such simple devolutionary premises.

East Indians, as we have seen, have often responded to cultural and political hegemony through resistance of various sorts. This response has taken shape in different ways at different times, but the general consensus today, even with an Indo-Trinidadian-dominated government at the helm, still seems to be that there is not enough autonomy to allow for the free and creative expression of "Indian" lifeways. *Indian* here must be put in quotation marks, for it should be clear at this point in my discussion that that which is subjectively perceived to be purely Indian has already gone through a steady process of creolization in urban St. James. We might want to talk of creolization as the strategic mixing of cultural forms to produce a distinctively modern form of Trinidadian society, replete with its own unique heritage. The heritage of the Republic of Trinidad and Tobago is usually perceived as transcending ethnic and religious boundaries associated with the former ruling class and outsiders. The reality of the situation, however, is much more complex.

Indians visiting from South Asia, for instance, often expect to find Indian culture as it is back home. When Indian tourists order a *roṭī* at a local roadside food stall or attend a Hindu or Muslim worship service, they usually expect to taste and experience things familiar to their own cultural world. They are often shocked by what they find, for even though terms from South Asian languages might be used for particular cultural items, the items themselves rarely live up to the expectations of Indian tourists, missionaries, and diplomats. I must admit that when I first arrived in Trinidad, directly from India, I was pleasantly surprised at how different local Indo-Trinidadian culture was. The same shattering of expectations also holds true when Indo-Trinidadian tourists visit India. They often comment that the food is not as good as it is in Trinidad, and they feel dismayed by what they perceive as rigid strictures imposed by Indian social norms. Consider, for example, the following quotation from an editorial sent to the *Trinidad Sunday Guardian* in 1991: "A relative, recently visiting family in India, describes Calcutta as a living hell. Another relative cried for hours on arrival in Bombay when a number of people were seen openly answering nature's call at the road side and the edge of ravines."[54]

We might raise the question, at this juncture, if an Indo-Trinidadian is

Indian when in Trinidad and Trinidadian when in India. However disconcerting the above differences and cultural misunderstandings may be, there is something intangibly Indian underlying Indo-Trinidadian cultural behavior that is difficult to observe externally in modes of dress, styles of cuisine, or rules pertaining to linguistic behavior and social interaction but is philosophically verifiable in the construction of an Indo-Trinidadian ontology. It is important to keep the notion of an emergent Indo-Trinidadian identity as explicated in the last section in mind when attempting to understand the extent to which Indo-Trinidadians perceive themselves to be bona fide Indians. We must remember that identity itself is not a static concept and needs to be used in the plural when discussing any polyethnic society in which many cultures co-exist in a creole environment of ongoing negotiation.

It is precisely at times when Indo-Trinidadians are criticized for being either too Indian or not Indian enough that many apologetically resort to the notion of tradition as a tool for the legitimacy of their own cultural practices and identities. Thus, outward signs of Indianness such as food and ritual observance may be spoken of as Indian, even though they might not be recognized as such by South Asians. When, for example, I once heard a visiting South Asian Indian comment on the mixture of spices in the local *masālā* as being different from that in the curry in India, the Indo-Trinidadian shopkeeper simply responded, "This is Trinidad, and you can't expect everything to be the same here as there!" Conversely, I overheard the same shopkeeper urging an American tourist to purchase the savory homemade Indian chutney, a concoction quite unlike any pickle that one would find in South Asia.

So the term *Indian* as a clearly demarcated category of ethnic identification must be seen in a relative way in diasporic communities such as Trinidad. The shifting nature of the hyphen between Indo- and Trinidadian is important here. When told that their form of Indianness is not quite authentic, Indo-Trinidadians often feel the need to assert their island identity. When they present their culture to those foreigners presumed to be unaware of South Asian culture, however, they may feel confident in their assertions regarding the quintessentially Indian nature of their social practices. Basically, this is a process of identity management, to which I intend to return shortly. First, we need to ask, what about the word *tradition* itself?

It seems that the word *tradition*, as well as the concept underlying it, is used to good effect in Trinidadian ethnic circles. For example, when criticized for performing a particular practice such as the *chutney wine*, a genre of song and dance perceived by many nonpractitioners to be lewd or sexually suggestive, Indo-Trinidadian performers engaged in this popular art medium can counter by saying that it is a traditional form of expression. They can make this claim because it is sometimes performed in so-called traditional contexts, one being the *batwaan*, or farewell celebration for the bride the night before a wedding.[55] The following line, for instance, though not traditional in any strict sense of the term—even though it parallels bawdy songs that are sung in eastern India on the same occasion—is performed in a traditional setting with unorthodox metaphorical props such as the *melongene* (eggplant) to allude to the sexual nature of the event: "De higher da mountain, de cooler da breeze. De sweeter da lovers, de tighter da squeeze."[56] Yet whose tradition are we talking about when popular dancers such as Sandra Beharry and Sherry Ramjit "give dem waist"? Do chutney music and dance belong solely to Indo-Trinidadians or do they belong to the populace-at-large that attends chutney functions?[57] Such emergent forms, historically arising out of vestiges of time-tested folk practices, are, of course, contested, at least in terms of ownership.

In this example, opponents to the *chutney wine* object primarily on moral grounds. Reynold Bassant and L. Siddhartha Orie recently stated in an editorial, "It is this sensuous element of the chutney shows that has provoked the moralists to mount their hobby horses and to be purveyors of the moral good of society. The performers would describe their act as nothing less than poetry in motion. But the critics see only sheer vulgarity on display."[58] Writers defending the *chutney wine* resort to tradition to justify its continued performance. The Indo-Trinidadian journalist Kamal Persad says that the pursuit of pleasure was a legitimate goal in Indian (that is, Hindu) *dharma*. Citing ancient Indian erotica such as the *Kāma Sūtra*, Persad makes the argument that the *chutney wine* is nothing to be morally ashamed of because it is only the local enactment of an age-old practice. His argument is, of course, both correct and incorrect simultaneously. It is correct in suggesting that the form is linked to an Indian performance tradition, but incorrect in suggesting that the genre is not an indigenous production of Trinidadian culture. Nonetheless, the important point here is that the rhetoric of tradition is drawn upon to legitimate something others perceive to be a deviant pattern of behavior among the Trinidadian descendants of East Indian indentured laborers.

The image of chutney, a foodstuff derived from the delicate mixing of ingredients, is an apt metaphor for the production of culture and identity among Indo-Trinidadians. The use of the term in this context is a subtle play on words, simultaneously suggesting a gastronomical dimension when referred to as a condiment and an artistic and visceral one in its performative gyrations and choreography.[59] Chutney as both a food and a performance genre is a viable indigenous model for cultural blending because it is currently spawning even more creole genres as the result of a gradual merger with other musical forms such as calypso and soca. Such a mixed-up attitude is apparent in a popular verse from Drupatee Ramgoonai's 1989 song "Indian Soca," in which she sings of Indian soca blending together in a perfect mixture the rhythms of India and Africa.

Sometimes, however, mixing cultures is regarded as a negative development, as is the case with the lyrics of calypsonian Gregory Ballantyne, whose artistic works are referred to pejoratively as a mutation.[60] But even so, these examples are clear evidence of yet another local cultural transformation taking place in the realm of popular culture. Here the appropriation of one performance style to suit the needs of another is not limited to a single ethnic group, for the genres just mentioned do not necessarily belong to one community or another, no matter how hard certain performers might lobby to make them their own. This is relatively clear with a popular, mass-mediated form such as the *chutney wine*, which is even performed in competitive displays and screened on television throughout the island, bringing it into national prominence. Yet emotions and opinions are much more marked when religion comes into play, as we have seen in the last section. Let us then return to *Hosay* and view it from within the discourse of tradition.

When a religious practice such as *Hosay* is criticized by orthodox Sunnis or overzealous missionaries for not conforming to their perspective, practitioners may offer a rebuttal that defends their practice in its local context, saying something akin to what Ibrahim Ali once told me when he became annoyed with my constant inquiries about the rite: "We are Trinidadians. We do not do things like they do in Iran, where it all started!" Notice that he points the finger at Iran—not India—for variation in ritual practice. He suggests that the changes that have taken place in the rituals occurred prior to their transportation to India from Persia in medieval times. In this case, the continuity of the rite from India to Trinidad is central to the way Indo-Trinidadian Shi'i Muslims use the term *tradition*, that is, to represent something unaltered, preserved through memory, and passed down orally from generation to generation.[61] As we saw in Chapter 4, the Shi'ah of Trinidad constantly say that they are practicing their religious rituals as their forefathers taught them to do. By drawing on the rhetoric of tradition, they are, to a certain degree, able to forestall the criticism of those who would like to see the rite banned.

As is the case elsewhere in the world, the biggest critics of the Shi'i

Muslims in Trinidad are the overwhelming Sunni majority, whose ideological attempts at religious hegemony have encompassed vehement criticism of Shiʻi ritual practice, mostly focusing on *muḥarram* observances.
One more supplementary example will suffice: "Hosay . . . is not considered a Muslim/Islamic festival. . . . The major resentment of [Sunni]
Muslims to Hosay on the basis of knowledge and investigations is its
polytheistic elements. Islam is the greatest soldier of monotheism and
urges its followers not only to resent polytheism but to fight it. . . . In the
eyes of the Shariah (Islamic Law), Hosay is totally harram (unlawful).
Hosay therefore is the antithesis of Islam."[62]

In this passage, the author, a Sunni Muslim, resorts to *fiqh* (jurisprudence) to question the legitimacy of the observance of *Hosay*. What
is most interesting to observe, however, as we did above, is the variety
of meanings that the phenomenon carries for the island's numerous
ethnoreligious communities. When analyzing the discourses about *Hosay*,
tradition very clearly becomes not the monolithic property of one specific community of believers or practitioners but a contested national emblem serving different needs for a broad range of interest groups and
individuals, each with its own agenda.[63] Thus the term *tradition*, when
used in conjunction with *Hosay*, becomes a multivalent word, lending itself to deep hermeneutic reflection on two levels: private and public. As I
have been arguing throughout, the two levels of interpretive reflection
can best be understood as corresponding to *bāṭin* and *ẓāhir* understandings that depend largely on the degree to which the interpreter is involved in the actual ritual process. In other words, some people, such as
audience members who watch the *tadjah* processions, would have a more
exoteric understanding of the event as a secular carnival-like pageant. In
stark contrast, those few Shiʻi practitioners who build the structures have
a guarded set of meanings about the rite and its practice. These inner
meanings are not common or public knowledge and are the joint property of only those families who continue the esoteric ritualistic practices
associated with *Hosay* in the private confines of the yards.

Because the whole observance is understood from these different vantage points, the Shiʻah must resort to a strategy that allows them to defend their central religious event of the year. This strategy is, as should
be clear by now, to focus on tradition, which has its counterparts in both
Hindu and Sufi notions concerning "chains of unbroken transmission"
(*saṃpradāya*, *silsilah*). When criticized for performing the controversial
Hosay rituals, Shiʻi spokesmen invoke the term *tradition* as a way of au-
thenticating and validating their practices. This is a deep subject for the
Shiʻah of Trinidad, which brings into play a number of theological and
cultural points that sacredly link this community of worshippers with

their Indian ancestors and then to the global community of Shi'ah, a point to which I will return in the following section.

The Sunni, being of both East Indian and African descent, object to the event altogether for ideological reasons that have plagued the overall sectarian relations between the two factions for more than a millennium on the global level. We saw this to be the case in both Iran and India as well. For others, however, the event is a secularized one reflecting national tradition. The adamant statement by the Afro-Trinidadian journalist quoted earlier, "Who say, I say, Hosay," implies that no single ethnic or religious group owns the public portion of the observance because it has become an integral part of Trinidadian patrimony. As *Hosay* increasingly becomes co-opted by other religious and ethnic groups on the island, the devout Shi'ah who are financially and spiritually responsible for its continued performance must, as I have been arguing, devise strategies to counter the claims of their critics.

The rhetoric of tradition thus can be utilized by all parties involved, be they East Indian Shi'ah, Afro-Trinidadian Christians, or others, in a legitimate yet contested fashion. Furthermore, an individual who engages in *Hosay* rituals also participates in other non-Shi'i activities during the rest of the year. Thus an individual who builds *tadjah*s or beats drums during *Hosay* might also build carnival floats, like Muggy Millette, or play in a steel band during Carnival, like Jit Samaroo, musical arranger of the well-known steel band called the Amoco Renegades.[64] In these two instances, the individuals concerned are exercising their personal rights to participate fully in other dimensions of Trinidadian life beyond their ethnic community of affiliation. In so doing, they may once again draw upon tradition to justify participation in these other events, which are, coincidentally, perceived to be national phenomena.

So the point is that while we as analysts might question the usefulness of a term as reified as *tradition*, it has a very useful function in societies that anthropologists used to call traditional. Indo-Trinidadians in St. James use tradition as a cultural category to be drawn upon as what Pierre Bourdieu calls "symbolic capital" for creating a coherent set of individual and group identities.[65] As an ethnic group, Indo-Trinidadians can draw upon their reservoir of expressive practices or traditions when necessary to make a statement about the authenticity of their diasporic culture. They may also draw upon the term in order to reassert their political, economic, and cultural roles in the greater arena of Trinidadian national life. On a more microethnographic level, subgroups such as the Indo-Trinidadian Shi'ah may also use the term *tradition* to discuss their own distinct religious culture within the island's broader, multicultural realm. One "mixed" Trinidadian, the son of an Indo-Trinidadian mother and an Iraqi father, rather ambiguously stated a few years ago in a letter to the *Trinidad Sunday Guardian* in reference to his own creole identity:

I have asked myself what this all means to an Indian/Trini/Iraqi like myself? How does it all transcribe to a man who wants to be a contribution and not a hindrance to the solution needed by his homeland T and T? Maybe it is that I must as an individual—build on the strength of 2,000 years of heritage by my father or maybe it is that I must learn the lesson of taking a risk and living for a brighter future—by the heritage of my mother—insofar as fortitude is the byproduct of an uprootment out of India to an unknown and uncertain future—or maybe it is that I must emulate those elements of Trinidadian society that can "accept" in the truest sense. Or perhaps it is that I must marry them all and live each day with that "callaloo bride."[66]

   The above examples indicate a number of intersecting spheres of sociological realities that must be dealt with on a daily basis. Occasionally, they must be handled in a context of conflict, as when physical brawls, riots, or worse, coup d'états, erupt, as was the case in 1990 during the month of Muharram.[67] This is when tradition becomes a most conspicuous tool for the resolution of difference through the propagation of tolerance. The usefulness of the term *tradition* in the context of Indo-Trinidadian society is to be found most readily in this dynamic and fluid sphere of identity negotiation and cultural production. The lengthy quote above, provided by a young man in London writing to a journal in his homeland Trinidad about his own dilemma of identity, symptomatically suggests the transnational arena within which the ongoing drama of *Hosay* continues to take shape on the periphery of the Islamic world. In the next section, I will consider the dialectical relationship between the local and the global as yet another angle from which we must view the observance. It is now becoming increasingly clear that *Hosay* as practiced in Trinidad is no longer an isolated phenomenon, a cultural relic cut off from the rest of the world. Then the final section of this chapter will provide an entrée into my epilogue, in which I discuss recent developments that challenge the manner in which *Hosay* is performed today.

Performing the Local, Thinking the Global

The concept of the "local" developed in the ethnographic fields as a way of offsetting ethnocentrism and the biases associated with comparative studies of cultural phenomena, as pointed out long ago by Melville Herskovits and his students.[68] Moreover, it remedied the dangerous tendency toward the construction of universals in the human sciences. From Boas and Malinowski onward, the notion of the specificity of cultural traits allowed for the gradual emergence of an anthropological theory of relativity, moving the discipline away from the banal generalizations about the nature of culture that plagued much of nineteenth-century speculation. Kenneth Pike's *emic* categories, it was thought, were better ways to understand the indigenous meanings attributed to things by specific people under investigation.[69] Indeed they were, for a while at least, and this emphasis allowed Geertz to craft carefully a subfield based largely on culturally relative epistemologies, a field he called "local knowledge."[70] One obvious constraint pointed out early on in the debate between relativists and generalists is that cultural relativism emphasizes difference at the expense of similarities and, in its most extreme form, negates comparison altogether.[71] Extreme cultural relativity, obviously, is not in line with the establishment of any general theory of culture and naturally has led to a wide range of criticism from humanists searching for common threads woven across national, linguistic, and ethnic borders.

More recently, the concept of the local has been interrogated by a number of writers dissatisfied with the idea of a bounded, monolithic, and superorganic form of culture impervious to external influences. The transnational anthropology advocated by Arjun Appadurai and Ulf Hannerz, among others, has taught social scientists to decenter the notion of culture, allowing us to seek out regional, national, and international connections within what Hannerz calls the "global ecumene."[72] Amy Shuman, for example, draws on Frantz Fanon's taxonomy of marked and unmarked categories to demonstrate that the local always serves "larger-than-local" interests because of its participation in a politics of culture that addresses issues of global relevance. As she states, "any definition of the local is marked and involves a contest with something outside it; even claims for homogeneity serve larger-than-local interests."[73] In a sense, a marked category such as Caribbean Islam tends to be marginalized and labeled as less authentic due to its marked status.[74] The issue of authenticity is, of course, a highly contested terrain in the politics of culture that becomes even more heated when religion is evoked to advocate or condemn the canonical nature of a given practice, rite, or custom. As we have seen repeatedly in the course of this study, ritual loci may thus become sites of contest where global concerns are debated and negotiated for political, economic, and ideological reasons.

Having stated this, the problem of positing a relationship between the local and the global is something that continues to vex scholars of Islam. Dale Eickelman signals a move in the direction of theorizing about the local while maintaining a sense of the global. The "main challenge for the study of Islam in local contexts," he writes, "is to describe and analyze how universalistic principles of Islam have been realized in various social and historical contexts without representing Islam as a seamless essence on the one hand or as a plastic congeries of beliefs on the other."[75] Clearly, there is a need for more reflection on how Islamic communities maintain a sense of local practice while participating in, and contributing to, the transnational flow of pan-Islamic philosophical values and performance traditions. Herein lies the need to bring together the work of the textual scholar in the field of the history of religions and the contextual scholar of ethnography.[76] However, the role of the "politics of place" in the study of Islamic communities, as noted by Lila Abu-Lughod, has hindered the development of an interdisciplinary field of study equipped to deal with the zigzagging contours of the local and the global dialectic.[77]

Eickelman's statement is certainly valid and needs critical attention in specific contexts throughout the world. Nonetheless, his major emphasis on class relations as the definitive marker between the transnational and the local, while well taken, hints at earlier unsubstantiated theories having to do with the unbridgeable divide between other questionable categories such as classical and folk. It seems to me that a more appropriate direction to take the study of the local is toward the study of ethnicity, because sociocultural realities in Islam, or any other so-called world religion, are never simply a question of economics or hierarchical status alone. The point just made is especially pertinent when we are dealing with diasporic communities. In diasporic communities a broad range of cultural matters interact in historically and geographically specific ways to create sets of indigenous meanings that force us to question universal models of culture and society on hermeneutic grounds alone. Yet there is also a continuing need to situate locally deduced meanings in their global settings.[78]

I personally do not see an opposition between the agendas of universalists and particularists. Instead, I would have to agree with Geertz's most recent statement on the matter. He argues that what we need instead of dichotomies is "a shifting focus of particularity" that acknowledges differences between one sort of local knowledge and another.[79] In this section, I intend to explore how the small community of Shi'i families in St. James creates its own form of local knowledge through discourses concerning the construction of ritual space and the subsequent presentation of self and community. In so doing, I also wish to suggest some ways in which Trinidadian Shi'i Muslims theologically and cognitively connect with their global brethren.

I do not want to argue that the local succumbs to the global in Trinidad, nor do I want to claim that the global has had no noticeable effect on the local. I merely wish to point out that there is a crisscrossing of interests, influences, ideas, and practices that forces us to consider the local in a broader transnational context. This context is difficult to unravel in the case of the Shi'ah, however, because of their tendency to conceal their practices and true beliefs through the employment of *taqiyyah*. I thus must approach the issue cautiously, with a concern for both local interests and the cultural complexity resulting from participation in a global drama. It is the intersections that result from the crisscrossing of the local and the global that I seek. These occasional intersections, mostly found on the ideological and symbolic level, do not necessarily translate as a permanent convergence of interests. Instead, I view them as moments of reflexivity during which local actors perform within a larger global drama that fits into the transnational Karbala paradigm discussed at the outset of this study.

One possible way to begin understanding how the local/global dialectic is construed among the participating families in question is to consider the main object of veneration, the *tadjah*. Being the central ritual objects of the processions in Trinidad, the *tadjah*s act as unifying symbols on many levels for the Indo-Trinidadian Shi'i community, albeit in an atmosphere of contention and terse competition. The objects can thus tell us much about the way citizens of the Republic of Trinidad and Tobago express their beliefs about the problem at hand. For example, the *tadjah* builders of St. James speak of the cenotaph's structure itself as hinting at the relationship between the local and the global. At the most basic level, the *tadjah* stands for family unity. Recall that there is a long-standing belief that misfortune can befall a family if it does not continue the building tradition in an unbroken fashion. The structure therefore acts as a symbolic "knot that binds" members of the nuclear family to each other.[80] This nuclear kinship bond then ties family members to the other yards involved in the ritual and further to the small group of Shi'ah on the island.

From the esoteric core, the local Shi'i community forms social links to other religious, ethnic, and national groups on the island. Through friendship networks, economic exchange, political affiliations, and, finally, participation in national expressive traditions such as steel drum ensembles and cricket, the local is connected to the regional and the national.[81] This essential series of island connections also allows, however, for a broader conceptual link with sectarian associates in India and Pakistan. Finally, the chain allows local Shi'ah to imagine an abstracted, ideological link with Shi'i Muslims throughout the world by remembering the master narrative of Husayn's passion and by participating in the Karbala paradigm through their ritual actions during the month of Muharram. In short, locally derived conceptions of transnational linkage begin at a commonly constructed center and move out in increasingly larger concentric circles of connection, ultimately engulfing the entire world. Essentially, we move from the individual and family at the emotional center to coreligionists, then to ethnic members of the Indo-Trinidadian community, and then to the level of the nation-state. From the nation-state, conceptual links to the original imagined homeland can be made and from there to the whole world as one interrelated community participating in the global drama of Husayn's martyrdom on an annual basis. The Shi'i master narrative is thus the tie that binds.

One can find further evidence of this transnational link in the ritualistic performances as well. First of all, I have been stressing throughout this study that there are abundant cultural continuities between Iran, India, and Trinidad with regard to the rituals performed during Muharram. I have shown that many of the rituals and customs performed in Trinidad have strong structural parallels in India that by extension link them to Iran. Second, the historical and legendary diffusion from one culture to the next establishes a fairly reliable, though not complete, chronology. The passage of rites from Iran to Trinidad via India is a sequential series of historical events not necessarily known consciously by most participants in the Caribbean. Nonetheless, the recall conjured up in the minds of participants when building the *tadjah* or viewing the rite in other geographical contexts suggests an important theoretical clue for linking such seemingly disparate observations. As Paul Connerton has suggested, the often informal institutionalization of ritual in its local contexts allows for a loosely conceived, "embodied" form of transnational Shi'i culture, collectively remembered and presented for self and other through the set of conventionalized performances that I have described in earlier chapters.[82]

Even though local meanings have been shaped by contextual exigencies, the ceremony's final moments hint at a larger transnational consciousness. One drummer standing near me during the immersion of the *tadjah*s on Teejah Day during a visit in 1997 poignantly stated, "You know, here we are in Trinidad and I think about people all over the world doing just what we're doing for Husayn." Perhaps not the same in practice, but similar in spirit. The cognitive reality to which I refer is a reality of symbolic connection. The symbolic connection allows for a link to be forged with a tradition that seems very alien to some of the local audience. The symbolic chain of traditions provides a common substratum of meaning to connect individuals as far afield as Trinidad and Jamaica on one end of the ritual spectrum to Iraq, Iran, and India on the other end. I have shown that while local culture asserts an overwhelming influence on *Hosay* as part of the creolization process, the Indo-Trinidadian Shi'ah can maneuver within the very confines of a national culture in the making to reconnect with a global community on the theological and performative levels. This is not to say that there are no contradictions within the local/global dialectic. Trinidadian practitioners of *Hosay* resist external missionary activities to conform to a normative global tradition dictated by Iranian clerics. Some, as mentioned earlier, find practices such as *mātam* and other forms of bodily mortification cruel and inhuman. They are also quick to point out that their way of thinking and acting is contextually appropriate for the island's lifestyle. As Hamdoo Emamali repeatedly emphasized to me, "This is Trinidad, not Iran. You can't expect us to act like them. Trinidad is a mini United Nations. You can't stop people from doing what they want."

What I want to suggest is that there is ample room for both conformity and dissent within the local constraints of a global tradition. At the same time, the Indo-Trinidadian Shi'ah participate in something so large—often so subtle—that they are not always fully aware of the transnational links providing the underlying meaning to their rituals. This is how I understand Ibrahim Ali's statement in Chapter 5 concerning the drumming narrative as telling a story so large that it cannot be comprehended fully. Although this small community of not more than two to three hundred people consisting of a handful of families acknowledges *Hosay*'s deep-rooted connection to rituals elsewhere in the world, participants insist in the end that they must be judged on their own terms: as Trinidadian Muslims. Here I would return to where I began this section.

At the beginning of this section, I suggested that the human sciences are currently engaged in deconstructing a marked category defined as the local to privilege much broader issues that affect people across national, ethnic, political, and geographic borders. Even though this is a necessary move in the postmodern world, there is still a great deal to be done on the local level to understand how global paradigms are reworked in a creative fashion for a specific community's own purposes. I have demonstrated that there are a number of alternative paths for a sociology of knowledge to take in the context of ritual performances, where both global continuities and local innovations can be displayed in public and negotiated between numerous ethnoreligious communities of interpreters. These paths intersect at various times and in various places but do not necessarily converge into a seamless whole. Here is precisely where Hannerz's "conversation of cultures" mentioned earlier comes to the fore. Intersection in complementary opposition to convergence highlights the need to study, as Geertz suggests, the relationship between one form of local knowledge and another.[83]

Perhaps the use of the plural for religious epistemologies, as suggested by Jonathan Z. Smith, makes more sense in our fragmentary world than a futile search for unity.[84] This, of course, moves us beyond the unquestionable Islamic category of *tawḥīd* (unity), forcing us to search for a system of signification to account for both universals and particulars in the study of world religions. It is all the more significant to underscore the resilient quality of the local in the face of globalizing forces in Trinidad because it is an area of the world where the practitioners of this particular faith are already perceived by their global brethren as being on the margins. In this sense, the Indo-Trinidadian Shi'ah are themselves a "marked" community, to use Fanon's term, removed from the mainstream of orthodox life. But local ritual practitioners believe strongly that through perpetuating their East Indian traditions they are practicing religion in the most authentic way possible, feeling no dire need to be overly apologetic for their customs. As Ibrahim told me repeatedly, "This is Trinidad, man! Don't judge us by what you see in other parts of the world."

I do not judge Ibrahim or his coreligionists, but others have questioned the authenticity of the rite. In recent years, missionaries have taken note of their practices from abroad and are now actively engaged in proselytizing activity to bring reform to the *Hosay* observance. In my epilogue, I conclude this study with the most recent transnational developments impinging upon the free and creative expression of the rite among the St. James community of Shi'ah. Let me first conclude this chapter, however, by addressing a question initially raised in the introductory section.

Is *Hosay* Shi'i, Indian, or Creole?

The question posed as the title to this section is not an easy one to answer, for there are many missing pieces to the puzzle. Nonetheless, based on the evidence presented in the earlier chapters, it is fruitful to make some educated guesses. On the simplest level, the answer depends upon the person giving it. An Indo-Trinidadian Shi'ah would certainly say that *Hosay* is both Shi'i and Indian. Some non-Shi'i Indo-Trinidadians would say that it is Indian, while some Afro-Trinidadians would say that it is Creole and therefore national. The previous hypothetical scenarios are, of course, overgeneralizations, and the picture is much more complicated because there are elements flowing together from all three of the streams. To disentangle the streams is my task in the remainder of this chapter.

We have seen in Chapter 1 that the Shi'i master narrative serves to provide the theological basis for the observances, yet the bulk of ritual action performed on the ground derives from similar practices in India. What remains constant from Iran to India to Trinidad beyond the underlying logic of the Karbala paradigm is the separation of private/ stationary and public/ambulatory rituals. I have argued that the private realm allows for the maintenance of the *bāṭin* level of understanding the commemoration through the employment of dissimulation, while the public realm allows for the expansion of meaning and interpretation of the *ẓāhir* level. It is precisely in the public realm where we notice the majority of accretions to the rite. This process of grafting elements from non-Shiʻi customs onto an imported substratum is one that clearly began in India, where the Iranian-inspired rituals began adapting to the South Asian cultural environment by allowing Sunni and Hindu practices into the observance as a method of survival.

In Chapter 3 I indicated that although one can speak of multiple sectarian *muḥarram*s existing simultaneously at different points in time, there is also abundant evidence to suggest mixed regional forms practiced in India today that cohere around a Shiʻi/Sunni/Hindu creolized form. The nineteenth- and early twentieth-century evidence from Bombay also provided in Chapter 3 suggests, however, that resistance to creolization can occur through the conscious maintenance of in-group practices; hence we saw the development of both private Shiʻi practices and public Sunni ones being performed separately. In my opinion, a similar scenario is apparent in Trinidad. Given this multicultural and multisectarian scenario, the question then becomes what exactly was transported to Trinidad. Because the record of evidence is far from complete, a kind of "archaeology of knowledge," as Michel Foucault terms it, has to be employed to make some sense of how the various rituals congeal on the island.[85] Such an intellectual archaeology is never unidirectional, which forces us to seek out both diachronic and synchronic factors to account for tentative genealogies of practices. On intellectual genealogies, Arjun Appadurai says, "Every genealogy is a choice among a virtually infinite set of genealogies that make up the problem of influence and source in intellectual history. Every idea ramifies indefinitely backward in time, and at each critical historical juncture, key ideas ramify indefinitely into their own horizontal, contemporary contexts."[86] Appadurai usefully points out that making influential cultural connections is not simply a matter of chronological and causal relationships. I therefore need to make certain temporal and spatial leaps and bounds in what follows to make my point salient.

In Chapter 4, I suggested that *Hosay* began shortly after the arrival of the first indentured laborers and that the Shiʻah among them were "hidden" and constituted a small minority. As a consequence of their small numbers, the Shi'ah could not control the direction that the public portion of the observance would take. Thus, it seems to me, many of the practices associated with the commemoration described in the historical literature are of Sunni and Hindu derivation. For example, elements such as immersing the *ta'ziyah*s, a fundamental aspect of the observance in Trinidad, is clearly Hindu, while the production and parading of the *sipar*s, the moons of Trinidad, are clearly Sunni in orientation. I would like to return to a more detailed discussion of this below, but first a word on Afro-Trinidadian participation in the event is necessary.

I suggested in Chapter 4 that the practices associated with *Hosay* came into contact with Afro-Creole culture on the estates quite early during the plantation period due to the racial and religious interactions of the polyethnic labor force. Johannes Fabian has suggested that such early ethnic and cultural encounters among subordinated peoples under colonial rule often constituted "pidgin contact cultures," in which a newly emergent form of communicative interaction developed to allow for social and cultural interchange.[87] Like language, culture writ large can be a means by which people in situations of encounter come to communicate with each other religiously, economically, and politically, often in opposition to the dominant, hegemonic control of the ruling class. Although Fabian's comments concern Zaire, I find his notion of a pidgin contact culture useful in discussing the development of a nascent creole form of the observance in Trinidad.

As we saw in Chapter 4, the coming together of Indo- and Afro-Trinidadians in ritual resistance to unfair labor practices during the plantation period led to the brutal suppression of *Hosay* on the island by the British government, which was backed by the plantocracy. Here perhaps we can speak of a basic pidgin form of *Hosay*, not yet fully creolized.[88] The developmental movement from pidgin to creole did not crystallize until well after the demise of the estate system and the freeing of the island's inhabitants by the British Crown. It is my contention that during the century-and-a-half-long development of *Hosay*, the gradual process of creolization came to its greatest fruition within an urban, cosmopolitan context after the island's independence. Conversely, independence, with less government intervention in the rite as a result, also allowed the Indo-Trinidadian Shi'ah to begin to "decreolize" the rituals in an accommodating response to the majority's efforts at racial integration and the creation of a national culture, a process not yet fully realized.

To return now to the first part of my question concerning whether *Hosay* is solely Shi'i or more generally Indian, let me explore some of the observance's elements that provide clues for a tentative answer. I have

been suggesting that because the Shi'ah were practicing *taqīyyah*, a preponderance of the public rituals associated with *Hosay* on the island are
of non-Shi'i derivation or are at least shared between sectarian groups. It
is only in contemporary times that the island's Shi'ah have started to assert their religious identity. In the past they continued practicing mixed
forms of the observance in public and concealing their esoteric practices
in the private realm. The evidence I have presented in previous chapters
bears this thesis out quite well, and I wish to review it now. First of all, recall that the majority of indentured laborers who came from India were
Sunni and Hindu. Secondly, this majority came from an area of north India where Muharram rituals were practiced not only by the Shi'ah but
also by other Indians. Indeed, we saw that these rituals were even practiced annually with great fervor in towns and villages where no Shi'ah
resided.

Many of the ostentatious public displays during *Hosay* bear strong Sunni
and Hindu markers. For example, the elements of competition and play,
though not completely lacking in Iranian and Indian Shi'i practice, are
prominent among Sunnis and Hindus. Further, it was among these sectarian groups that we found professional *ta'zīyah* builders from whom
the Shi'ah would purchase their models for procession in India. It was
also predominantly from the lower economic classes and low castes that
drummers were recruited to accompany the parades, and Hindus most
often served as vendors of material goods and foodstuffs for public
consumption during the event. So it is in St. James, where the street vendors who set up shop during *Hosay* are also primarily of Hindu descent.
Such economic activity has provided a festival-like aura to the solemnity
of this paramount Shi'i observance, which has also encouraged the
consumption of liquor by both Sunnis and Hindus. Moreover, it has
stimulated the general commodification and consumption aspects of
the observance as a whole, which has signaled a gradual co-optation
of the rite by the majority from the Shi'i minority. A good example of this
is the *sipar*. A uniquely Sunni aspect of the observance is the innovative
addition of this shield of Husayn, which I have argued is based on an
Iranian Shi'i prototype that was introduced into Indian practice by
Sunnis from Bihar, from where a good portion of the original indentured laborers hailed.

Rather than laboriously recounting each and every morphological feature of the rite, it will be useful to summarize the evidence in graphic
form and then review the data before turning to the vexing issue of creolization. Table 1 represents a breakdown of the rite's core elements into
categories that identify the extent to which they are shared or are exclusively the domain of one or another sectarian group.

TABLE 1. CORE ELEMENTS OF *HOSAY*

Feature	Shi'i	Sunni	Hindu
burial of flowers	less	more	less
burning frankincense	+	+	+
cloth offerings for vows	+	+	+
competition and play	less	more	more
curative power of the cenotaphs	+	+	+
demarcating *cauks*	+	+	+
dirge/lament recitations	more	less	less
drumming	+	+	+
earth-pit rituals	less	more	more
festivelike atmosphere	less	more	more
food offerings	+	+	+
horse processions	+	+	−
liquor consumption	−	+	+
master narrative	+	less	less
mātam	more	less	less
piety	more	less	less
private/public distinction	+	less	less
sipar	−	+	−
standards	+	+	+
ta'zīyah builders	less	more	more

Note: In instances where it is possible to indicate either the distinct presence or absence of a practice or trait, I use plus and minus symbols. Where distinctions are less clear or blurred, I opt for the words *less* or *more* to indicate the degree of frequency.

Perhaps it is fruitless to attempt a strict sectarian demarcation between practices performed by one religious community or the other because the long historical process of co-optation and borrowing has blurred the lines considerably. Indeed, it would be unwise to attempt this, for as Jayawardena contends, if we assume culture to be changing constantly, it becomes extremely difficult, if not impossible, to pinpoint a moment in time and a place in space to use as points of departure for comparison.[89] But the reduction in Table 1 is useful insofar as it demonstrates the absence, presence, or shared nature of key features pertaining to the observance to the extent possible under such difficult circumstances.

To me, the table suggests an overwhelming number of shared features, some of which are continuities from Iran, such as the cloth offerings for vows and the use of standards. I do not want, however, to go into a tedious comparison here for the purposes of a pointless attempt to map a course of unidirectional diffusion. Instead, I opt for the multidimensional approach discussed in my Introduction. I want to make clear that there is obviously a great degree of fluidity in religious practice across sectarian boundaries, a point that I emphasized in Chapters 3 through 5.

Based on the evidence I have presented, there is no good reason to assume that creolization and decreolization affects Muharram rituals only in Trinidad. Instead, it is better to see the process of mixing as an ongoing one along a global cultural continuum that has allowed for the rite to remain vital in a world of creolization. This perspective provides us with the possibility of understanding that the phenomenon is not the sole product of either localizing or globalizing forces. What we rather see is a fluid convergence of cultural streams stemming from the Middle East, South Asia, and the Caribbean, and neither of the three should be privileged over the others in determining the relative authenticity of practices associated with the rite. *Hosay* is far too complex to be explained in the simplistic terms of binary either/or frameworks. It must thus be understood as unfolding over time through a process of sociocultural negotiation that is tempered by political and economic power relationships and by majority/minority status ratios. From my perspective, it is at the intersection of these two opposite poles that dynamic creativity occurs, and this makes it difficult to discern one pole from the other.

In cases where Iranian Shi'i elements become the shared property of other sectarian groups, for example, we notice customs moving from the minority group to the majority. This fact reinforces not only the dialogic nature of the event that I have been stressing but also the quintessential point that creolization moves in both directions, not necessarily from the majority to the minority. What this suggests to me is that the process of co-opting Muharram rituals from the minority Shi'ah was well under way in India prior to the advent of Indians in the Caribbean. As I have been stressing, the Shi'ah needed to adopt practices from the majority communities as a strategy of ritual survival. Again, the mechanism and motive force of this strategy was the artful deployment of dissimulation within a private/public dialectic. The strategy allowed for both accommodation to cultural change on the public level and resistance to creolization in the private realm.

Now, given that I have been emphasizing that creolization occurred for centuries in India, I need to address the extent to which this process continues in Trinidad. First, I must point out again that we notice a preponderance of customs heavily associated with Sunnis and Hindus being practiced during *Hosay* in Trinidad. It is my contention that because the observance had already become carnivalized by Sunnis and Hindus in India before it was brought to the island, the majority Sunni/Hindu faction already wielded a heavy hand in propagating the rite on the island during the plantation period. Sunni/Hindu ritual dominance is easily confirmed by the simple fact that the headmen, the major culture brokers involved in organizing and perpetuating the event during the colonial period, were non-Shi'ah. The Shi'ah presumably had very little to say in the matter because their voices do not echo throughout the historical record.

There can be no doubt, however, that the Shi'ah continued to participate both privately and publicly in the phenomenon. Privately, they continued the esoteric dimension still apparent today, and publicly they participated in a form that was heavily Sunni and Hindu in orientation. In other words, it was more Shi'i internally and more Indian externally. In the latter case, the rite was a shared symbol of Indian ethnicity that aided members of the community to connect with the imagined homeland. In the former, it was the esoteric and religious property of the Shi'ah, allowing them the opportunity to participate in the global drama of Husayn's passion, which is seen as a universal tragedy applicable to the whole human experience. The splitting of ritual practices into private and public domains for these purposes is still a critical feature of the observance today, as we saw in Chapter 5.

We may now turn to the third part of my opening question in this section. Is *Hosay* Creole? Again, a tentative answer is a contentious yes and no, depending on whose opinion one cites. I have been arguing that certain features of the rituals such as yard organization, rules of street performance, and technical terminology bear strong resemblance to Afro-Creole practices. Phenomena such as drumming, drinking, and fêting most likely attracted Afro-Creole participation in the event during the pidgin contact phase on the plantations. Then, as the rite continued to develop on the island after the estate period and well into the era of independence, the changing balance of power and relative ethnic autonomy brought about by freedom allowed for a more variegated social and cultural context within which to interpret the rituals. This is especially true in urban areas such as St. James, where we notice the most pronounced Afro-Trinidadian participation. It is my belief that the process of keeping the rite intact involved the use of a decreolization strategy on the part of the small Shi'i community. They did so to resist full absorption into the majority Afro-Trinidadian population, which included many proponents of a national culture based on practices perceived to be derived from Africa.

Recall from above that decreolization involves a reinterpretation of preexisting practices to make sense of, and draw parallels with, the culture of the dominant group. The dominant group in postcolonial Trinidad is, of course, not the British but the African-descended majority of the island's population. So it is to their cultural influence that Indo-Shi'i Trinidadians needed to respond. During the estate period, what we noticed was a sort of "cultural diglossia," to continue the linguistic metaphor, in which Afro- and Indo-Trinidadians communicated through their own distinct cultural repertoires, while participating in an emergent pidgin contact culture.[90] This can be illustrated most readily by recalling the "Black Tadjah" phenomenon of British Guiana discussed in Chapter 4, during which exclusively Afro-Guianese plantation workers performed their own public processions on Good Friday. But as the performance of *Hosay* moved off the plantations and continued to develop into more complex and creolized forms in St. James prior to and after independence, it seems to me that a dire need arose among the small community of Shi'ah to deal with Afro-Creole accretions.

A strategic response was necessary to allay the criticisms posed first by the colonial regime and later by other members of the nation's citizenry. This mode of accommodation was accomplished by way of decreolization. To quote Bickerton again, decreolization "occurs wherever a creole language is in direct contact with its associated superstrate language."[91] He also suggests that the dynamic process involved leads to progressive change, resulting in a surface resemblance between the subordinate and dominant grammar.[92] Translated into cultural terms, through the artful use of decreolization, Indo-Shi'i Trinidadians have been fairly successful in making their subordinate cultural performance *(Hosay)* appear to resemble the dominant cultural performance (Carnival) on the surface without actually making a complete turn in the direction of the lexifier. In so doing, they have been able to appear to creolize on the external level, while continuing to resist creolization internally within the confines of the yards. One is tempted here to speak of crypto-Shi'ism based on the analogy of crypto-Judaism as practiced in the American Southwest. Concealing their faith in times of persecution has allowed the Jews of New Mexico to continue practicing their ancestral religious customs, as they understand them, for hundreds of years, even under enormous pressure to conform to a predominantly Hispano-Catholic culture.[93]

Let me provide a few illustrations from previous chapters to exemplify this basic point. In Chapter 5, I noted that there are striking similarities between the organization of yards in Afro- and Indo-Trinidadian culture. These similarities offered the St. James *tadjah* builders the possibility of drawing parallels in both behavioral and terminological ways that allowed them to maintain the distinctiveness of their practices while simultaneously opening up the observance to outside participation, thereby accommodating the Afro-Trinidadian majority. A number of authors have also pointed out the strong parallels between the organization of pan yards during the Afro-Trinidadian Carnival and the Indo-Trinidadian *Hosay*, which led many to think of the latter as an Indian carnival.[94] Both require widespread participation in assembly-line fashion to produce the objects required for the successful performance of the respective events. Similar terminology is also used to describe the spaces within which men work. For example, the term *tent* that refers to the sacred enclosure within which the *tadjah*s are constructed is an obvious Carnival term applied to *Hosay*, as is the use of the term *camp* for the yard itself. Similarly, the wearing of uniform jerseys with the name of the *Hosay* yard on the front and the sponsor's name printed on the back, as well as the naming of musical instruments, is strongly reminiscent of Carnival culture, as are intoxication, competition, and play.

The open borrowing of practices and terms described above are conscious choices made by Indo-Trinidadians to accommodate Afro-Trinidadian customs under pressure to acculturate. I would argue that such liberal borrowing is a reinterpretation of preexisting practices to suit contemporary needs, a strategy that I earlier identified as central to the process of decreolization. Whereas many theorists of decreolization see in it a move toward the superstrate by the substrate, I see it as a veiled strategy working in tandem with *taqīyyah* to resist the ideological pull toward standardization. Hence to the outsider it may seem that *Hosay* has become creolized over time on the exoteric level. It is precisely this exoteric level that finds expression in the many accounts I have cited from colonial and postcolonial periods. In contrast, precious little has been written about the esoteric level. For this very reason, the island's Indo-Shi'ah, with their reluctance to engage in extensive rhetorical rebuttals against their critics, have been easy targets for criticisms levied by both the orthodox members of the Sunni community and Afro-Trinidadians. The scenario has changed somewhat in recent times, but largely has followed past tendencies. To ignore the internal level of belief and practice is a grave injustice to the small community of practitioners who have so piously and lovingly nurtured the esoteric dimension under trying conditions for centuries.

I suggest that we can only admit to *Hosay* being a purely creolized phenomenon if we ignore the esoteric dimension of the rite, which is so crucial for the Shi'ah. It is in the inner, private, and domestic dimension that is maintained and nurtured in secrecy that I see resistance to creolization. Recall the forceful words of Hamdoo Emamali in Chapter 5, where he stated that the public portions of the rite would be meaningless without the private. In my opinion, the dialectic just described is a wonderful example of dissimulation in action. By externally conforming to majority pressures, the Shi'ah have been able to continue the practice of their esoteric rituals in private, even as they seem to conform to the demands of Creole culture in public. The dual process of inner maintenance and outer change is the defining strategy of what I theorize to be the underlying mechanism of adaptation that has allowed for the continuance of *Hosay* even under constant pressure from the majority Sunni community to abolish it. By allowing the participation of the Afro-Trinidadian majority and by externally appearing to creolize, thereby minimizing criticism from the latter for being too Indian, the Indo-Trinidadian Shi'ah are also able to stave off Sunni criticisms of their religious practices by rallying the support of their Afro-Trinidadian fellow participants. Decreolization thus works well in tandem with *taqiyyah* to guard against total assimilation and to insure the rite's continuation. As a strategy to deal with the delicate game of representation politics, the Indo-Shi'ah on the island have, to a large extent, succeeded in allowing *Hosay* to survive and flourish in St. James. I would even go so far as to argue that the rituals in Trinidad are every bit as complex as their South Asian and Middle Eastern counterparts, when viewed from a Caribbean vantage point. Lest I be misunderstood, I do not see creolization as a simplification, as an earlier generation of researchers on creole languages did, for I see it as involving immense complexification.

I have taken great pains to argue that the oscillation between creolization and decreolization is densely layered and enormously complex when it comes to negotiating *Hosay*. Unfortunately, some critics still do not view it this way. The greatest threat and challenge to the free expression of *Hosay* in performance today comes not from the orthodox Sunni sector of the Trinidadian population, which has recently toned down its anti-*Hosay* rhetoric, but from foreign Shi'i missionaries who have started to attend the rite from abroad. Using the same critical idiom of viewing *Hosay* as being degenerated as the result of creolization, this outside force now wishes to bring about ritual reform in St. James by transforming the rite into a more Iranian and pan-Shi'i mode of observance. Such recent global developments are the topic of my final reflections in the epilogue that closes this volume.

Epilogue

You really have to be in it to understand it!
—*Ibrahim Ali*[1]

New Developments

The words of Ibrahim Ali quoted above have come back to haunt me numerous times over the years since I began my project. How well did I really understand what was going on during *Hosay* time? After all, I was a floater, as he called me, constantly moving from one yard to the next to get a feel for how the whole dynamic process took shape throughout St. James. Having accomplished the task of being in numerous places to gather data on the overall event over a period of several years, I now thought that I had to heed his words and be "in it." To this end, I made plans to return to Trinidad during the *Hosay* preparatory season in May 1997. I expected things to be quite the same as they had been during previous visits, but little could I imagine the kinds of changes that were sweeping through the *Hosay* community.

"A lot of changes have been occurring to *Hosay* over the last few years," Noble told me over the telephone prior to my departure for the island. I had been to Trinidad the year before to attend Carnival and had had the opportunity to dine with Noble and his family. He told me then that Shi'i missionaries from Canada had started attending *Hosay* in 1994 to, as he put it, "set the record straight." He related how one member of the Canadian delegation was so devout that he even pulled the Balma *tadjah* to QRC single-handedly on Karbala Day. Since then, the Bilal Muslim Mission of the Americas, a nonprofit organization based in Ontario and New York, has been making inroads into the community to propagate the "real" meaning of *Hosay*.[2]

In leaflets that this organization has prepared, they state that Flag Night is held in honor of Abbas, whose famous and tragic water-skin incident plays such a major role in the Iranian observances. In the Mission's attempt to propagate the global and doctrinal meaning of the event, the master narrative of the Karbala paradigm is made public, rendering the esoteric in a form consumable by a mass audience. But no mention is provided in the leaflets of the promises associated with the flags that are made by those who believe in the power of *Hosay*. The latter remains part of the private and esoteric tradition of the yards but is ignored by this newly rendered reinterpretation based on a more globally inspired understanding.

The leaflets also explain that Small *Hosay* Night is held in remembrance of Ali Asghar, the infant son of Husayn, who is said to have hopped out of his cradle to aid Husayn in his hour of need when no one else would or could. With great panegyric flair, the leaflet prosaically taps into the poetic traditions of Iran and India. The emphasis in this second leaflet is on the standard, transnational understanding of this night's significance. But excised from the narrative is any mention of the local interpretation of the event. Gone is any mention that the small *tadjah* commemorates Husayn's older brother Hasan. Here again we see the Mission actively endeavoring to fix meaning and to shape public understandings of the event from a global perspective at the expense of local innovations that may have deeper roots in Indic traditions.

Last, the flyer distributed on Big *Hosay* Night focuses on the martyrdom of Husayn. It ends by imploring us to remember that "Islam is reborn after every Kerbala. Trinidad is Kerbala also. Every day is Ashura."[3] No mention, however, is made of the moons, which are still so difficult for an outsider to explain. I mention the missionary leaflets to illustrate how the Mission wishes to standardize the meanings of the observance, while simultaneously ignoring local understandings of the event. Naturally, such an attempt to usurp and control meaning has led to even more contested debates, but curiously missing from the current discourse thus far have been the formerly vocal Sunni clergy, which for some is a blessing in disguise. Debate notwithstanding, there is also a certain openness to receiving information from those in the know. "The participating yard families do not seem especially averse to learning the 'true' meaning," I wrote in my journal on May 5, 1997. Some elite members of the community, such as the spokesman for the organizing committee, Hamdoo Emamali, have embraced the visitors. Hamdoo is now the Trinidad and Tobago representative for the missionary association. Yet one could feel a palpable tension underlying the extreme courtesy being shown to the foreign visitors by yard members.

The other major change that has occurred is that a faction has developed at Balma. Disputes in the yard led to the landmark founding of a fifth *Hosay* yard, with Noble, former Balma master builder, at the helm.

The decision to start a new yard raised economic issues as well as questions concerning yard loyalty. One of Noble's brothers, Terry, took it upon himself to become headman of the new yard. As headman, it was his responsibility to raise funds, because the new crew had no cash reserve. So Terry organized a curryque to raise money. He sold over nine hundred tickets and raised more than TT$6,000, but that was far less than had been spent on the rituals in previous years. The year 1997 was thus the start of a new venture and a new era, but questions lingered. At whose house should the new yard be established? What should it be called? How could a crew be assembled without causing undue rivalry and discontent at Balma? Soon Noble, two of his brothers, and his youngest son Jameel were joined by other long-time members of Balma as well as younger boys who had been only observers in years past. They also managed to assemble a drum crew of eight basses and ten *tassa*s. After they decided to use a relative's house on Bournes Road, across the street from Ghulam Hussein Yard, the site was founded and given the hyphenated name Bis-Ali, which combines the surnames of the headman (Bisnath) and the yard's owner (Ali). In this way, the Bis-Ali Yard was born. Bill Ali, owner of the home, took over duties as the head of the adjacent drum room.

Other changes had occurred as well. Early last year the St. James/ Cocorite *Hosay* Association voted Bunny Emamali, headman of Balma Yard, out as chairman and replaced him with a Hindu named Ronald "Gobi" Lakhan.[4] The *tadjah*s are also changing. Gone is the elaborate *roseau* frame, probably due to scarce funds and a shortage of labor; it has been replaced with 2" x 4" planks and plywood to be reused annually.[5] Gone also are the complex inner frames of the cylindrical minarets, which have been replaced by large cardboard tubes upon which the usual elaborate ornamentation is now glued. The length of time now required to build the structure has also increased because of a smaller and less experienced crew. Hence the dire need to cut corners. Noble began work on his *tadjah* on March 28 and what little *roseau* was used in the frame was cut on April 17. Last, one must also note a change in the construction of the *tassa*s. Due to the rising price of shells and skins, Ghulam Hussein's drum crew is experimenting with other materials. They now have four drum shells made of recycled metal airplane fuselages. They also wish to experiment in the future with PVC tubing to replace the drum's bamboo slip.[6]

I was naturally drawn to the new yard to lend assistance, partly because I knew they could use the help and partly because Noble and his crew had always befriended me during the course of my fieldwork. I felt extremely comfortable among them. My first task was to make the usual rounds before settling in to work the night shift with Noble's crew. At Balma, the *tadjah* design had been created by bass-maker Brian (aka Shabby), but because he was busy with drums, his design had been being implemented by one of Bunny's sons, who used to assist Noble in former years. At Ghulam Hussein, Aziz still manned the drum room, but Raiez told me that the younger builders are taking over the *tadjah*. He was sitting this one out because of a torn cartilage but still kept a watchful eye over the proceedings from a cot on the veranda. Across the bridge at Cocorite, many of the same personnel were building their usual "castle" with lights, but it was a colossal 15'-high one with a 10' x 12' base. Everyone seemed to be ignoring the 12' height ordinance, saying that they could lift the wires with a long pole to allow the *tadjah*s to pass underneath them. Muggy was also building a huge structure with a 15' x 15' base. He told me that not everyone was cooperating these days. To compensate for this turn of events, he has been forced to begin work on the project in New York, where his children help. Buying his materials at a huge discount in the garment district during after Christmas sales, he now assembles as much of the structure as he can before leaving the States and ships down the sections in pieces, which are then put together at Bay Road.

It seems that the presence of the Bilal Mission has been having quite an impact, both pro and con. One headman, for example, is now worried that they will attempt to take over the rituals. Some also fear that they are fanatics, citing the zeal with which one delegate pulled the Balma *tadjah* on a rope in 1995. Still others (an elite minority) believe their presence to be a good thing. At any rate, the Mission's facts have unleashed a guilt or inferiority complex. As Muggy explains it to me, he thinks that people have been ignorant and now the truth is out. In fact, Muggy went so far as to say that my presence and that of my colleagues during a 1992 film shoot "opened up their eyes." Terry later told me that my 1991 television spot to defend the historicity of the rite altered the negative perceptions of some orthodox Sunnis, and the more vociferous opponents have remained silent in recent years.[7] I was flattered by this redeeming praise, but it raised in my mind other issues of reflexivity. Am I altering the natural progression of things? Did the international exposure of *Hosay* to which I contributed directly result in the current missionary activities that further threaten the traditional event? I am not alone in thinking like this. When Muggy states that their eyes have been opened, what he seems to mean is that community members involved in *Hosay* are now becoming more self-reflexive than they ever were in the past. What if we aren't doing it correctly? Should we accept the changes that the missionaries are proposing? If so, what of our long tradition of doing it as our forefathers taught us? These are the kinds of questions that are now on everyone's minds in the *Hosay* yards.

Only time will tell in which direction *Hosay* will go. Will outside organizations such as the Bilal group succeed in co-opting the event? Will continuous factionalism lead to more and more *Hosay* yards? And further, will the new push by the Trinidad Tourism and Industry Development Company (TTIDCO) lead to a greater carnivalization of the event? If so, will *Hosay* eventually become a staged and judged display like Carnival? All of these are remote possibilities at present. TTIDCO, for example, is pushing to make the event more international once again.[8] To set the stage, it commissioned Noble to design a green archway at the entrance to St. James on Western Main Road, upon which have been placed green onion domes reminiscent of his *tadjah* designs. St. James is now an icon visibly marked as *"Hosay* town," a kind of living heritage museum that contributes to national patrimony. It is through these same arches that revelers must pass on the final night of Carnival for "last jump." What does this say to the average audience member and tourist?

Clearly some radical changes are occurring, and the next few years could be decisive in terms of *Hosay*'s future. With all the external invasions shaping the course of the observance, anything is possible, but as mentioned in the previous chapter, such external influences are not new because Dr. Eric Williams attempted to folklorize the event some decades ago. The question is whether the participants currently embody the same sort of resilience and will as the previous generation did. Less labor and finances may mean that crews will have to succumb to a certain amount of external pressure if they wish to keep the tradition vital, especially since the Bilal Mission is eager to contribute money to the organizing committee. On the other hand, this most recent assault could blow over, as previous ones did. Many, however, are less optimistic. With the serious investment made by the Bilal Mission, some believe that more considerable changes could occur.[9] Hamdoo, for example, notes that the Mission's first goal is to establish a Shi'i cultural center. Then it eventually wishes to build a religious school *(madrāsah)* and Shi'i mosque in St. James. Such actions, from the point of view of those like Hamdoo who wish to see them succeed, would authenticate the Shi'i minority and provide them a greater voice in Trinidadian Muslim affairs, after more than a century and a half of silence and concealment. Hamdoo insists that this is not a bad thing, and he does not think that the Mission intends to take over, as some suspect.

After all the buzz I had been hearing about the Mission, I finally had the opportunity to meet Ashiq Keramalli, the secretary of the group, on the second of Muharram (May 10, 1997). Keramalli is a diasporic Gujarati Indian from East Africa who has settled in North America and now volunteers as the Mission's secretary. The Mission was founded in 1964 in Tanzania, where Keramalli first became familiar with its work.[10] He states that his initial reaction when witnessing *Hosay* was shock at the way the rituals were performed on the island, but then he gave in to a spirit of resignation. Realizing that change does not come easily, he now practices a strategy of tolerance. Essentially, he wishes to impart knowledge of the "real" meanings over a period of years. Thus, this year there are the leaflets and an open offer to match any funds raised by Hamdoo for the cultural center. Gradually, he wishes to introduce more standardized global practices into the observance.[11]

Although the Mission has enticed a small number of wealthy intellectuals from the Indo-Trinidadian community such as Hamdoo, the general feeling in the yards is one of skepticism. Ironically, Keramalli's Mission has thus far had a greater impact on a little-known Afro-Trinidadian Shi'i community called the Imame Zamana Brotherhood, which is located on Prince Street in Port of Spain, an area with an Afro-Trinidadian majority population. In the last chapter, I mentioned a group of Afro-Trinidadian Muslims that had brought out a counter-*Hosay* procession in 1992; authorities halted them because they had no parade permit. The group was incorrectly identified by the press as belonging to coup leader Abu Bakr's faction, but they were actually Shi'ah who converted from Sunni Islam around the time of the Iranian Revolution. That group is located in the remote countryside and is currently less visible in St. James. The Imame Zamana, however, has been much more visible in the years since the Bilal Mission has been present on the island. According to Brother Hasan, who owns a tire repair shop underneath this group's center, many members of the congregation were originally Catholics who converted first to Sunni Islam during the Black Power Movement in the 1970s but then became inspired by Shi'ism during the Islamic Revolution in Iran.[12] Brother Hasan and Keramalli estimate that there are approximately three hundred people in the congregation, which may well outnumber the Indo-Shi'i population.

Because of ethnic mistrust, underlying racial tension, politics, and prejudices, the Indo-Trinidadian Shi'ah and the Afro-Trinidadian Shi'ah have been cautious to engage in dialogue with each other. Stereotypically, some within the Indic-community consider the Imame Zamana to be too fanatical and revolutionary, wrongly believing them to be sympathetic to the radical politics of Abu Bakr. Therefore they have never really had a strong presence during *Hosay* up until now. In the past, they have had their own private Muharram observance on the tenth, from 10 a.m. until 3 p.m., which has included prayer, *mātam*, and dirge singing, followed by a communal meal. In addition, their practice is much stricter than the Indo-Trinidadian form. They consume only *ḥalāl* foods, pray five times per day, and the female members wear veils, which is why some of the more liberal practitioners of *Hosay* view them as being fanatics. They are misunderstood by the general public because they have kept a very low profile since their conversion in the late seventies. Now, however, inspired by Keramalli's Mission, they are beginning to be more assertive and are visible on the streets, as I note below, when I describe the 1997 *Hosay* processions.

All these factors have forced *Hosay* participants to become more reflexive about their practices. Hindus who participate, for example, are now even questioning whether *Hosay* was ever Islamic, or even should be. Some assert that there are just as many Hindu elements in the rituals as there are Islamic ones. Needless to say, this has revived and intensified the kinds of debates discussed in the last chapter over religion versus culture. But now there is more contention than ever within the yards, and opinions are heated.[13]

Without question, the infiltration of the Bilal Mission has had the greatest impact on the observances in many years. Many practitioners outside the elite circle that embraces the Mission believe that outsiders have no right to tell them how to perform their own tradition. "I don't like people telling me what I should do," one said, while another *tadjah* builder said that he is carrying on the tradition as he understands it and finds it offensive when others tell him how to do it. One tactic used by the Mission to gain the confidence of the yards is to donate money to the organizing committee for redistribution to the yards. One builder refuses to accept the money, but others do, which causes further divisiveness between the yards, setting apart those people who accept donations from those who do not.

The presence of the Mission has affected the evening prayers as well. Kermalli has been invited to lead the prayers at Cocorite, but the others still prefer to employ itinerant *imam*s. Hamdoo seems to be making an exerted effort to spread the customary meanings of the ritual objects used on the *chowk*s. Each evening he visits a different yard and gives a sermon after the prayers to explain the Indian meanings of the various customs practiced during *Hosay*. Although sympathetic to the Mission, he stresses that yard members should continue to practice the customs of their ancestors. In acknowledging both interpretations as valid and complementary, he strives for a middle ground between the missionaries and the practitioners. In so doing, Hamdoo continues his role as a culture broker mediating disputes between the opposing camps, just as he previously did between the Sunni and the Shiʻiah. The difference is that now he must negotiate within the Shiʻi congregation to reach a resolution that balances scriptural authority and customary practice. Meanwhile, Keramalli is attempting to convince the participants to wear homogeneous black clothing to be like the other observers all over the world. Gobi, the new head of the organizing committee, confided in me that he thinks it is worth a try and that everyone should stop and pray in front of the St. James mosque during the processions. Of course, drummers are reluctant to do this because they spend all the time leading up to the mosque working up momentum for the clashes. Again, there is disagreement.

Throughout the days of preparation that May, the Mission's presence dominated the discourse in the *imambaras*. Everyone had an opinion, whether pro or con. So when Flag Night was upon us on May 15, there was tension in the air. The Bis-Ali yard members were nervous because it was their first time out on the road. Because they are new, they will have to wait on the corner of Bournes Road until all the other *tadjah*s pass. Bis-Ali was to emerge behind Balma at the rear. Flag Night got off to a confusing start because the *imam* was accompanied by Keramalli, who was with him to give sermons after the prayers in each yard. Because Keramalli's sermon took an extra thirty minutes in each yard, the pair did not arrive at Bis-Ali's compound until after 10 p.m. By the time they were ready to move, Ghulam Hussein's members were already on the road. At the other end of Western Main Road, Balma pulled out at about 11 p.m. but did not move from its spot for more than an hour. Balma's *tadjah* just sat there, refusing to move. By midnight Balma still had not passed, so Gobi and Hamdoo gave Noble permission to move onto the road. Not wishing to cause a confrontation, however, Bis-Ali waited until Balma finally passed at 1:30 a.m. Clearly there was some animosity being displayed, and the terse confusion set the tone for the remainder of the evening's procession, when Balma again refused to move at the turnaround. Balma's unexpected tactic forced Bis-Ali to turn around early, putting us back in the yard thirty minutes before the others.

The tension and confusion of the first night gave way to more cooperation on Small *Hosay* Night. Balma kept apace, and everyone was on the road at the usual time, but the crowds were small. Things became even more relaxed on Big *Hosay* Night on the surface, but personal animosities fueled greater competition. Keramalli visited the Bis-Ali yard wearing a traditional long, flowing black robe and tried to convince yard members that they too should don the garment for the tenth. In typical Trini fashion, one yard member responded, "I can't beat the drum if I'm wearing that!" The verbal jest was a pleasant show of defiance against adopting ways alien to local tradition. Scripture may be authoritative, but tradition is conservative. Rebuked by yard members, Keramalli took solace in his more enthusiastic Afro-Trinidadian congregation, which had earlier completed a four-mile procession from Port of Spain to St. James. Now the Imame Zamana members were seated on the ground in a small park adjacent to the St. James police station. Also dressed in black, they eagerly awaited his sermon. Later, members of the congregation performed *mātam* as the *tadjah*s passed, but not one member of the Afro-Trinidadian congregation joined in the Indo-Trinidadian procession.[14]

Crowds on this night were nominally large, but the general consensus was that the audiences are shrinking in size. Many blame this on the interventions taking place. Some revelers in the crowd with whom I spoke claimed that it was not fun anymore now that they were being requested to respect the religious nature of the event and not jump up. Many of the flyers handed out by the Mission could be seen strewn about on the road, but some people who accepted them were reading what the Mission had to say. When all was said and done, the talk in the Bis-Ali yard was that this year's *Hosay* was successful, despite the tension and competition on the streets, especially between Balma and Bis-Ali.

The 1997 experience was a highly personal and subjective one for me. I labored day and night to make *Hosay* a success, but the long hours of work tired me, as they did the other *Hosay* members. I better understand now what *Hosay* means because I have participated fully in it. I was presented with a small *tassa* drum of my own and told repeatedly that I was now one of the guys. Now I know on an experiential level what yard allegiance means, and I know what Ibrahim meant when he said that the drums tell a story so large that one cannot explain it or even begin to describe it accurately. Articulating the meaning is difficult because participation is so deeply personal and intense. The whole story of *Hosay*, therefore, cannot be told in its entirety. What I have attempted in this book is to situate the observance in its broader historical and ethnographic context to make sense of a phenomenon that bewilders so many.

Ten years have passed since I first began to work on the topic of this book. The 1997 *Hosay* made me feel somewhat melancholy and nostalgic for the good old days. I was not alone in this feeling. Numerous others longed for a *Hosay* of the past. Hamdoo, for example, lamented that earlier *tadjah*s were prettier, and Aloh remarked that "we need to return to the past." But those days seem to be gone forever, and change is in the air. Although my experience is relatively brief compared to those who have grown up in the tradition, I have seen small boys turn into men and become full participants. I have seen new children born into the yards, and I have seen some dramatic changes over the past few years that will more than likely only accelerate in the coming decades. Perhaps it is because of the external pressures to conform to globally construed normative practices that participants now yearn for the past. In the face of transnational forces that will inevitably shape the rituals in the future, participants may feel the need to revitalize the observance based on a search for missing elements located in the past. Aloh was firm on this point: "We have to obey the rules," by which he meant that as the older, more pious generation passes, the younger practitioners are no longer adhering strictly to Indic custom and tradition. Of course, it should by now be clear that any pure Indic past is an impossibility, but the fact that older participants yearn for this imagined past reconfirms that the cultural struggle for interpretive rights continues to the present day.

Concluding Thoughts

The future shape of *Hosay* hangs in the balance. As I was making my rounds to say good-bye to all of my friends in St. James, I ran into Gobi at the Bis-Ali yard, my last stop. He coerced me into going with him to have a talk at his home. As head of the organizing committee, he has big plans for *Hosay*. He would like to see it expand even more and would like to see Aloh Dookuwa, long since retired, start building again. He thinks that the larger the event becomes, the more political and cultural support he could muster for it. He wants to "build things up." He also thinks that the cultural center would be a good idea. That way the older generation could teach the younger ones to beat drums and build *tadjah*s in a more formal environment. He is also interested in learning more about the history and meaning of *Hosay*, but he has very strong, dichotomous views on the subject. For him, something is either right or wrong. For example, the fact that Bay Road places only two wick lamps on the *chowk* and Bis-Ali has five is an incongruity to him. Either one has to be wrong and the other right, or both are wrong. He is not willing to concede that both can be correct. With a more intensified search for absolute truth, there is now little room for relative truths and multiple meanings. If Gobi has his way, standardization will be inevitable, which would impinge upon artistic creativity. It is very unlikely, however, that his voice alone can sway the opinions and practices of yard members. What his leadership does do, however, is create yet one more set of contemporary voices contributing to the contentious debate over *Hosay* that has existed ever since the observance began on the island.

Now that there has been a significant amount of external awareness

created by foreign researchers and Shi'i missionaries, internal participants are becoming more self-conscious and reflexive about the way they
perform *Hosay*. They are asking questions about authenticity that have
never been raised before in such a vocal and forceful manner. What the
current scenario suggests is a very strong case for the dynamics of folk
religion in the textbook sense of the term, that is, a local form of religion
in creative tension with the official version.[15] As the official version
gradually begins to take root in St. James, there could be a trend to conform to textual practice and adopt foreign models that would be more in
keeping with a transnational form of Shi'ism mandated by foreign clerics
and oriented around canonical rules. The broader implication is that
strict adherence to orthodox practices would leave less interpretive room
for the further development of local customs. On the other hand, there
could be a resurgence of defiance, an old Muharram theme that is already being voiced by many yard members.

We have seen in Chapter 2 that popular interpretation and practice
was not always accepted by Shi'i clerics in Iran, Lebanon, and Syria,
which led to hermeneutic tension, but not the elimination of practices
performed by the masses. There is therefore no reason to take an alarmist
position and assume that a similar heterogeneous situation of ongoing
contention could not continue in Trinidad. Simply stated, there could
emerge the kind of passive attitude that was customary in the past that
would advocate a refrain from rhetoric but accommodate new trends,
such as allowing the Afro-Trinidadian Shi'i congregation to hold its own
sermons and conduct its own processions as a parallel congregation. The
latter scenario bears strong resemblance to the nineteenth-century example from Bombay discussed in Chapter 3, where we saw the development of two independent *muharram*s: one popularly oriented around the
public and transcommunal processions of the model cenotaphs and the
other privately confined to an elite Shi'i intelligentsia. There it was a case
of Indian (public, transcommunal) versus Persian (private, Shi'i). Now in
Trinidad it is a case of predominantly Indo-Trinidadian expression (both
private and public, but also transcommunal) versus Afro-Trinidadian expression (private, but now becoming public, Shi'i).

In this regard, though, Gobi points out that there is suspicion and
hesitation on both sides to accept the other. The island's Afro-Shi'ah of
Prince Street are wary of being incorporated into the St. James model
because they feel discriminated against. They are also cautious for fear of
being even more confused with Abu Bakr's radical band than they already are.[16] On the other hand, the many Indian *Hosay* participants are
skeptical of the Afro-Shi'ah because they fear that "they are up to no
good and harboring criminal elements from that part of town," as one

person put it. Much of the fear is unsubstantiated, in my opinion, for there is no evidence to suggest the need for such suspicion.[17] Old racial animosities and ethnic stereotypes die hard.

Much of the Indian paranoia has to do with Abu Bakr's legacy, which leads some to think that all Afro-Muslims are fanatics. A more passive Indo-Trinidadian attitude is manifest in quieter statements by some, such as "We don't associate with them" or "We keep our distance from them." Many Afro-Trinidadians who are not Muslims freely mingle and help in the yards, however, partly because they are members of the extended *Hosay* family and conform to tradition, which is defined by the yard. In other words, they pose no threat because they grew up in the tradition and have proven themselves trustworthy and respectful of Indic customs. Here again arises the issue of culture/ethnicity versus religion/race, the rhetoric that suggests the St. James *Hosay* maintains and propagates something Indian, not (just) Shi'i or Islamic. Gobi concedes that the St. James *Hosay* is "our contribution to the Indian culture in Trinidad." He goes on: "Whereas other areas, such as the sugar or rice belts, are more heavily populated by Indians, they contribute to other aspects of Indian culture. But this 'Coolie Town,' is famous for *Hosay*, and that is our only contribution to local Indian culture."[18] *Hosay*, in other words, is an icon of ethnicity for him. His assessment is a fairly typical justification, coming from a Hindu participant.

As for the Shi'ah, the added prestige and support, both economic and ideological, afforded by foreign missionaries provides a feeling of empowerment to an embattled elite that believes it has been silent too long. What this means, however, is that as the esoteric knowledge nurtured by the Shi'ah all these years becomes public knowledge through lectures, sermons, and pamphlets, the private/public distinction could gradually dissolve into a relatively meaningless dichotomy. As a result, there would no longer be a need to practice dissimulation. Perhaps this is what the intellectuals siding with the Mission crave: legitimacy, power, and authority. Yet where does that leave the average participant who places more authority on the power of custom and tradition? Clearly there is resistance within the yards, and the dynamic process of questioning authority could possibly continue through healthy dialogue, leading to ever more creative responses. My assessment deviates very little from Thaiss's preliminary musings on *Hosay*'s authenticity in 1994, which he wrote just prior to the missionary arrival in Trinidad. Commenting on Brackette Williams's discussion of cultural ownership in Guyana, he argues that authenticity and multivocality are central issues. He rhetorically asks, If various groups participate and provide idiosyncratic meanings, do they not have just as much right to the rituals as the organizers and sponsors?

Can truth be fixed? Thaiss indicates that "In a very real sense the *Hosay* is an articulation of social and cultural differences and similarities and in the discursive process a ritual and social world is given meaning; but a meaning which is always contestable and open to re-articulations. It is a never-ending process of negotiation. What it was in India, it is not today; and what it is today, it will not be tomorrow, although in that process various participants try to fix its meaning to reflect their view of the world."[19]

Thaiss here points to the emergent quality of culture in the making, with which I certainly agree. The phrase *culture in the making* indicates a mutual appropriation of practices from the various parties involved that results in a shared cultural repertory. I have already suggested at the end of the last chapter that it would be speculative at best to attempt to attribute specific practices definitively to one community or another at this late point in the rite's development. It is precisely because of the pattern of mutual appropriation that we have seen unfolding during the course of this study that we must see Trinidadian culture, here reflected in *Hosay*, as an emergent phenomenon continuously constructed in a dialogical fashion by all communities inhabiting the island. Similar to a house that is never completed, the Republic of Trinidad and Tobago's citizens individually contribute to the process of creating an emerging national culture.

Culture in the making in diasporic contexts is what I alluded to earlier in this study as a conversation of cultures. One could also add that the formulation of diasporic consciousness is a collision of cultures, as I did at the very outset by quoting James Clifford's poignant observation.[20] For mutual appropriation is not always equal in distribution, which causes not only contentious debate but also conflict and resistance, as we have seen repeatedly throughout our long journey from Karbala to Caroni. The issues of intellectual property rights and whose opinions and interpretations matter most in the battle for cultural autonomy are heavily influenced by power relationships.[21] Who is in a position to determine what is real or not? In the past, the answer to this question was provided by influential members of society who could sway government opinion in their favor, and this resulted in severe consequences for the survival of *Hosay* elsewhere in the Caribbean. The issue of ownership must be raised again today in Trinidad because it is the central question that has to be debated even more sharply now that a fairly influential transnational intervention has occurred, one that is not likely to be a flash in the pan.

I remain optimistic, however, that the resilience of local actors is vital enough to allow for innovation and change in response to the new global challenges that confront their small *Hosay* community, just as it has been in the past.[22] This is not to deny, however, that religious, cultural, ethnic, and racial groups will continue to lobby for their own specific agendas as the ongoing interrogation about the politics of representation and who owns *Hosay* continues into the uncharted waters of future generations.

Notes

Introduction

1. Van Gennep (1961); Turner (1977).
2. Turner (1977): 95. I am aware that Turner's concept is inadequate to explain social relationships during periods of liminality because of his emphasis on egalitarianism resulting from communitas. See, for example, Sallnow (1981). Indeed, I want to argue that during Muharram differences in status are emphasized and dramatically played out. Nonetheless, his characterization of liminality suits my purposes nicely here.
3. On this point, see Waugh (1977).
4. See Fischer (1980).
5. See Jameson (1981).
6. Kumar (1988): 211–17 provides an earlier description of the social role of the rite in this city.
7. Sadiq (1964): 145–63 discusses the importance of this genre's performance.
8. See the entry on *muḥarram* in the *Shorter Encyclopedia of Islam* (1965): 409–10.
9. For a trenchant critique, see Baird (1971). See also my comments in Korom (2000): 25–26.
10. *OED* (1971.2:3): 210
11. Howard and Mageo (1996): 4; Thomas (1992).
12. Howard and Mageo (1996): 4.
13. For example, Bettelheim and Nunley (1988).
14. See Bakhtin (1984).
15. Bateson (1958): 230–31.
16. Robertson (1995).
17. See Singer (1972). For an exemplary study employing Singer's notion of cultural performance as a strategy for placing public rituals in the contemporary sociopolitical contexts in which they are enacted, see Guss's (2000) recent volume on the festive state in Venezuela.
18. These two indigenous conceptual categories of analysis have broader application to spatial arrangements as well. For example, citing the Islamic architectural historian Hakim, Geertz ([1995]: 194, n. 162) argues for the different social uses of inner and outer space in the Islamic world.
19. Langacker (1977); Bickerton (1980): 112.

20. Jourdan (1991): 202.

21. See Gibson (2001). Although Gibson argues against the standard view of decreolization, his findings are still consonant with my own in that neither of us sees the evidence to suggest that there is a movement toward standardization in the direction of the dominant culture.

22. See LePage and Tabouret-Keller (1985). Their multidimensional model has received some criticism, however, for being too unconstrained, which implies that every individual has the absolute freedom to choose. See Gibson (2001): 216–21. I am well aware that economic and political constraints impinge upon free will. Such constraints thus lead to the kinds of contested discourses that I discuss throughout this book.

23. For a useful overview of the debate, see Vertovec (1991).

24. Hall (1993): 362.

25. On imaginary homelands, see Anderson (1991).

26. A number of scholars have used Connor's (1986) broad definition of anyone living outside of their homeland to define diaspora. Safran (1991): 83 has suggested that we extend the notion to include any group that retains "a collective memory, vision, or myth about their original homeland." This is certainly true of Indo-Trinidadians. For discussions, see Korom (2000) and Baumann (2000).

27. For a recent overview of studies on cultural hybridization, see Kapchan and Strong (1999): 239–53.

28. Mitchell (1997): 533 suggests that the term's fuzzy contours "are attractive because of the inherent instability" associated with them. She goes on to state that the term is even more appealing than "modernist paradigms" or "either/or frameworks," which seemingly places hybridity in a position to offer scholars "a satisfyingly unstable and ambivalent alternative." See also Young (1995): 27, where he writes that "There is no single, or correct, concept of hybridity; it changes as it repeats, but it also repeats as it changes."

29. Young (1995). See also Werbner (2001), who argues that hybridity theory does not account for indigenous forms of transgression and the critical reflexivity necessary for resisting the impositions of hegemonic forces.

30. See Bhabha (1994): 193.

31. For example, see Anzaldúa (1987): 81.

32. Both are, in the senses described above, forms of what Carolyn Cooper (1995) calls (h)ideology.

33. For a masterful study of creolization, see Brathwaite (1971). The first linguist, to my knowledge, who used hybridization with reference to creolization, however, was Whinnon (1971). The term's journey from biology to cultural studies via linguistics has recently been documented historically and conceptually by Stross (1999).

34. Hannerz (1987): 551. See also Drummond (1980).

35. On the s/x factor, see Jansen (1959). On taqqīyah, see Goldziher (1906) and Kohlberg (1975).

36. For critical histories of the development of pidgin and creole studies in anthropological linguistics, see Bickerton (1976) and Jourdan (1991).

37. On the dynamism of convergence, see Hymes (1971) as well as Gumperz and Wilson (1971). Further, we must acknowledge that judging a creole as less complex or inferior to the dominant form is based on power relationships. See

DeCamp (1971): 16, where he writes, "A creole is inferior to its corresponding language only in social status." See also Hall (1966): 132–35.

38. See Bishop and Korom (1998).

39. See Davis's (1986) work on parades in Philadelphia.

40. Abrahams (1982): 161.

41. See Canclini (1995): 200ff.

42. On the *bricoleur*, see Lévi-Strauss (1966): 17. On the need for multisited ethnographies, see Marcus (1998).

43. See Rabinow (1986).

Chapter 1

1. Mottahedeh (1986): 141.

2. See the *New York Times Magazine* (February 15, 1987): 39. See also Chelkowski (1987b): 559–60. Persian and Arabic sources vary on the number of martyrs killed at Karbala, but popular tradition favors 72; see Ayoub (1978): 105. The dating used in this chapter refers to the Islamic calendar (A.H.), followed by corresponding Gregorian dates (C.E.).

3. For more on visual propaganda in Iran, see Chelkowski (1989).

4. See Fischer (1980): 13, who writes that "Its focus is on the emotionally potent theme of corrupt and oppressive tyranny repeatedly overcoming (in this world) the steadfast dedication to pure truth; hence its ever-present, latent, political potential to frame or clothe contemporary discontents."

5. Abrahams, personal communication, 1986.

6. Fischer (1980): 21.

7. See Ameed (1974).

8. Ayoub (1978): 148

9. Canetti (1978): 153.

10. The term is inspired by Hjortshoj (1977).

11. Chelkowski (1986b): 209.

12. Ayoub (1978): 145.

13. This popular slogan, attributed to the sixth *imām*, was revived and propagated in the 1960s at the outset of the Iranian Islamic Revolution by Ali Shari'ati (1933–77). For a volume of his lectures and speeches, see Algar (1979). On *muḥarram* and revolution, see Chelkowski and Dabashi (1999).

14. Kippenberg (1984): 126–27.

15. See Connor (1988): 12.

16. For example, see Chelkowski's (1986b) survey.

17. Scott (1990).

18. For the full texts of both speeches, see Algar (1981): 174–80.

19. Algar (1981): 242.

20. Lincoln (1989): 35–36.

21. Ibid., 36.

22. Algar (1981): 131. Preachers and poets of the historical tragedy should "firmly fix the issue of government in their minds."

23. I am grateful to Peter Chelkowski for providing me with this point.

24. The political uses have been noted elsewhere. Norton and Safa (2000): 26, with reference to southern Lebanon, point out that the commemoration is "not merely grassroots practice of religion, it is also a political event, an opportunity

for the rivals Amal and Hizbollah to show their strength and demonstrate their solidarity."

25. The term is based on the Hebrew word *'asor* and is mentioned in Leviticus 16:29. See the entry on *'āshūrā'* in Wensinck and Kramer (1941): 59–60.

26. Sunni sources cite various interpretations from the Old Testament for this. The tenth day of Muharram is believed to be the day that Noah left the ark and also the day that Moses led the Israelites out of Egypt. See Goldziher (1894): 82–84. Ayoub (1987): 31–32 recounts that Noah's ark was disrupted by turbulent waters as it floated over Karbala at the spot where Husayn would later be slain. Noah wept and then cursed the murderers, after which the ark safely came to rest on the mountain on *'āshūrā'*.

27. The Twelvers, known as *Imāmīyah* or *Ithnā 'Asharīyah*, place the greatest emphasis on the succession of the twelve *imāms*; hence they have developed the most elaborate hagiographic tradition to elevate Husayn's status. It is largely their views that I present below.

28. Muir (1963): 5. At the time of Muhammad's death, Fatimah was his only surviving child.

29. See Ayoub (1978): 50.

30. Two other caliphs ruled during the intervening period between Abu Bakr's death in 634 C.E. and Ali's election in 656 C.E. These were Umar and Uthman. For details, see Madelung's (1997) masterful account.

31. The Kharijites were not just rebelling against Ali, for they also attempted to assassinate Muawiyah on the same day. Some speculate that the real reason for Ali's assassination was revenge for those Kharijites slain by him at the "massacre" of Nahrawan. See Williams (1987): 288–90.

32. Muir (1898): 303.

33. Hasan lived in Medina for eight more years and died at the age of forty-five in 49 A.H., when he was supposedly poisoned by one of his wives.

34. Geertz (1968) has noted this distinction in his intrinsicalist/contractualist definition of Islamic leadership. Recently, however, Madelung (1997) has forced us to rethink this dichotomy.

35. Ayoub (1978): 94.

36. Muir (1898): 322; Ayoub (1978): 95.

37. Ayoub (1978): 95.

38. Ibn Ziyad is reviled as the epitome of evil in popular Shi'i tradition because of his supposed illegitimate birth and his ruthless exterior. See Ayoub (1978): 100ff.

39. Ayoub (1978): 109 notes that "Sending Ibn Sa'd against Ḥusayn was no doubt a political tactic aimed at placing the blame for Ḥusayn's death squarely on the shoulders of one of the tribe of Quraysh"—that is, within the Prophet's own fold. This would absolve Ibn Ziyad of any wrongdoing if members of the House of the Prophet were killed.

40. Ayoub (1978): 110.

41. Ibid.

42. Ibid., 117.

43. Ibid., 114.

44. One source notes that even Husayn's infant son Ali Asghar, who was dying of thirst, was shot through the neck by an arrow while Husayn, holding the child, asked the enemy for a drink to save the baby's life.

45. In Iran and India, it is popularly held that Hasan's last request was to have his own son Qasim married to Husayn's daughter Fatimah Kubra. Narratives relate that Husayn performed the wedding ceremony after the initial parley on the morning of the tenth. On the importance of Qasim's wedding in Iran and India, see Humayuni (1979) and Pinault (1992): 131–36.

46. See Muir (1898): 327. The only male member to survive was Husayn's youthful son Ali Zayn al-Abidin, who was thought to be dying of fever but survived to become the fourth *imām*.

47. Ayoub (1978): 118, citing the historian Tabari, reports that Husayn's body was later found with thirty-three spear wounds and thirty-four sword slashes.

48. Ayoub (1978): 119.

49. Ibid.

50. Tales of the severed head's luminous and miraculous powers are preserved in Persian and Arabic hagiography. On severed heads in the Indo-European tradition, see Nagy (1990).

51. Fischer (1980): 20.

52. See Amir-Moezzi (1994).

53. Ayoub (1978): 54.

54. Ibid. The image of light is a pervasive theme in Islamic mysticism. See, for example, Corbin (1978) and Rubin (1975).

55. Nasr (1966): 161.

56. On *ta'vil* in Shi'ism, see Pinault (1992): 27–46.

57. This refers to the *da'irat al-wilāyah*, a cycle of initiation that was inaugurated at the beginning of time and issues through the Prophet into the phenomenal world. See Nasr (1966): 161.

58. Nasr (1966): 162.

59. Ayoub (1978): 68.

60. Ibid., 109.

61. Ibid., 23–52.

62. This final vindication will occur with the return of the Mahdi, the twelfth and last *imām* who will return from occultation to take revenge for Husayn's cruel murder.

63. Ayoub (1978): 85, citing Ibn Shahrashub.

64. The term comes from a saying of the Prophet in which he states that "whoever makes himself resemble a group is in the category of that group." In this sense, the concept unites practitioners by serving as a vehicle for common experience through self-realization, transforming spectators into participants performing as a global community, as Baktash (1979): 95–120 has argued.

65. Baktash (1979): 101.

66. Quotes are from Pelly (1879.2): 100–101, 343, 346, and 347 respectively. *Hawd al-kawthar* is the body of water in Paradise that is the source of eternal life. See Ayoub (1978): 206.

67. See Nakash (1994): 168–83 and Fernea (1969): 216–50.

68. Fernea (1969): 230.

69. White (1987).

70. See Chelkowski (1986a). The tradition of honoring Husayn during private commemorative services *(majālis al-'azā')* is much older, however, as is the public remembrance led by a professional mourner *(na'ih)*. See Ayoub (1978): 153.

Chapter 2

1. As cited in Nakash (1993): 165.

2. Fernea (1969): 241–42.

3. See Nakash (1993).

4. The term is derived from the Arabic verbal noun *'azīya*, showing condolence, and is mentioned in all schools of Islamic jurisprudence in connection with public observances for the dead, in which Muslims "are exhorted to condole with the relatives." See the entry on *ta'zīya* in the *Shorter Encyclopedia of Islam* (1965): 590–91.

5. Chelkowski (1979): 9.

6. See Wirth (1979): 32–39. There are, however, other forms of European drama performed in Iran. See Asgar (1963): 146.

7. For example, see Azarpay (1975) and (1981): 128–32, Benveniste (1932): 245–93, Eerdmans (1894), Jamasp-Asana (1897), Monchi-Zadeh (1981): 129, Tavadia (1956): 135–37, and Yarshater (1978).

8. As cited in Azarpay (1981): 129.

9. For the most recent assessment, see Nakash (1993).

10. Many hold that Iraq already had a firmly embedded tradition of divine hereditary kingship in pre-Islamic times. Madelung (1997), however, has provided compelling evidence to complicate this point of view.

11. I am grateful to Peter Chelkowski for this point.

12. Ayoub (1978): 152. Moreover, he goes on, popular tradition holds that women in the house of Yazid joined the survivors of Husayn's party in seven days of lamentation. Later, as the survivors were being escorted back to Medina, it is said that they made a pilgrimage to the site of Husayn's burial forty days after his death, which would mark the beginning of the custom of the fortieth-day pilgrimage *(zīyārat al-arba'īn)*. As Ayoub notes, however, this latter belief is historically questionable. See Ayoub (1978): 278, n. 32.

13. Ayoub (1978): 152.

14. Ibid., 153.

15. Nakash (1993): 169.

16. Chelkowski (1979): 3.

17. Ibid.

18. Lincoln (1989): 35.

19. Chelkowski (1979): 3.

20. Kashifi is said to have finished his book in 908 A.H./1502 C.E. See Mahdjoub (1988): 74.

21. Waseem (1995): 15.

22. See Chelkowski (1987b): 220.

23. Cited in Schimmel (1986): 29. See also Browne (1953): 180–81.

24. Unvala (1927): 86.

25. On the flagellation, see Ende (1978).

26. See Chelkowski (1979): 4. Beeman (1981): 286–87 writes, "The principal 'sympathetic' characters chant their parts in lines of elegant verse to traditional classical Persian musical modes, while the 'villainous' characters declaim their lines in exaggerated speech contours."

27. Pelly (1879). The martyrs of Karbala are often compared to Joseph,

"leaving their bloodied cloaks 'of many colors' (bodies) behind while they go on to a world of plenty"; Fischer (1980): 21.

28. Litten (1929).

29. Ayoub (1978): 231.

30. Ibid., 154.

31. See Chelkowski (1979): 4–6 and (1988); van Vloten (1892): 107.

32. See, for instance, Ameed (1974).

33. See Beeman (1981): 290. In reality, the Shah's move was motivated by the fear that these powerful public displays could be easily converted into massive political demonstrations.

34. On *ta'ziyeh* and social change, see the seminal works of Thaiss (1971, 1972a, 1972b, 1973, and 1978). Aspects of change can be observed in the incorporation of new characters into the performance as well as in shifts in dialogue to accommodate new religious and political issues. For example, British ambassadors sporting pith helmets were introduced previously into the drama and can still be seen today.

35. On *dasteh* as theater, see Haery (1982): 33–41.

36. See Steingass (1973): 525.

37. See Chelkowski (1985): 24–26.

38. Caron (1975): 4.

39. Fischer (1980): 170.

40. Canetti (1978): 150–51. Also cited in Chelkowski (1985): 27.

41. Caron (1975): 5.

42. As quoted in Haery (1982): 35.

43. Again, I have to thank Peter Chelkowski for this observation.

44. Fischer (1980): 262–63.

45. See Cejpek (1968): 683.

46. Beeman (1981): 289–90.

47. See Ende (1978). Compare with Adam (2001).

48. Moreover, the text still circulates in India. Pinault (2001): 30–31 points out that the text is being used currently by Shi'i scholars in Ladakh to reform the rite's bloodier side.

49. Thaiss (1971): 192–93.

50. For brief accounts of the *nakhl* in Iran, see Chelkowski (1985): 24 and van Vloten (1892): 109.

51. Fischer (1980): 170–80 indicates that Yazd had two *nakhl*s in the late 1970s.

52. Chelkowski, personal communication, 1993.

53. According to Professor Ali Mizarchi, the structure is called a *nakhl* all year long except on the day of '*āshūrā*'. When the structure is actually being moved, it is referred to as a *naql*. Steingass (1973): 1420 notes that the word can also mean "acting" or "story," which suggests the object's movement to be a mimetic narrative. Fischer (1980): 170–71 prefers *naql* rather than *nakhl*, as does Momen (1985): figures 43, 44, 45. I am indebted to Peter Chelkowski, personal communication, 1993, for Mizarchi's subtle interpretation.

54. Browne (1953): 176.

55. Ayoub (1978): 169.

56. Cowan (1976): 636.

57. Fischer (1980): 171.

58. Browne (1953): 182.

59. Ibid., 184–85.

60. Beeman (1981): 304. Caron (1975): 4 adds, "There was no lack of humour in this very vivid theatrical art, the tense atmosphere being relieved at suitable moments by comic interludes and the appearance of buffoons." See also Haery (1982): 46–51.

61. Beeman (1981): 304.

62. Fischer and Abedi (1990): 14.

63. Ibid.

64. Ibid., 14–15.

65. Norton and Safa (2000): 26 confirm this reversal for southern Lebanon as well, when they write that "despite the heavy stench of blood there was a carnival-like atmosphere."

66. Norton and Safa (2000): 26.

67. Reza (1994): 10.

Chapter 3

1. Saiyid (1981): 113. Pinault (2001) was the first to undertake a comparative study of *muḥarram* in India.

2. Masselos (1982): 64.

3. Naqvi (n.d.): 128 identifies a class of texts called *Tazk-e Taimuri* but fails to locate the relevant passages in any of them to account for the legend.

4. Schubel (1993): 110. The assertion that Timur converted to Shi'ism is pious speculation. Momen (1985): 98 points out, however, that he retained Shi'i vassals and favored the descendants of Ali even at times when they revolted against him.

5. de Tassy (1995): 33.

6. See Cole (1988): 115–17.

7. Saiyid (1981): 115.

8. The Mughals, although largely champions of Sunni Islam, "were not without Shi'i influences," according to Momen (1985): 122. He concludes that "During the whole of the Mughal period, the court was divided into two factions, Irāni, which was in effect the Shi'i faction, and Tūrāni, which was the Sunni faction."

9. Founded by a governor of the Mughal emperor, the principality enjoyed sovereign status as a kingdom under the British from 1819 to 1856.

10. Smaller Shi'i dynasties in the Deccan, south India, that nurtured *muḥarram* are the Adil Shahs (1489–1686), Nizam Shahs (1490–1599), and Qutb Shahs (1512–1687). The Chaks of Kashmir in northernmost India ruled less than three decades (1561–85).

11. Hasan (1990): 210–11. Halm (1991): 137, however, indicates that "The number of Indian Twelver Shiites is difficult to assess because, on the one hand, many practice *taqiyya* in the Sunni environment and, on the other hand, the Muḥarram rites are even partly observed by the Sunnis." For population statistics, see Momen (1985): 277–78.

12. Ayoub (1978): 151.

13. See, for example, Egnor (1986) and Blackburn (1985) respectively.

14. See Korom (1999b).

15. Hollister (1953): 177.

16. Vedantam (1975): 5.

17. See Freitag (1984): 132–52.

18. As quoted in Waseem (1995): 21.

19. For an exception, see Masselos (1976): 81 and (1982): 52.

20. The day varies because in some places the *ta'zīyah*s are not buried until the twelfth, which is also referred to as *zīyārat* (pilgrimage). See Sharīf (1975): 184.

21. See Qureshi (1972 and 1981).

22. For Urdu, see Karrar (1986), Naim (1983), and Sadiq (1964); for Sindhi, see Schimmel (1979); for Bengali, see Sāklāyen (1969) and Dunham (1997); for Balti, see Sagaster (1993): 309.

23. Naim (1983): 101–2.

24. Vedantam (1975): 3.

25. This is the Urdu equivalent to *arba'īn*.

26. Fruzzetti (1981): 105 reports that in Bishnupur, West Bengal, the work commences from the first of Muharram. Saiyid (1981): 118 reports that in Fatehpur, Maharashtra, it begins on the fifth, and in Chanorba, Uttar Pradesh, it is carried on throughout the year. See also Burman (1965): 9.

27. The belief is based on a popular legend that Husayn arrives in India each year during the period of mourning. It was codified in a verse by the poet Mir Taqi Mir, in which Husayn swears an oath to restore his honor by making India *(hind)* his abode. See Cole (1988): 98.

28. Hollister (1953): 172.

29. Sharīf (1975): 163.

30. Hollister (1953): 167.

31. Sharīf (1975): 164.

32. Oman (1907): 299–300.

33. Burman (1965): 52.

34. See Jaffri (1979): 225–26; Hasnain and Husain (1988): 156. Vedantam (1975): 1, however, suggests that it was simply a titular designation for Brahmin families who organized functions associated with the rite.

35. This belief has arisen because ibn Sad, who was sent to intercept and apprehend Husayn, was from the tribe of Quraysh.

36. Burman (1965): 15–16.

37. On this issue, see Wolf (2000). Cole (1988): 115 makes a similar point in his assertion that Sunnis in eighteenth- and nineteenth-century Avadh held mourning assemblies, but without performing *mātam*.

38. See also Vedantam (1975): 4.

39. Fischer and Abedi (1990): 15.

40. Two *ta'zīyeh*s are devoted solely to the conversion of European Christians to Shi'ism. See Pelly (1879.2): 222–40, 286–302.

41. As quoted in Hasnain and Husain (1988): 152.

42. This publication also influences less formal domestic gatherings for female recitations, in which inexpensive printed pamphlets popularize and standardize verses recited by women, as Bard (2000) suggests.

43. This list was abbreviated from Burman (1965): 6, but is the same in Vedantam (1975): 20–21, with minor variations for day five.

44. Qureshi (1981): 45.

45. See the works of Hegland (1995, 1997, 1998).

46. Ali (1917): 17

47. Hasnain and Husain (1988): 156.

48. Hollister (1953): 177.

49. Cole (1988): 119. He goes on to say that "where Muslim villagers were a small minority surrounded by unbelievers, the Umayyad armies attacking Husayn came to be portrayed as Hindus."

50. For a description from the 1920s, see Sharīf (1975): 158. On the trench symbolism, see Oman (1907): 296.

51. *Bāṛā,* according to Platts (1977): 121, can be any enclosed space or cemetery. An alternate spelling in Persian is *bārah,* according to Steingass (1973): 97. In south India these shelters are known as *'ashurkhānah*s (tenth houses) or *tābūtkhānah*s (coffin houses). See Naqvi (1982).

52. See Kumar (1988): 212.

53. Sharīf (1975): 159.

54. See Vedantam (1975): 14.

55. Sharīf (1975): 166.

56. Oman (1907): 300–301. Also cited in Pinault (1992): 73, but for different purposes.

57. Platts (1977): 1067.

58. Sharīf (1975): 160.

59. Saiyid (1981): 136.

60. Sharīf (1975): 161.

61. Ali (1917): 32.

62. Hjortshoj (1977): 154.

63. As in many cultures, drumming plays an important role in acting as a catalyst for ecstasy. See Needham (1967): 606–14. Oman (1907): 302 notes that drummers known as *pūrbīya*s (easterners) from the eastern districts of the United Provinces were especially prized. Ali (1917): 50 also notes the use of kettle drums in Lucknow.

64. de Tassy (1995): 50.

65. Hjortshoj (1977): 156–57.

66. This incident is reported to have happened during the days of the Adil Shahi dynasty (1489–1686 C.E.).

67. Lemons are classified as cool foods. Because of the "heat" created by the event it is necessary to have these cooling agents on hand to maintain a healthy balance of hot and cold. If an imbalance were to occur, there would be potential danger to all in the room.

68. In other parts of India, the possession is more spontaneous, and anyone can become possessed by the groom. For the most part, the interpretation given to me by participants in Banaras is consonant with that found in Hollister (1953): 175–76. See also Sharīf (1975): 158–59.

69. Hjortshoj (1977): 161 and Jain (1970).

70. See Ayoub (1978): 34.

71. Ibid., 126.

72. On Zuljanah rituals in India, see Pinault (2001).

73. *Shahnāī* is a north Indian instrument in the oboe family that is used in almost all public rituals and rites of passage.

74. See Burman (1965): 3, 8 and Vedantam (1975): 16.

75. Sharīf (1975): 161.

76. Hasan (1997): 117.

77. It should be noted here that the evening provides a transition from one day to the next when the moon is sighted. Thus the ninth of the Gregorian calendar would become the lunar tenth at dusk.

78. Sharīf (1975): 162.

79. Ibid., 163.

80. Clive (1798): 179–81.

81. Sharīf (1975): 162.

82. I am indebted to Shakeel Hossain and Mushirul Hasan for bringing these objects to my attention.

83. I have witnessed the running phenomenon in Calcutta as well. In Banaras this might be a Hindu accretion because a running *parikrama* (circumambulation) of the city is performed annually by unmarried Hindu men.

84. See also Hollister (1953): 172.

85. In south India it is more common for the *ta'zīyah*s to be immersed in a river or tank of water. Immersion also occurs in such coastal cities as Mumbai (Bombay) and Calcutta. Elsewhere in north India, flowers are buried instead of the *ta'zīyah*s, which are later reused.

86. Sharīf (1975): 182.

87. This is the case in Lucknow as well. See Hjortshoj (1977): 177 and Burman (1965): 18.

88. Burman (1965): 37.

89. Hjortshoj (1977): 245.

90. Clive (1798): 182–84.

91. For instance, Sharīf (1975): 161.

92. Oman (1907): 299, 305.

93. On the issue of praying or playing at a Sufi shrine in Gujarat, see van der Veer (1992).

94. My summaries are based on Saiyid (1981): 113–42 and Fruzzetti (1981): 91–112 respectively. For another contemporary example of the carnivalesque in Sunni *muḥarram* performances held in Darjeeling, West Bengal, see Pinault (2001): 87–108.

95. Compare with Benson (1983): 48–51.

96. Saiyid (1981): 114.

97. Ibid., 120.

98. Ibid., 128.

99. Fruzzetti (1981): 109.

100. Hollister (1953): 177.

101. Hjortshoj (1977): 252.

102. As Masselos (1976, 1982) demonstrates for Bombay, Freitag (1988) for Kanpur, and Cole (1988): 101–249 and Hasan (1990, 1997) for Lucknow (1984), and Pandey (1989) for Banaras. Freitag (1989) synthesizes a large amount of data on the same issue for all north India.

103. Oman (1907): 298–99.

104. Clive (1798): 79–80.

105. Oman (1907): 305.

106. Pinault (1992): 76

107. See Hasnain and Husain (1988): 157–200.

108. Grandpré (1803): 178–79.

109. Sherring (1975): 191–92.

110. Ibid., 193–94.
111. Freitag (1984): 133.
112. Ibid., 135–43. Masselos (1982): 50–51, however, notes that *tabbara'* was already being performed in Bombay in the late eighteenth century, when Persian Shi'i Muslims entered the city and introduced Zuljanah processions, *mātam,* and cursing of the caliphs.
113. Masselos (1982): 52.
114. Ibid., 50–52.
115. Ibid., 57.
116. Ibid., 54.
117. Pinault (1992): 65.
118. Masselos (1982): 63.
119. Cole (1988): 118.

Chapter 4

1. As cited in Singh (1988): 42.
2. Hall (1978): 14. Hall (1978): 10–11 notes that scholars have generally given "less consideration to the 'push' factors, which influenced ex-slaves to leave the estates, and to emphasize the extent to which 'pull' factors, such as the availability of land or alternative employment, attracted the ex-slaves away from estate labor." See also Khan (1995): 101.
3. See again Hall (1978): 11 and 14, where he states, "Many of those who removed their residences from the estates continued to give estate labour, though not regularly; and many of those who remained on the estates were not to be depended on to labour there five days a week. . . . those who left did not entirely withdraw their labour and those who remained did not always give it."
4. See Wood (1968): 108. Also invaluable is Cumpston (1953).
5. Brereton (1979): 177–78. On Indian indentured labor in the Caribbean, see Kale (1998). On Trinidad specifically, see Weller (1968).
6. Brereton (1979): 178.
7. For an account of the Spanish period, see Ottley (1955). Of the 468 estates functioning during the waning years of Spanish rule, 159 were in sugarcane, while the remainder produced coffee, cotton, cocoa, and indigo. See Smith (1963): 11.
8. East Indians began arriving earlier on the French island of Bourbon (now Réunion) in 1829. The first Indians in Mauritius date from 1839, while the first in the Caribbean landed in British Guiana during 1838.
9. Wood (1968): 113 lists the total at 225, with six dying in transit. For the first voyage's passenger manifest, see Brereton (1992): 221–22, in which 211 names are included. Add to this the six deaths, and we have 217.
10. Brereton (1979): 177. See Weller (1968): 151–53 for a numerical breakdown by year.
11. Brereton (1979): 177.
12. Ibid. Smith (1963): 22. In 1907 the total population of Trinidad was 338,992, of which 102,849 were East Indians. See also Dey (1962) for overall population figures.
13. Oxaal (1968): 22.

14. Ibid.

15. Khan (1995): 34.

16. Wood (1968): 131.

17. Smith (1963): 154. More recent researchers such as Kasule (1986) also fail to mention the Shi'ah. But Crowley (1954): 208 has reported that "Up until a few years ago, a mosque in San Fernando had a plaque which read 'This is for the Shias, not for Sunnis.'"

18. Brereton (1979): 176.

19. Wood (1968): 145.

20. Hasan (1990): 210.

21. Wood (1968): 145. More recent statistical research based on the protector of emigrants records corroborates this. See the tables in Vertovec (1989): 160–66.

22. Smith (1963): xxix.

23. Wood (1968): 151. On *Hosay* in other former British island-colonies, see Beckwith (1924) for Jamaica, Mangru (1993) for Guyana, and McCarry (1993) for Mauritius, where it is called *Yamse*.

24. Wood (1968): 144.

25. Tinker (1974).

26. Brereton (1979): 180.

27. As rendered in Mahabir (1985): 45–50. The phrase "sara bara anna rogh" refers to twenty-five cents. On the theme of trickery, see Khan (1997): 131–36.

28. On Trinidadian Bhojpuri's current state, see Bhatia (1982 and 1988), Durbin (1973), Mohan (1978), and Mohan and Zador (1986).

29. Brereton (1979): 178.

30. Wood (1968): 158; Brereton (1979): 179.

31. See Brereton (1979): 179.

32. Ibid., 181.

33. On East Indian rice culture and economy in Trinidad, see Taitt (1999).

34. See de Verteuil (1989): 235–57.

35. For example, see Ehrlich (1971).

36. Brereton (1979): 182. On the decline of caste, see Schwartz (1967). On the transformation of the family, see MacDonald and MacDonald (1973) and Schwartz (1965).

37. Wood (1968): 139.

38. See Richardson (1975).

39. Khan (1995): 125.

40. For the background and history of the Canadian Presbyterian Mission, see Mount (1977) and Samaroo (1972).

41. Grant (1923): 67, 70.

42. Khan (1995) also stresses that during the premodern period there was not a strong division between Hindu and Muslim.

43. The nonsectarian public school system in Trinidad was started in 1851, but by 1870 Christian discourse was firmly implanted in the curriculum. East Indian Hindus and Muslims did not have the right to establish their own religious schools until 1949. See Smith (1963): 94. On Muslim schools in Trinidad, see MacKenzie (1989).

44. On the impact of the oil boom, see Vertovec (1990). For an account of economics and social mobility among Indo-Trinidadians, see Nevadomsky (1983).

45. Khan (1995): 134–135.

46. During the plantation period, participants spoke of "playing *Hosay*." As Bharath, an Indian indentured laborer put it, "nobody na humbug wha you doing / hosay making / barrick / estate gi money / hosay / play hosay." He goes on to say that he never participated in Carnival: "carnival nah / cyan go dat one / dat one kaper one." As rendered in Mahabir (1985): 135.

47. Brereton (1979): 184. On Morton's career in Trinidad, see Morton (1916).

48. Included in Singh (1988): 45–46

49. Wood (1968): 153.

50. The term *taʻzīyah* went through a phonetic shift from Urdu to Bhojpuri, during which /z/ became /j/, thus producing *tadjah*. Today the *tadjah* is often called *hosay*, which means that the rituals and objects have been combined into one conceptual field.

51. Grant (1923): 69–70.

52. Grant (1923): 69. De Verteuil (1989): 91 adds that from the Phillipine estate, "It spread to other estates and areas and was officially recognized by the government in 1863. Queen Victoria granted permission for *Hosay* to be celebrated in the colony, as long as there were Indian residents."

53. Wood (1968): 152.

54. Ibid., 152–53.

55. Brereton (1979): 182.

56. Wood (1968): 152–53.

57. Ibid., 153.

58. Included in Singh (1988): 43–44.

59. See Wood (1968): 152.

60. Jaywardena (1968a): 420 and also (1963).

61. My summary is based primarily on Mangru (1993): 43–58. See also Comins (1893) and Williams (1990).

62. Comins (1893): 80.

63. Ibid. Cothonay (1893): 236 also refers to *Hosay* as a fête "without a mood of sadness." Hence he negates *Hosay*'s religious authenticity. I thank Keila Diehl for bringing Cothonay to my attention.

64. On this issue, see Kale (1995).

65. Mangru (1993): 46. Here we notice again the process by which the marginal Chinese became incorporated into *Hosay*. First, they were the object of violence, then they became the instrument of violence, which ultimately led to their incorporation into the creolization process. I am grateful to Regina Bendix for this point.

66. Mangru (1993): 51.

67. Section 5 of Ordinance No. 16 of 1869, by command of J. M. Grant, government secretary, as quoted in Comins (1893): 81.

68. Comins (1893): 80–81.

69. See Mangru (1993): 52.

70. Singh (1988): 1.

71. My summary relies mainly on Ali (1976), Haraksingh (1974), Jha (1972 and 1975), Norman (1885), and Singh (1988).

72. Singh (1988): 8.

73. As rendered by Mahabir (1985): 60.

74. Singh (1988): 11.

75. De Verteuil (1989); 91. See also Ali (1976): 17.

76. Ali (1976): 16. For an insightful analysis of these Carnival-related riots, see Cowley (1996): 84–90.

77. Wood (1968): 151.

78. On the impact of the mutiny on Trinidad, see Jha (1972).

79. Norman (1885): 4.

80. There was a series of 25 strikes between 1882 and 1884 at Naparima, Tacarigua, and El Socorro: 7 in 1882, 6 in 1883, and 12 in 1884. See Jha (1972): 430.

81. Cowley (1996): 56.

82. Brereton (1979): 184.

83. See Cowley (1996): 61.

84. Singh (1988): 17; Cowley (1996): 103.

85. As quoted in de Verteuil (1989): 94 and 95 respectively. For the full petition and response, see Singh (1988): 82–83.

86. This decision was no doubt further fueled by disturbances involving East Indians at Brothers and Cedar Hill estates in Williamstown, at Perseverence and Brechin Castle in Naparima, and at Couva and El Socorro in San Juan, which culminated in police intervention on October 14, 1884, at Union Hall estate, according to a notice published in the *San Fernando Gazette* on October 18, 1884. See Ali (1976): 15.

87. De Verteuil (1989): 98.

88. Singh (1988): 18.

89. Ibid.

90. For a European eyewitness account, see Cothonay (1893): 175f. Cothonay, a missionary, then proceeded to the hospital in an attempt to convert the wounded, but like Grant, he found it useless to attempt converting the Muslims among them.

91. Singh (1988): 1–41; Wood (1968): 152.

92. On the former, see Jha (1972): 428–30 and on the latter, see Ali (1976): 16.

93. Brereton (1979): 184; Cowley (1996): 61.

94. Singh (1988): 18.

95. Kale (1995) places the disturbances and their aftermath in the broader context of imperial rule: the declining role of the Caribbean in British policymaking, the consolidation of governmental administration in India, and bourgeois agitation for various sorts of social reform in England.

96. On October 30, 1986, however, 102 years after the *Hosay* riots, a commemoration of the historical event was reenacted in San Fernando with displays of a *tadjah*, crescent moon, *panjah*, *'alam*, and a *sabīl* stand. The *Sunfest 86* flyer of the San Fernando Arts Council states that "the heroism and courage displayed then, remains a glorious landmark in the continuing struggle of the people of our country for genuine cultural sovereignty. On Oct. 25th 1986, honoring the memory of thousands who stood against cultural suppression, and inspired by the blood of martyrs, we, symbolically, complete the procession through the streets of San Fernando, marching to the thunder of the tassa drums." The reenactment was repeated in 1987. See the *Trinidad Guardian* (November 21, 1987): 14.

97. Singh (1988): 32.

98. Ibid., 31–32.

99. de Verteuil (1989): 87 notes that there seems to have been a general rule in place to assign Muslims to plantations in the north and central regions, rather than to the south.

100. Singh (1988): 32.

101. See, for instance, Mahabir (n.d.). See also Gibbons (1979): 23–28.

102. See Cowley (1996): 82–83, 92–93.

103. See Ali (1990): 4.

104. On early Afro- and Indo-Trinidadian Muslims, see Samaroo (1996).

105. Koss (1959): 151.

106. Niehoff and Niehoff (1960): 145 note stick fighting during *Hosay* in the 1950s, and Ahye (1978): 63 mentions it in Couva as late as 1967. Brereton (1992): 218 includes an early twentieth-century photograph of a turbaned man carrying a bass drum mounted on a white horse at the head of a procession. These practices, however, have not survived to any great extent into the present century.

107. Cothonay (1893): 236 mentions girls screaming loudly and beating their breasts.

108. See Appadurai (1981) on the logic of the "past as a scarce resource."

109. *Hosay* has sometimes been banned temporarily in some minor locations on the island where it is occasionally performed. In 1989 it was banned in Point Fortin under Sunni pressure. But in Longdenville it was held for the first time in twenty years during 1987. See the *Trinidad Guardian* (September 14, 1989): 1 and (October 19, 1987): 1 respectively.

110. Smith (1963): 15 argues that Trinidadian "Hindus, possibly because of caste bonds, showed more interest in, and knowledge of, the original homes of their forebears. Muslims, on the other hand, feel a strong spiritual bond to all co-religionists and not to specific locales."

111. On the concept of "Indianness," see Eriksen (1992): 122–23.

112. For example, see Gibbons (1979): 23–28.

113. Ahye (1978): 72 includes a British West Indian Airlines advertisement stating that "BWIA recognizes the solemn significance of the Feast of *Hosay*, as the nation's Muslims celebrate the legacy of Imam Hosein."

114. Sporadic, small-scale *Hosay* observances are also to be found in other places such as Tunapuna and Couva, where "forty-day *tadjahs*" are paraded on the occasion of *arbaʿin*.

115. On religious oscillation in postcolonial contexts, see Stewart (1956): 71–76.

116. For example, see Beck (1982).

117. For a description, see Troll (1988): 44.

118. *Roseau*, a grass known as *Arundo donax L.*, is commonly called "giant reed."

119. Personal communication, February 2001.

120. One structure built in 1991 was covered with 24,000 knot roses, alternatively called *batassah*.

121. On the southern observance, see Chelkowski (1992–93).

Chapter 5

1. In actuality, the color of the green moon and shirts that the yard members wear is blue. Mr. Ramgoonan, a retired member of the green yard, says that

when he was a young man, their moon was called the blue moon. The green *sipars* paraded in nineteenth-century Bihar were in fact blue.

2. The word *camp*, however, is discouraged. One senior yard member quipped that "it sounds too much like 'Boy Scout camp!' " His sardonic sense of humor, always appreciated by fellow yard mates, might be a comical way of guarding against associations with Carnival, during which the term *camp* is also used to refer to the yards in which neighborhood teams design costumes and floats. For a discussion of *mas* camps, see Burton (1997): 156–220; Hill (1993): 64–113; and Mason (1998): 79–120.

3. For the first half of the 1990s, the headmen were Farley Muhammad (Bay Road), Raiez Ali (Ghulam Hussein), Bunny Emamali (Balma), and Sammy Ali (Cocorite).

4. Cocorite is the exception, being located just across a traffic bridge bordering St. James, where Western Main Road continues onward to the northwest.

5. Mr. Ali is the great-grandnephew of Ghulam Hussein, the yard's founder, who came from Allahabad, Uttar Pradesh, according to family tradition.

6. Khan (1995): 10, for example, writes of the multivalence of religious discourse as a "rhetorical language" of mutual exclusiveness in practice and mutual inclusiveness of belief. In the case of the St. James *Hosay*, however, there is less exclusiveness on the level of practice because people of various racial and ethnic backgrounds continue to participate today. Elsewhere in her study (46ff), Khan refers to "boundary crossings" of belief and practice, which her southern field consultants generally viewed in a negative light.

7. Joseph (1996): 15 attributes this potential decline to lack of patronage, concluding that "it is quite possible that by the turn of the century the event would not confine itself to the commemoration of the killing of the martyrs, but the death of the very festival itself." Fortunately, he was wrong.

8. Hill (1993): 22–23. See also Abrahams (1983): 98–108, 133–56.

9. Wilson (1973). See also Burton (1997): 158–73.

10. Abrahams (1983): 99. See also Eriksen (1990): 23.

11. Abrahams (1983): xvii.

12. For a review of the literature, see Burton (1997): 158–68. On Trinidad specifically, see Stewart (1989).

13. The only period during which activity was permissible was between the hours of one and three in the afternoon. During this time all *Hosay* activity took place in the yards, but not on the streets. The *tadjah*s were brought out from the *imambara*s and placed on the sacred squares in front of them, at which time an *imām* said the appropriate prayers. After prayers, the sacred drums were played, but only within the yard compounds and only during the officially sanctioned two hours.

14. During Muharram in 1990, Bonasse and St. Mary camps in the southern Trinidadian region of Cedros brought out their *tadjah*s in defiance of the police curfew, but the police were helpless to do anything about it. The event proceeded peacefully and without any violence there, despite the coup.

15. Derived from the Hindi *cauk*, which can refer to any four-cornered object or a town square. This is same term used for the square in front of the *imambara*.

16. Another builder from the south told me that he dreams his *tadjah* design each year, while the late Abdool Hani (aka David Ali), the grandfather of Sammy Ali and former Cocorite headman, stated that "God sticks that design in my head."

17. The term derives from the Hindi *chauṅk*, which means "seasoning with oil and spices." See Chaturvedi and Tiwari (1984): 228.

18. Builders in the south say that a term of seven years is compulsory.

19. The current Balma master builder, Noble Bisnath, also mentioned that he was once afflicted with warts. He says that he didn't make a promise, but they suddenly disappeared one day when he was busily engaged in building a *tadjah*. He also attributes his recovery to the object's healing power.

20. For example, John Cupid, an Afro-Trinidadian employed by the Trinidad Carnival Commission, told me in 1997 that all the pregnant women of Point Fortin, where he grew up, would come out to touch the *tadjah*, regardless of race or creed.

21. The term comes from the north Indian word *pañcāyat* for a village council, traditionally consisting of five men, who would be responsible for local arbitration. Hamdoo explains it as "a group of people coming together for a common purpose." In estate days the community *tadjah* was called the company *tadjah*, according to the late David Ali, the "king" of *Hosay* who was seventy-two in 1991.

22. According to oral history, the community *tadjah* entered its 101st year in 1964, which means that the tradition dates to 1863. As of the year 2001, the community *tadjah* is 138 years old.

23. This is confirmed by an indentured laborer named Shankar: "e have a man building hosay / dey collect money / manager / pay day / oman twelve cent / six cent / sometime a half shilling / a man one shilling / if e nuh gi im / dey take it out / dey take it out in de plate / everybody / three estate / three estate people / dey putting money an ting to buy paper / an e go build it." As rendered in Mahabir (1985): 177.

24. See Joseph (1997): 19. Indian involvement in Carnival is an understudied topic. While it is generally discouraged within the Indo-Trinidadian communities located in rural areas, there are notable exceptions in the urban milieu. Sukhu, for example, from Balma Yard, plays in a steel drum band, and Darryl, another member of Balma, makes masks at a camp during Carnival. When I asked the latter in 1997 if he ever mixes the two, he looked at me in astonishment and replied, "No, man, they are totally different. I don't mix them up!" On Indian participation in, and influence on, Carnival, see Mason (1998): 160–61.

25. A Hindu builder from the south, Mr. Ganpat, once added, "without prayer, *Hosay* is meaningless."

26. Two of the sites (Balma and Ghulam Hussein) are normally used as garages/work rooms, while the other two (Cocorite and Bay Road) are constructed out of bamboo and cardboard solely for this purpose.

27. These are, of course, ideals that are not always achieved, especially the restriction against smoking. Smoking is said to lessen cravings for meat and sex, so participants do, in fact smoke while they are building the *tadjah*s. The consumption of alcohol is less tolerated, however.

28. In 1991, for example, two bars on Western Main Road in St. James took out an advertisement in a local newspaper using a photo of Balma's 1989 *tadjah* without permission. The caption read: "The College Rest. and Bar and Smokey and Bunty Sports Bar extends best wishes to THE MUSLIM COMMUNITY on the occasion of the HOSAY FESTIVAL in St. James July 20th–23rd." See the *Trinidad Guardian* (July 19, 1991).

29. On rum *tadjah*s, see Williams (1990).

30. Rampersad (1987): 21.

31. To this end, I hesitatingly appeared on radio and television on numerous occasions to defend their rights to practice their rites. See also Korom (1999a and 2001).

32. The fixing of the date for *Hosay* according to a solar date has also occurred in Jamaica, the only other place remaining in the Caribbean where the event is currently observed. I thank Jake Homiak for pointing this out to me.

33. Although I realize that it is not a reliable way to account for the elusive number of Shi‘ah on the island, the 1997 Trinidad and Tobago telephone book lists seven and a half pages of names carrying the surname Ali and two and a half with Hosein/Hussein.

34. The plants and glass of water represent the Euphrates River environment near the historical stage of events at Karbala. In this sense, the *chowk* parallels the Iranian *ta‘ziyeh* stage, which also bears representations of vegetation and water. On the latter, see Mamnoun (1967).

35. Mandal says he left Calcutta in 1941 to join his two brothers in a business venture. His work as an *imām* is a secondary source of income for him. His sacred duties represent the office of the itinerant *imam* mentioned in the previous chapter.

36. The community *tadjah* is actually located on the corner of Carlton and Mathura Roads but still bears the Bay Road name because that is where it was first located until that property was sold. The late Asghar Ali, brother of Ibrahim, suggested that the *chowk* was originally outside the city during plantation days at a site called Tollgate. It was later moved to the original Bay Road site after the latter was incorporated into the Port of Spain municipality.

37. A criticism levied against *Hosay* by orthodox Sunnis is that it is too Hindu. The use of *jhandee* (*jhanḍi*) flags to mark a house that has had a *pūjā* performed is an ostentatious visual aspect of Trinidadian Hinduism. Moreover, Hindus sometimes make promises when such services are performed. Therefore Sunni critics say that the *Hosay* flags are a part of this same tradition, making it un-Islamic and polytheistic because the *tadjah*s are treated as objects of veneration. The criticism can be easily dissolved by pointing out that the flags are squarely within the tradition of standards carried during processions in South Asia and Iran.

38. An older female yard member said red is the color offered for sickness and green and white for prosperity. A male head from another yard told me, however, that the symbolism's meaning has been lost.

39. When teasingly asked by a male friend during a lime what she does while her husband is abstaining, the wife of a yard member mockingly replied that she keeps a long broomstick by the bed.

40. The only ingredient that drummers willingly shared with me is the castor oil seed, which is pressed to provide the central congealing agent for the mixture.

41. On steel band clashes during Carnival, see Stuempfle (1995): 60–64. Here again we notice an example of a preexisting practice from India paralleling an Afro-Trinidadian one, which suggests mutual influence and supports the argument I wish to make for decreolization in the next chapter.

42. Debe, in the Penal area, is said to be quintessentially Indian by locals,

which is to say, more authentic, but also more backward as a result. A skin can run from anywhere between TT$60 and TT$100, which would have been approximately U.S.$13–22 in 1991.

43. From the Hindi *baddh*, which means "tied," "bound," "closed," or "fixed." See Chaturvedi and Tiwari (1984): 499.

44. Wolf (2000): 100 writes that "*Muharram* drumming can communicate textually even while a living tradition of liturgical recitation continues to flourish."

45. Beckwith (1924): 7. The tune to which she refers may be what Shair Ali identifies as the drum of sorrow.

46. Beckwith (1924): 13–17 provides a sample text and musical annotation.

47. See Dournon and Kartomi (1984): 532.

48. In my estimation the term *mahatam* is a conflation of *mahā* (great) and *mātam*. Recall from South Asia that many Sunni drummers in India refer to the playing of the drums as a form of *mātam*; hence, the war hand can be understood as a great lamentation. On drumming as *mātam* in South Asia, see Wolf (2000): 90–95 and 98ff. Although both north and south talk of four (plus one in the north) natural hands, the style differs dramatically. In the south the drumming is slower but freer and the *tassa*s used have a larger circumference (approximately 16") but a shallower bowl, resembling more closely the *tāsā*s of South Asia.

49. The sequencing, terminology, and corresponding English translations vary from yard to yard and from performer to performer. Moreover, local pronunciation of Bhojpuri terms varies from person to person, making most of them virtually impossible to trace back to an original term. The spellings I use here are mere approximations based on variations provided to me by numerous drummers. It is important to bear in mind that much of this lore is oral, not written, so there is considerable variation in both interpretation and pronunciation. This fact makes it difficult to make educated guesses about possible derivations. The only hand I can identify with certainty is the *kabulkana*, which has to come from the Arabic *tabal khānah* (military band music), which is considered to be a legitimate *(halāl)* genre of rhythm because it is not considered *mūsiqā* (music). See Nasr (1997): 222. *Teen chropa* (sometimes pronounced *chopra*) may be *tīn* (three) *thaperā* (a violent blow or stroke) or possibly *thappar* (a slap) or *jhāpar*, (a full-blooded slap), referring to the basic repeat of the three-beat pattern of the open palm on the female side of the bass. See Chaturvedi and Tiwari (1984): 298, 255 respectively. *Nubie salbat* could be *nabī* (prophet) *ṣifat* (attribute), a term used in Persian *radīf* music. See Platts (1977): 788. But a knowledgeable older drummer who still speaks some Bhojpuri told me that *salbat* is from *sharbat*, the sweet drink given out after a funeral to all attendees. This could certainly be true because /r/ is often replaced by /l/ and /sh/ by /s/ in the local jargon used by participants in *Hosay* (for example, *turbat* becomes *tulbat*; *bishnath* becomes *bisnath*). But *sarvar* (chief, head, leader, principal, lord, master; see Platts [1977]: 657) also exists in Urdu poetry about Karbala. I am grateful to Amy Bard for pointing out the latter. Lastly, *chalta kabulkana* is simply the moving *(calṭā)* march.

50. The term is obviously related to *dingolay*, a dance style or expression of exuberance associated with Carnival. I thank Steve Stuempfle (personal communication, 2001) for this insight.

51. An alternative term is *foolayer*. The term is most probably of West African origin (that is, *fula*), and this term, along with cutter, was used identically in

tamboo bamboo bands, the precursors of steel bands. Again, my thanks go to Steve Stuempfle (personal communication) for providing me with this point.

52. Although they are widely accepted to be of African origin (i.e., *kata*), alternative folk etymologies were given to me by older Indo-Trinidadians. According to them, the term *cutter* literally comes from the Hindi/Bhojpuri infinitive *kaṭnā* (to cut). The nominal form *kaṭā-marī* (violent quarreling, bloodshed) and the nominal verb *kaṭ marnā* (to battle to the death) add further to the martial imagery. See Chaturvedi and Tiwari (1984): 112.

53. The analogy is reaffirmed in a statement by an elderly Indo-Trinidadian drummer of Hindu descent in the south who provided me with a folk etymology of the word *tassa*. According to Bachu Bhagwandeen, the word comes from the Hindi word for "taste." Although I question the etymology, his point is well taken. On the etymology of the term, see Dournon and Kartomi (1984): 532.

54. Originally, there were only four hands. The fifth, *chalta kabulkana*, was introduced by Ibrahim Ali, and it was only played by him as the *tadjahs* and moons approached QRC. After his death, the hand was not played for a few years in honor of his memory, but by 1997 it was played incessantly on the slow approach to the grounds.

55. Wolf (2000): 108 cites a Shi'i Indian, Professor Bilgrami, as saying that in his hometown of Bilgram three styles of drumming are performed: marching, attack, and death, which would basically correspond to the Trinidadian core sequence.

56. On the drums communicating verbal messages in South Asia, see Wolf (2000): 95 and 97ff. Citing an interview with a *tāsā* player from Hallaur, U.P., he writes, "From the sound of the drums . . . [we play to] disseminate the message of Husain" (p. 98).

57. Sharar (1994), cited in Wolf (2000): 91.

58. In this regard, I am most indebted to Peter Chelkowski.

59. Bettelheim and Nunley (1988): 132, however, provide some documentary evidence from Hyderabad that the moons might be linked to the *'alam* associated with the *na'l ṣāhib* described in Chapter 3. The crescent shape of the moons and some of the symbolism of their ornamentation make the link plausible. Nonetheless, I still believe that they can be linked even more closely to the Iranian *nakhl*.

60. I should note here that at least one moon man, Joey Miller, told me that he does not like the word *dancing*. He prefers *playing*, which would be consistent with the verbal noun used in reference to performing *Hosay* during the plantation period by indentured Indo-Trinidadians. The use of the term *dancing* is, however, widespread, so I will continue to use it here.

61. An oral legend still circulates that when Hasan was poisoned the moon turned green, and when Husayn was beheaded the moon turned red.

62. The first red moon builder was William Deen Mohammad. His grandson Ralph "Sonny Boy" Abdool was the headman during my ethnographic present. Casim Juman, who was 76 at the time, was the head of the green moon camp. Each yard has roughly twenty to twenty-five moon men.

63. The reason that the green moon is larger is that Hasan is the older brother. This is the reverse of the *tadjahs*, where the smaller *tadjahs* represent Hasan and the larger ones Husayn.

64. Although I have not been able to verify this due to the secrecy of the moon

guilds, I have been told that the men bark and howl at the moon when they cut the first *roseau*. In 1991 the red moon yard cut their bamboo on July 7 and began building on July 13. The blue moon yard cut at the same time, but started construction on the fourteenth.

65. Due to the noticeable difference in size, the red moon has twenty-one knives, whereas the blue moon has twenty-six knives.

66. The sword in the middle most likely represents the one used to behead Husayn. The others symbolize the slashes he received in battle prior to his death.

67. Older retired dancers who still have some knowledge of Hindi use the word *jhārāl*, most likely a Trinidadian Bhojpuri variant of *jhālar* (festoon, frill, or gather). See Chaturvedi and Tiwari (1984): 255.

68. It could also be derived from *'ainī* (of or related to the eye). See Platts (1977): 768. This etymology would tie it even closer to the Iranian *nakhl*, which, we have already seen, is in the shape of a teardrop, a substance "of or related to the eye."

69. This is the exoteric interpretation, however. When I pursued the number of *tawa*s further, a member of the green yard admitted that some people believe that five represents the members of the Prophet's family, but the sixth, which is not visible on the surface of the moon because it is covered by the *makna* (see below), represents the *mehdī*, or hidden *imām* in Shi'i tradition. Further, if one adds the five from the red and the six from the blue, one arrives at eleven, with one lacking for the twelfth and hidden *imām*. I believe this numerology to be correct on the *bāṭin* level because another *tawa* was not added by the green moon in 1997 when a new *Hosay* yard was founded.

70. The term most likely derives from either the Perso-Arabic Urdu term *maqna'* (a veil of fine linen or muslin worn over the head) or *maknūn* (hidden, concealed, secret). See Platts (1977): 1056, 1059 respectively. Given the fact that a veil is also used to cover or conceal the face or body, the Trinidadian Bhojpuri term could be a very clever play on both terms. Each of the *tadjah*s also has a *makna* in the form of a concealed compartment at the base of the *tadjah*. Each yard places flowers inside these as well, which are later buried in Ghulam Hussein's *chowk*. Recall that flowers are also buried at many Indian locations where *muharram* is performed.

71. This information comes from an anonymous newspaper blurb in the *Trinidad Guardian* dated February 2, 1972, and titled "*Hosay* Hangs in the Balance."

72. This belief is prevalent in Jamaica as well. See Beckwith (1924): 6.

73. At Bay Road, the yard members also circumambulate their *chowk* counterclockwise seven times, with hands on each other's shoulders.

74. The order of procession was Balma, Ghulam Hussein, Cocorite, Red Moon, and Bay Road.

75. In the 1940s the *tadjah*s were cordoned off so that only family members had direct access to the objects of veneration.

76. What is not generally known is that this evening is referred to by some as "dirt night " (*mati keh rat*, from Hindi *miṭṭī kī rāt*). Although not all are in agreement about this, there is a precedent, following the Shi'i legend that the Prophet ordered the angel Gabriel to bring him a handful of dirt from Karbala so that he could see the soil upon which his grandson would be slain. He then ordered one of his wives to place it in a clean bottle and observe it until it turned red, which

would be a sign that Husayn had been killed. See also Ali (1976): 8. On dirt rituals during *Hosay* in Jamaica, see Beckwith (1924): 6. For south Trinidad, where effigies of the martyrs are molded out of earth, see Chelkowski (1992–93): 60–63.

Cognate rites are performed in St. James. Shair Ali, for example, told me that dirt from QRC is dug up and placed in the *makna* of Ghulam Hussein's *tadjah* while the processions are going on. The dirt is then buried in the *chowk*'s hole on the final evening along with the flowers offered by the other *tadjahs* and the moon. Shair also mentioned that Ghulam Hussein brought over to Trinidad a clod of earth from his local *karbalā'* near Allahabad in Uttar Pradesh, which itself is believed to have had dirt from Karbala in Iraq placed in it. Hamdoo, however, said that no dirt is dug up. It is already in the hole, stored in an urn from the time that the *chowk* was transferred from Bay Road. What he suggests is that the urn is taken out and then reburied on the final evening of prayers. Asghar Ali further elaborated by stating that even before the *karbalā'* was moved, women of Ghulam Hussein Yard used to carry dirt from Bay Road in a pot, while singing sad songs, and deposit it in Ghulam Hussein's *chowk*. On cognate dirt rituals brought to Sumatra from India, see Feener (1999) and Kartomi (1986): 150–51.

77. For a personal account of these performances from Dinsley village in Tacarigua as observed in the 1920s, see Alladin (1971). Beckwith (1924) reports similar occurrences in Jamaica.

78. It is also known to some as *Chotka Chowk* (Hindi *choṭe kā cauk*), the little *chowk*.

79. Sometimes a white cock is also sacrificed, and its blood is drained into a hole next to the family dwelling. The same ritual used to occur in Jamaica. See again Beckwith (1924): 6. Now only the goat's blood is drained into the hole.

80. The term is derived from the Urdu *bakhsh* (imparting, bestowing, forgiving). See Platts (1977): 138.

81. In the absence of moons in Cedros, the *tadjahs* themselves kiss.

82. One green moon yard member told me that samples of the ornaments are also inside the *makna* along with flowers. Thus the symbolic gesture of transferring these to the hole suggests an actual burial of the *imam*'s body, confirming that Ghulam Hussein's *chowk* is the actual *karbalā'*.

83. The pattern is somewhat different in Cedros, however. There the *tadjahs* are moved to their appointed places at approximately six in the evening on Karbala Day. The *mojawir*, as the *imam* is called in the south, says a short prayer, after which the *tadjahs* are carried to the sea and immersed. Immersion is performed sooner in Cedros because the beginning of the month is reckoned differently. Therefore the event usually begins one day earlier than in St. James.

84. The swords are not in view during the procession because they are slid horizontally into the frame of the Ghulam Hussein *tadjah*.

85. The phenomenological effect of this experience is what one might call "disposable sacred art." Gill (1972): 6–13 calls it "disenchantment."

86. Eriksen (1990).

87. Ibid., 25. Eriksen, however, is more concerned with informal limes that simply happen on street corners or in rum shops, mostly among Afro-Trinidadians. But he does concede that nowadays the term is used for any leisure-time activity, which is more in line with the beach lime I describe here.

Chapter 6

1. Speaking in the film *Hosay Trinidad*. See Bishop and Korom (1998).
2. DeCamp (1971): 15.
3. Bickerton (1976): 169.
4. Mühlhäusler (1980): 19.
5. See the discussion in Jourdan (1991): 197f. Holm (1989): 459–66 provides a useful overview of linguistic creolization in Trinidad and Tobago.
6. DeCamp (1971): 27.
7. See Brathwaite (1971): 296.
8. Ibid., 310. Prothero (1996): 7–13 usefully extends the model to the "Protestant Buddhism" of Henry Steel Olcott.
9. Drummond (1980). Jayawardena (1980): 448 has warned that the model of cultural creolization can be developed fully only "against the backdrop of prestige, economic and political interests that motivate the actors." I have attempted to account for these factors earlier in my study, and I pursue them in what follows.
10. On the continuum, see Bickerton (1973). For critiques of it, see Chaudenson (1981) and Gilbert and Makhudu (1987).
11. Hannerz (1987): 551.
12. Ibid., 550–52.
13. Ibid., 555–56.
14. Bickerton (1980): 109, for example, points out that decreolization occurs wherever a creole language is in direct contact with its associated superstrate language and that it involves a progressive change in which the basilectal (subordinated) grammar gradually comes to resemble the output of the acrolectal (dominant) grammar. See also Bailey and Maynor (1987) for a critique.
15. Jourdan (1991): 195.
16. Ibid., 200.
17. Hannerz (1987): 555.
18. For overviews, see Banks (1996), Bentley (1981), Cohen (1978), and Sollers (1989). Yelvington (1993) presents a uniquely Trinidadian point of view on the phenomenon.
19. Banks (1996): 190. Sollers (1989) also indicates the "invented" nature of the concept.
20. Banks (1996): 190.
21. See Barth (1969).
22. See Cohen (1978): 387–89 and Stern and Cicala (1991).
23. I employ the term *emergent* here in the sense used by performance theorists such as Georges (1969), Bauman (1975), Hymes (1981), and Schieffelin (1985) to account for the constantly changing notions and definitions of cultural phenomena in their appropriate contexts.
24. On this rationale, see Abrahams (1981).
25. See the *Trinidad Guardian* (September 3, 1974): 3.
26. Mohammad (1985): 9.
27. Ali (1988): 9. UWBP is the conventional English abbreviation for the refrain "Upon Whom Be Peace," which is always uttered after mention of the Prophet's name.
28. See Wilson (1992): 4. Bunny Emamali, former head of the *Hosay* organiz-

ing committee, is of the same opinion: "people ought to show more respect for the religious ceremony. We can't stop people from drinking, . . . but we would like them to remember that this is a religious festival and insist that it be maintained as such." See the *Express* (July 19, 1991): 21.

29. Leader (1983): 9.

30. Ibid.

31. Ibid.

32. Ibid. Ibrahim Ali (interview, May 1991) voiced a similar sentiment: "All religious festivals end up in a fête because of Trinidadian carnival mentality." Crowley (1954): 202 explains this mentality by stating that the fête is the "keystone" of Creole culture: the "fete is what makes life worth living; it is the focus of Trinidadian culture."

33. Leader (1983): 9.

34. Ali (1990): 4. For a remarkably similar rationale defending a mixture of happy and sad feelings during the rite in India, see Wolf (2000): 94.

35. *Trinidad Guardian* (July 24, 1991). In support of this viewpoint, ASJA published an advertisement explaining the true nature of the observance. The ad ends with the following statement: "So it is that the height of mockery and a particularly gross insult, that some people . . . palm it off on the country as the 'Islamic' or 'Muslim' festival of *Hosay*. Let us inform the country about this mockery and insult."

36. See the *Express* (July 24, 1991): 2. It is probably no coincidence that the coup attempt occurred during the month of Muharram as an act of defiance, which is, as we have seen repeatedly, an old historical Muharram theme. But the placard-bearing group led by Abdul Kareem Abraham was not a splinter group of Abu Bakr's faction, as the newspapers misleadingly claimed.

37. Jacobs (1964): 1. Although well intentioned, Jacobs's statement offended many of St. James's Shi‘ah, for he was not aware of the praying and fasting that always occur among participants in the community during the preparatory phases of the event. Here we see a good example of the s/x factor in action.

38. See Cohen (1978): 387–89, Moerman (1965, 1974), and Handelman (1977).

39. Bauman (1972) uses this term with specific reference to contested identities.

40. As one Indian Muslim intellectual living in the United States recently put it, "no matter what I call myself, two facts stand out: by my presence here I demand that the host people change their definition of themselves as Americans, and secondly, my presence here requires that I strenuously re-examine the question of my Indianness, not only in relation to this country but also in relation to what I imagine I left behind, as if frozen forever in time." See Naim (1993): 77–78.

41. See, for example, Adorno (1967), Cantlie (1979), Honko (1983a, 1983b), and Shils (1981).

42. See Eisentstadt (1969), Handler and Linnekin (1984), Hobsbawm and Ranger (1983), Korom (1989), Thomas (1992), and Zerubavel (1994) respectively.

43. Ben-Amos (1984). On tradition and religion, see Brown (1994).

44. For a classic example, see Lerner (1958).

45. In Hindu India, for example, the term that approximates the English *tradition* most closely is the Sanskrit word *sampradāya*, the composite meaning of which could be rendered as "that which is given forth unaltered." On the

etymology of the term, see Böhtlink and Roth (1966): 579. For a discussion, see Claus and Korom (1991): 8–11.

46. Stewart (1984): 151.

47. See Eisenstadt (1973) and Rudolph and Rudolph (1967).

48. Handler and Linnekin (1984): 273.

49. For useful discussions of authenticity, see Appiah (1994), Berman (1972), and Thaiss (1994).

50. But it can also be co-opted in colonial contexts by the colonizers to (mis)interpret the colonized group as well, as has been demonstrated with regard to the British understanding of Indian tradition by Raheja (1996). Kale (1995) provides a similar argument with reference to *Hosay* specifically.

51. On the state's co-optation of local cultural practices for the purpose of creating national culture, see Bowen (1986).

52. See the discussion in LePage and Tabouret-Keller (1985): 119–200.

53. For one extended case study of religious revivalism on the island, see Klass (1996).

54. *Trinidad Sunday Guardian* (July 28, 1991): 12.

55. The term *wine* (derived from *wind*) is known as early as 1790 from Jamaica, as is evidenced in the following lyrics sung by a slave while dancing for her master's pleasure: "You no shake like-a me! You no wind like-a me"; as cited in Burton (1997): 166, n. 18. On *chutney wine* specifically, see the comments in Manuel (1995): 216–20 and (2000): 168–95.

56. On complementary genres in Trinidad and India, see Myers (1998).

57. This seemingly simple question becomes even more complex when we consider that some chutney lyrics are composed by Afro-Trinidadians, as is the case with Rikki Jai's 1993 hit "Cry for Unity," which was composed for him by Ras Shorty I (formerly Lord Shorty). See Manuel (1995): 219.

58. Bassant and Orie (1991): 27.

59. A primarily Afro-Trinidadian parallel exists in the word *callaloo (kyalalou, kalalou)*, a viscous soup made from boiling okra, a kind of taro named dasheen *(Colocsia esculenta)*, and crabmeat or pigtail in coconut milk. As Hill (1993): xiii states, "It is a blend of unlikely ingredients. The word also refers to a 'confusion,' a 'fix,' or a 'stew' of the sort in which a person becomes entangled. In a more positive way, it may even refer to Caribbean culture, with its many different ethnic groups and their special histories."

60. Even more serious is the ongoing problem of ignoring minority input to Trinidadian national culture, as when the singer Stalin brought out "Caribbean Man," which won the Calypso Monarch Competition that year and started a national debate about Trinidad's cultural and ethnic composition. In the chorus he sings that the Caribbean Man represents one race which came from the same place. A response to Stalin's lyrics by a Reverend Hamid is indicative of the overall Indo-Trinidadian community's response: "The fact of the matter is that right here in Trinidad not all come from the same place, nor belong to the same race, nor come on the same ship, not make the same trip." See Deosaran (1987): 113.

61. This understanding is somewhat parallel to what Bausinger (1990): 117 refers to as cultural relics in the context of exile culture, which "are assumed to express a continuity with communal culture, which is unchanging and genuine in its substance."

62. Rahaman (1997): 9.

63. As has been shown to be the case for the Taos fiesta by Rodríguez (1997), where a celebratory tradition initiated by Anglos for the stimulation of tourism leading to economic revitalization has been taken over gradually by Hispanos.

64. More on the cross-fertilization of cultural performances in Trinidad can be found in Hill (1993): xiv–xv and Stuempfle (1995): 219–36.

65. See Bourdieu (1977): 171–83.

66. Al-Rawi (1997): 36.

67. See Ryan (1991).

68. Herskovits (1973). Recently the concept has been challenged by Norris (1996). See also Spiro (1986) and Fernandez (1990).

69. Pike (1954). For assessments of the term and its current usefulness, see Harris (1976), Headland, Pike, and Harris (1990), and Baumann (1993). Gothóni (1981) provides an application of the *emic* concept to the religions of "foreign" cultures.

70. See Geertz (1983).

71. See Downs (1971): 15–28.

72. See Appadurai (1991) and Hannerz (1987 and 1989).

73. Shuman (1993): 357. See also Fanon (1990).

74. On the question of religious authenticity in Trinidad with special reference to *Hosay*, see Thaiss (1994). On the perils of inauthenticity in the Caribbean, see Williams (1990).

75. Eickelman (1982): 1–2.

76. On this issue, see el-Zein (1977).

77. See Abu-Lughod (1989).

78. See Lawrence (1995).

79. Geertz (1992): 129.

80. The religious significance of the symbolic knot is discussed by Eliade (1961): 92–95.

81. On steel drums, see Stuempfle (1995), and on cricket, see Yelvington (1990).

82. See Connerton (1989). Here I would want to distinguish between globalization and transnationalism, as Kearney (1995): 548 does, for the former is a territorially decentered geographical phenomenon, while the latter is grounded in the social, economic, political, and religious interrelationships between one or more nation-states. See also Hannerz (1989).

83. Geertz (1992): 129.

84. See Smith (1990).

85. Foucault (1972).

86. Appadurai (1988): 40.

87. See Fabian (1978): 317.

88. In positing this, I do not want to suggest an evolutionary model of pidgin leading to creole, for as Jourdan (1991): 194 clearly suggests, the relationship is much more complex, and both forms may exist simultaneously in the same social niche on the continuum. Instead, I use pidgin to refer to the initial contact situation and creole to refer to the lengthier and ongoing encounter that results in constant and ever-more complex negotiations in the cultural sphere.

89. See Jayawardena (1968b).

90. On diglossia, see Ferguson (1959).

91. Bickerton (1980): 109.

92. Ibid.

93. That is, external conversion, while continuing to practice the original faith of their forefathers as it was passed down to them. This is the case with crypto-Jews, the descendants of Spanish Jewry currently residing in New Mexico and southern Colorado. See Tobias (1990).

94. See, for example, Gibbons (1979): 23ff and Mahabir (n.d).

Epilogue

1. Interview with Ibrahim Ali, May 1991.

2. The Mission was incorporated as a nonprofit organization in October 1993.

3. The full texts of the leaflets are available at http://al-islam1.org/organizations/bmma/.

4. Gobi (interview, May 1997), by his own admission, is a practicing Hindu. Yet he says that he believes in the *Hosay*. He thinks that one does not have to be Muslim to participate, so long as one has respect for the rituals. "As a child," he says, "you grow up in it, you are drawn to the drums, regardless of sectarian affiliation. At a young age you don't make distinctions about religion; you just do it." This is the logic underlying the whole tradition. As he says, "It is an Indian thing." Here his sentiments echo the religion versus culture debate discussed in the previous chapter.

5. Ghulam Hussein Yard is also considering the construction of a metal *tadjah* frame that could be reassembled quickly and easily each year.

6. Other changes to the drums include using nylon twine to replace the deer-skin cord used in earlier years. Again, the reason is financial.

7. Nevertheless, the anti-*Hosay* editorials keep on being printed as the tenth approaches each year.

8. For example, in 1996 they arranged for the BBC to telecast the rituals live in the United Kingdom, and in 1997 it was broadcast live throughout the island on the radio, much as Carnival is.

9. Other female members of the yards argue that the event is fragmenting because of familial discord, which weakens the whole observance and makes it easier for the missionaries to lure participants to their side.

10. Shi'ism spread from India and Zanzibar into East Africa at the end of the nineteenth century. The spread of Shi'ism in the area was accomplished by traders from Gujarat. The Twelver community in Tanzania was founded at the beginning of the twentieth century by Khojas who united local communities (*jamā'at*) into an African confederation in 1945. Since then, the *jamā'at* has been successful in developing education and religious instruction by constructing schools and *madrāsah*s. See Halm (1991): 137. The work of the Bilal Mission now continues in the spirit of that tradition in the Americas. For a brief overview of the Khojas, see again Halm (1991): 190–91.

11. Keramalli's perseverance has already paid off, for the event is now officially known as the "*Hosay* Procession." The term *festival* has been dropped from the official literature.

12. When I asked Brother Hasan what inspired him to convert, he simply responded, "The Truth." There may also be political reasons, however, for why so

many have converted. Unfortunately, I cannot delve deeply into this issue here. By and large, however, many of those who have converted are from the dispossessed class residing in the economically depressed area of the city named Laventille, which led one Indo-Trinidadian to state that people convert just for the free room and board. Perhaps hopes of solidarity and a better economic future within the group have influenced many to join. Indeed, the organization's official website reports that every week a new convert joins. On the background of the Black Power Movement in Trinidad, see Oxaal (1971). On East Indians and Black Power, see Nicholls (1971).

13. As recent as 2001, a new fortieth-day *Hosay* with a large *tadjah* was staged in the village of Curepe to coincide with Indian Arrival Day. The organizer, Nagib Ghany, claims to be Shi'ah but "christened" Hindu. For him the rite has both cultural and religious significance because it simultaneously memorializes Husayn and Ghany's Indian ancestors. The St. James *Hosay* community has denounced the event as a "mockery," and Hamdoo adamantly opposes it. Interestingly, here we see the St. James Shi'ah using the same rhetoric against the Curepe Shi'ah that has been used by the island's Sunni majority against the St. James Shi'ah in the past. See Kalipersad (2001).

14. Keramalli, perhaps due to his own upbringing in Tanzania, realizes that bringing the two racial groups together as one congregation is unrealistic. His solution is, therefore, to strive for two mosques, one for the Indo-population and another for the Afro-population. The first step in this direction has already been taken. The Mission has recently put down a deposit for purchase of the building now housing the Prince Street congregation. The 5,000-square-foot property will serve as a place of prayer, study facility, daycare center, vocational training school, and source of revenue for the congregation's brothers and sisters, "the majority of whom," as the Mission's website explains, "are unemployed at present in Trinidad." This fact lends credence to the idea that some convert out of necessity or convenience, as suggested in several places throughout this study.

15. See Yoder (1974): 11, in which he minimally defines the term as follows: "Folk religion exists in a complex society in relation to and *in tension with* the organized religion(s) of that society."

16. Some may very well be converts from that faction, now that Abu Bakr has become stigmatized, but most converted from Sunnism or Catholicism, as noted above. On this question, Gobi has reconfirmed something stated earlier in my study: conversion is often a matter of convenience on the island.

17. One knowledgeable person who wishes to remain anonymous told me that such groups as the Imame Zamana are under government surveillance and if they were doing anything illegal, it would have been exposed by now.

18. Personal communication, 1997.

19. Thaiss (1994): 55.

20. Clifford (1994): 319.

21. Concerning property rights in relation to religion, see Brown (1998) and Harrison (1992).

22. Moreover, *Hosay*, being a "national treasure," also has economic value to the government, which ensures that measures will be taken by authorities to guarantee that it continues in one or more public forms.

Glossary

Language designations refer to the way the term is cited in the text, not to etymology: [A] = Arabic, [H] = Hindi, [P] = Persian, [T] = Trinidadian, [U] = Urdu.

'alam: flag, badge, signpost, distinguishing mark [P]
'ādat: custom, habit, manner, practice [U]
ahl al-bayt: the five holy members of the Prophet's family [A]
āinā: mirror [H]
'ainī: of or related to the eye; refers to the silver plates decorating the *Hosay* moons of Trinidad [U]
alāvā: a fire pit around which people dance during *muḥarram* in India, a bonfire [U]
arba'īn: the fortieth-day observance of Imam Husayn's martyrdom on the twentieth of Safar [P]; same as *cahallam* [U]
'azā': ceremony of mourning, solace, consolation, comfort [A]
bāṛā: enclosed space, area, cemetery, enclosure [H, U]; same as *bārah* [P]
bāṭin: internal, not visible, esoteric [P]
bida': innovation in matters of religion, new original, novel [A]
chauṅk: seasoning with oil and spices [H]
dasteh: procession, an assemblage of people, a division of an army, a brigade [P]
du'ā': petitionary prayer, invocation, salutation [P]
fātiḥah: commencement, the first part of something, opening chapter, prayers for the dead [U]
fatvā: a judicial decree, judgment, settlement award decision [U]
gummaj: cupola, a large dome, specifically the one at the center of the *tadjah* [H]
ḥadīs: sayings of the Prophet, history, tradition [P]
imāmbāṛā: an enclosure within which mourning sessions are held and in which replicas of Imam Husayn's tomb and other ritual paraphernalia are constructed and displayed [U]
jhālar: festoon, frill, fringe; refers to the ornamental bolts of cloth gathered around the crescent of the *Hosay* moons [H]
khuṭbah: discourse, sermon, oration [U]
lobān: frankincense [U]; same as *lohban* [T]
maknūn: concealed, hidden, or secret [U]

malīdah: a cake made of pounded meal (or flour), milk, butter, and sugar [P]; same as *maleedah* [T]

marṣiyah: a genre of poetic elegies recited to lament the death of a martyr [U]

mātam: breast beating, an assembly of mourners, a misfortune [U]; same as *mā'tam* [P]

muḥallā: neighborhood [U]; variant of *muḥallah* [U]

nakhl: date palm, symbolic bier of Imam Husayn [P]

naql: transporting, carrying from one place to another, transplanting, translating, copying, transcribing, imitating, mimicking, acting, relating, telling, history, tradition [P]

nauḥah: lamentation, moaning, wailing (over the dead) [U]

naẓar: vow, endowing with beauty and every ornamental excellence [P]

qiyāmat: Day of Judgment, last day, the resurrection, confusion, tumult, calamity [P]

rauẓat: flower garden, Paradise, a tomb, a funeral prayer [P]; same as *rawḍat* [A]

rauẓeh khvān: a eulogist, one who prays over the dead, a performer of martyrdom poetry [P]

rauẓeh khvānī: a gathering for the recitation of martyrdom narratives [P]

sabīl: water or sherbet given to the thirsty during the month of Muharram; way, road, path [U]

shamshīr: a sword, scimitar, saber, blade, the light of the morning sun [P]

shamshīrzan: striking with a sword, warlike, a gallant soldier [P]

silsilah: chain of transmission, a chain, series, succession, descent, inheritance, genealogy, unbroken tradition [A]

sinehzan: chest beater [P]

sipar: shield, a ritual object carried in *muḥarram* processions symbolizing the *imām* Husayn's courage [U]

tabarra': the practice of cursing the first three caliphs [U]

tamāshā: entertainment, spectacle, exhibition, sport, amusement, fun [U]

tashabbuh: imitation, resembling, likeness, similitude [P]

ta'ziyeh: Iranian dramatic performances of Imam Husayn's passion [P]

ta'ziyah: model tombs of Hasan and Husayn paraded in South Asia; same as *tadjah* [T]

tijā: third day after the death of a relative on which offerings are made [U]

visarjan: immersing a deity's image in water after a *pūjā* [H]

ẓāhir: external, exterior, outer, apparent, clear, visible, manifest, exoteric [P]

zarīh: a permanent replica of Imam Husayn's tomb; sometimes used interchangeably with *ta'ziyeh*; a railing or latticework surrounding a temple or tomb [U]

ziyārat karnā: to make a pilgrimage or religious visitation [U]

Bibliography

Abrahams, Roger D. 1981. Shouting Match at the Border: The Folklore of Display Events. In R. Bauman and R. D. Abrahams, eds., *"And Other Neighborly Names": Social Process and Cultural Image in Texas Folklore*. Austin: University of Texas Press, pp. 303–21.

———. 1982. The Language of Festivals: Celebrating the Economy. In V. Turner, ed., *Celebration: Studies in Festivity and Ritual*. Washington, D.C.: Smithsonian Institution Press, pp. 161–77.

———. 1983. *The Man-of-Words in the West Indies: Performance and the Emergence of Creole Culture*. Baltimore, Md.: Johns Hopkins University Press.

Abu-Lughod, Lila. 1989. Zones of Theory in the Anthropology of the Arab World. *Annual Review of Anthropology* 18: 267–306.

Adam, Volker. 2001. Why Do They Cry? Criticisms of Muḥarram Celebrations in Tsarist and Socialist Azerbaijan. In R. Brunner and W. Ende, eds., *The Twelver Shia in Modern Times: Religious Culture and Political History*. Leiden: Brill, pp. 114–34.

Adorno, Theodor W. 1967. Thesen über Tradition. In *Ohne Leitbild: Parva Aesthetica*. Frankfurt am Main: Suhrkamp Verlag, pp. 29–41.

Ahye, Molly. 1978. *Golden Heritage: The Dance in Trinidad and Tobago*. Petit Valley, Republic of Trinidad and Tobago: Heritage Cultures Ltd.

Algar, Hamid, ed. 1979. *On the Sociology of Islam: Lectures by Ali Shari'ati*. Berkeley, Calif.: Mizan Press.

———, ed.1981. *Islam and Revolution: Writings and Declarations of Imam Khomeini*. Berkeley, Calif.: Mizan Press.

Ali, Imtiaz. 1988. *Hosay* Has Lost Its Meaning. *Express* (Trinidad), August 19: 9.

Ali, Mrs. Meer Hassan. 1917. *Observations on the Mussulmauns of India*. London: Oxford University Press.

Ali, Shair. 1990. *Hosay*: Symbols of Martyrdom. *Trinidad Guardian*, July 17: 4.

Ali, Zobida. 1976. *Hosay Riots, 1884*. M. Phil. thesis, University of the West Indies–St. Augustine.

Alladin, M. P. 1971. *A Village in Trinidad*. Maraval, Trinidad: M.P. Alladin.

Al-Rawi, Faris. 1997. No Mother India nor Mother Africa. *Trinidad Sunday Guardian*, May 18: 1, 36.

Ameed, Syed Mohammad. 1974. *The Importance of Weeping and Wailing*. Karachi: Peermohamad Ebrahim Trust.

Amir-Moezzi, Ali. 1994. *The Divine Guide in Early Shi'ism: The Sources of Esotericism in Islam*. Albany: State University of New York Press.

Anderson, Benedect. 1991. *Imagined Communities: Reflections on the Origin and Spread of Nationalism* (revised and expanded). London: Verso.

Anzaldúa, Gloria E. 1987. *Borderlands: The New Mestiza = La Frontera*. San Francisco: Spinster/Aunt Lute Press.

Appadurai, Arjun. 1981. The Past as a Scarce Resource. *Man* 16/2: 201–19.

———. 1988. Putting Hierarchy in Its Place. *Cultural Anthropology* 3: 36–49.

———. 1991. Global Ethnoscapes: Notes and Queries for a Transnational Anthropology. In R. G. Fox, ed., *Recapturing Anthropology: Working in the Present*. Santa Fe, N.M.: School of American Research Press, pp. 191–210.

Appiah, Anthony. 1994. Identity, Authenticity, Survival: Multicultural Societies and Social Reproduction. In A. Gutmann, ed., *Multiculturalism: Examining the Politics of Representation*. Princeton, N.J.: Princeton University Press.

Asgar, Jalal. 1963. *A Historical Study of the Origins of the Persian Passion Plays*. Ph.D. diss., University of Southern California.

Ayoub, Mahmoud. 1978. *Redemptive Suffering in Islam*. The Hague: E. J. Brill.

Azarpay, Guitty. 1975. Iranian Divinities in Sogdian Painting. In J. Duchesne-Guillemin, ed., *Acta Iranica, Monumentum H. S. Nyberg I*. Leiden: E. J. Brill, pp. 19–29.

———. 1981. *Sogdian Painting: The Pictorial Epic in Oriental Art*. Berkeley: University of California Press.

Bailey, Guy, and Natalie Maynor. 1987. Decreolization? *Language in Society* 16: 449–63.

Baird, Robert. 1971. *Category Formation and the History of Religions*. Mouton, The Netherlands: Mouton Publishers.

Bakhtin, Mikhail. 1984. *Rabelais and His World*. Bloomington: Indiana University Press.

Baktash, Mayel. 1979. Ta'ziyeh and Its Philosophy. In P. J. Chelkowski, ed., *Ta'ziyeh and Ritual Drama in Iran*. New York: New York University Press, pp. 95–120.

Banks, Marcus. 1996. *Ethnicity: Anthropological Constructions*. London: Routledge.

Bard, Amy. 2000. "To Whom Shall I Sing Lullabies Now?" Form, Function, and Feeling in "Women's Songs" as Poetic Genres of the Shi'i Mourning Assembly. Paper presented at the *Annual Conference on South Asia*, Madison, Wisc., October.

Barth, Fredrik, ed. 1969. *Ethnic Groups and Boundaries: The Social Organization of Cultural Difference*. London: Allen and Unwin.

Bassant, Reynold, and L. Siddhartha Orie. 1991. Understanding the Chutney Phenomenon. *Trinidad Guardian*, July 26: 27.

Bateson, Gregory. 1958. *Naven*. Stanford, Calif.: Stanford University Press.

Bauman, Richard. 1972. Differential Identity and the Social Base of Folklore. In A. Paredes and R. Bauman, eds., *Toward New Perspectives in Folklore*. Austin: University of Texas Press, pp. 31–41.

———. 1975. Verbal Art as Performance. *American Anthropologist* 77/2: 290–311.

Baumann, Martin. 2000. Diaspora: Genealogies of Semantics and Transcultural Comparison. *Numen* 47: 313–37.

Baumann, Max Peter. 1993. *Emics and Etics in Ethnomusicology*. Berlin: International Institute for Traditional Music.

Bausinger, Hermann. 1990. Relics and What Can Become of Them. In *Folk Culture in a World of Technology*. Bloomington: Indiana University Press, pp. 116–60.

Beck, Brenda E. F. 1982. *The Three Twins: The Telling of a South Indian Folk Epic*. Bloomington: Indiana University Press.

Beckwith, Martha W. 1924. *The Hussay Festival in Jamaica*. Poughkeepsie, N.Y.: Vassar College.

Beeman, William O. 1981. A Full Arena: The Development and Meaning of Popular Performance Traditions in Iran. In M. E. Bonine and N. Keddie, eds., *Continuity and Change in Modern Iran*. Albany: SUNY Press, pp. 285–305, 342–46.

Ben-Amos, Dan. 1984. The Seven Strands of Tradition: Varieties in Its Meaning in American Folklore Studies. *Journal of Folklore Research* 21/2–3: 97–131.

Benson, Janet E. 1983. Politics and Muslim Ethnicity in South India. *Journal of Anthropological Research* 39/1: 42–60.

Bentley, G. Carter. 1987. Ethnicity as Practice. *Comparative Studies in Society and History*. 29/1: 24–55.

Benveniste, E. 1932. Le mémorial de Zarér. *Journal Asiatique* 220/2: 245–93.

Berman, Marshall. 1972. *The Politics of Authenticity*. New York: Atheneum.

Bettelheim, Judith, and John Nunley. 1988. The *Hosay* Festival. In J. Nunley and J. Bettelheim, eds., *Caribbean Festival Arts*. Seattle: University of Washington Press, pp. 119–36.

Bhabha, Homi. 1994. *The Location of Culture*. London: Routledge.

Bhatia, Tej K. 1982. Trinidad Hindi: Three Generations of a Transplanted Variety. *Studies in the Linguistic Sciences* 11/2: 135–50.

———. 1988. Trinidad Hindi: Its Genesis and Generational Profile. In R. K. Barz and J. Siegal, eds., *Language Transplanted: The Development of Overseas Hindi*. Wiesbaden: Otto Harrasowitz, pp. 179–96.

Bickerton, Derek. 1973. The Nature of a Creole Continuum. *Language* 49: 640–69

———. 1976. Pidgin and Creole Studies. *Annual Review of Anthropology* 5: 169–93.

———. 1980. Decreolization and the Creole Continuum. In A. Valdman and A. Highfield, eds., *Theoretical Orientations in Creole Studies*. New York: Academic Press, pp. 109–28.

Bishop, John, and Frank J. Korom. 1998. *Hosay Trinidad* (video). Watertown, Mass.: Documentary Educational Resources.

Blackburn, Stuart. 1985. Death and Deification: Folk Cults in Hinduism. *History of Religions* 24/3: 255–74.

Böhtlink, O., and R. Roth. 1966. *Sanskrit Wörterbuch*, 1–3. Osnabruck: Otto Zeller Verlags Buchhandlung.

Bourdieu, Pierre. 1977. *Outline of a Theory of Practice*. Cambridge: Cambridge University Press.

Bowen, John. 1986. On the Political Construction of Tradition: Gotong Royong in Indonesia. *Journal of Asian Studies* 45/3: 545–61.

Brathwaite, Edward. 1971. *The Development of Creole Society in Jamaica, 1770–1820*. Oxford: Clarendon Press.

Brereton, Bridget. 1979. *Race Relations in Colonial Trinidad, 1870–1900*. Cambridge: Cambridge University Press.

———. 1992. The Indians and Indentureship, 1845–1917. In G. Besson and

B. Brereton, eds., *The Book of Trinidad*. Port of Spain, Trinidad: Paria Publishing Company Limited, pp. 212–26

Brown, Delwyn. 1994. *Boundaries of Our Habitations: Tradition and Theological Construction*. Albany: State University of New York Press.

Brown, Michael F. 1998. Can Culture Be Copyrighted? *Current Anthropology* 39/2: 193–222.

Browne, Edward G. 1953. *A Literary History of Persia*. Vol. 4, *Modern Times (1500–1924)*. Cambridge: Cambridge University Press.

Burman, B. K., ed. 1965. *Moharram in Two Cities: Lucknow and Delhi*. Census of India 1961, Monograph Series, no. 3, vol. 1, pt. 7–B. New Delhi: Ministry of Home Affairs.

Burton, Richard, D. E. 1997. *Afro-Creole: Power, Opposition, and Play in the Caribbean*. Ithaca, N.Y.: Cornell University Press.

Canclini, Néstor García. 1995. *Hybrid Cultures: Strategies for Leaving and Entering Modernity*. Minneapolis: University of Minnesota Press.

Canetti, Elias. 1963. *Crowds and Power*. New York: Viking Press.

Cantley, Audrey. 1979. The Concept of Tradition. In R. J. Moore, ed., *Tradition and Politics in South Asia*. New Delhi: Vikas Publishing House.

Caron, Nelly. 1975. The Ta'zieh, the Sacred Theatre of Iran. *World of Music* 17/4: 3–10.

Cejpek, Jiri. 1968. Iranian Folk-Literature. In J. Rypka, ed., *History of Iranian Literature*. Dordrecht, Holland: D. Reidel Publishing Company, pp. 607–709.

Chaturvedi, Mahendra, and Bholanath Tiwari. 1984. *A Practical Hindi-English Dictionary*. New Delhi: National Publishing House.

Chaudenson, Robert. 1981. Continuum intralinguistique et interlinguistique. *Etudes Créoles* 4/1: 19–46.

Chelkowski, Peter J. 1975. *Ta'ziyeh: Indigenous Avant-Garde Theatre of Iran*. Tehran: NIRT Publications.

———. 1979. Ta'ziyeh: Indigenous Avant-Garde Theatre of Iran. In P. J. Chelkowski, ed., *Ta'ziyeh: Ritual and Drama in Iran*. New York: New York University Press, pp. 1–11.

———. 1985. Shia Muslim Processional Performances. *Tisch Drama Review* 29/3: 18–30.

———. 1986a. From Maqātil Literature to Drama. *Al-Serāt* 12/1: 227–64.

———. 1986b. Popular Shī'ī Mourning Rituals. *Al-Serāt*. 12/1: 209–26.

———. 1987a. Rawẓah-Khvānī. In Mircea Eliade, ed., *The Encyclopedia of Religion*, vol. 12. New York: Macmillan Press, pp. 220–21.

———. 1987b. Stamps of Blood. *American Philatelist* 101/6: 556–66.

———. 1988. When Time Is No Time and Space Is No Space: The Passion Plays of Husayn. In Milla Riggio, ed., *Ta'ziyeh: Ritual and Popular Beliefs in Iran*. Hartford, Conn.: Trinity College, pp. 13–23.

———. 1989. In Ritual and Revolution: The Image in the Transformation of Iranian Culture. Views: *Journal of Photography in New England* 10/3: 7–11.

Chelkowski, Peter, and Hamid Dabashi. 1999. *Staging a Revolution: The Art of Persuasion in the Islamic Republic of Iran*. New York: New York University Press.

Chelkowski, Piotr (Peter). 1992–93. Muharram in South Trinidad. *Folia Orientalia* 29: 55–64.

Chokolingo, Patrick. 1965. Why Hosein Is Banned from the Towns. *Daily Mirror* (Trinidad), May 11.

Claus, Peter J., and Frank J. Korom. 1991. *Folkloristics and Indian Folklore*. Udupi, India: Regional Resources Centre for the Folk Performing Arts.

Clifford, James. 1994. Diasporas. *Cultural Anthropology* 9/3: 302–38.

Clive, Charlotte Florentina. 1798. *Journal of a Voyage to the East Indies and During a Residence There a Tour Through the Mysore and Tanjore Countries, etc. and the Return Voyage to England*. London: India Office Library, manuscript no. WD4235.

Cohen, Ronald. 1978. Ethnicity: Problem and Focus in Anthropology. *Annual Review of Anthropology* 7: 379–404.

Cole, Juan. 1988. *Roots of North Indian Shi'ism in Iran and Iraq: Religion and State in Avadh, 1722–1859*. Berkeley: University of California Press.

Comins, D. W. D. 1893. *Note on Emigration from India to British Guiana*. Calcutta: Bengal Secretariat Press.

Connerton, Paul. 1989. *How Societies Remember*. Cambridge: Cambridge University Press.

Connor, Walker. 1986. The Impact of Homelands Upon Diasporas. In G. Sheffer, ed., *Modern Diasporas in International Politics*. New York: St. Martin's Press, pp. 16–46.

———. 1988. The Interrelated Histories of Shi'i Islam and Persian Nationalism. In Milla Riggio, ed., *Ta'ziyeh: Ritual and Popular Beliefs in Iran*. Hartford, Conn.: Trinity College, pp. 9–12.

Cooper, Carolyn. 1995. *Noises in the Blood: Orality, Gender, and the "Vulgar" Body in Jamaican Popular Culture*. Durham, N.C.: Duke University Press.

Corbin, Henry. 1978. *The Man of Light in Iranian Sufism*. Boulder, Colo.: Shambhala.

Cothonay, R. P. M. 1893. *Trinidad: Journal d'un Missionaire Dominicain des Antilles Anglaises*. Paris: Victor Retaux et Fils.

Cowan, J. Milton, ed. 1976. *The Hans Wehr Dictionary of Modern Written Arabic*. Ithaca, N.Y.: Spoken Language Services.

Cowley, John. 1996. *Carnival, Canboulay, and Calypso: Traditions in the Making*. Cambridge: Cambridge University Press.

Crowley, Daniel. 1954. East Indian Festivals in Trinidad Life. *Caribbean Commission* 7/9: 202–8.

Cumpston, I. M. 1953. *Indians Overseas in British Territories*. Oxford: Oxford University Press.

Davis, Susan G. 1986. *Parades and Power: Street Theatre in Nineteenth-Century Philadelphia*. Berkeley: University of California Press.

DeCamp, David. 1971. The Study of Pidgin and Creole Languages. In D. Hymes, ed., *Pidginization and Creolization of Languages*. Cambridge: Cambridge University Press, pp. 13–39.

Deosaran, Ramesh. 1987. The "Caribbean Man": A Study of the Psychology of Perception and the Media. In D. Dabydeen and B. Samaroo, eds., *India in the Caribbean*. London: Hansib Publishing, pp. 81–118.

Dey, Mukul K. 1962. The Indian Population in Trinidad and Tobago. *International Journal of Comparative Sociology* 3/2: 245–53.

Dournon, Genevieve, and Margaret J. Kartomi. 1984. Ṭāśa. In S. Sadie, ed., *The New Grove Dictionary of Musical Instruments*, vol. 3. New York: Macmillan Press, p. 532.

Downs, James F. 1971. *Cultures in Crisis*. Beverly Hills, Calif.: Glencoe Press.

Drummond, Lee. 1980. The Cultural Continuum: A Theory of Intersystems. *Man* 15/2: 352–74.

Dunham, Mary Francis. 1997. *Jarigan: Muslim Epic Songs of Bangladesh*. Dhaka: University Press Limited.

Durbin, Mridula Adenwala. 1973. Formal Changes in Trinidad Hindi as a Result of Language Adaptation. *American Anthropologist* 75/4: 1290–1304.

Eerdmans, B. D. 1894. Der Ursprung der Ceremonien des Hosein-Festes. *Zeitschrift für Assyriologie* 9: 280–303.

Egnor, Margaret T. 1986. Internal Iconicity in Paṟaiyar "Crying Songs." In S. Blackburn and A. K. Ramanujan, eds., *Another Harmony: New Essays on the Folklore of India*. Berkeley: University of California Press, pp. 294–344.

Ehrlich, Allen S. 1971. History, Ecology, and Demography in the British Caribbean: An Analysis of East Indian Ethnicity. *Southwestern Journal of Anthropology* 27/2: 166–80.

Eickelman, Dale F. 1982. The Study of Islam in Local Contexts. *Contributions to Asian Studies* 17: 1–16.

Eisenstadt, S. N. 1969. Some Observations on the Dynamics of Tradition. *Comparative Studies in Society and History* 11: 451–475.

———. 1973. *Tradition, Change, and Modernity*. New York: Wiley.

Eliade, Mircea. 1961. *Images and Symbols: Studies in Religious Symbolism*. Princeton, N.J.: Princeton University Press.

Ende, Werner. 1978. The Flagellations of Muḥarram and the Shiʿite ʿUlamāʾ. *Der Islam* 55: 19–36.

Eriksen, Thomas Hylland. 1990. Liming in Trinidad: The Art of Doing Nothing. *Folk* 32: 23–43.

———. 1992. *Us and Them in Modern Societies: Ethnicity and Nationalism in Mauritius, Trinidad, and Beyond*. Oslo: Scandanavian University Press.

Fabian, Johannes. 1978. Popular Culture in Africa: Findings and Conjectures. *Africa* 48: 315–34.

Fanon, Frantz. 1990. The Fact of Blackness. In D. T. Goldberg, ed., *Anatomy of Racism*. Minneapolis: University of Minnesota Press, pp. 108–26.

Feener, R. Michael. 1999. Tabut: Muharram Observances in the History of Bengkulu. *Studia Islamika* 6/2: 87–130.

Felix, Paul. 1996. *Hosay* an Islamic Farce. *Trinidad Guardian* May 27: 14.

Ferguson, Charles A. 1959. Diglossia. *Word* 15: 325–40.

Fernandez, James. 1990. Tolerance in a Repugnant World and Other Dilemmas in the Cultural Relativism of Melville Herskovits. *Ethos* 18/2: 140–64.

Fernea, Elizabeth W. 1969. *Guests of the Sheik: An Ethnography of an Iraqi Village*. Garden City, N.Y.: Anchor Books.

Fischer, Michael M. J. 1980. *Iran: From Religious Dispute to Revolution*. Cambridge, Mass.: Harvard University Press.

Fischer, Michael M. J., and Mahdi Abedi. 1990. *Debating Muslims: Cultural Dialogues in Postmodernity and Tradition*. Madison: University of Wisconsin Press.

Foucault, Michel. 1972. *The Archaeology of Knowledge*. New York: Vintage.

Freitag, Sandria. 1984. Sunnīs and Sīʿa: From Community Identity to Communal Sectarianism in North Indian Islam. In P. Gaeffke and D. A. Utz, eds., *Identity and Division in Cults and Sects in South Asia*. Philadelphia: University of Pennsylvania Department of South Asia Regional Studies, pp. 132–52.

———. 1988. The Roots of Separatism in South Asia: Personal Practice and Public Structures in Kanpur and Bombay. In E. Burke III and I. M. Lapidus, eds.,

Islam, Politics and Social Movements. Berkeley: University of California Press, pp. 115–45.

———. 1989. *Collective Action and Community: Public Arenas and the Emergence of Communalism in North India.* Berkeley: University of California Press.

Fruzzetti, Lina M. 1981. Muslim Rituals: Household Rites vs. Public Festivals in Rural India. In I. Ahmad, ed., *Ritual and Religion Among Muslims in India.* New Delhi: Manohar, pp. 91–112.

Geertz, Clifford. 1968. *Islam Observed: Religious Development in Morocco and Indonesia.* New Haven, Conn.: Yale University Press.

———. 1983. *Local Knowledge.* New York: Basic Books.

———. 1992. "Local Knowledge" and Its Limits: Some *Obiter Dicta. Yale Journal of Criticism* 5/2: 129–35.

———. 1995. *After the Fact: Two Countries, Four Decades, One Anthropologist.* Cambridge, Mass.: Harvard University Press.

van Gennep, Arnold. 1961. *Rites of Passage.* Chicago: University of Chicago Press.

Georges, Robert A. 1969. Toward an Understanding of Storytelling Events. *Journal of American Folklore* 82: 313–28.

Gibb, H. A. R, and J. H. Kramer, eds., 1965. *Shorter Encyclopedia of Islam.* Ithaca, N.Y.: Cornell University Press.

Gibbons, Rawle. 1979. *Traditional Enactments of Trinidad: Towards a Third Theatre.* M. Phil. thesis, University of the West Indies–St. Augustine.

Gibson, Kean. 2001. *Comfa Religion and Creole Language in a Caribbean Community.* Albany: SUNY Press.

Gilbert, Glenn, and Dennis Makhudu. 1987. Le continuum créole en Afrikaans. *Etudes Créoles* 10/2: 15–24.

Gill, Sam D. 1972. Disenchantment. *Parabola* 1/3: 6–13.

Goldziher, Ignaz. 1894. Usages juifs d'après la littérature religieuse des musulmans. *Revue des Etudes Juives* 28:75–94.

———. 1906. Das Prinzip der *taķijja* im Islam. *Zeitschrift der Deutschen Morgenländischen Gesellschaft* 60: 213–26.

Gothóni, René. 1981. Emic, Etic and Ethics: Some Remarks on Studying a "Foreign" Religion. *Studia Orientalia* 50: 29–41.

de Grandpré, Louis. 1803. *A Voyage in the Indian Ocean and to Bengal, Undertaken in the Years 1789 and 1790.* London: G. and J. Robinson.

Grant, Kenneth J. 1923. *My Missionary Memories.* Halifax, Canada: Imperial Publishing Company, Limited.

Gumperz, John, and Robert Wilson. 1971. Convergence and Creolization: A Case from the Indo-Aryan/Dravidian Border. In D. Hymes, ed., *Pidginization and Creolization of Languages.* Cambridge: Cambridge University Press, pp. 65–90.

Guss, David M. 2000. *The Festive State: Race, Ethnicity, and Nationalism as Cultural Performance.* Berkeley: University of California Press.

Haery, Mahmoud M. 1982. *Ru-Howzi: The Iranian Traditional Improvisatory Theatre.* Ph.D. diss., New York University.

Hall, Douglas. 1978. The Flight from the Estates Reconsidered: The British West Indies, 1838–1942. *Journal of Caribbean History* 10/11: 7–24.

Hall, Robert A. 1966. *Pidgin and Creole Languages.* Ithaca, N.Y.: Cornell University Press.

Hall, Stuart. 1993. Culture, Community, Nation. *Cultural Studies* 7: 349–63.

Halm, Heinz. 1991. *Shiism*. Edinburgh: Edinburgh University Press.

Handelman, Don. 1977. The Organization of Ethnicity. *Ethnic Groups* 1: 187–200.

Handler, Richard, and Jocelyn Linnekin. 1984. Tradition: Genuine or Spurious. *Journal of American Folklore* 97/385: 273–90.

Hannerz, Ulf. 1987. The World in Creolisation. *Africa* 57/4: 546–59.

———. 1989. Notes on the Global Ecumene. *Public Culture* 1/2: 66–75.

Haraksingh, Kusha R. 1974. When Police Fired on a *Hosay* Procession. *Sunday Guardian* (Trinidad), November 14: 5.

Harris, Marvin. 1976. History and Significance of the Emic/Etic Distinction. *Annual Review of Anthropology* 5: 329–50.

Harrison, Simon. 1992. Ritual as Intellectual Property. *Man* (NS) 27/2: 225–44.

Hasan, Mushirul. 1990. Sectarianism in Indian Islam: The Shia-Sunni Divide in the United Provinces. *The Indian Economic and Social History Review* 27/2: 209–28.

———. 1997. Traditional Rites and Contested Meanings: Sectarian Strife in Colonial Lucknow. In V. Graff, ed., *Lucknow: Memories of a City*. Delhi: Oxford University Press, pp. 114–35.

Hasnain, Nadeem, and Sheikh Abrar Husain. 1988. *Shias and Shia Islam in India: A Study in Society and Culture*. New Delhi: Harnam Publications.

Headland, Thomas N., Kenneth L. Pike, and Marvin Harris, eds., 1990. *Emics and Etics: The Insider/Outsider Debate*. Newbury Park, Calif.: Sage Publications.

Hegland, Mary. 1995. Shi'a Women of Northwest Pakistan and Agency Through Practice: Ritual, Resistance, Resiliance. *PoLAR: Political and Legal Anthropology Review* 18/2: 65–79.

———. 1997. A Mixed Blessing: The Majales-Shi'a Women's Rituals of Mourning in Northwest Pakistan. In J. Brink and J. Mencher, eds., *Mixed Blessings: Gender and Religious Fundamentalism Cross Culturally*. New York: Routledge, pp. 179–96.

———. 1998. Flagellation and Fundamentalism: (Trans)forming Meaning, Identity, and Gender Through Pakistani Women's Rituals of Mourning. *American Ethnologist* 25/2: 240–66.

Herskovits, Melville. 1973. *Cultural Relativism*. New York: Vintage Press.

Hill, Donald R. 1993. *Calypso Calaloo: Early Carnival Music in Trinidad*. Gainesville: University of Florida Press.

Hjortshoj, Keith G. 1977. *Kerbala in Context: A Study of Muharram in Lucknow, India*. Ph.D. diss., Cornell University.

Hobsbawm, Eric, and Terence Ranger, eds., 1983. *The Invention of Tradition*. Cambridge: Cambridge University Press.

Hollister, John N. 1953. *The Shi'a of India*. London: Luzac and Co.

Holm, John. 1989. *Pidgins and Creoles: Reference Survey*, vol. 2. New York. Cambridge University Press.

Honko, Lauri. 1983a. On the Analytical Value of the Concept of Tradition. In L. Honko and P. Laaksonen, eds., *Trends in Nordic Tradition Research*. Helsinki: Finnish Literature Society, pp. 233–50.

———. 1983b. Research Traditions in Tradition Research. In L. Honko and P. Laaksonen, eds., *Trends in Nordic Tradition Research*. Helsinki: Finnish Literature Society, pp. 13–22.

Howard, Alan, and Jeannette Mageo. 1996. Introduction. In J. M. Mageo and A. Howard, eds., *Spirits in Culture, History, and Mind*. London: Routledge, pp. 1–10.

Humayuni, Sadeq. 1979. An Analysis of the Ta'ziyeh of Qasem. In P. J. Chelkowski, ed., *Ta'ziyeh: Ritual and Drama in Iran*. New York: New York University Press, pp. 12–23.

Hymes, Dell. 1971. Introduction. In D. Hymes, ed., *Pidginization and Creolization of Languages*. Cambridge: Cambridge University Press, pp. 65–90.

———. 1981. Breakthrough into Performance. In *"In Vain I Tried to Tell You": Essays in Native American Poetics*. Philadelphia: University of Pennsylvania Press, pp. 79–141.

Jacobs, Carl. 1964. Who Say? I Say, Hosay! *Trinidad Guardian*, March 31: 1.

Jaffri, Syed Husain Ali. 1979. Muharram Ceremonies in India. In P. J. Chelkowski, ed., *Ta'ziyeh Ritual and Drama in Iran*. New York: New York University Press, pp. 222–27.

Jain, Mirjhar. 1970. *Religious Festivals and Traditions of the Muslims of Lucknow*. Master's thesis, Lucknow University.

Jamasp-Asana, J. M. 1897. *Pahlavi Texts*, vol. 1. Bombay: Fort Printing Press.

Jameson, Fredric. 1981. *The Political Unconscious: Narrative as a Socially Symbolic Act*. Ithaca, N.Y.: Cornell University Press.

Jansen, Hugh William. 1959. The Esoteric-Exoteric Factor in Folklore. *Fabula: Journal of Folktale Studies* 2: 205–11.

Jayawardena, Chandra. 1963. *Conflict and Solidarity in a Guianese Plantation*. London: Athlone Press.

———. 1968a. Ideology and Conflict in Lower Class Communities. *Comparative Studies in Society and History* 10/4: 412–46.

———. 1968b. Migration and Social Change: A Survey of Indian Communities Overseas. *Geographical Review* 58/3: 437–39.

———. 1980. Culture and Ethnicity in Guyana and Fiji. *Man* 15/3: 430–50.

Jha, J. C. 1972. The Indian Mutiny-Cum-Revolt of 1857 and Trinidad (West Indies). *Indian Studies, Past and Present* 13/4: 419–30.

———. Hosay Is Not Always a Peaceful Festival. *Express* (Trinidad), August 10: 3.

Joseph, Terry. 1996. Poor Hosay. *Express* (Trinidad), May 29: 15.

———. 1997. The Tadjahs Take Shape. *Daily Express* (Trinidad), May 7: 19.

Jourdan, Christine. 1991. Pidgins and Creoles: The Blurring of Categories. *Annual Review of Anthropology* 20: 187–209.

Kale, Madhavi. 1995. Projecting Identities: Empire and Indentured Labor Migration from India to Trinidad and British Guiana, 1836–1885. In P. van der Veer, ed., *Nation and Migration: The Politics of Space in the South Asian Diaspora*. Philadelphia: University of Pennsylvania Press, pp. 73–92.

———. 1998. *Fragments of Empire: Capital, Slavery, and Indian Indentured Labor Migration in the British Caribbean*. Philadelphia: University of Pennsylvania Press.

Kalipersad, Dominic. 2001. Hosay or Not Hosay? *Trinidad Guardian*, May 31: n.p.

Kapchan, Deborah, and Pauline Turner Strong. 1999. Introduction: Theorizing the Hybrid. *Journal of American Folklore* 112/445: 239–53.

Karrar, Husain. 1986. The Social and Spiritual Significance of Urdu *Marthīya*. *Al-Serāt* 12/1: 265–74.

Kartomi, Margaret. 1986. Tabut-A Shi'a Ritual Transplanted from India to Sumatra. In D. P. Chandler and M. C. Ricklefs, eds., *Nineteenth and Twentieth century Indonesia: Essays in honor of Professor J. D. Legge*. Clayton, Victoria, Australia: Centre of Southeast Studies, Monash University, pp. 141–62.

Kasule, Omar. 1986. Muslims in Trinidad and Tobago. *Journal. Institute of Muslim Minority Affairs* 7/1: 195–213.

Kearney, Michael. 1995. The Local and the Global: The Anthropology of Globalization and Transnationalism. *Annual Review of Anthropology* 24: 547–65.

Khan, Aisha. 1995. *Purity, Piety, and Power: Culture and Identity among Hindus and Muslims in Trinidad*. Ph.D diss., City University of New York.

———. 1997. Migration Narratives and Moral Imperatives: Local and Global in the Muslim Caribbean. *Comparative Studies of South Asia, Africa, and the Middle East* 17/1: 127–44.

Kielstra, Nico. 1985. Niveaus van Religieuze Ervarung in het Iraanse Shi'isme. In W. Jansen, ed., *Lokale Islam: Geloof en Ritueel in Noord-Afrika en Iran*. Muiderberg, Netherlands: Dick Coutinho, pp. 91–108.

Kippenberg, H. G. 1981. Jeder Tag 'Ashura, jedes Grab Kerbala. Zur Ritualisierung der Strassenkämpfe im Iran. In K. Greussing, ed., *Religion und Politik im Iran*. Berlin: Syndikat, pp. 217–76.

———. 1984. How Dualistic Beliefs Are Performed by Shi'is: The Stages of Kerbala. In H. G. Kippenberg, ed., *Struggles of Gods: Papers of the Groningen Work Group for the Study of the History of Religions*. Amsterdam: Mouton Publishers, pp.125–42.

Klass, Morton. 1996. *Singing with Sai Baba: The Politics of Revitalization in Trinidad*. Prospect Heights, Ill.: Waveland Press.

Kohlberg, Etan. 1975. Some Imāmī Shī'ī Views on *Taqiyya*. *Journal of the American Oriental Society* 95/3: 395–402.

Korom, Frank J. 1989. Inventing Traditions: Folklore and Nationalism as Historical Process in Bengal. In D. Rihtman-Auguštin and M. Povrzanović, eds., *Folklore and Historical Process*. Zagreb: Institute of Folklore Research, pp. 57–84.

———. 1999a. Empowerment Through Representation and Collaboration in Museum Exhibitions. *Journal of Folklore Research* 36/2–3: 259–64.

———. 1999b. "To Be Happy": Ritual, Play, and Leisure in the Bengali Dharmarāj *pūjā*. *International Journal of Hindu Studies* 3/2 (1999): 113–64.

———. 2000. South Asian Religions and Diaspora Studies. *Religious Studies Review* 26/1: 21–28.

———. 2001. Introduction: Fieldwork, Ethnography, and the History of Religions. *Method & Theory in the Study of Religion* 13/1 (2001): 3–11.

Korom, Frank J., and Peter J. Chelkowski. 1994. Community Process and the Performance of Muharram Observances in Trinidad. *The Tisch Drama Review* 38/2: 150–75.

Koss, Joan D. 1959. *Hindus in Trinidad: A Survey of Culture Change and Cultural Continuity*. Master's thesis, University of Pennsylvania.

Kumar, Nita. 1988. *The Artisans of Banaras: Popular Culture and Identity, 1880–1986*. Princeton, N.J.: Princeton University Press.

Langacker, R. W. 1977. Syntactic Re-analysis. In C. N. Li, ed., *Mechanics of Syntactic Change*. Austin: University of Texas Press, pp. 57–139.

Lawrence, Bruce B. 1995. *Toward a History of Global Religion(s) in the Twentieth Century: Parachristian Sightings from an Interdisciplinary Asianist*. Sixteenth Annual

University Lecture in Religion. Tempe: Arizona State University, Department of Religious Studies.

Leader, Winston. 1983. The 2 Faces of Hoosay. *Sunday Express* (Trinidad), October 16: 9.

LePage, R. B., and Andrée Tabouret-Keller. 1985. *Acts of Identity: Creole-Based Approaches to Language and Ethnicity*. Cambridge: Cambridge University Press.

Lerner, David. 1958. *The Passing of Traditional Society: Modernizing the Middle East*. New York: Free Press.

Lévi-Strauss, Claude. 1966. *The Savage Mind*. Chicago: University of Chicago Press.

Lincoln, Bruce. 1989. *Discourse and the Construction of Society: Comparative Studies of Myth, Ritual, and Classification*. New York: Oxford University Press.

Litten, Wilhelm. 1929. *Das Drama in Persien*. Berlin: Walter de Gruyter and Co.

MacDonald, John, and Beatrice MacDonald. 1973. Transformation of African and Indian Family Traditions in the Southern Caribbean. *Comparative Studies in Society and History* 15: 171–98.

MacKenzie, Clayton. 1989. Muslim Primary Schools in Trinidad and Tobago. *The Islamic Quarterly* 33/1: 5–16.

Madelung, Wilfred. 1997. *The Succession to Muḥammad: A Study of the Early Caliphate*. Cambridge: Cambridge University Press.

Mahabir, Noor Kumar. N.d. *The Influence of the Tassa on the Making of the Steelband: The East Indian Contribution to the Trinidad Carnival*. Unpublished paper.

———. 1985. *The Still Cry: Personal Accounts of East Indians in Trinidad and Tobago during Indentureship (1845–1917)*. Tacarigua, Trinidad: Calaloux Publications.

Mahdjoub, Mohammad-Dja'far. 1988. The Evolution of Popular Eulogy of the Imams Among the Shi'a. In Said Amir Arjomand, ed., *Authority and Political Culture in Shi'ism*. Albany, N.Y.: SUNY Press, pp. 54–79.

Mamnoun, Parviz. 1967. *Ta'zija, Schi'itisch-Persisches Passionsspiel*. Ph.D. diss., Universität Wien.

Mangru, Basdeo. 1993. Tadjah in British Guiana: Manipulation or Protest? In Basdeo Mangru, *Indenture and Abolition: Sacrifice and Survival on the Guyanese Sugar Plantations*. Toronto: TSAR Publications, pp. 43–58.

Manuel, Peter. 1995. *Caribbean Currents: Caribbean Music from Reggae to Rumba*. Philadelphia: Temple University Press.

———. 2000. *East Indian Music in the West Indies: Tān-Singing, Chutney, and the Making of Indo-Caribbean Culture*. Philadelphia: Temple University Press.

Marcus, George. 1998. *Ethnography Through Thick and Thin*. Princeton, N.J.: Princeton University Press.

Mason, Peter. 1998. *Bacchanal! The Carnival Culture of Trinidad*. Philadelphia: Temple University Press.

Masselos, Jim. 1976. Power in the Bombay "Mohalla," 1904–15: An Initial Exploration into the World of the Indian Urban Muslim. *South Asia* 6: 75–95.

———. 1982. Change and Custom in the Format of the Bombay Mohurrum During the Nineteenth and Twentieth Centuries. *South Asia* 5/2: 47–67.

McCarry, John. 1993. Mauritius: Island of Quiet Success. *National Geographic*, April: 110–32.

Mitchell, Katharyne. 1997. Different Diasporas and the Hype of Hybridity. *Environment and Planning. D. Society and Space* 15: 533–53.

Moerman, Michael. 1965. Who Are the Lue: Ethnic Identification in a Complex Civilization. *American Anthropologist* 67: 1215–30.

————. 1974. Accomplishing Ethnicity. In R. Turner, ed., *Ethnomethodology*. New York: Penguin Press, pp. 54–68.

Mohammad, A. N. 1972. Ban *Hosay* as Celebrated in Trinidad. *Trinidad Guardian*, February 26: 2.

Mohammad, Afzal. 1985. Why Celebrate *Hosay*? *Express* (Trinidad), October18: 9.

Mohan, P. R. 1978. *Trinidad Bhojpuri*. Ph.D. diss., University of Michigan.

Mohan, P. R., and P. Zador. 1986. Discontinuity in a Life-Cycle: The Death of Trinididad Bhojpuri. *Language* 62/2: 291–319.

Momen, Moojan. 1985. *An Introduction to Shiʻi Islam: The History and Doctrine of Twelver Shiʻism*. New Haven, Conn.: Yale University Press.

Monchi-Zadeh, Davoud. 1981. *Die Geschichte Zarér's*. Uppsala: Almqvist and Wiksell International.

Morton, Sarah E., ed. 1916. *John Morton of Trinidad: Journals, Letters, and Papers*. Toronto: Westminster Company.

Mottahedeh, Roy. 1985. *The Mantle of the Prophet: Religion and Politics in Iran*. New York: Pantheon Books.

Mount, Graeme. 1977. The Canadian Presbyterian Mission to Trinidad, 1868–1912. *Revista/ Review Interamericana* 7: 30–45.

Mühlhäusler, Peter. 1980. Structural Expansion and the Process of Creolization. In A. Valdman and A. Highfield, eds., *Theoretical Orientations in Creole Studies*. New York: Academic Press, pp. 19–56.

Muir, William. 1963 [1891]. *The Caliphate: Its Rise, Decline and Fall*. Beirut: Khayats Oriental Reprints.

Muller, Anesha. 1996. Who Say? Hosay! *Trinidad Guardian*, May 21: 7.

Myers, Helen. 1998. *Music of Hindu Trinidad: Songs from the India Diaspora*. Chicago: University of Chicago Press.

Nagy, Joseph F. 1990. Hierarchy, Heroes, and Heads: Indo-European Structures in Greek Myths. In L. Edmunds, ed., *Approaches to Greek Myths*. Baltimore, Md.: Johns Hopkins University Press, pp. 200–238.

Naim, C. M. 1983. The Art of the Urdu Marṣiya. In M. Israel and N. K. Wagle, eds., *Islamic Society and Culture: Essays in Honour of Professor Aziz Ahmad*. New Delhi: Manohar Publications, pp. 101–16.

————. 1993. Displacement, Hijrat—What's in a Name! *Toronto South Asian Review* 11/2: 74–78.

Naipaul, V. S. 1982. *Among the Believers: An Islamic Journey*. Middlesex, U.K.: Penguin Books.

Nakash, Yitzhak. 1993. An Attempt to Trace the Origins of the Rituals of 'āshūra'. *Die Welt des Islams* 33: 161–81.

————. 1994. *The Shiʻis of Iraq*. Princeton, N.J.: Princeton University Press.

Naqvi, Ali Naqi. N.d. *Azadari: A Historical Review of Institution*. Karachi: Peer Mohammad Trust.

Nasr, Seyyid Hossein. 1966. *Ideals and Realities of Islam*. Boston: Beacon Press.

————. 1997. Islam and Music: The Legal and the Spiritual Dimension. In L. Sullivan, ed., *Enchanting Powers: Music in the World's Religions*. Cambridge, Mass.: Harvard University Press, pp. 219–36.

Needham, Rodney. 1967. Percussion and Transition. *Journal of the Royal Anthropological Institute* 2/4: 606–14.

Nevadomsky, Joseph. 1983. Economic Organization, Social Mobility, and Changing Social Status Among East Indians in Rural Trinidad. *Ethnology* 22/1: 63–79.
New York Times Magazine. 1987. Postage Size Propaganda. February 15: 38–41.
Nicholls, David. 1971. East Indians and the Black Power Movement. *Race* 12/4: 443–59.
Niehoff, Arthur, and Juanita Niehoff. 1960. *East Indians in the West Indies*. Milwaukee: Olson Publishing Company.
Norman, Henry W. 1885. *Correspondence Respecting the Recent Coolie Disturbances in Trinidad, at the Mohurrum Festival*. London: Eyre and Spottiwoode.
Norris, Christopher. 1996. *Reclaiming the Truth: Contributions to a Critique of Cultural Relativism*. Durham, N.C.: Duke University Press.
Norton, Augustus Richard, and Ali Safa. 2000. 'Ashura in Nabatiyya. *Middle East Insight* May–June: 21–27.
Oman, John Campbell. 1907. *The Brahmans, Theists, and Muslims of India*. Philadelphia: George W. Jacobs and Company.
Ottley, C. R. 1955. *An Account of Life in Spanish Trinidad*. St. Ann's, Trinidad: Government House.
Oxaal, Ivar. 1968. *Black Intellectuals Come to Power: The Rise of Creole Nationalism in Trinidad and Tobago*. Cambridge, Mass.: Schenkman Publishing Company, Inc.
———. 1971. *Race and Revolutionary Consciousness: A Documentary Interpretation of the 1970 Black Power Revolt in Trinidad*. Cambridge, Mass.: Schenkman Publishing Company, Inc.
Oxford English Dictionary. Compact Ed. 1971. Oxford: Oxford University Press.
Pandey, Gyan. 1989. The Colonial Construction of "Communalism": British Writings on Banaras in the Nineteenth Century. In R. Guha, ed., *Subaltern Studies VI*. New Delhi: Oxford University Press, pp. 132–68.
Pelly, Sir Lewis, trans. 1879. *The Miracle Play of Hasan and Husain*, 1–2. London: William H. Allen and Co.
Pike, Kenneth L. 1954. *Language in Relation to a Unified Theory of the Structure of Human Behavior*. The Hague: Mouton.
Pinault, David. 1992. *The Shiites: Ritual and Popular Piety in a Muslim Community*. New York: St. Martin's Press.
———. 2001. *Horse of Karbala: Muslim Devotional Life in India*. New York: St. Martin's Press.
Platts, John T. 1977. *A Dictionary of Urdū Classical Hindī and English*. New Delhi: Oriental Books Reprint Corporation.
Prothero, Stephen. 1996. *The White Buddhist: The Asian Odyssey of Henry Steel Olcott*. Bloomington: Indiana University Press.
Qureshi, Regula. 1972. Indo-Muslim Religious Music: An Overview. *Asian Music* 3/2: 15–22.
———. 1981. Islamic Music in an Indian Environment: The Shi'a Majlis. *Ethnomusicology* 25: 41–71.
Rabinow, Paul. 1986. Representations Are Social Facts: Modernity and Post-Modernity in Anthropology. In J. Clifford and G. E. Marcus, eds., *Writing Culture: The Poetics and Politics of Ethnography*. Berkeley: University of California Press, pp. 234–61.
Rahaman, Mohammed K. 1997. Muslims Should Distance Themselves from Hosay. *Newsday* (Trinidad), May 5: 9.

Raheja, Gloria Goodwin. 1996. Caste, Colonialism, and the Speech of the Colonized: Entextualization and Disciplinary Control in India. *American Ethnologist* 23/3: 494–513.

Rahman, Haji Tawfiq-ur. 1964. Hosay? Nothing but an Ironical Observance. *Sunday Guardian* (Trinidad), May 17: 6.

Rampersad, Sheila. 1987. "Hosay" Festival Is a Way of Life. *Express* (Trinidad), August 27: 21.

Reza, Rahi Masoom. 1994. *The Feuding Families of Village Gangauli*. New Delhi: Viking Penguin Books India (P) Ltd.

Richardson, Bonham. 1975. Livelihood in Rural Trinidad in 1900. *Annals of the Association of American Geographers* 65/2: 240–51.

Robertson, Roland. 1995. Glocalization: Time-Space and Homogeneity-Heterogeneity. In M. Featherston et al. eds., *Global Modernities*. London: Sage Publications, pp. 27–44.

Rodríguez, Sylvia. 1997. The Taos Fiesta: Invented Traditions and Infrapolitics of Symbolic Reclamation. *Journal of the Southwest* 39/1: 33–57.

Rubin, U. 1975. Pre-existence and Light: Aspects of the Concept of Nūr Muḥammad. *Israel Oriental Studies* 5: 62–119.

Rudolph, Lloyd L., and Susanne H. Rudolph. 1967. *The Modernity of Tradition*. Chicago: University of Chicago Press.

Ryan, Selwyn. 1991. *The Muslimeen Grab for Power: Religion, Race, and Revolution in Trinidad*. Port of Spain: Inprint Publications.

Sadiq, Muhammad. 1964. *A History of Urdu Literature*. Oxford: Oxford University Press.

Safran, William. 1991. Diasporas in Modern Societies: Myths of Homeland and Return. *Diaspora* 1/1: 83–99.

Sagaster, Ursula. 1993. Observations Made During the Month of Muharram, 1989, in Baltistan. In Charles Ramble and Martin Brauen, eds., *The Anthropology of Tibet and the Himalayas*. Zürich: Ethnological Museum of the University of Zürich, pp. 308–17.

Saiyid, A. R. 1981. Ideal and Reality in the Observance of Moharram: A Behavioural Interpretation. In I. Ahmad, ed., *Ritual and Religion among the Muslims in India*. New Delhi: Manohar, pp. 113–42.

Sāklāyen, Golām. 1969. *Bāṅglāy Marsīyā Sāhitya*. Ḍhākā: Pākistān Buk Karpareśan.

Sallnow, Michael J. 1981. Communitas Reconsidered: The Sociology of Andean Pilgrimage. *Man* 16: 163–82.

Samaroo, Brinsley. 1972. The Presbyterian Canadian Mission as an Agent of Integration in Trinidad During the 19th and Early 20th Centuries. *Caribbean Studies* 14/4: 41–55.

———. 1996. Early African and East Indian Muslims in Trinidad and Tobago. In D. Dabydeen and B. Samaroo, ed., *Across the Dark Waters: Ethnicity and Indian Identity in the Caribbean*. London: Macmillan Education Ltd., pp. 201–12.

Schieffelin, Edward. 1985. Performance and the Cultural Construction of Reality. *American Ethnologist* 12/4: 707–24.

Schimmel, Annemarie. 1979. The Marsiyeh in Sindhi Poetry. In P. J. Chelkowski, ed., *Ta'ziyeh: Ritual and Drama in Iran*. New York: New York University Press, pp. 210–21.

———. 1986. Karbalā' and Ḥusayn in Literature. *Al-Serāt* 12/1: 29–39.

Schubel, Vernon. 1993. *Religious Performance in Contemporary Islam: Shi'i Devotional Rituals in Islam.* Columbia: University of South Carolina Press.

Schwartz, Barton. 1965. Patterns of East Indian Family Organization in Trinidad. *Caribbean Studies* 5/1: 23–36.

Schwartz, Barton, ed. 1967. *Caste in Overseas Indian Communities.* San Francisco: Harper.

Scott, James C. 1990. *Domination and the Arts of Resistance: Hidden Transcripts.* New Haven, Conn.: Yale University Press.

Sharar, Abdul Haim. 1994. *Lucknow: The Last Phase of an Oriental Culture.* Delhi: Oxford University Press.

Sharīf, Ja'far. 1975 [1921]. *Islam in India or the Qanun-i-Islam: The Customs of the Musulmāns of India.* London: Curzon Press Ltd.

Sherring, Matthew A. 1975 [1868]. *Benares, the Sacred City of the Hindus.* Delhi: B. R. Publishing Corp.

Shils, Edward. 1981. *Tradition.* Chicago: University of Chicago Press.

Shuman, Amy. 1993. Dismantling Local Culture. *Western Folklore* 52: 345–64.

Singer, Milton. 1972. *When a Great Tradition Modernizes: An Anthropological Approach to Indian Civilization.* Chicago: University of Chicago Press.

Singh, Kelvin. 1988. *Bloodstained Tombs: The Muharram Massacre, 1884.* London: Macmillan Publishers Ltd.

Smith, Jonathan Z. 1990. *Drudgery Divine: On the Comparison of Early Christianities and the Religions of Late Antiquity.* Chicago: University of Chicago Press.

Smith, Robert J. 1963. *Muslim East Indians in Trinidad: Retention of Ethnic Identity Under Acculturative Forces.* Ph.D. diss., University of Pennsylvania.

Sollors, Werner. 1989. Introduction. In W. Sollors, ed., *The Invention of Ethnicity.* New York: Oxford University Press, pp. ix–xx.

Spiro, Melford. 1986. Cultural Relativism and the Future of Anthropology. *Cultural Anthropology* 1/3: 259–86.

Steingass, F. 1973. *A Comprehensive Persian-English Dictionary.* New Delhi: Oriental Books Reprint Corporation.

Stern, Stephen, and John A. Cicala, eds. 1991. *Creative Ethnicity: Symbols and Strategies of Contemporary Ethnic Life.* Logan: Utah State University Press.

Stewart, John O. 1989. *Drinkers, Drummers, and Decent Folk: Ethnographic Narratives of Village Trinidad.* Albany, N.Y.: SUNY Press.

Stewart, Omer. 1956. Three Gods for Joe. *Tomorrow: Quarterly Review of Psychical Research* 4/3: 71–76.

Stewart, Susan. 1984. *On Longing: Narratives of the Miniature, the Gigantic, the Souvenir, the Collection.* Baltimore, Md.: Johns Hopkins University Press.

Stross, Brian. 1999. The Hybrid Metaphor: From Biology to Culture. *Journal of American Folklore* 112/445: 254–67.

Stuempfle, Stephen. 1995. *The Steelband Movement: The Forging of a National Identity in Trinidad and Tobago.* Philadelphia: University of Pennsylvania Press.

Taitt, Glenroy. 1999. Rice, Culture and Government in Trinidad, 1897–1939. In B. Brereton and K. Yelvington, eds., *The Colonial Caribbean in Transition: Essays on Postemancipation Social and Cultural History.* Gainesville: University Press of Florida, pp. 174–88, 294–96.

de Tassy, Garcin. 1995. *Muslim Festivals in India and Other Essays.* Delhi: Oxford University Press.

Tavadia, Jahangir C. 1956. *Die Mittelpersische Sprache und Literatur der Zarathus-trier*. Leipzig: Otto Harrassowitz.

Thaiss, Gustav. 1971. Religion and Social Change in Iran: The Bazaar as a Case Study. In E. Yarshater, ed., *Iran Faces the Seventies*. New York: Praeger Publishers, pp. 189–216.

————. 1972a. Religious Symbolism and Social Change: The Drama of Hussein. In N. Keddie, ed., *Scholars, Saints and Sufis: Muslim Religious Institutions in the Middle East Since 1500*. Berkeley: University of California Press, pp. 349–66.

————. 1972b. Unity and Discord: The Symbol of Ḥusayn in Iran. In C. J. Adams, ed., *Iranian Civilization and Culture*. Montreal: McGill University Institute of Islamic Studies, pp. 111–19.

————. 1973. *Religious Symbolism and Social Change: The Drama of Husain*. Ph.D. diss., University of Washington.

————. 1978. The Conceptualization of Social Change Through Metaphor. *Journal of Asian and African Studies* 13/1–2: 1–13.

————. 1994. Contested Meanings and the Politics of Authenticity. In A. S. Ahmad and H. Donnan, eds., *Islam, Globalization and Postmodernity*. London: Routledge, pp. 38–62.

Thomas, Nicholas. 1992. The Inversion of Tradition. *American Ethnologist* 19/2: 213–32.

Tinker, Hugh. 1974. *A New System of Slavery: The Export of Indian Laborers Overseas, 1830–1920*. New York: Oxford University Press.

Tobias, Henry J. 1990. *A History of the Jews in New Mexico*. Albuquerque: University of New Mexico Press.

Troll, Christian W. 1988. Muslim Festivals and Ceremonies. In P. Jackson, ed., *The Muslims of India: Beliefs and Practices*. Bangalore: Theological Publications in India, pp. 34–63.

Turner, Victor. 1977. *The Ritual Process: Structure and Anti-Structure*. Ithaca, N.Y.: Cornell University Press.

Unvala, J. M. 1927. The Moharram Festival in Persia. *Studi e Materiali di Storia delle Religioni* 3: 82–96.

Vedantam, T., ed. 1975. *Moharram in Hyderabad City* (Census of India 1971, series 2, Andhra Pradesh, part 11). New Delhi: Ministry of Home Affairs.

van der Veer, Peter. 1992. Praying or Playing: A Sufi Saint's Day in Surat. *Journal of Asian Studies* 51/3: 545–64.

de Verteuil, Anthony. 1989. *Eight East Indian Immigrants*. Port of Spain, Trinidad: Paria Publishing Company Limited.

Vertovec, Steven. 1989. Hinduism in Diaspora: The Transformation of Tradition in Trinidad. In G. D. Sontheimer and H. Kulke, eds. *Hinduism Reconsidered*. New Delhi: Manohar, pp. 157–86.

————. 1990. Oil Boom and Recession in Trinidad Indian Villages. In C. Clarke, C. Peach, and S. Vertovec, eds., *South Asians Overseas: Migration and Ethnicity*. Cambridge: Cambridge University Press, pp. 82–112.

————. 1991. East Indians and Anthropologists: A Critical Review. *Social and Economic Studies* 40/1: 133–69.

van Vloten, M. G. 1892. Les drapeaux en usage à la fête de Huçein à Téhéran. *Internationales Arcgive für Ethnographie* 5: 105–11.

Waseem, M. 1995. Introduction. In G. de Tassy, *Muslim Festivals in India and Other Essays*. Delhi: Oxford University Press, pp. 1–27.

Waugh, Earle H. 1977. Muḥarram Rites: Community Death and Rebirth. In F. E. Reynolds and E. H. Waugh, eds., *Religious Encounters with Death: Insights from the History and Anthropology of Religions*. University Park: Pennsylvania State University Press, pp. 200–213.

Webster's Ninth New Collegiate Dictionary. 1986. Springfield, Mass.: Merriam-Webster Inc., Publishers.

Weller, Judith Ann. 1968. *The East Indian Indenture in Trinidad*. Rio Piedras, Puerto Rico: Institute of Caribbean Studies.

Wensinck, A. J., and J. H. Kramer, eds. 1941. *Handwörterbuch des Islam*. Leiden: E. J. Brill.

Werbner, Pnina. 2001. The Limits of Cultural Hybridity: On Ritual Monsters, Poetic License and Contested Postcolonial Purifications. *Journal of the Anthropological Institute* 7/1: 133–52.

Whinnon, Keith. 1971. Linguistic Hybridization and the "Special Case" of Pidgins and Creoles. In D. Hymes, ed., *Pidginization and Creolization of Languages*. Cambridge: Cambridge University Press, pp. 91–115.

White, Hayden. 1987. *The Content of Form: Narrative Discourse and Historical Representation*. Baltimore, Md.: The Johns Hopkins University Press.

Williams, Brackette F. 1990. Nationalism, Traditionalism, and the Problem of Cultural Inauthenticity. In R. G. Fox, ed., *Nationalist Ideologies and the Production of National Cultures*. Washington, D.C.: American Anthropological Association, pp. 112-29.

Williams, John A. 1987. Khārijīs. In Mircea Eliade, ed., *The Encyclopedia of Religion*, vol. 8. New York: Macmillan Press, pp. 288–90.

Wilson, Fulton. 1992. Close Bars in St. James. *Express* (Trinidad), July 8: 4.

Wilson, Peter J. 1973. *Crab Antics: The Social Anthropology of English-Speaking Negro Societies of the Caribbean*. New Haven, Conn.: Yale University Press.

Wirth, Andrez. 1979. Semeiological Aspects of the Ta'ziyeh. In P. J. Chelkowski, ed., *Ta'ziyeh: Ritual and Drama in Iran*. New York: New York University Press, pp. 32–120.

Wolf, Richard Kent. 2000. Embodiment and Ambivalence: Emotion in South Asian Muharram Drumming. *Yearbook for Traditional Music* 32: 81–116.

Wood, Donald. 1968. *Trinidad in Transition: Ten Years After Slavery*. Oxford: Oxford University Press.

Yarshater, Ehsan. 1979. Ta'ziyeh and Pre-Islamic Mourning Rites in Iran. In P. J. Chelkowski, ed., *Ta'ziyeh: Ritual and Drama in Iran*. New York: New York University Press, pp. 88–94.

Yelvington, Kevin. 1990. Ethnicity "Not Out": The Indian Cricket Tour of the West Indies and the 1976 Elections in Trinidad and Tobago. *Arena Review* 14/1: 1–12.

Yelvington, Kevin A., ed., 1993. *Trinidad Ethnicity*. Knoxville: University of Tennessee Press.

Yoder, Don. 1974. Toward a Definition of Folk Religion. *Western Folklore* 33/1: 2–15.

Young, Robert. 1995. *Colonial Desire: Hybridity in Theory, Culture, and Race*. London: Routledge.

el-Zein, Abdul Hamid. 1977. Beyond Ideology and Theology: The Search for the Anthropology of Islam. *Annual Review of Anthropology* 6: 227–54.

Zerubavel, Yael. 1994. The Historic, the Legendary, and the Incredible: Invented Tradition and Collective Memory in Israel. In J. R. Gillis, ed., *Commemorations: The Politics of National Identity*. Princeton, N.J.: Princeton University Press, pp. 105–26.

Index

Acknowledgments

Hosay Trinidad began as a team project in 1990 to produce a film and monograph under the auspices of the Smithsonian Institution's Center for Folklife Programs and Cultural Heritage. The work was initially conceived as a thorough comparative study of *muharram* practices in Iran, India, and Trinidad. My project codirector, Peter Chelkowski, a Persianist, was to handle the Iranian context, while I, a South Asianist, would deal with the Indian side of the story. Together we planned to venture onto new Caribbean terrain. As the project developed, the destruction of the Babri Masjid in Ayodhya foiled our attempts to receive government sanction to film in north India. We thus reconceived the film as a more in-depth visual study of the Trinidadian variant. In 1991, Peter Chelkowski and Guha Shankar joined me to engage in initial fieldwork and to set up the film shoot. For a part of the period in 1991, Aisha Khan also joined us. Then in 1992 cameraman John Bishop and soundman John Terry joined us to shoot the film. As the project continued to evolve and members of the team pursued their own interests, it was left to John Bishop and me to complete the film *Hosay Trinidad*, which the reader should consult as a companion to this work. It was released in 1998 and is currently distributed by Documentary Educational Resources.

Peter Chelkowski deserves special mention. It was his work on *ta'ziyeh* in Iran that initially stimulated my interest in *muharram*, and he was a patient mentor and friend throughout. In the early stages of research, we published a few cursory articles together, but gradually our interests diverged and I undertook the long-term commitment to complete this study as a solo project. Peter's input and thoughts on the topic, however, are quite pervasive, especially in the first two chapters on the Iranian material. It was Peter who taught me much of what I know about the rite there, and in some places his words and thoughts are intermingled with my own.

Research is always a collaborative enterprise, and feedback from numerous individuals has shaped the present work. In particular, I wish to thank Ravina Aggarwal, Martin Baumann, Ken Bilby, Naomi Bishop, Peter Bräunlein, the late Dan Crowley, John Cupid, Fred Denny, M. David Eckel, David Edwards, Michael Feener, Jonathan Friedman, Henry Glassie, Peter Gaeffke, David Gilmartin, André Gingrich, Kathryn Hansen, Clare Harris, Jake Homiak, Shakeel Hossein, Joyce Ice, Norman Yoffe, Ivan Karp, Corinne Kratz, Nancy Owen Lewis, Philip Lutgendorf, Jan Magnusson, Peter Manuel, Margaret Mills, Pat Mora, Jozsi Nagy, Kirin Narayan, A. Richard Norton, Amelia Parkes, Carla Petievich, David Pinault, Gloria Raheja, Milla Riggio, Brinsley Samaroo, Vernon Scarborough, Richard Schechner, Laurel Seth, Kelvin Singh, Fred Smith, Christopher Steiner, Tony Stewart, Khachig Tölölyan, and Jenny White. In addition, Roger Abrahams, Amy Bard, Regina Bendix, Peter Chelkowski, Louis Komjathy, Richard Kurin, Charles Lindholm, Steven Stuempfle, Merlin Swartz, and Richard Wolf read parts or all of the manuscript prior to publication. I am extremely grateful for their comments. Peter Agree, my editor, also deserves a note of gratitude for his support.

Generous funding for the work was provided on numerous occasions. It gives me great pleasure to thank the following institutions and people. The shooting and production of the film was funded by the Center for Folklife Programs and Cultural Heritage. Another grant from the Smithsonian's Office of Scientific Research in 1993 allowed me to undertake archival research at the India Office Library in London, where Graham Shaw greatly facilitated my work. Patricia Kattenhorn of the Prints and Drawings Division also provided invaluable assistance. The Committee on Excellence of the Museum of New Mexico, Trinity College, and the Trinidad and Tobago Carnival Commission provided funds for research during Carnival season in 1996. Another return trip in 1997 was made possible by grants from the American Philosophical Society and the International Folk Art Foundation. The National Endowment for the Humanities provided a faculty summer stipend in 1998 to work on a first draft, which was completed while I was a resident summer scholar at the School of American Research in Santa Fe. My thanks to SAR's past president Douglas Schwartz for his generosity and hospitality. A grant from the American Academy of Religion in 1993 enabled me to make reproductions of some of the illustrations included in this book. A fellowship from Boston University's Humanities Foundation in the fall of 2001 allowed for a semester off to complete the final draft.

Special mention must be made of Kim Gransaull, head archivist at the West Indiana Archives in St. Augustine, who always provided cheerful assistance when I needed it. Lastly, this volume could not have been completed without the cooperation of numerous people involved in *Hosay*. Warm thanks goes out to the entire St. James community. Many people involved in *Hosay* have passed away since this work began, but their spirits live on in the children who have been born into the *Hosay* yards to carry on their legacy. May they follow in their ancestors' footsteps, just as their parents continued the work of those who crossed the *kālā pānī* (black waters) to toil on the plantations prior to independence. For all of them, I say *Hosay*!